"An engaging and heartbreaking account of the tragic circumstances girls and women find themselves in today as they struggle to find a body they can feel secure with."
—Susie Orbach, author of *Fat Is a Feminist Issue*

"Reading this book, I said to myself, 'If only.' If only girls were demanding applause instead of starving for food, thirsting for knowledge instead of hungering for support, and knowing how perfectly perfect they are in every way instead of letting doubt run rampant. Fortunately, Martin is here to move women in the right direction. She writes about body image with passion, intelligence, savvy, and curiosity. Best of all, readers will know that this will be just the first of Martin's many worthy reads."
—Wendy Shanker, author of *The Fat Girl's Guide to Life*

"Original, passionate, and important . . . shines a light on a troubling trend in young women's development. Martin's gripping stories give us a new way to understand the plight of the struggling young women we love."   —Rachel Simmons, author of *Odd Girl Out*

"I'm the mother of two teenage girls, so *Perfect Girls, Starving Daughters* hit me like a hardcover punch in the gut . . . Martin sounds a clarion call for all of us—mothers, daughters, pundits—to stop counting calories and start changing the world."
—Arianna Huffington, author of *Fanatics and Fools*

"Courageous, intelligent, and provocative . . . Thoughtfully researched and rich with trenchant insights, compelling interviews, and eye-opening anecdotes, it is something I will recommend without reservation to patients and colleagues alike."
—Brad Sachs, Ph.D., author of *The Good Enough Teen*
and *The Good Enough Child*

continued . . .

"Great news! The vexed knot of eating disorders, body image, and self-esteem gets updated with fresh analysis and new examples for a new generation. Martin's take on her peers' new experiences of pressures around beauty and thinness will bring insight to a whole new group of teenagers and young women."

—Naomi Wolf, author of *The Beauty Myth*

"These beautifully written, sensitive, and empathetic stories tell the heart-wrenching truth about the critical, harmful way women and girls regard themselves—with normalized self-hate. Martin gives voice to so many who are suffering, many whose self-hatred has insidiously become part of everyday conversation. She offers the reader deep insight based on extensive research and authentic interviews, and demands that we stop settling for self-hate. *Perfect Girls, Starving Daughters* will undoubtedly change lives."

—Dr. Robin Stern, author of
The Gaslight Effect

"An inspirational collection of research and stories about the problem young girls are tormented by in today's society. No ethnic group is excluded from this epidemic. Perfect girls are not anorexic daughters. The desire to be thin is masking the true underlying problem—the desire to be loved and acknowledged. This book is an invaluable tool for all of us. A must-read!"   —Laura E. Corio, M.D., author of
The Change Before the Change

"A courageous, intelligent, warm, and insightful deconstruction of the complicated experience of becoming a woman for this generation . . . relentlessly honest . . . Anyone wanting to know the truth of how our vital, brilliant, talented young female generation is slowly being eroded, and also wanting to travel the road to re-empowerment, must read this."

—Ellen M. Boeder, M.A., L.P.C., former primary therapist,
Eating Disorder Center of Denver

"For health professionals, Courtney Martin gives an indispensable guide to food behavior. Using compelling personal insights, she effortlessly conveys the tangle of nutritional health and disordered eating. Stories of dieting daughters and young women seeking their worth in weight are told with uncommon wit and wisdom. Tragicomic accounts of Martin's college experience combine with sharp analysis that anyone can enjoy and employ, from dietitians and physicians dealing with full-blown eating disorders to parents and their children who face the impossible paradox of perfect girls and starving daughters."

—Sharron Dalton, author of *Our Overweight Children*

"Shatters society's perception of perfectionism. Through the collection of personal stories and interviews, she reveals an extensive impression of females with eating disorders."

—Ira M. Sacker, M.D., author of *Regaining Your Self* and *Dying to Be Thin*

"It was inspiring, necessary, and revolutionary for me to read this book . . . One of the most important, comprehensive looks into the malnourished souls of today's girls and women. You owe it to yourself to read this book and give it to every daughter, mother, and woman you know."

—Jessica Weiner, author of *Life Doesn't Begin 5 Pounds from Now*

"Martin asks some deep questions, ones that are both obvious and suppressed: Is women's obsession with weight and what we eat a major contributor to women's lack of liberation as well as evidence of it? What would happen if our minds weren't constantly focused on how many calories we took in and whether we were 'being good' and not eating too much? Pulling from an army of feminist thinkers (from poet Nicole Blackman to Anna Quindlen), she makes a significant—and desperately needed—move forward in the theorizing around body image and eating disorders."

—Jennifer Baumgardner and Amy Richards, coauthors of *Manifesta* and *Grassroots*

Perfect Girls, Starving Daughters

*How the Quest for Perfection
Is Harming Young Women*

COURTNEY E. MARTIN

THE BERKLEY PUBLISHING GROUP
Published by the Penguin Group
Penguin Group (USA) Inc.
375 Hudson Street, New York, New York 10014, USA
Penguin Group (Canada), 90 Eglinton Avenue East, Suite 700, Toronto, Ontario M4P 2Y3, Canada
(a division of Pearson Penguin Canada Inc.)
Penguin Books Ltd., 80 Strand, London WC2R 0RL, England
Penguin Group Ireland, 25 St. Stephen's Green, Dublin 2, Ireland (a division of Penguin Books Ltd.)
Penguin Group (Australia), 250 Camberwell Road, Camberwell, Victoria 3124, Australia
(a division of Pearson Australia Group Pty. Ltd.)
Penguin Books India Pvt. Ltd., 11 Community Centre, Panchsheel Park, New Delhi—110 017, India
Penguin Group (NZ), 67 Apollo Drive, Rosedale, North Shore 0632, New Zealand
(a division of Pearson New Zealand Ltd.)
Penguin Books (South Africa) (Pty.) Ltd., 24 Sturdee Avenue, Rosebank, Johannesburg 2196, South Africa

Penguin Books Ltd., Registered Offices: 80 Strand, London WC2R 0RL, England

Published by agreement with Free Press, a division of Simon & Schuster, Inc. Previously published in hardcover as *Perfect Girls, Starving Daughters: The Frightening New Normalcy of Hating Your Body.*

PUBLISHER'S NOTE: While the author has made every effort to provide accurate telephone numbers and Internet addresses at the time of publication, neither the publisher nor the author assumes any responsibility for errors, or for changes that occur after publication. Further, publisher does not have any control over and does not assume any responsibility for author or third-party websites or their content.

Certain names and identifying characteristics of individuals in this book have been changed.

Copyright © 2007 by Courtney E. Martin.
Cover design by Lesley Worrell.
Cover photograph by James Connelly/Veer.
Text design by Tiffany Estreicher.

PRINTING HISTORY
Free Press hardcover edition / April 2007
Berkley trade paperback edition / September 2008

Library of Congress Cataloging-in-Publication Data

Martin, Courtney E.
    Perfect girls, starving daughters : how the quest for perfection is harming young women / Courtney E. Martin.
        p. cm.
    Originally published: New York : Free Press, c2007.
    Includes bibliographical references and index.
    ISBN 978-0-425-22336-9 (alk. paper)
    1. Body image in women.   2. Eating disorders in women.   3. Self-esteem in women.   I. Title.
    BF697.5.B63M37 2008
    306.4'613—dc22

                                                                                            2008003801

PRINTED IN THE UNITED STATES OF AMERICA

10 9 8 7 6 5 4 3 2 1

For my momma,
Jere E. Martin,
whose body was my first home
and whose spirit continues to be my hearth.
You are the most powerful
human being I have ever known.

And for the brave women who share
their stories in this book.
You are my hope.

Contents

Preface

I have carried this book around inside of me for years. At age twenty-five, far from the gluttony of college and even further from the angst of adolescence, I suspected I might finally be rid of the gagging noises echoing in dorm bathrooms and the scrape of plates sliding against Formica tables. I thought I might be able to feign ignorance about the next wave of thirteen-year-old girls discovering the ritual language of self-hatred—*fat, disgusting, weak, worthless.*

But then my best friend—one of the few girls I had ever been close to who had not had an eating disorder—looked at me, eyes wet with tears, and admitted that she had been making herself throw up after meals. I felt the hope leak out of me, like air out of a punctured balloon.

Then my small-town cousin came to visit me in the big city, and as we wandered the echoing halls of the Met, she admitted that she felt, as I had in college, often on the edge of an eating disorder. I felt rage.

Over coffee and some history homework, a fourteen-year-old girl I mentor told me that her friends thought about nothing so much as their weight. I felt dread.

My students at Hunter College, working-class, first-generation American, ethnically diverse, shocked me by standing up in front of the class and admitting to struggling with undiagnosed eating disorders for years and watching their mothers take out loans for tummy tucks.

It wasn't just my private world either. Though few talked about it, Terri Schiavo was suspected to have had a heart attack and gone into a coma as a result of her battle with bulimia. Lindsay Lohan and Nicole Richie shrank down to nothing in plain view. Anorexic fashion models in Uruguay and Brazil, both in their early twenties, died. On websites, girls from all over the country pledged their devotion to Ana (aka anorexia) and Mia (aka bulimia)—sharing starvation tips with anyone old enough to type in a URL.

Evidence was everywhere, yet people were not talking about the cultural causes or the larger implications. Few were expressing public outrage at the amount of time, energy, and emotion being displaced onto diets and disease. When I thought about starting the conversation, it scared me. I could already hear the critics in my own head: *You are making vast generalizations. You are unprepared, untrained, unqualified. How can you tell other people's stories for them? What about men with eating disorders? What about older women? Queer folks? What about the obesity epidemic?*

But the critics could not speak louder than the voices of my best friend, my cousin, my mentee, my students. The risk of having critics, I realized, could be no greater than the risk of losing more young women—metaphorically or physically. And so I sat down at my computer and did the only thing I know how to do when I am in great pain and feeling powerless: I wrote.

In the process of writing and reading and talking and thinking, I have been compelled to make generalizations. I know no other way to talk about culture. I recognize that there are women, young and old, who feel great about their bodies and won't connect with the mental and physical anguish I describe in this book. These lucky, rare women have sidestepped the cultural imperative to be perpetually unsatisfied with their form. I hope they will share their secrets of self-protection with the rest of us.

I am not an expert on eating disorders, nutrition, health, or psychology, but I do have expertise in quiet desperation. I can spot the light fuzz that covers an anorectic's body, the mysterious disappearances that signal bulimia, the dull cast in the eyes of a teenage girl who feels bad for eating too many cookies, the real story behind the stress fractures sustained by an avid runner who can't take it easy. In this book, I act as an observer, an outraged idealist, a story-teller, a bleeding heart, an eavesdropper, and an ordinary young woman.

A writer takes great responsibility when trying to speak for another—whether that other is a best friend or a whole generation of women. While some of the stories in this book are based on my memory of past events, I am also honored to have been trusted by many women whose interviews fill this book. I can only hope that I do their stories and their beauty justice. Most of them have asked for pseudonyms (signaled throughout the text by asterisks). In some cases, certain identifying characteristics have been changed. A few of them have bravely opted to use their real names. I not only welcome but implore other young women to add their voices to this conversation. I do not intend to be a voice in the wilderness; I intend to be instead the first note in a chorus.

So many are suffering from food and fitness obsessions—the victims are becoming younger and younger, older and older, male, gay, lesbian, and transgender. In order to explore even a fraction of this terrain with any clarity, I had to construct limits (however artificial), and so focus on the ways in which young, heterosexual women feel and fear. What they believe men find "hot" feeds their obsessions with food and fitness. A version of this dynamic exists also between lesbian women and between gay men, but I have not gathered the evidence necessary to address the ways in which it is undoubtedly different. This is intended to be not the definitive book on food and fitness obsession, but a beginning.

The obesity epidemic, which I explore in Chapter 8, is in truth the flip side of the same coin. Being underweight or overweight so often stems from the same roots: a society of extremes, struggles for control, learned behavior, self-hatred. I talk throughout this book about food and fitness obsessions as existing along a spectrum. Being on either end of the spectrum—totally obsessed or completely unengaged—is hazardous to your health. These extremes are crippling our society's collective economic, intellectual, and even spiritual health.

Perfect Girls,
Starving Daughters

Introduction

When we try to pick out anything by itself, we usually find it is hitched to everything else in the universe.

—John Muir

Eating disorders affect more than 7 million American girls and women, and up to 70 million people worldwide. Ninety-one percent of women recently surveyed on a college campus reported dieting; 22 percent of them dieted "always" or "often." In 1995, 34 percent of high school–age girls in the United States thought they were overweight. Today, 90 percent do. Over half the females between the ages of eighteen and twenty-five would prefer to be run over by a truck than be fat, and two-thirds surveyed would rather be mean or stupid. The single group of teenagers most likely to consider or attempt suicide is girls who worry that they are overweight. A survey of American parents found that one in ten would abort a child if they found out that he or she had a genetic tendency to be fat.

We live in a time when getting an eating disorder, or having an obsession over weight at the very least, is a rite of passage for girls. Terms such as *saturated fat* and *aerobic workout* roll off twelve-year-old tongues. One friend told me of a group of girls in her college dorm who set dates for group bingeing. They would fill a large serving bowl with their favorite forbidden foods—ice cream, bread, cookies—then eat them, and throw them up, in tandem. An eighteen-year-old girl I met during a summer enrichment program said her friend justifies not eating bread not because she is on Atkins—which would be embarrassingly clichéd—but because she "doesn't like the taste of carbs." A writer for a popular women's magazine tells me that one of her interns chews on Styrofoam peanuts because doing so gives her the experience of consuming food without any of the calories. Another friend of a friend calls up the Tasti D-Lites throughout the island of Manhattan to find out where the best flavors are so she can hit them for her daily dinner of frozen yogurt. Many women, even those who consider themselves healthy, classify what they have eaten or how much they have exercised as a marker of their worth in the world.

It is not our kindness or courage that we count at the end of the day, it is our caloric intake.

I look at the driven, diverse, brilliant, courageous, and beautiful women around me and am devastated by how many struggle with these issues. At age twenty-five, I can honestly say that the majority of the young women I know have either full-blown eating disorders or screwed-up attitudes toward food and fitness. Jen wills herself to eat, even though she still craves the high of a hollow stomach. Bonita* abandons her homework to go the gym with her sisters, listening to their banter about fad diets all the way there. Susan* avoids making dates that include food so she won't have to explain her rigid restrictions. Jane* wakes up in the middle of her liposuction surgery to the haunting sound of a sucking machine. This is the daily reality of the women in my immediate circle of friends. Even those who I thought might be safe from the powerful distraction of the scale turn out to be affected once I start asking. Big and beautiful Felice starved herself skinny, only to realize that life still wasn't perfect. Gareth, my brave fat-activist best friend, admits to me that she too has stuck her finger down her throat when the guilt over what she ate was too much to bear.

Connect the dots, and you have a tangled, paralyzing web of obsession. Seemingly isolated cases—the gagging sound in the bathroom, the family-style bowl of pasta disappearing in the night, the meticulous food diary—seen together are evidence of a larger picture of pathology. My generation is expending its energy on the wrong things. We are holed up in our bedrooms doing Google searches on low-fat foods, churning away on stationary bikes in torturous spinning classes, and feeling guilty, inadequate, shameful, and out of control in the process. We thought we would save the rain forest and find a cure for AIDS. Instead we are doing research on the most accurate scales and the latest diet trends.

Professors, sociologists, and parents have called us apathetic, but really we are distracted. We don't have time to think about the war in Iraq, because we can't get past the war in our own minds: Should I be "bad" and have pizza, or should I be "good" and have a salad? We can't look up and out because we are too busy looking down, scrutinizing our bodies in magnifying full-length mirrors. Delilah* planned her day around the bathrooms on campus that were least utilized so she could vomit in peace. Jen couldn't carry the groceries into her first house because she was too thin and had no energy. Girls and women across America turn down invitations to go to the beach because they don't want anyone to see them in their bathing suits.

How did this happen? Is this okay with everybody else? What can we do about it?

For a long time, these questions nagged at me, but I kept silent, thinking it was just the young women I knew who were starving themselves. Those to whom I did try to reach out were often dismissive. A friend studying psychology said, "Eating disorders are very individual psychological diseases, Courtney. You can't think of them as a social problem."

She was only partially right. Recent research does indicate that eating disorders have significant genetic and biochemical components, but other research confirms that our culture is very much an influence.

I push further: "But what about the fact that eating disorders disproportionately affect women? And what about all the girls who don't have diagnosable eating disorders but just obsess about every little thing they put in their mouths? That may not be a disease, but it definitely affects their lives in a significant way."

"That's America, Courtney. That's normal." With that, she took another sip of her Diet Coke.

One smart feminist to whom I talked about my concerns and ideas for this book told me, "It's been done, Courtney. Try to think of something new." I thanked her and shut my mouth, but inside I was screaming, *But this is what I'm living with! This is what I wake up in the morning to, what I walk around all day resisting, what I go to bed sad and hopeless about! Doesn't that matter to you?*

During an alumni event at Barnard College, I spoke to one of the older women at my table about my impressions of an epidemic of disordered thinking about food and fitness, how it seemed to be taking over young women's lives. "Oh, that's nothing new, honey," she responded. "That's womanhood. Women have always obsessed. They always will."

Many women have normalized food and fitness obsessions and collectively accept that "it is just part of being a woman" to count calories or feel guilty after every ice cream cone. We feel secretly pleased when we get sick because we know we will lose a few pounds. We eat healthy portions in social situations or out on dates, but when we are home, we feel relief that we can go back to our skimpy dinners without feeling observed—a nutrition bar, a small salad with a few crackers, a bowl of spinach and a piece of dry toast, a chicken breast plain and cold. "Everybody does it," a friend tells me. "It's just normal now."

But does that mean it's okay? Does that mean I should watch a generation of promising young women devote the better part of their intellects to scheduling visits to the gym and their next meal? Does it mean that we should just continue to watch it happen and chalk it up to individual psychology, something out of our control, no chance of prevention? Is this really what it means to be a woman?

I was raised by two feminists—my mom a clinical social worker and community activist, my dad a Buddhist bankruptcy lawyer—who told me that being a woman was about freedom of choice, a culture of care, a spirit of resilience and courage. My grandmother muscled her way through the premature death of her husband and learned to pay her own bills, make her own friends, travel her own path. When I rubbed her arthritic knuckles, I knew I was touching the hand of a soldier. From watching my mom move through the world, I concluded that being a woman meant spending time on the important things—community building, learning, teaching, loving, listening, birthing, caring for the dying. When my grandmother grew frail and out of it, it was my mother who dressed her, fought for her last wishes, cried without covering her face. Womanhood, they told me and showed me, was about something solid and beautiful right in the core—a vulnerable yet unbreakable center of strength and openness.

At the center of most of the young women I know today are black holes. Next to the brilliance, and the creativity, and the idealism is a bubbling, acid pit of guilt and shame and jealousy and restlessness and anxiety. It isn't that they aren't driven or brilliant or powerful or determined. To the contrary, most of the women I know between the ages of nine and twenty-nine (the age range I focus on in this book) are complete dynamos. In a recent study of thirteen hundred women, half of those with eating disorders described themselves as having been "obsessive perfectionists" as early as age eight. They dominate the classrooms, score higher on the MCATs and the LSATs than their older brothers, have exhausting social schedules, run marathons, devote time to volunteer work and artistic projects, and seek out mentors far more often than their boyfriends do. From the outside, these women look like they are just about to take over the world. But on the inside is a far less powerful picture.

Anna Quindlen, in her 2005 short book aptly titled *Being Perfect,* wrote: "Someday, sometime, you will be sitting somewhere. A berm overlooking a pond in Vermont. The lip of the Grand Canyon at sunset. A seat on the subway. And something bad will have happened: You will have lost someone you loved, or failed at something at which you badly wanted to succeed. And sitting there, you will fall into the center of yourself. You will look for some core to sustain you. And if you have been perfect all your life and have managed to meet all the expectations of your family, your friends, your community, your society, chances are excellent that there will be a black hole where that core ought to be."

My friends and I, girls and young women across the nation (and even, I have learned, across the world), harbor black holes at the center of our beings. We, the perfect girls, try to fill these gaping holes with food, blue ribbons, sexual attention, trendy clothes, but no matter how hard we try, they remain. We have called this insatiable hunger by many different names—ambition, drive, pride—but in truth it is a fundamental distrust that we deserve to be on this earth in the shape we are in. A perfect girl must always be a starving daughter, because there is never enough—never enough accomplishment. Never enough control. Never enough perfection.

Our mothers had the luxury of aspiring to be "good," but we have the ultimate goal of "effortless perfection." This was the term that young women at Duke University used to describe "the expectation that one would be smart, accomplished, fit, beautiful, and popular, and that all this would happen without visible effort" in a series of discussions held in 2001 as part of their Women's Initiative. This is not, of course, just a Duke thing. "Effortless perfection" has become the unattainable and anxiety-producing ideal for women across the country and across the world. We must not only be perfect—as in accomplished, brilliant, beautiful, witty—but also appear as if we achieve all this perfection through an easygoing, fun-loving approach. Perfect girls are powerfully afraid of seeming too uptight, rigid, or moralistic. We don't just want to achieve; we also want to be cool.

The "perfect" part of this equation gets us in trouble with eating disorders, or obsessions with food and fitness. The Herculean effort to appear effortless keeps us silent or nonchalant about the pain we are in.

In truth, "effortless perfection" is a hell of a lot of work. Calories, workouts, pounds, new diet trends, feeling guilty, shameful, inadequate, out of control. Imagine—no, seriously, close your eyes and imagine—the time that you spend each day thinking about food, fitness, and the size and shape of your body:

- One minute debating whether to have a bagel and be "bad" or a protein shake and be "good"; two minutes chastising yourself for choosing the bagel; two minutes contemplating how fattening the cream cheese was

- Three minutes poking your face in the mirror, feeling bad about the dark circles under your eyes

- Four minutes reading that Lindsay Lohan lost a bunch of weight; another minute chastising yourself for being so vulnerable to the media; five minutes thinking about how crazy it is that women as smart as you spend so much of their days obsessing about food and fitness

- Two minutes contemplating whether to head for the salad bar at lunch or get the chicken sandwich you actually crave; one minute thinking how hungry you still are after your salad; three minutes milling around the snack bar wondering if you should get one more little thing

- Two minutes trying to figure out when you should go the gym

- One minute standing in front of the coffee counter, trying to figure out what drink is sweet enough that it tastes good but doesn't contain a lot of hidden calories

- Ten minutes talking to your friend in the student union about how much crap you drank (i.e., keg beer) and ate (i.e., 2:00 A.M. pizza) over the weekend and how gross you're feeling

- Five minutes lying on your bed contemplating whether to go to the gym or take a nap, which you really want to do; five minutes wondering if your body looks anything like that of the girl on the treadmill directly in front of you; two minutes hating her when you decide you are much rounder

- Three minutes debating with your roommate whether to go down to the cafeteria and risk major overeating or to go out for sushi and risk major overspending; five minutes wandering around the cafeteria trying to decide what to eat that sounds good but isn't going to make you blow up; two minutes debating whether taking the top slice of bread off of your tuna sandwich makes you look lame

- One minute resisting the temptation to get frozen yogurt; one minute recounting everything you've eaten that day in order to justify to yourself that you haven't been that "bad" and deserve it; five minutes arguing with your roommate about the actual calorie content of frozen yogurt, the nutritional value of soy, and the Atkins diet

- Five minutes talking shit about the really skinny girl getting a few pieces of lettuce and pouring balsamic vinegar over it

- One minute pledging to yourself that you won't eat one more thing the rest of the night; two minutes thinking about how little willpower you have when you eat some gummy bears out of the care package your mom sent; three minutes trying to get other people to eat some with you

- Three minutes distracted from your poli sci reading while you think about how thin you want to be by the summertime; two minutes recounting, again, what you ate all day and chastising yourself for the bagel, the frozen yogurt, and the gummy bears while trying to fall asleep; one minute planning what you will eat and when you will exercise tomorrow

Sound familiar? So many women spend at least this much time— about a hundred minutes a day—scrutinizing instead of loving their bodies. That's one hundred minutes a day they could spend admiring the impressive curve of their shoulders, the width of their hips, the way their hair falls to one side, the baffling work of their organs and muscles. That's one hundred minutes they could spend celebrating their creativity, curiosity, dedication, and openness. That's one hundred minutes they could spend reading an amazing book, feeling grateful for family and friends, memorizing a poem, considering concepts of God, or taking action against global warming.

Many women waste even more time on their bodies. If the average woman spends about an hour a day contemplating her size, her calorie intake, and her exercise regimen starting at the age of twelve and she lives for eighty-five years, she will have lost over three years of her life. Three years! Most women I know get irritated if they spend more than five minutes waiting for a bus or talking to an uninteresting guy at a bar. Three years of inefficiency, powerlessness, and sheer waste should make us furious!

Yet many of the women I have spoken to over the years seem resigned to their fate of caring too much about the shapes of their bodies, despite realizing that it is a shallow pursuit. Most of them shrug when I ask the hard question: What can we do to close the gap between what we know—that body obsession is a waste of time and spirit—and how we actually lead our lives and think about ourselves? One of my mom's wild and wonderful friends told me, "When you're my age, you don't give a shit about what other people think. You can eat whatever you want, wear whatever you want. Courtney, you can be whoever you want."

"But I don't want to wait until I'm fifty to feel that way," I told her. And many women fifty and older still don't feel that way.

I turned to books in hope of finding some answers. Many older women don't understand the depth of my generation's despair. In fact, many older women (mothers, teachers, coaches, bosses) give younger women positive feedback for their obsessive dedication to thinness or their imbalanced, insatiable drive for perfection. I certainly perceived that most of my mentors were thrilled that I felt compelled to write faster, stay longer, and sacrifice balance in pursuit of achievement. An otherwise brilliant boss once said to me, "Oh, you're skinny, you don't have to worry." Does this mean, I wondered, that if I wasn't "skinny," I *would* have to worry? What exactly should I be worrying about?

Much has been written by many insightful, brave women about media and body image, food and emotions, perfectionism and eating disorders, the complexity of family and identity. In *Unbearable Weight,* Susan Bordo takes an academic but authentic stab at drawing parallels between the body and the culture. Kim Chernin dives into the depths of our psyches and discovers that our relationships with food reflect our relationships with our mothers and our femaleness in general. Geneen Roth, author of *Feeding the Hungry Heart,* reveals ways for women to become self-aware and embrace pleasure. The late Caroline Knapp's anorexia memoir, *Appetites,* pushes women to consider the almost universal female struggle with "hunger." Naomi Wolf rails against the system that grants beauty a greater value than intelligence in the influential *Beauty Myth,* written when she was twenty-five. The psychologist Marion Woodman quotes Shakespeare, Jung, and Donne in her books on the deadly imbalance of the feminine and masculine in modern culture and writes: "To move toward perfection is to move out of life." Marya Hornbacher's eloquent memoir, *Wasted,* is proof of Woodman's claim—a terrifying true story of one young woman's plunge into oblivion.

To all of these courageous writers, I am deeply indebted. This book is my own answer to the unsettling feeling I was left with even after experiencing their wisdom. I didn't want to read psychological theory or history on eating disorders and obsessions. I felt uninspired by the fashion-magazines-are-rotting-your-mind theory, for which the filmmaker Jean Kilbourne is the pied piper in *Killing Us Softly* and *Slim Hopes.* Painting the mass media and advertising as the ultimate, deliberate evil is too simplified and unconvincing on a personal level. I'm smart. So are my friends. We were familiar with marketing and media literacy from a young age, hip to the fact that Barbie, supermodels, and the beauty industry were dangerous for our psyches.

We need a new analysis about the ways in which pop culture and the Internet age are covertly shaping our ideas about beauty and femaleness. Given all of our media training, how do fads and fasting celebrities still manage to weasel their ways into our brains and influence our ideas about our own bodies? How can we still engage with pop culture in fun and ironic ways, and even reclaim it, without being brainwashed by it?

I wanted to read a book that tried to answer these questions—a book that traced girls back to their beginnings and looked for the vulnerable moments, the tipping points. I wanted to read a book in which I could see my childhood, adolescence, and young adulthood in other women's stories. I wanted a book that communicated the complexity and danger involved in growing up a girl now, right now, a book that told the truth about my generation's tumultuous love affair with perfectionism and showed why it is not all good.

I wanted to read Harriet the Spy–like observations of mothers and fathers and how they influence attitudes toward beauty and success. I wanted a clear picture of the tightrope on which every adolescent girl precariously balances—that feeling of never wanting to be too sexual or too prudish, too forward or too timid, too fun or too rigid. I wanted to read descriptions of the thick and sultry beat of hip-hop as it seeped out of her first boyfriend's car, a music that would initially seduce and ultimately silence her. I wanted my generation to confirm our collective disappointment with the contemporary parade of bimbo pop stars. I wanted to read raw, honest answers to the question: What do guys *really* want? I wanted to read something that untangled our all-or-nothing nation's incredibly messy knot of spin about fat, health, and willpower. I wanted to put into words the soaring sisterhood of team sports and also find admissions to the often dangerous level of dedication. I wanted to read the real truth about college—the lurking around the salad bar, the cosmetics kits full of laxatives—and the feeling of floating nowhere that came afterward. I wanted a call to action.

But I didn't find that book. I found memoirs about anorexia and bulimia, painful accounts of weight obsessions taken to the extreme. I found psychological and spiritual polemics, women my mom's age spouting hard-earned wisdom about the sacredness of the body and the goddess within. I found histories of eating disorders that revealed that problems are not new but are showing up in different, more pernicious forms. I found self-help books with bright, flashy covers whose celebrity authors exhorted us to "take back your life."

So at age twenty-five, I figured—why not me? Why don't I write down what I want to know—what I know others are longing to know—so that the next time a girl in Colorado Springs or Corvallis or Hartford goes searching her sister's shelf for something that makes sense of the world, she finds a story that reminds her of her own. That makes her pain real. That makes all of our pain real.

I want this book to move us all—the prom queens and the hip-hop heads, the volleyball stars and the newspaper editors, the investment bankers and the social workers—to admit that we are sick. Because on some level, in some way, we *are* sick. And we are also really, truly sick of being sick.

In this book, I extricate myself from the rat race for thinness, stand still and look around, describe the textbook-case eating disorders that surround me as well as the supposedly healthy girls who spend their days writing in food diaries and feeling bad about themselves. I suggest that maybe things can be different, that maybe food obsession isn't a necessary part of being a woman.

This book is filled with stories of my friends and my friends' friends, and sometimes even my friends' friends' friends. For several years, I have sat in coffee shops and bars and taken long road trips to talk with these girls and women. I have read revealing, brave e-mails and letters from women all over the country—Hara from Jersey, Elizabeth from Southern California, and Lorie from Portland, Maine.

What I first thought was an American problem turns out to be insidious almost anywhere that food is not scarce and MTV appears; Tatijiana from Germany, Hiromi from Japan, and Anna Rose from London told me how weight obsession plays out in their home countries. Recent research confirms that more than forty countries report eating disorders, including seemingly unlikely locales such as Nigeria, India, South Africa, and Mexico.

Japan's "culture of cute" (*kawaii bunka*) encourages rampant eating disorders; a 2001 National Nutrition Survey reported a 100 percent increase in the rate of underweight Japanese women since 1990. A 2003 study of high school girls in Hong Kong found that though only 4.80 percent of them were overweight, 85.16 percent wanted to weigh less. Another in an all-female kibbutz in northern Israel found that 85 percent of adolescent girls were dissatisfied with their figures, 63 percent were considering a diet, and 60 percent were afraid of "losing control over their weight." Almost a quarter of girls from the United Arab Emirates, according to a recent study there, are unhealthily preoccupied with food and fitness. *The Independent,* a London paper, recently reported that more than 1 million people in Britain now suffer from eating disorders. An unprecedented law passed in Buenos Aires requires retailers to carry sizes above the U.S. equivalent of a size six after the government recognized that healthy women in this eating disorder–infested country couldn't even find clothing to fit them.

I have spent hours on the phone with women as young as eleven and as old as eighty, mulling over this undeniable problem and possible solutions. Many of their stories echo one another despite biographical differences.

Many conversations I have had recently with women my age and younger start out centered on "a friend." *You know who you should really talk to*, they tell me, *is my high school best friend, Olivia. She was really screwed up about food.* Or *I mean I'm not totally happy with my body, but I would never starve myself. Unlike my cousin— now, that's who you should really interview if you want an intense story.* If I stick with it long enough and explain that I am actually interested in talking to women with a range of perspectives, the pronouns shift—*she* becomes *I*. Sometimes this shift happens unconsciously: *Yeah, she got into really bad cycles with fasting and exercising excessively. It's like you try to eat right and avoid bad foods, and then I feel guilty when I cheat and I'll go the gym and work out a lot to try to make it right again.* I rewind, listen again, and wonder at the seamlessness of the transition.

I have mined my own childhood for the defining moments when I learned that my body was a currency and my ability to control, confine, and cultivate it one of my most difficult charges as a girl. I have used my story as a backdrop throughout the book, a benchmark to understand what is peculiar to my middle-class suburban white background, and what speaks to a larger truth about growing up a girl in the dusk of the twentieth and the dawn of the twenty-first centuries. I realized, as I gathered the vulnerable, emotional stories, that I would have to be just as open and revealing as the women I interviewed.

Some of the experts I respect most, the ones who seem most attuned to the lives girls are actually leading rather than stuck to old theories or misleading statistics, heard about my project and said,

"Finally. Finally, your generation is finding its own voice." These psychologists and nutritionists care more about healing people than about being right. They are expert at sitting with someone else in pain, being quiet, telling their own stories if it helps. They informed my thinking greatly.

In swimsuit dressing rooms, Girls Inc. summer camps, conventions for eating disorder specialists, third-wave feminist work groups, Overeaters Anonymous meetings, and high school dances, I have taken furious notes on the ways in which women's ideas about their own bodies dictate their behavior. At the recent wedding of a childhood best friend, I went into the bathroom and heard the distinct sounds of a girl making herself throw up. When I told my boyfriend, he joked that he was surprised I didn't crawl up the side of the stall next to her, peer over, and ask, "Do you want to be in a book?"

Girls understand their own bodies and their power in the world through a strange and complicated mix of influences—television, radio, magazines, movies, health class, their mothers, their fathers, their siblings, their boyfriends, their genetics, the Olympics, porn, the prom, et cetera. Television reflects this culture, from *I Want a Famous Face* on MTV to the constant references to size and shape on talk shows and sitcoms. And women's magazines, with rare exception, are notorious incubators of the worst of our fears and phobias. As Pink so pointedly satirized in her 2006 "Stupid Girls" video, the vacuous lyrics and political personas featured in Top 40 fare are rife with messages about the preeminent importance of women's bodies with little mention of their minds.

Further, a variety of experts—including psychologists, spiritual advisers, self-help gurus, and Girl Scout leaders—profess to have the answer to girls' problems. But the true authority on a young woman's battle with her own body is the woman herself.

I have listened to the stories of the girls I met and asked them personal, necessary questions, trying to understand the larger implications of their suffering. Sometimes I have tried to understand the importance of the things they cannot see or say. Their stories paint an authentic, sometimes unexpectedly funny, sometimes painful, often powerful, and ultimately hopeful picture of what it is like to grow up in this body-preoccupied time.

I believe in the possibility of a world where a girl doesn't learn how to count calories at the same age she learns algebra. I believe that my generation can raise our daughters to believe they can be anything but that they do *not* have to be perfect at everything. There is room to believe that you, the reader, can see yourself in some of the stories contained within this book and find some kind of peace in that recognition.

I set out asking: How did we become so obsessed with perfection, so preoccupied with food and fitness, and what can we do to reclaim our time and our energy? *Perfect Girls, Starving Daughters* is my attempt to answer, one story at a time.

1

Perfect Girls, Starving Daughters

There is a girl, right now, staring in a mirror in Des Moines, scrutinizing her widening hips. There is a girl, right now, spinning like a hamster on speed in a gym on the fifth floor of a building in Boston, promising herself dinner if she goes two more miles. There is a girl, right now, trying to wedge herself into a dress two sizes too small in a Savannah shopping mall, chastising herself for being so lazy and fat. There is a girl, right now, in a London bathroom, trying not to get any vomit on her aunt's toilet seat. There is a girl, right now, in Berlin, cutting a cube of cheese and an apple into barely visible pieces to eat for her dinner.

Our bodies are the places where our drive for perfection gets played out. Food is all around us, as are meals and the pressure that goes with them. Well-intentioned after-school specials teach us, from a very young age, how to purge our snacks. We are inundated with information about "good" and "bad" foods, the most effective workout regimens, the latest technological advancements in plastic surgery. We demand flawlessness in our appearance—the outer manifestation of our inner dictators.

To some degree, this makes sense. People in general like to look at a pretty face—which means they also like to be friends with a pretty face, do business with a pretty face, and marry a pretty face. Attractive people are desired and coddled in our society; they have an easier time getting jobs, finding boyfriends and girlfriends, getting parts in music videos, simply getting the average waiter's attention. Even smart girls must be beautiful, even athletes must be feminine. Corporate CEOs, public intellectuals, and even accountants must be thin. Lorie, an eighteen-year-old from Portland, Maine, wrote, "Everyone wants to be skinny, because in life the skinny one gets the guy, the job, the love." A ten-year-old girl I interviewed in Santa Fe, New Mexico, broke it down for me even further: "It is better to be pretty, which means thin and mean, than to be ugly, which means fat and nice. That's just how it is."

The body is the perfect battleground for perfect-girl tendencies because it is tangible, measurable, obvious. It takes four long years to see "summa cum laude" etched across our college diplomas, but stepping on a scale can instantly tell us whether we have succeeded or failed.

The cruel irony is that although we become totally obsessed with the daily measures of how "good" or "bad" we are (refused dessert = good; didn't have time to go to the gym = bad), there is no finish line. This weight preoccupation will never lead us anywhere. It is a maniacal maze that always spits you out at the same point it sucked you up: wanting. We keep chasing after perfection as if it is an achievable goal, when really it is the most grand and painful of all mirages.

Beauty is the first impression of total success. Social psychologists call this the halo effect: We see one aspect of a person—such as her nice hair—and assume a host of other things about her—that she is wealthy, effective, and powerful. Looking good indicates control, dedication, grace. If you are beautiful, we learn, you are probably rich, lucky, and loved. You are probably sought after, seen, envied. You probably have ample opportunities for dates and promotions. Our generation does not generally equate beauty with stupidity the way our parents or grandparents sometimes did. Beautiful, to us, has come in savvy packages—Tyra Banks creating her own empire, Candace Bushnell writing her way into four-hundred-dollar Manolo Blahniks.

If you are beautiful, we have concluded, you can construct the perfect life—even if you are not brilliant, well educated, or coura-geous—because the world will offer itself up to you. By contrast, if you are overweight—even if you are brilliant, dynamic, funny, and dedicated—you have no chance at the perfect life. Thinness and beauty are the prerequisites for perfection, which to my generation appears to be the only road to happiness.

From a very young age, we see weight as something in our con-trol. If we account for every calorie that we consume, if we plan our fitness schedule carefully and follow through, if we are exacting about our beauty regimen—designer makeup, trendy clothes—then, we con-clude, we will be happy. And we can be beautiful if we are just com-mitted enough—no matter our genetics, our bank account, or our personality—as we have learned from advertising and the American Dream ethos. This logic leads us to believe that, if we are unhappy, it is because of our weight and, in turn, our lack of willpower. We are our own roadblocks on this road to twenty-first-century female per-fection and happiness.

The Jungian psychologist Marion Woodman has our number:

> In an effort to be mature and independent . . . a woman tries to be more and more perfect because the only way she can allevi-ate her dependence on that judgmental voice is to be perfect enough to shut it up. Thus the opposites meet in a terrifying contradiction. As she runs as fast as she can for independence via perfection, she runs into her own starving self, totally dependent and crying out for food.

Was I just your average temperamental, overcommitted teenage girl in the middle of America? On some level, yes. I grew up in a middle-class household with a lawyer daddy, a homemaker/community volunteer/consulting therapist mommy, and a Nordic-looking, over-protective older brother (captain of the tennis, lacrosse, and basketball teams and math genius). I rode my bike around the neighborhood, sold lemonade on the corner, and sneaked out of the house at midnight to toilet-paper big Victorian houses. The first time I told my boyfriend, who is from Bed-Stuy, Brooklyn, that I used to get to middle school by carpool, he scoffed: "I thought those only existed in television sitcoms. Oh my God, you really do come from the Beaver Cleaver family!"

Colorado Springs, Colorado, was suburbia to the nth degree, home of strip malls, chain restaurant heaven, and Focus on the Family. *Normal* doesn't begin to describe how homogenous my hometown was.

Perfect Girls

But as in any American town with picket fences this white, something dark lurked underneath. Like *American Beauty*'s psychopathic real estate agent, the mothers I knew were often grinding their teeth and trying to outdo one another in landscaping and SUVs. The fathers—mostly doctors and lawyers—were socially accepted workaholics who attended big games and graduations still in their suits. The sons were out on the field 24/7, dreaming of Big Ten schools. And the girls . . . were perfect.

Yet these perfect girls still feel we could always lose five more pounds. We get into good colleges but are angry if we don't get into every college we applied to. We are the captains of the basketball teams, the soccer stars, the swimming state champs with boxes full of blue ribbons. We win scholarships galore, science fairs and knowledge bowls, spelling bees and mock trial debates. We are the girls with anxiety disorders, filled appointment books, five-year plans.

We take ourselves very, very seriously. We are the peacemakers, the do-gooders, the givers, the savers. We are on time, overly prepared, well read, and witty, intellectually curious, always moving.

We are living contradictions. We are socially conscious, multi-culti, and anticorporate, but we still shop at Gap and Banana Republic. We listen to hip-hop, indie rock, and country on our iPods. We are the girls in hooker boots, wife beaters, and big earrings. We make documentary films, knit sweaters, and DJ. We are "social smokers," secretly happy that the cigarettes might speed up our metabolisms, hoping they won't kill us in the process.

We pride ourselves on getting as little sleep as possible and thrive on self-deprivation. We drink coffee, a lot of it. We are on birth control, Prozac, and multivitamins. We do strip aerobics, hot yoga, go five more minutes than the limit on any exercise machine at the gym.

We are relentless, judgmental with ourselves, and forgiving to others. We never want to be as passive-aggressive as our mothers, never want to marry men as uninspired as our fathers. We carry the old world of guilt—center of families, keeper of relationships, caretaker of friends—with the new world of ambition—rich, independent, powerful. We are the daughters of feminists who said "You can be anything" and we heard "You have to be everything."

We must get A's. We must make money. We must save the world. We must be thin. We must be unflappable. We must be beautiful. We are the anorectics, the bulimics, the overexercisers, the overeaters. We must be perfect. We must make it look effortless.

We grow hungrier and hungrier with no clue what we are hungry for. The holes inside of us grow bigger and bigger.

This quintessentially female brand of perfectionism goes on all over America, not just in suburban enclaves but in big cities, mountain towns, trailer parks. And perfect girls abound in Vancouver, Rio, Tokyo, and Sydney. Their compulsion to achieve constantly, to perform endlessly, to demand absolute perfection in every aspect of life is part of a larger, undeniable trend in the women of my generation all over the world.

I satisfied my hunch that this was the case by consulting more than twenty-five experts in the fields of food, fitness, and psychology, interviewing twice as many girls and young women about their personal experiences (sometimes multiple times), and conducting focus groups with girls on the topic across the country. When I sent out an informal survey via e-mail to all the women I knew and asked them to forward it on to all the women they knew, I got more than one hundred echoing responses in my in-box. Here are just a few:

I am DEFINITELY a perfectionist. To the extreme. Everything I do has to be perfect—whether it be school, gymnastics, working out, etc. I do not allow myself to be the slightest bit lazy. I think if I heard someone call me lazy, I would cry!

—Kristine, Tucson, AZ, 22

Perfectionists were rampant at my all-women's high school, as were eating disorders. I think I can remember two women in my class who really didn't have body issues and I always admired them. I never had an eating disorder, but I definitely didn't get away without disordered ideas about food.

—Tara, Beirut, Lebanon, 27

I have always been and always will be a perfectionist in almost everything I do. It creates a struggle within me to truly define or determine when I will be good enough.

—Melissa, McKinney, TX, 21

I do not consider myself a perfectionist, but others describe me that way. There is always room for self-improvement with my body, no matter how thin I am.

—Kelly, Denver, CO, 28

People who know me call me an overachiever. I am hard on myself. My body fits into this mentality because I'm tall, long, lean, but that is the result of strict diet and lots of exercise.

—Kathleen, Jersey City, NJ, 28

I am quite a perfectionist. If I put on weight, I would be very upset. I would see it as a sign of failure on my part to control myself.

—Michelle, Dublin, Ireland, 24

Our bodies, our needs, our cravings, our sadness, our weakness, our stillness inevitably become our own worst enemies. It is the starving daughter within who must be shut down, muted, ignored . . . eventually killed off.

Starving Daughters

A starving daughter lies at the center of each perfect girl. The face we show to the world is one of beauty, maturity, determination, strength, willpower, and ultimately, accomplishment. But beneath the façade is a daughter—starving for attention and recognition, starving to justify her own existence.

The starving daughter within annoys us, slows us down, embarrasses us. She is the one who doubts our ability to handle a full-time job and full-time school. She gets scared, lonely, homesick. She drinks too much, cries too loud, is nostalgic and sappy. When neglected, she seeks comfort in cookies, coffee ice cream, warm bread—transgressions that make the perfect girl in us angry.

The starving daughter emerges in midnight confessions, a best friend's sudden tears, a suite mate buried in mountains of covers, shades drawn, eating ice cream in the middle of the day, and watching *Buffy* reruns in the dark.

Starving daughters are full of self-doubt. We don't want to worry so much about making other people happy but feel like we can never say thank you enough times, never show enough humility, never help enough, never feel enough shame. We feel guilty. We fear conflict. We are dramatic, sensitive, injured easily. We are clinging to all kinds of attachments that, in our minds, we know we should let go of, but in our bodies, we feel incapable of relinquishing. We are self-pitying, sad, even depressed.

We are tired of trying so hard all the time. We feel like giving up. We feel hopeless. We want love, acceptance, happy endings, and rest. We wish that we had faith, that we weren't ruled by our heads and could live in our hearts more often. We want to have daughters—little girls who will love us unconditionally. We steal small things, such as candy bars and bras—that make us feel special for just a moment. We try to fill the black holes inside of us with forbidden foods. We never feel full. We always feel cold. We starve for a god.

We don't like to talk about this part of ourselves. Our whole lives, we have received so much affirmation for the perfect part that the starving-daughter part feels like an evil twin. Sometimes we can even convince ourselves that the sadness, self-doubts, and hunger don't exist, that we *like* to be this busy, that we *like* to eat small, unfulfilling portions or work out constantly.

For a while . . . but then the phone doesn't ring when we want it to or we get passed over for a job or a fellowship. Then the starving daughter makes herself known like an explosion. We collapse from exhaustion, or pick fights with our boyfriends or families, or sob inside the locked bathroom stall. Some girls experience their deep sadness in going on binges (food or alcohol), sleeping all day, sleeping around, buying a lot of clothes they don't need, ignoring professional or relational opportunities, dropping out of the race altogether. Some of my best friends have retreated inside themselves in this way, refused help, wasted away, or cloaked themselves in excess weight. We get mono and can't move for weeks. We hate losing control. We hate being "wimps." We fight these breakdowns, but the starving daughter emerges, young and scared and sick of our shit.

Young women struggle with this duality. The perfect girl in each drives forward, the starving daughter digs in her heels. The perfect girl wants excellence, the starving daughter calm and nurturance. The perfect girl takes on the world, the starving daughter shrinks from it. It is a power struggle between two forces, and at the center, almost every time, is an innocent body.

The Art of Diagnosis

The degree to which women channel their anxiety and ambition into their bodies varies. Some are subtle about the strain between their drive and vulnerability. They would rather pretend that they are above the inane calorie counting or messy bingeing and purging that other girls do. They would prefer to be skinnier but are not going to starve themselves to get there. That would be embarrassing.

Others go through peaks and valleys of obsession, spending months at a time churning through a cycle of destructive self-talk about how unsatisfied they are with their body size and shape, how lazy and weak, then rebounding when they get too busy or too in love to think so much about their imperfections. Their body obsession is seasonal, tolerable, easily brushed under the rug.

I'm one of the girls who has been on the edge of an eating disorder but lucky or scared enough that I have not crossed the line. Yet since the age of about sixteen, I have felt as if I have a common cold. It's sometimes worse, sometimes better, and I always have this underlying fear that the cold could lead to a more serious, even deadly disease. Sometimes I feel worse about my body than others, but I can generally muffle the nasty bitch in my head who tells me that my butt is too big or my stomach too round. She doesn't scream the way she does at some of my friends who have full-blown, diagnosable eating disorders.

There are currently three eating disorders in the *Diagnostic and Statistical Manual of Mental Disorders* (DSM-IV)—the big book that psychologists use to label what kind of crazy everyone is. They are anorexia nervosa (which made its DSM debut in 1980), bulimia nervosa (1987), and binge-eating disorder (1994).

Anorectics starve themselves until they are 15 percent or more below a normal body weight for their height and lose their periods. Even when they are skeletally thin, many of them still see themselves as fat—a phenomenon called "body dysmorphic disorder," which scientists are just beginning to understand is associated with blood flow in the parietal cortex of the brain. The girls who develop anorexia are often poster girls for perfectionism: control freaks, straight-A students, big-time pleasers. Many have a genetic predisposition as well, a component being explored by clinicians and scientists. Anorexia nervosa is the most deadly psychological disease;

5 percent of those who have anorexia for up to ten years and 20 percent of those who battle the disease for twenty years eventually die as a result of it.

With both bulimia nervosa and binge-eating disorder, women eat large amounts of food, far more than they need, in one sitting. Bingeing is defined, in the DSM-IV, as eating an amount of food that is larger than what most people eat in a relatively short period of time, such as an hour or two. The size of a binge varies according to a woman's size, but the average is fifteen hundred calories. To be diagnosed as bulimic, one must vomit twice a week minimum.

Usually these women mistake emotional hunger for physical hunger. Women who suffer from bulimia take drastic and immediate measures to purge after a binge. Most commonly they make themselves throw up, but some use laxatives or extreme exercising to get the food (and the associated feelings of guilt, shame, sadness, and anger) out of their systems. Women with binge-eating disorder usually eat and wallow in their guilt, refraining from any of these alternatives.

Psychologists are beginning to realize that perfect girls don't like to be pigeonholed. A lot of young women suffer from combinations of these diseases depending on the time of life (or the time of day). Professionals often describe these women as suffering from bulimiarexia, though it is not an official diagnosis in the DSM-IV.

A grab-bag category called "eating disorder not otherwise specified" (EDNOS for short) does appear in the bible of psychological diagnosis and is applied to those who don't satisfy all the requirements outlined for the other diseases. Binge-eating disorder was distinguished from this category in 1994, when enough research indicated that it was a separate disease. Experts expect that the DSM-V may feature similar additions or, alternatively, a revision of the rigid restrictions on current diagnoses. For example, large numbers of young women binge and purge once a week and therefore don't "qualify" for a bulimia nervosa diagnosis. But clearly these women need the same intensity of attention as those who happen to purge once more. Many young women starve themselves but don't lose their periods, a requirement for the official diagnosis of anorexia nervosa.

The very existence of the EDNOS option is a telling indication of the "art," as opposed to "science," of diagnosing eating disorders.

Those women who have a more extreme version of the common cold—i.e., a time-wasting, confidence-draining obsession, a binge and purge a month, a tendency to undereat—get lumped together in a category called "partial-syndrome eating disorder." They are not likely to see their neurosis as anything other than a nagging preoccupation. It's normal. In fact, you would be hard-pressed to find a woman who doesn't think more than she would like to about food and fitness. This is especially scary because repeated studies have proven that the gateway to a full-blown eating disorder is the simple trendy diet. "Oh, I'll just go on Atkins for a little while" quickly shifts into "If I'm not eating bread, I might as well cut out lunch altogether." In my informal e-mail survey of more than a hundred women, not one said that she was satisfied with how much she thought about her diet or her workout regimen every day. Each described too much obsession and too little action, the internal battle of the perfect girl with a militaristic agenda and the starving daughter who is too tired to satisfy her.

Another interesting tendency emerged in my survey. One of the early questions was "Have you ever had or do you now have a diagnosable eating disorder? Please elaborate, i.e.: When did it start? Are you still struggling with it? Please describe in as much detail as you are comfortable." Over half the women answered "No, *but . . .*" and then went on to describe a time in their lives when they stopped eating, ran ten miles every day, started throwing up a few times a month, or sometimes, every once in a while, used laxatives. A few examples:

No, but I threw up food for a couple of days after I realized I had been gaining weight. I told my boyfriend (in tears) after blood came up, and he made sure I stopped.

—Jenna, Bloomington, MN, 18

I never had a diagnosed eating disorder, but in seventh grade I attended an all-girls Catholic school and I stopped eating altogether. I guess I am still struggling with it because I still have a bad relationship with food.

—Debbie, New York, NY, 26

No, as a teenager I would crash diet, eat 800 calories a day, but I'm over that. 25% of the girls in my high school class had eating disorders and I didn't want to be one of them.

—Lauren, Atlanta, GA, 27

These women's responses indicate that the way we have been socialized to think about food and fitness obsessions is to "otherize" them. It makes us feel safe to think that *those* girls, over *there,* the ones with the really serious problems and the really screwed-up families, are the ones who develop full-blown disorders. *They* are the ones who have to go to the hospital and all that. *They* are the ones who need therapy. The rest of us are just dealing with the everyday "stuff" of being a girl in this society. We can live with it. (We don't consider that we don't *have* to.)

The media have contributed to this inaccurate notion that food and fitness obsessions are dangerous only when they reach a lethal level. Shows such as *Entertainment Tonight* and magazines such as *Us Weekly* show skin-and-bones shock photos of anorectic models, dramatize the glass jars filled with vomit hidden in bulimic girls' closets, reenact their grotesque binges with actresses paid to look like wild animals. Unless we are seriously debilitated by our obsession—dropping out of school, fading away into skeletal form, or throwing up after every single meal—the media make us feel as if we are okay. We aren't like *those* girls we've seen on TV. We're not *that* out of control.

The media have an obvious love-hate relationship with these disorders. Magazine editors know that publishing Fergie's latest diet sells copy, just as entertainment tabloid shows have proof that footage of skeletal women boosts ratings. The media moguls, however, don't like the idea of analyzing their own role in promulgating these images. In an analysis of the women's magazine coverage of eating disorders since 1980, the Drexel University communications professor Ronald Bishop found that "treating eating disorders as aberration allows the editor to deal with a serious problem while at the same time sustaining a discourse that contributes to the problem."

Many health care professionals—doctors especially—also encourage this me-versus-them attitude when it comes to eating and exercise pathology. Some are so weary of the concurrent epidemic of obesity that they have put on blinders when dealing with the other extreme. These doctors encourage rigorous exercise and restraint in diet, regardless of the profile of the individual patient. A good friend of mine recently had a doctor recommend that she avoid carbs for breakfast and eat boiled eggs instead, despite the fact that she solicited no advice on how to lose weight, has a history of anorexia, and was in for a routine checkup. The doctor was a woman. Another girl I interviewed talked about seeing a doctor in college, secretly praying that he would notice her dwindling weight, but as she left his office, he hollered after her, "Keep up the good work. Lookin' great!" My former gynecologist showed me the body mass index in her office and pointed out how many pounds I had to go before I was overweight. She didn't mention a thing about the other end of the scale. I wondered if she was trying to subtly let me know that I needed to "watch it" (as if every girl isn't already).

The media and so many doctors would have us believe that eating disorders are like the chicken pox: Either we have one or we don't. But there is no blood test we can take to confirm that we are misdirecting our energy, time, and money. There is no urine sample that proves your life is being watered down by your focus on the inanity of counting calories. Susie Orbach, a feminist psychologist who has helped thousands of women with her 1978 book, *Fat Is a Feminist Issue,* argues that eating disorders are many and varied in the way they manifest themselves, and women should not consider themselves "out of the woods" because they don't fit the textbook diagnoses.

I'm with Susie. Eating disorders are more extreme versions of what nearly every girl and woman faces on a daily basis—a preoccupation with what they put in their mouths and how it affects the shape and size of their bodies. We all have some degree of obsessiveness about food and our bodies. A lucky few feel guilty only for major

Thanksgiving binges or when they haven't been to the gym in months. Some of us are relatively healthy, doing a decent job of avoiding the cultural influences that make us feel bad about ourselves, making choices about what we want to eat based on what we are hungry for. Others are somewhere in the middle—sometimes obsessing, sometimes coasting. And the majority are struggling somewhere beyond what we know is healthy but shy of having a diagnosable eating disorder. We struggle in limbo because we can convince ourselves that, as long as we don't hit starvation, full-blown self-hate, or weekly purges, we are average. We find comfort in being almost as screwed up as everyone else.

A History of Eating Disorders, CliffsNotes Style

One of the first questions that skeptics ask about the prevalence of eating disorders is: Haven't eating disorders been around for years in one form or another? This is nothing new, is it?

Yes and no. Joan Jacobs Brumberg, feminist author, Cornell professor, and badass historian, provides a thorough, surprisingly entertaining education in the social history of women's relationships with food, fitness, and their own bodies in her 1997 book, *The Body Project: An Intimate History of American Girls.*

Religious martyrs sometimes exhibited eating-disordered tendencies. Joan of Arc wouldn't have called herself anorectic, of course (the term hadn't been invented yet), but she did starve herself to make a point. Bingeing and purging was actually a communal ritual at some ancient Greek feasts, where people would rock out so hard and eat so much that they had to make themselves throw up. Yet this did not amount to diagnosis, just debauchery.

During the 1870s, however, doctors in France and England scrambled to name and develop treatments for a new crop of girls who came into their offices with the mystifying tendency to reject food altogether. Charles Laségue, from France, and William Withy Gull, from England, competed head-to-head to be the first to name the disease the starving girls suffered from. France won with *anorexia,* perhaps because "Gull disease" didn't catch on. Gull suggested that young women needed "parentectomies" in order to heal properly. Both doctors employed artists to draw before and after versions of their patients—eerie portraits of an anomaly that predicted a future epidemic.

It isn't surprising that the Victorian era marks the birth of modern eating disorders. As they are today, control and thinness were characteristics of wealthy, attractive women. Food, by contrast, brought to mind sexuality, appetite, and indulgence—all things that the prim-and-proper woman was supposed to steer clear of. Victorian gals even converted to vegetarianism, because meat was considered carnal. (Funny, my boyfriend says that there is nothing sexier than me taking a big bite of a cheeseburger.)

Around the same time in America, lunatic asylums were reporting the presence of starving girls suffering from "sitophobia"—literally translated from the Greek as "fear or loathing of bread" (and Atkins hadn't even been invented!). The word *image* started appearing in American girls' diaries in the 1920s—the same time movies became a public obsession. Brumberg explains that "girls learned that images could be malleable" from Hollywood actresses, who changed identities and looks as fast as moving pictures could be produced.

Anorexia would not become a household term in the United States until much later. In fact, Brumberg herself remembers returning to her eastern college dorm after her first day at a hospital internship and telling her roommates about this strange woman who was starving herself. That was 1965, and none of them had heard of anorexia.

I believe that Brumberg's discovery is representative of the experiences of many women my mom's age. I've been cornered frequently by middle-aged women who tell me stories, after they hear the subject of this book, about the mysterious sorority girl who used to throw up after meals or the disappearing sister whom no one knew how to treat. In the 1960s and most of the '70s, anorexia and bulimia were still exotic and undiscussed. They were seen not as diseases so much as aberrations, phases, sounds: the roommate who always rushed to the bathroom immediately after meals, the little sister who always picked at her plate and avoided mealtimes, the best friend who got depressed and shrank to the size of nothing.

One of the first public memories of eating disorders that many middle-aged women have is of the singer Karen Carpenter, who first dieted in 1967 and by the fall of 1975 weighed just eighty pounds. After collapsing on a Las Vegas stage and being rushed to the hospital, she was diagnosed with anorexia (though she suffered from a combination of fasting, purging, and laxative abuse). The headlines were a shock to the average American. Karen Carpenter died in 1983, though most of her fans mistakenly thought she had been cured.

The 1980s brought on the era of fitness and food obsession: Jazzercise, fad diets, consumerism, and extravagance. Eating disorders were still not diagnosed at the level they are today, but they became a familiar phenomenon, less a sound than an image: another Christie Brinkley ad, skinny blondes in rock videos, *Mommy & Me* workout tapes. Brumberg asserts that the biggest changes in our collective consciousness have been the increased tolerance for thinness and ambivalence about excessive exercise: "In the nineteenth century a woman running through public parks in spandex would be locked up." Today, of course, she is lauded.

Catherine Steiner-Adair, a specialist in eating disorder treatment and prevention at Harvard Medical School (*and,* as she adorably puts it in her e-mails, "the real world"), argued as early as 1986 that perfectionism was correlated with eating-disordered behavior. The "superwoman," she wrote, often has a "vision of autonomy and independence that excludes connection to others and a reflective relationship with oneself." In other words, we are so keyed in to achievement, over and above attachment, that we have a hard time being in relationships with others and are not conscious about our own bodies' needs. Steiner-Adair is now developing prevention models with great success, which she documents in her latest book, *Full of Ourselves: A Wellness Program to Advance Girl Power, Health, and Leadership.*

Dr. Janell Lynn Mensinger, a young researcher and a survivor of anorexia herself, has carried the torch of Steiner-Adair's work by developing a "superwoman scale" aimed to prove statistically that perfectionism, coupled with pathological independence, often leads to eating disorders. Though the results of her initial study were inconclusive, she writes, "We are forced to question whether the concept of the Superwoman as being doubly burdened has essentially become outdated for adolescents coming of age in the twenty-first century." I would say Superwoman is not outdated as much as eclipsed—we are perfect girls before we even have the chance to become "superwomen."

So no, eating disorders are nothing new. But yes, the extreme form that they have taken on is very much new and characteristic of our time. Today you don't have a small percentage of white, upper-class women starving themselves; you have a generation of girls obsessed with the shape of their bodies, the number of calories they consume, and their fitness regimens. I challenge you to find a female between the ages of nine and twenty-nine who doesn't think about these issues more than she would like to, who doesn't feel racked by guilt and unsatisfied with her body a lot of the time.

Eating disorders no longer discriminate. Research suggests they now affect poor women and women of color in nearly equal numbers. For example, Dr. Ruth Striegel-Moore, chairwoman of psychology at Wesleyan University, found that young black women were as likely as white women to report binge eating in a 2003 study. Two Latina women in the Intro to Women's Studies course at Hunter College that I teach stood in front of the class and confessed to having eating disorders. One, a working-class woman, the first in her family to go to college, admitted to making herself throw up multiple times a week so she can look more like her aunt, who has had liposuction.

Ours is a time of dramatic addictions. Besides textbook anorexia and bulimia, excessive exercising, plastic surgery addiction, and laxative abuse have also grown common. The "starving disease" is no longer whispered about behind closed doors but is sensationalized by media coverage of celebrities openly wasting away. Diet and fitness information is everywhere; messages of wellness and authentic health are nowhere. Fad diet headlines can be found on just about every issue of every magazine aimed at a female demographic. At home, women are surrounded by the latest cookbooks and health guides; they print new recipes off the Internet, but food is an indulgence they won't let themselves have in real life. Reality shows promote our dissatisfaction with ourselves and our lives: Extreme makeovers of houses, children's behavior, marriages, and careers are big business. We are conditioned to believe that everything is within our grasp, that the only thing between us and perfection is, well, us.

Yes, eating disorders have a long history, but what was once a strange and rare disease has become a modern and dire epidemic. Girls today grow up with the knowledge that part of their inheritance is a more gender-equal world but a sicker and more unhealthy one as well. They are trained early in the typical female language of guilt and shame at the dinner table: "Oh, I really shouldn't." They watch the women around them obsess and judge and despair. They hear them vomit and lament and deny. They sense their mothers' dissatisfaction and self-hate and become younger versions of them, the perfect girls and the starving daughters of a broken culture.

The Brain Drain

The 7 million American women and girls currently suffering from diagnosed eating disorders are just the tip of the iceberg. A quantity of evidence shows that women in their twenties are increasingly vulnerable to out-and-out anorexia or bulimia. Beneath that evidence lie more women who are harder to diagnose but who show evidence of widespread shame, guilt, self-hate, obsession, and deprivation. This borderline behavior is what I am most committed to talking about in this book. I want you to see it for what it is—not a normal part of being a girl, not an acceptable way of moving through the world, but a destructive pathology that is stripping us of our potential. Obsessing over every little thing we put in our mouths may not lead to death or some of the other tangible side effects of diagnosable eating disorders (osteoporosis, infertility, depression), though it does take away our ability to control our own thoughts, our inalienable right to feel good about ourselves regardless of the size of our thighs. It takes away our time, our pleasure, our energy, our vision, our joy.

We are not our bodies. Our souls are not our stomachs. Our brains are not our butts. A lot of women have lost track of the truth that how we feel about our bodies does not have to be indicative of how we feel about ourselves. My friend's therapist recently asked her, "So how are you?" She answered, "Oh, I'm okay, feeling kind of fat this week."

"No, but how are *you*?" he asked again.

"What do you mean?" she questioned. "I just answered that."

"No, how are *you*?" he asked for a third time.

"I'm okay, I told you," she spat back, frustrated with what appeared to be a weird psychological game.

"You realize that you are not your body?" he finally explained. "You realize that your body is only one aspect of who you are?"

"Yeah, of course I . . ." She was stunned speechless.

This exchange was a revelation to me. I could feel completely fat and out of shape and gluttonous but say to myself, *Man, I feel bad about my body right now, but I feel great about my career and my relationships and my talents and my intellect and my . . . and my . . . and my . . .* Almost every girl I know lives as if how she feels about her body is representative of how she feels about everything else. It doesn't matter how successful or in love or at peace she is in the rest of her life, if she feels overweight, she is unhappy.

You don't need to have a diagnosable eating disorder to be power-fully affected by these issues. If you spend precious time and energy worrying about your weight instead of your soul, you have been cheated. If you waste your sharp intellect on comparing and contrast-ing diet fads instead of on the state of the world, we are all cheated. Brumberg has identified body preoccupation as a dangerous "brain drain" on our society. We are the most highly educated generation of young women ever. We now outnumber men in law schools, are creeping toward the 50 percent mark in medical schools, and receive more Ph.D.'s than any generation of women scholars before us. Some of this, no doubt, is thanks to our perfect-girl mentality—the work of achieving is never done. But what is the point of all this learning if we don't use it to its full potential to make the world a better place? Some of us already have the yet-to-be-solved conundrum of how to raise kids and have a fulfilling career ahead of us. Why would we add to that mix the full-time job of worrying about our weight?

Even if you don't feel like you have a disease, the quality of your life is diminished if you think about food and fitness obsessively. That, in turn, diminishes the quality of all of our lives.

2

From Good to Perfect: Feminism's Unintended Legacy

> I had no doubt that if they could have, my mother and her sisters and my grandmother would have left their skins draped like pantyhose over their unsatisfactory furniture and floated up above us all: the men who never failed to oppress them; the children who'd ruined their beautiful bodies; and the boxy little houses fit to bursting with the leftover smells of their cooking and the smoke from their cigarettes, curling up and hanging just above our heads like ambition.
>
> —Lorene Cary, *Black Ice*

The frizzy-haired feminist Carol Gilligan stands in front of a packed hotel conference room of therapists, psychologists, nutritionists, dietitians, social workers, and nurses, the peacekeepers on the front line of women's war on their own bodies. She is giving the keynote address at the national conference of the Renfrew Center, one of the leading eating disorder clinics in the nation. I'm trying to catch a glimpse of the women (and a few token men) who dedicate their lives to healing women like me and my friends.

In her soothing voice, Gilligan reminds us of her 1982 feminist sensation, *In a Different Voice,* in which she first asserted that Erik Erikson's model of human development—that kids become grown-ups when they assert independence—works for only half of the population. Girls, she argued, face the impossible choice of retaining their authentic voices and being socially shunned or becoming "good-girl" ventriloquists and retaining their connections to family and friends. In her observation, almost all choose the latter.

She reviews this argument for the nodding, scribbling therapists packed hip to hip in the Marriott ballroom. Nowadays, as a professor at NYU, she urges her students to create "psychological maps" for themselves in order to understand how their voices have developed in their private (puberty, divorce, depression) and political (shoulder pads, the Internet, war) lives. Gilligan asks each of us in the audience to draw on a piece of paper a river—"the river of your life"—with the date and place of our birth at the mouth. At the end of the river, we write the current date, November 11, 2005. "Now take your hovercraft back," she says, "to when you were eight or nine. Where were you? What were you doing? How did you feel?"

I close my eyes, trying to block out the sounds of shuffling papers and shifting bodies.

———

I am reaching into a pile of chiffon scarves in Ms. Barbara's Monday evening ballet class. She is standing near me, at the stereo, putting on Pachelbel's Canon. I love her. She is small and made of bones and muscles, jet-black hair, little wisps of which try to escape her pink headband when she spins fast and straight across the wood-floored studio. She has tiny feet that point into perfect arches.

At the end of every class, she announces, "And now we go to Pikes Peak Center," with that slow gravitas adults use to signal that they are capable of pretending too. Pikes Peak Center is the biggest and most prestigious theater in Colorado Springs, admittedly not the arts and culture capital of the world. But all of us, the round-bellied, flat-footed, side-ponytailed little girls of the class, don't know this yet. We scurry to the mirror, slide down it, and plop our tiny butts in a line to watch. Then she chooses one of us to begin. Today it is me. I pick the blue scarf, hurry to the middle of the room, throw my hands in the air, and look down to the right—a dramatic beginning pose surely borrowed from secret viewings of my mom's *Flashdance* video.

I had thirty long seconds to dance to my heart's content for the audience of thousands that I imagined sat before me, on the edges of their seats to see what my skilled and beautiful body would do next. I turned at will, maybe threw in a teetering arabesque or a clunky leap—eight-year-old stream of consciousness in motion. I thought I was beautiful, invincible, unstoppable. In those moments, I felt huge—not fat huge, but profound huge.

Gilligan brings us back. A therapist near me puts down her pen and picks up her knitting. Another covertly checks her BlackBerry. This eight-year-old girl, Gilligan explains, gets slowly buried beneath the pressure of being female in a society that is ambivalent about everything female. The round-bellied, dancing little girl becomes a sucking-in, gossiping, teenage "good girl."

As I listen to Gilligan describe some of the fabulous eight-year-olds she has interviewed who devolve into miserable "good girls" by thirteen, something keeps catching in my brain. This term, *good girl,* doesn't fit. It doesn't resonate. "Good girls" are polite, traditional, asexual, cute, cheerful, obedient. They are concerned with pleasing their parents, not challenging them. They want to be voted sweetest senior in the yearbook, not most likely to be president. The term makes me think of the faded photograph of my mom's sophomore prom—her beehive uncomfortably tall and her dress too tight and not at all her style, clearly picked out and forced on her by my grandmother. She wore it, as a "good girl" should. Her effort to cast off this good-girl identity was the primary project of her twenties.

I, by contrast, would never let my mother dictate my dress (though, looking back at some of my choices, I see I should have). By four years old, I insisted on dressing myself, and some of my creations were hideous—leg warmers, jeans, tutus, crimped hair, torn tights, and American Ballet Theater sweatshirt . . . all at once. I stole lacy homecoming bras from JCPenney, taking piles of them into the dressing room with my best friends and layering them under our clothes. I did any dirty trick necessary to get a rebound under the basket. At house parties, the most popular girls were not good girls but the ones who drank the most, cheated on tests to get better grades, stepped on toes to get boyfriends, defied their parents' wishes and applied to colleges in faraway big cities, such as New York and Los Angeles.

My generation did not strive for goodness or politeness, blindly ascribe to our parents' values, or muffle our opposition to their rules. In stark contrast, most of us were brazenly vocal, sometimes antagonistic. We were "perfect girls," composing our picture of the perfect female life—well educated, daring, unsentimental, and of course, thin. But Gilligan—as do many of the feminists who follow her—uses *good girl* and *perfect girl* synonymously.

At first I thought it was a matter of semantics, something I shouldn't make a fuss about. But the more I read it and heard it, the more I realized that the issue behind the semantics is exactly what needs to be fussed over. We are not our mothers, not "good girls." We are "perfect girls," obsessed with appearing ideal. We aren't worried about doing things "right." We are worried about doing things "impeccably."

We are the unintended side effects of feminism, the products of unfinished business (work-family balance, equal parenting, comprehensive sex education). We are the inheritors of an often unspoken legacy of body hatred and the manifest undiagnosed anxiety, depression, and eating disorders of our mothers. We interpret our parents' contradictions (gourmet cooks who don't eat their own creations; feminists who diet in secret; CEOs who cower at home; gender-conscious fathers who leave the housework to their wives). We are the children of the now-faster eighties and the anything-is-possible nineties, the daughters of visionary superwomen with buried bitterness. We are the perfect girls and the starving daughters.

Good to Perfect

My mom was raised to be "good." Period.

Jere Elizabeth was born on March 27, 1948, in Omaha, Nebraska, to a tight-lipped Episcopalian schoolteacher—my grandmother—and a jolly, big-bellied traveling salesman—my grandfather. In their house, my mother and her little sister were allowed one piece of fruit each as a snack after school, nothing more, while their brother, Scott, could eat as he pleased. Boys and girls got different portions of their always homemade meat-and-potatoes dinners as well. Scott was expected to be physical, smart, and insatiable. Jere and Janice were to be polite, agreeable, quiet, and thin—all, of which, it turned out, my mother was not.

A voracious reader and talker, a lover of everything dirty and outdoors, she had potentially fatal asthma but would sneak out of the house and into the neighbor's field, where they had a horse perfect for secret riding. Eventually her asthma got so bad that the whole family up and moved to Colorado, where the air was thinner and more forgiving to her stubborn little lungs. She grew into a verbose, voluptuous young woman, despite my grandmother's attempts to keep her quiet and small. By sixth grade she was five foot ten, irascible, and perpetually at odds with my grandmother.

My mother pretty much fit the bill for the 1950s all-American girl—middle-class, from the middle of the country, from a nuclear family. Something brilliant and sometimes angry—a sense that she was essentially not "good" (i.e., polite, timid, asexual)—lurked within her, and many women of her generation identify with it. They felt that it was worthwhile and perhaps even revolutionary to be not good, but were unable to express that feeling for fear of judgment, reprisal, ostracization.

When my mom went off to college at a nearby state school, she registered as a home economics major in a last-ditch attempt to be the quintessential "good girl" her mother so hungered for. When my mom first told me her major, I was incredulous. Home ec? Mom melted the burners making tea; she left the sugar out of her Nana's Famous Chocolate Cake and had to throw away the whole thing. The closest moment she had to a craft phase was when she started spray-painting Halloween pumpkins in fluorescent colors and attaching plastic jewels to them "just to be different"; to my horror as a fourteen-year-old, they stayed on our porch until they rotted into soft lumps of glittering plastic and seed. My mom as a home ec major is all the evidence I need that the repressed culture of the 1950s and early '60s made women (and men) totally insane. Despite her being Mensa-brilliant, my mom's biggest dream in her early college years was to become a secretary because she had heard that girls who got their work done fast enough were welcome to read for the remainder of the day. She could imagine nothing better. Her world, like her aspirations, was small.

But then Vietnam happened and the world expanded. My mom was politicized, outraged, getting less "good" all the time. The word *feminism* penetrated even her small town of Fort Collins, Colorado, and she was an immediate convert. Gloria Steinem, Betty Friedan, Janis Joplin—each confirmed that Mom had been right all along: being a "good girl" was boring, unfair, and frankly, unnatural. She traded in her required home ec uniform—skirts, sweaters, girdle—for bell-bottom jeans and peasant shirts. She took military history courses, smoked grass with her social theory professors, and protested to her heart's content. She read about the suffragist movement in the 1920s (the "first wave") and attended consciousness-raising groups where she and her friends, the self-described "second wave," spilled their long-held-in frustrations with femaleness. She was ecstatically liberated from goodness.

My parents first met in sixth grade and started dating as sophomores in high school. They fell in love all over again under new auspices—they would be equal partners in this war against the establishment. My dad adored my mom, not because she was "good," but because she *wasn't*. She was full-figured and bighearted. He was attracted to her fearlessness, her brilliance, even her stubbornness. The same qualities that had once made her mom's head shake and her teachers put "disruptive" on her report cards now constituted her sex appeal. She was no longer "good," but life sure was. In 1969, their summer of love, they were married.

But as my dad now openly admits, "We wanted to change the world, and instead we just got rich." (Rich, to my dad, who grew up opening the door for bill collectors, is upper-middle-class). Mom put Dad through law school, then Dad put Mom through social work school, and they both moved to Colorado Springs, where Dad got an offer to join a firm. My mom hated the idea of living in a practically artless, cultureless town, but she bit the bullet. They spent most of the seventies working like crazy, discovering Jung and Buddhism, going to therapy, and having a lot of fun.

And then my brother and I came along.

Despite what most women of my generation have been taught by sensationalistic media, feminism was not about burning bras, becoming lesbian, or hating men. It has always been and will always be about two things: equality and educated choice. The second-wave feminist movement that blazed in the late 1960s and early 1970s was fueled by the idea that being a "good girl" was actually an oppressive, unnatural state—that it endangered women's capacities to develop real personalities and genuinely happy lives. Much of the activism that took place in the sixties and seventies can be traced back to this assertion. Raising their consciousness in groups, women shared their frustrations over "good-girl" expectations and brainstormed ways to defy them. The sexual revolution was, in theory, about freeing women from their pleasure-phobic personalities and finding out how fun being bad could be. Storming the *Ladies' Home Journal* offices and protesting the Miss America pageant were just some of the ways buttoned-down, clammed-up "good girls" came out of their shells. Even the impassioned, ultimately unsuccessful attempt to get the Equal Rights Amendment passed was just another way for women to argue that neither "goodness" nor maleness should be a prerequisite for opportunity; only humanness should.

As bright young things, the baby-boomer feminists fared pretty well with this new identity. My mom certainly did and remembers her late twenties as some of the best years of her life—earning her own money, constructing intellectual and political arguments, reenvisioning traditional notions of marriage, love, and sex. She was traveling the world and taking on activist projects at home. She taught her own classes, made her own meat loaf, even changed her own tires.

Not surprisingly, my dad had to convince her to have kids. She had a sinking feeling that she wouldn't be a "good" mother (the first time in a long time that she'd worried about being "good"). She thought she was too independent, introspective, and spontaneous to behave responsibly, associated maternity with her own rigid and passionless mother, and had no model for an alternative.

Now, of course, she swears that my brother and I were the biggest gifts of her life. She turned out to be an incredible mother—loving, generous, innovative, fun. She was fascinated by my brother's and my development, our quirks and nascent personalities, and took the opportunity to put into practice all of her psychological training and feminist ideology. She was determined to teach me, her little girl, that I did not have to be "good" or quiet or sweet or cute. She would never tell me I couldn't climb trees or talk loudly at the dinner table. She raised my brother in her feminist image as well; she encouraged all of his sensitivities, teaching him that being a "real man" meant being vocal, emotional, relationship-oriented. She enrolled him in ballet lessons (he went because NFL players danced to increase agility) and seriously disciplined him when he shot a bird in the backyard with our neighbor's BB gun.

Despite her best intentions, things didn't work out quite as planned. My mom bought me overalls and I asked for skirts. She signed me up for soccer and I did cheers and cartwheels in the field. She resisted Barbies and I pursued them with fierce determination. She banned toy guns from the house and my brother constructed Uzis out of sticks and rubber bands in the backyard. He was hyperactive and aggressive. I was shy and passive. My feminist, hippie mother got a daughter who wanted to dance ballet and have a canopy bed with pink trim, and a son who was a cross between Alex P. Keaton from *Family Ties* and your average sports-obsessed all-American boy.

She also got another thing she hadn't bargained for: a frequently absent partner. Even though my parents had the most visionary of equal-parenting plans, my dad had a lot to prove at the firm, where the senior partners were white-haired, cigar-smoking, and unaware of terms such as *paternity leave*. Mom's field of choice was more flexible and her parenting skills more intuitive. Our whole young family slid down the slippery slope of compromise and landed in a loving dog pile of flailing appendages, hungry bellies, and dirty clothes. My momma, of course, was at the bottom.

Second-wave feminists hit a series of brick walls when they became mothers circa 1980. The first was the illusion of shared parenting in a world unaccustomed to the idea. Throw in some residual 1950s conditioning, a traditional workplace or two, and some crying, needy babies, and you have the recipe for failed experiments in shared parenting. My dad meant well, but when push came to shove, he was at the office sweating over a brief and my mom was at home, doing all the ten thousand unrecognized tasks that have to be done to keep a family going. This wasn't how it was supposed to be.

Shared parenting is a lot harder than equal relationships sans kids. When it is just Mom and Dad together, they have things pretty well figured out. If I cook, you clean. I'm not your laundress, cleaning lady, or secretary, and you aren't my sugar daddy, protector, or father. But having kids throws all that equanimity into a tailspin, until what is left is a smattering of empty promises, faulty systems, cold dinners—what feminists call the second shift.

This inequality is one of the most widely shared stories of my generation's upbringing and has been confirmed by psychologists. A study appearing in the *Journal of Family Psychology,* for example, confirmed that wives' marital satisfaction decreased when they became mothers. Researchers hypothesize that the shift "likely reflects the high stress associated with taking care of children." Those of us who heard our fathers say "Oh, I could have done that, sweetie!" right as our mothers put the last dish in the cabinet will be unsurprised that the same study shows that husbands-turned-fathers experienced no such decrease in satisfaction.

Women with jobs outside the home still spend about twice as much time as men taking care of children and household chores, according to the U.S. Department of Labor. The average American woman spends one hour and twenty minutes on household chores every day. The average man, by contrast, spends under forty-five minutes. Most of my friends saw this, whether they grew up rich or poor, in the suburbs or the city, with their biological parents or three half brothers, an adopted sister, a stepdad, and a grandma. Regardless of the peripheral players, the story starring our moms also features undone chores, a few unrealized dreams, and muffled outrage.

The failure to share parenting meant mothers went into major superwoman mode, overdrive. Already sold on careers and community activism, they made the bulk of parenting responsibilities one more hat on the rack. Women in my mother's generation still had the notion that "having it all at once" was a very real possibility (silly, silly girls), so they heaved the weight of the world onto their shoulders and tried to run around with it (gracefully, of course). And guess who was watching the whole time?

Our mothers learned, albeit too late, that "superwoman" is simply a superhero fantasy that, when attempted in the real world, spells disaster. Your mother may have, indeed, appeared to be "faster than a speeding bullet, more powerful than a locomotive" on the outside, but inside she was stressed out, often sick, and more than a little pissed off.

The second brick wall that many superwomen mothers ran into in raising us watchful daughters was pop culture. No matter how much my mom worked to make our home a "hate-free zone" (we actually had a sign in our front window with these words emblazoned on it), the misogyny crept in. She couldn't keep me from Get in Shape Girl! or *Dirty Dancing* or *YM,* any more than she could keep my brother from NBA games or *Mike Tyson's Punch Out!* or gangsta rap. We were American kids watching American television, playing American video games, and reading American magazines, i.e., having our minds filled with backlash, booty dancing, and unrealistic body ideals.

We were also into good old-fashioned rebellion. My brother didn't declare himself a Republican at seven years old because he understood Reaganomics (he has since recanted); his affiliation had more to do with the fact that my parents stuck a Jimmy Carter sign in the front yard. The second the word *feminism* escaped my mother's lips, I had a built-in reason to avoid it like the plague.

––––––––––

After I went to grade school, I became insufferably precocious and ambitious. The tender little girl got buried beneath layers of drive and curiosity. I wanted to be great at everything, better than everyone else (especially the boys), and I believed in the power of my own intellect at the tender age of eight, whereas it took my mom until eighteen even to begin to entertain the idea that she might not be destined for a dead-end job. Holding our lives up side by side like this makes mine seem even further from the "good-girl" paradigm in which she had been caught.

While discovering the fun of being smart, I certainly didn't lose my interest in being pretty. When I raised my hand to answer one of Mrs. Fanning's questions, I hoped my friends would notice my new shirt. I still liked to wear skirts, but I didn't mind getting them dirty on the playground. Friday flip-up day fascinated and horrified me, my first indication that there was something under my skirt a boy would want to try to see. I started to understand how sweetness could be a useful tactic rather than a benign quality. I was shy but not scared. I didn't act out, not because I was worried about being "bad" but because I was so damn determined to be the best.

My generation grew up with Title IX. According to the Women's Sports Foundation, a New York–based advocacy group for women's athletics, girls who are active in athletics have higher self-esteem, more confidence, higher achievement test scores, less depression, improved mental health, more academic success, and as if that weren't enough, greater lifetime earning potential.

My little pack of girlfriends and I valued achievement over attachment, bravery over manners, beauty over kindness. We wanted to be fierce competitors and understood early on that fierce competitors could not care too much about the next girl's feelings. We craved attention, sought it by trying out for school plays and sports teams, winning spelling bees and finishing our timed math tests the quickest. This all meant beating out other people, making them cry behind the backstop, being self-focused and determined.

When Mom wasn't "consulting"—which I understood in terms of babysitters—she was pumping artistic and cultural life into Colorado Springs by running the Rocky Mountain Women's Film Festival (which she cofounded in her "free time"). She was the queen of multitasking— informal therapist to all of her friends, bona fide therapist to strangers, president of the film festival, cooker of meals, cheerer at sports games, coordinator of social lives, house repairs, and holidays. Somehow she never appeared particularly ruffled. Part of her responsibility, in fact, seemed to be to hide the blood, sweat, and tears involved in all of this running around—to make it appear "effortless." In retrospect, I see that this let her pursue her varied aspirations without leaving her kids feeling she was overburdened or bitter about our arrival. In fact, when my mom came down with a chronic immune illness when I was around twelve, she used to wake up with a smile on her face, chat happily during the carpool, and then head back to bed for hours on end, trying to sleep off the excruciating ache of her muscles and the pain in her head. When I got home at four, she was back on her feet, whistling as she made dinner. Womanhood, I was acutely observing and intuitively sensing, was characterized by a lot of rushing around, a lot of responsibility, and a lot of accomplishment—all dressed up in a pretty, seemingly easy package. We were supposed to deny the ugliness of exhaustion or pain.

My mom, like most, never said "Do what I do," of course; it was all "Do what I say." She told me that I could go after any goal I set for myself, but that I didn't have to excel at everything. I begged to be signed up for pottery wheel throwing, basketball, ballet, drama, Brownies, and Cotillion (yes, the kind with the white gloves), and was horrified if I wasn't immediately adept at every activity. My mom said that what was most important was my personal best. I cried my eyes out when I got an A– in algebra because I knew Katie got an A. My mom emphasized that honesty is important, beauty complex, and creativity vital. It all sounded too sweet and idealistic in a world of celebrity scandal, Cindy Crawford, and underfunded art classes.

My mother taught me not to be "good," but this lesson fit into my sense that perfection was necessary. Goodness was a shade short of perfection, and being "good" was not good enough to be competitive. She told me that I should always stand up for myself, that I should value speaking my truth above protecting relationships. She taught me that it was sometimes fun to let a swear word fly if the situation called for it. I didn't have to make nice. I didn't have to say "sorry" if I wasn't. I didn't have to go out with boys, but if I felt like it, that could be fun.

In the 1980s, even women who didn't ascribe to feminism and thought of it as the F-word were benefiting from the fallout and seeing the world through feminist-colored glasses. They too were teaching their daughters that they could do anything they wanted, that they were as smart and capable as the boys, though they may not have identified feminism as the source of their teachings or of their own increased capacity for earnings and independence. According to the Bureau of Labor Statistics, between 1970, when the second wave of feminism was sparked, and 2004, women increased their participation rate in the formal workforce from 43 to 59 percent. Likewise, in 2004, 33 percent of women ages twenty-five to sixty-four had four-year-college degrees, compared with 11 percent in 1970. Seems like more than a coincidence to me.

Nonfeminist feminists—who believe in choice and equality but deny they are feminists—may have clung to the "good-girl" script a bit, but I challenge you to find an '80s mom who didn't have a suit coat with some serious shoulder pads and an oft-repeated "Go, girl" speech for her daughter.

Remnants of these speeches made it into many of the surveys I received:

> I was taught that I had all the potential in the world—I could accomplish anything I wanted. My parents always told me I was capable of anything. They told me I was "special."

> Both my parents always told me I could do and be whatever I wanted. As a child, this was reinforced through being accepted and enrolled into "gifted and talented" education in grade school, and more or less succeeding in everything I tried in high school. Both my parents still tell me I'm "special."

> When I was younger I was a perfectionist, because I was told I was "a gifted child." I always felt compelled to be the best in school, in sports, and to never be wrong in general.

And this response, from a nineteen-year-old in Newark, Delaware, traced the trajectory of her current obsession with food and fitness back to her first motivational pushes from her parents:

> Mediocrity is a large pet peeve of mine. To be average is not acceptable. I am an only child and sometimes I feel that my parents feel unsatisfied with their own education and lived vicariously through me. I was pushed to always succeed in academics. A B was fine, but it wasn't an A.
>
> I believe the academic aspect really shifted my whole personality into perfectionism. I was very independent and things needed to be done exactly how I pictured them. While taking notes, if we needed to draw a shape, I would erase it until it was symmetrical. It did not matter if I wasn't caught up with what the teacher was saying. The lopsided circle would bother me.

This obsession with getting the two-dimensional shape right on paper evolved into an obsession with getting her three-dimensional shape right in real life—a pressure that many young women feel from their parents. A survey of almost six hundred tenth-graders found that 41 percent of girls thought their fathers wanted them to be thinner, and a whopping 45 percent thought their mothers wished their daughters weighed less. The Delaware native went on:

> I was a chubby child but when my parents divorced, my weight skyrocketed. During my freshman year of college, I decided enough was enough and dieted extremely to drop weight. Every day, what I can and cannot eat is a problem. I would rather go hungry than eat something with several calories or even something as simple as a sandwich. My body is starting to become ideal.

Not all trajectories are so obvious, not everyone's parents so vocal. My mom, for example, never explicitly held up achievement or busyness as virtues the way she did independence, honesty, or fun, but her actions were the boldest statements. My most immediate model of womanhood was whizzing past me faster than a speeding bullet, in many different directions from sunup to sundown, accomplishing all of her variable tasks with efficiency, excellence, and emotional presence. My dad was busy at work but chilling out at home.

Hard work is often associated with generations past, but the Puritan ethic certainly hasn't died. If anything, our generation has brought it to a whole new level. Dr. Jean Twenge, author of *Generation Me*, reports that "in a 2000 survey, young people were 50 percent more likely than older people to say that working hard was 'the most important thing for a child to learn to prepare him or her for life.'"

A recent report by the National Council for Education Statistics confirms that girls are internalizing their mothers' lessons about obsessive activity and achievement. Girls consistently outperform boys on reading and writing tests. In the United States, girls score an average of eighteen points higher on the Progress in International Reading Literacy Study. Even in math and science, fields previously dominated by men, young women are making their mark. Female high school graduates in 2000 were more likely than their male peers to have taken algebra II, biology, AP/honors biology, and chemistry. Young women dominate extracurricular activities as well. In 2001 females were more likely than their male peers to participate in music or other performing arts, belong to academic clubs, work on the school newspaper or yearbook, or hold offices in student council or government. Women outnumber men on college campuses by at least 2 million, and their majority is growing. In a *New York Times* op-ed, "To All the Girls I've Rejected," the Kenyon College admissions officer Jennifer Delahunty Britz admitted relying on the equivalent of affirmative action for boys in an attempt to create a gender-balanced class. Responses flooded the paper, including one from the career educator Vaughn A. Carney, who said that " 'gender norming' is the dirtiest little secret in higher education."

The daughters of baby boomers have driven straight on past equality to dominance when it comes to achievement—academic or otherwise. Unlike our brothers and boyfriends, who settle for being great at certain things and uninterested in others—a style borrowed perhaps from their fathers—we desire, like our mothers, to do it all and do it all near perfectly. Mediocrity is for sissies, and as inheritors of Title IX and "go-girl" feminism, we despise nothing more than weakness (except perhaps fatness, which we equate with weakness).

Every time I did well in school or had a good-hair day (rare as that was)—the world gave me glowing praise. I quickly learned that the question "Have you lost weight?" actually means "You seem like you're doing well" in female-speak, even if a person clearly hasn't changed a physical inch. The evidence was conclusive—real women were busy, accomplished, thin, and perpetually chasing after perfection at a mind-numbing speed without so much as a grunt.

My mom stacked my shelves with *Our Bodies, Ourselves,* books on financial literacy, Mary Oliver poetry, weathered feminist tomes that I would not crack until I was far away from home, and blank journals waiting to be filled with angst-ridden scrawls. She told me: "You can be anything that you want to be."

My translation: "I have to be everything."

Unspoken Legacy

So that is how we went from good to perfect, but how did we get from Jane Fonda to bulimia? Easy: Jane Fonda *was* bulimic.

In her 2005 memoir, *My Life So Far,* Fonda writes: "How much better I might have been back in those early movies had I been able to show up fully in the roles rather than work half-crippled by a disease that no one knew I suffered from!?" Sweet Jane, like so many of our mothers, *thought* no one knew she suffered. In fact, like women in general (perhaps more than women in general), young girls are highly perceptive and intuitive. As I watched my mom bounce maniacally on the mini-trampoline to Olivia Newton-John's "Physical," I wondered what bad feelings could lead to such self-torture.

Many young women I interviewed admitted that they knew intuitively their mothers hated their own bodies or, worst-case scenario, their own lives. Tara, a twenty-seven-year-old living in Lebanon, explains, "I think mothers saying lines like 'my thighs look huge in this' takes a toll on the daughter because unconsciously you look at yourself and see your mother's shape and start having the same issues with it, even if you really aren't built the same way."

Even if their moms adopted the trademark superwoman smile— forced and tense around the edges—their daughters picked up on the little signs that spelled desperation. Nancy Friday, author of *My Mother/My Self,* describes this discovery: "The girl is left with the perception of the gap between what mother says, what mother does . . . and what the girl detects mother feels beneath it all. Nothing mother really feels ever escapes us. Our problem is that because we try to live out all parts of the split message she sent us, our behavior and love all too often represent a jangled compromise." We read the messages, as cryptic as some of them may be: a smaller portion of food on Mom's plate, a whispered epithet at the mirror, a blanket refusal of birthday cake or Christmas cookies.

For some, the unspoken legacy was handed down in more obvious ways.

Karen's* mom did everything that was supposed to be kept secret in the bathroom. With the door shut and the lights off, she would light up her cigarettes and blow the smoke out the little window above the toilet, but Karen smelled it. Sometimes, after dinner or in the late morning, Karen would hear the sounds of her mom gagging behind the closed door. Karen tried crying, hoping that it would make her mother emerge from the secret place and stop doing whatever it was she was doing in there, but the sounds of the toilet flushing repeatedly were much louder than her tears.

Sela's* mom was a workaholic, a flash of muted silks always running past her to get to the car in the morning. Sela was ticked off that her mom was so much skinnier and less available than the other moms. Even if her mother had possessed one of those wide, comforting laps, Sela never would have had a chance to lie in it. Instead, she spent most of her time with her nanny—a kind maternal substitute. When her mother was home, she always refused food but insisted that Sela eat. "But I want to eat with you, Momma," she would whine. "Don't be difficult," her mother would order.

Heather's* mom was a feminist therapist. She marched around with scarves flying, flowing skirts dragging on the dusty floors (she wasn't much for cleaning). Heather was embarrassed by all the talk of feminism but liked that her mother was more liberal than her friends' uptight, out-of-touch moms. She could talk to her mom about boys or fights with girlfriends, sometimes even hint at sex. What Heather didn't find so comforting was the discrepancy between what her mom said to her—"Heather, you are a gorgeous goddess! Don't let anyone ever tell you different"—and what she said to herself. After catching a glimpse of herself in the full-length bedroom mirror, her mother scoffed, "Jesus, how did I get so round? Disgusting." It was just a passing comment, but it burned into Heather's brain. If her mom was "disgusting" and Heather—who looked like her mom—anticipated growing up to have her mom's body, what did she have to look forward to?

Not all of our mothers had undiagnosed eating disorders, but many did. And many of those who didn't still had unhealthy patterns with food (fad or yo-yo dieting), new and twisted fitness regimens, and distorted views of and relationships with their own bodies. Second-wave feminists politicized the idea that unrealistic beauty standards are dangerous, certainly, but they clearly didn't internalize their own cultural critique. The more enlightened Jane Fonda reflects: "Up until then I had been a feminist in the sense that I supported women, brought gender issues into my movie roles, helped women make their bodies strong, read all the books: I had it in my head. I thought I had it in my heart—my body—but I didn't; not really."

This is not a blame game. My mother's generation taught mine to be questioning, critical, outspoken, unafraid. Well, here we are: looking back on our childhoods and trying to understand how we acquired such bottomless hunger for achievement and perfection and such resistance to balance, wellness, and satisfaction.

Most mothers do the best they can so that they do not pass on their pathologies to their daughters and sons. Even the moms who say one thing but model another are hoping their children won't discern the difference. Mothers with serious eating disorders may have chosen not to talk about them because they thought that ignoring them would help them go away and keep them from becoming part of their daughters' lives. Or maybe they were so sick they didn't even know they were sick, so separated from their bodies that they didn't feel the pain. *AARP: The Magazine* recently revealed that "more and more midlife women are being diagnosed with anorexia, bulimia, and other eating disorders." Remuda Ranch, a treatment center in Arizona, reports a 400 percent increase in female patients over forty since it opened in 1990. William Davis, vice president of research and program development at the Renfrew Center, which has sites all over the country, reports that about half of the older women now seeking help have struggled with food issues for years, untreated.

Just getting through the day with double or triple duty was probably all most mothers could handle. As long as they put on the happy face and kept providing, comforting, cooking, and cleaning, they hoped they could keep their intimate and destructive "body issues" to themselves. Yet we soaked up what they did and how they felt. Fifty years of attachment theory—the psychology of the unique physiological and emotional bonding that goes on between mother and child—confirm that no connection is more intimate than that between a mother and a daughter, no bond of bodies more tangled and powerful.

Interpreting Our Mother's Bodies

My own mother is tall. In sixth grade she had a tremendous growth spurt and shot up to her full height of five feet ten inches. My dad likes to tell stories about this giraffe of a girl who sat in front of him, swinging her ponytail in his face until he would yell at her and then, in turn, get yelled at by the teacher, Mrs. Lamb. Though my dad was smitten from the first swing of that ponytail, he decided not to ask her out until he was taller than she. Finally, right before sophomore-year homecoming, he approached her in the hallway, stood back to back with her, and declared himself worthy. My grandmother made my mom go.

What my grandmother said was law, a lot of which was disastrous to my mom's self-image. She grew up knowing that her mother disapproved of her. My mom represented everything that my grandmother was not; her most obvious differences were in her body. My mother is tall and athletic, was a fierce competitor when she played semipro softball, and is a generous and spontaneous flirt. My grandmother was petite, private, and pious. She believed that God liked women who were steadfast and internally strong but not showy, not women like my mom.

I pieced all this together little by little, through snatches of phone conversations I overheard, the under-the-breath complaints traded between my parents on the ride home from Grandma's house, the way my mom's eyes got watery sometimes when she talked about her adolescence. At one of my mother's birthdays, as we all sat around the dining room table in my grandmother's pristine condo staring at the giant cake she had made from scratch, my grandmother announced:

"I made German chocolate because that's Jere's favorite, and we all know how much Jere likes cake!" Everyone laughed, but I saw the discomfort behind my mom's smile.

These scraps of memory, seemingly inconsequential in isolation, constitute an important quilt of meaning that I painstakingly sewed together as a young observer. My mom's presence, her personality, her body made my grandmother uncomfortable. My grandmother, in turn, made my mom feel too big, physically and otherwise.

My mom *was* a little overweight when I was growing up, but when I was a little girl, this extra weight seemed like an essential part of her vast repertoire of mothering—a warm lap for sleeping on, big, fleshy hands for smoothing the hair off my forehead, a shelf of breast to rest my head on when I crept into the nook of her arm. My mom still has a Mother's Day gift that my brother made for her when he was six years old: It is a plate with a picture of her, jumping on the mini-trampoline, two long, winding coils springing from either side of her stick body. "Those are your boobs, Mommy! When you bounce up and down!" This hilarious but telling memento sums up how my brother and I understood our mom's body back then. It was big and wonderful, a toy and a talisman.

Eventually I wanted a voice-over for all the nuanced scenes I had witnessed over the years, an explanation of the subtext. I could sense that it was a language of pain.

One lazy summer afternoon, I asked my mom about it: "Why was Grandma mean to you?"

I could tell from my mom's expression that she was taken aback. "What do you mean, Courtney?"

"I mean, how did she make you feel back when you were young?"

"She was critical, that's all. She was critical, and she really liked men better in general."

"What do you mean, 'liked men better'?"

"Well, it's kind of hard to explain. There were a lot of women back then like your grandma, who were more accepting, more forgiving of men, and more interested in men."

"Weird," I said, the eloquent summary of a nine-year-old. I had never thought about such a thing—women liking men more than women. It seemed that all the women I knew spent hours talking on the phone to other women, going out for lunch, congregating in little groups at family picnics or after school as they waited for their kids to come running out with backpacks hanging off their shoulders.

"Mom, will I look like you when I grow up?"

Quickly she responded, "I think you have your father's frame. You'll look like me in the face, maybe."

I knew what she was doing, even then. I knew she was trying to reassure me that I wouldn't be "bigger," like her, that I would grow into a female equivalent of my lanky dad. That seemed safe. Becoming wide-hipped and big-breasted, like her, could get me criticized. Staying thin and tall, like him, could get me respect. I have lived in the shadow of this conversation since then—always wondering if I am becoming my mother, in spirit and body. I am wide-hipped like her, big-assed like her, slight in the shoulders like her. I am not big-breasted or round-bellied. I lurk at the edges, always afraid that I will unconsciously slip across the line into her burdens and her body. I pray that it is not a self-fulfilling prophecy.

At twelve I named our new kitten Murphy, after Murphy Brown. There was something contained, autonomous, inarguably successful about that quintessential eighties sitcom character that stood in opposition to my fear of becoming my mother. Murphy Brown represented a mix of independence, authority, and humor—a combination I wasn't seeing in my real life.

My generation sees our mothers' lives for what they are—often well-intentioned but failed experiments at being superwomen. Their bodies were the casualties of so many of these experiments. In my mom's case, her worst nightmare came true; this energetic, ambitious, and optimistic woman was suddenly trapped in a body weakened by chronic fatigue syndrome. Slowing down, of course, is death for a perfect girl. It was certainly a hot, silent hell for my supermom.

It is widely known that women are more prone to depression than men, but in recent years studies have confirmed that they suffer disproportionately from a variety of illnesses. Panic disorders are also twice as likely in women. There are 1.2 million more American women than men who have diabetes. For reasons researchers still don't understand, about 75 percent of autoimmune diseases occur in women, most frequently during the childbearing years. Women's relationships with their bodies are fraught, not simply with the pressure to be thin but with the most basic pressure of all: just to keep up.

Some mothers wear stress like a badge of honor, acting as if being stressed is a sign of a good woman. Others deny it even exists: "No, you've got it all wrong, sweetie. I love juggling ten things at once, having the same 'discussions' [never fights] with your father over and over again, and scheduling in 'me time.'" Stress, like weight preoccupation, had begun to look like a necessary landmark in women's country to girls at the border. In fact, studies show that women's bodies are affected by stress differently than men's, and further, that the toxins in pesticide-treated food and even cosmetics may be contributing to the rise in autoimmune illnesses among women in the last few decades. Despite early evidence that our mothers' bodies were breaking down under so much responsibility and expectation, few young women even know about the critical connections among stress, health, and body weight. We have watched our mothers "emotionally eat" when stressed out, but few of us have seen them draw the parallels between their busy schedules and their ailing bodies.

Feeling as if there is an unspoken subtext to our relationships with our mothers and, additionally, to their relationships with food is common among the young women in my survey. Their mothers feel comfortable talking all day about protein, saturated fat, Jazzercise, Atkins, Olivia Newton-John, and their daily sit-up regimen, but when it comes to having a down-and-dirty conversation about how they feel about their own bodies or their daughters', they become mute. It is as if they anticipate that the impact of the truth would be seismic—that they have hated their bodies since their mothers first taught them to, that they are doing everything in their power not to make the same mistake—as if their words would shatter a delicate pane of glass between their daughters and the ugly world outside. Yet the daughters pay the price of their mothers' well-intentioned silence in their own physical symptoms.

How much of our obsession with food and fitness, our daily evaluation of our bodies, even our textbook eating disorders is an unconscious expression of our loyalty to or rejection of our mothers? We speak with our bodies as well.

To reject the pressure to be thin is to reject our mothers' lifelong efforts. On the one hand, to extricate yourself from the culture of dieting and overexercise is to miss out on a huge part of female bonding—the dieting promises exchanged between mother and daughter, sisters, friends; the self-disparaging watercooler talk about that holiday weight; the chats at the gym. On the other hand, some girls starve themselves expressly to avoid growing into adult female bodies and inheriting their mothers' lives. Some girls overeat and get fat to wound their weight-conscious mothers. Some girls become sports-obsessed, in part, to drive home the point that they will not be dainty and domestic like their powerless moms.

We see that our mothers cannot love their own bodies, and this translates, albeit unintentionally, to a lesson about femaleness, about form, about our own futures. Marion Woodman writes: "Because our mothers could not love themselves as complete feminine beings, they could not love us as feminine beings. So our fear is archetypal, monstrous. We have a tremendous sense of something within being shut off, abandoned."

All daughters say to all mothers—sometimes in words, more often with our own bodies as a substitute for words—I came from you, your body was my first home, and you didn't suspect I sensed how you felt about it? Your genes imprinted themselves indelibly on the moment of my birth, creating an equation for what I would look like when I emerged. It was you. Even if I have Dad's knock-knees or Grandpa's curly hair, it is you that I become.

———————

My grandmother died two years ago. She shrank into a fraction of her former size, all wrinkles and bones, and stopped breathing. It was a long, drawn-out dying—she was diagnosed with a rare disease that virtually turned her lungs to stone. My mom took care of her every step of the way, made sense of her nonsensical requests, negotiated her do-not-resuscitate order with the doctors, held her hand, watched the breath leak out of her one last time. The memorial service was beautiful; a giant-winged bird flew great arcs behind the picture window at the altar of her church in the mountains.

In the months that followed my grandmother's death, my mother herself started shrinking. The funeral was in February, and by August, when I came home for a visit, my mom was svelte. Where there had been a generous, ample lap, there were now taut muscles. Where there had been tricep wings—the "evils" of old age—there were now strong arms. Her upper chest, always one of the most beautiful parts of her, was even more striking—tan and freckled, the skin stretched across her collarbones like a drumhead. She wasn't too thin, but she was the smallest I had ever seen her. She looked young. She looked, truth be told, more like me—her twenty-two-year-old daughter.

On one of our ritual walks in the park, I questioned her about it: "Mom, did you set out to lose all this weight? Have you been exercising a ton? Have you been eating enough?"

She gave me a "don't mother me, girl" look and replied, "Honestly, Courtney, nothing changed. I am walking with my friends in the park, eating generally healthy stuff, taking my vitamins—the usual."

"So what happened? I mean, I don't get it," I countered, incredulous. I had spent too much time around too many closet dieters and overexercisers in college to swallow her claim.

"I don't know. I honestly don't know. I think Mom's death had something to do with it, but I can't explain it in any rational way. There was some emotional block that disappeared, I guess—one of those strange, inexplicable phenomena."

Let me clarify that my mother did exercise and eat a little differently. It was unconscious, for sure, but her relationship to food and fitness shifted in small, barely noticeable ways. Yet at the heart of it, what really happened is that she became less hungry. My grandmother bicycled into that eternal light with a basket full of judgment, rules, and rigidity. She left my mom a clock with singing birds at each hour on the hour, an emerald ring, some Maya Angelou books, but the most precious gift she gave her was release. The day my grandmother died, a part of my mom died too—the part that still believed there would never be enough, that she could never do enough, that she was fundamentally never going to *be* enough.

My charge as her daughter, I know, is to convince myself of the same thing without such great loss.

Unfinished Business

By high school, almost every one of my girlfriends in our picture-perfect suburb was falling apart. It was basically your after-school-special potpourri: abusive relationships, rape, teen pregnancy, bourgeoning alcoholism, drug dealing, gun-carrying boyfriends, car accidents, verbally abusive mothers, and yes, eating disorders galore. After four years of enduring this roller coaster of teenage dysfunction, my big plan was to hightail it out of Colorado Springs as fast and as far as I possibly could—essentially to escape the drama (I thought I was holding it all together—that, of course, was my drama).

When I stepped onto the Barnard campus, I breathed a sigh of relief. Now I could get down to the business of becoming brilliant, unaffected, and beautiful. Now I could take my pledge of perfection to a new level, free from the distraction of high school drama. I could read the great books, gallivant in the great clubs and bars, develop the perfect body undisturbed by teenage petty concerns like . . .

But wait, was that gagging in the dorm bathroom? Was that really all my friend was going to eat for dinner? Was that girl down the hall going to the gym for the second time in one day? Was the short story with the starving heroine that another student submitted in my writing workshop really a cry for help?

The collection of addictions and compensating behaviors that I had chalked up to teenage angst were actually permanent conditions of womanhood. Damn. Now I would have to read *The Second Sex* and *The Feminine Mystique*. I could hear my mom's voice in my head, sweetly cooing, "I told you so."

Okay, so I'm a feminist. I had to be. When I figured out that some of the smartest women I knew were also starving themselves, sticking their fingers down their throats, spending the majority of their time on a treadmill and the majority of their brainpower hating themselves, I had no choice. In a time of incessant question marks, it seemed the only answer.

I attempted to find a feminism of my own. Jennifer Baumgardner and Amy Richards's *Manifesta: Young Women, Feminism, and the Future* showed that feminism didn't have to include formless jumpers and Birkenstocks but could be sexy, lighthearted, brilliant. I went to see them speak and was immediately heartened by Jennifer's vintage skirt and fishnet stockings and Amy's laid-back laugh and informal style.

My feminist generation is the "third wave" (the first having been the suffragists in their petticoats, the second having been the hippies in their aviator glasses). I imagine a huge ocean wave rolling in with an army of young women with trendy, layered haircuts and vintage glasses riding surfboards expertly to shore. *BUST* and *Bitch* magazines, the Third Wave Foundation, and feminist bookstores such as Bluestockings on the Lower East Side of New York are the cultural hallmarks of my generation.

I felt, finally, a part of something, but I wasn't just looking for a community. I want answers. I am looking for third-wave feminism to be a plank that I can smack down over the abyss between my intellect—*bodies come in all shapes and sizes, I don't have to be good at everything, there is time*—and my behavior—*eating neurotically, wanting more all the time, immediately*. I don't want to grow bitter, frustrated, and even sick as a result of a superwoman lifestyle.

Second-wave feminism accomplished sweeping, grand social change. Despite this life-altering transformation, neither our mothers nor we can eat without feeling guilty. We still can't seem to eradicate the idea that a woman must be physically perfect, in addition to being liberated, brilliant, funny, stylish, and capable—all effortlessly. We still can't be authentically sexual—only raunchy like our brothers or asexual like our mothers. We still don't appear to be adept at creating egalitarian families where men are not just "picking up the slack" or "helping out" but are in all ways sharing the responsibilities. We still haven't created institutions that support these kinds of families. We still don't have a spiritual or political orientation that emphasizes presence instead of speed, joy instead of accomplishment, the beauty of aberration instead of perfection. We still can't look in mirrors without a wave of self-recrimination and anxiety.

Our mothers bravely threw out the need for us girls to be "good." They also modeled some dangerous lessons through their actions. We watched "good girls" turned superwomen accomplish themselves into frenzies, deny their glaring contradictions, and hold firm to dangerous delusions—*it will all get done, he can't help it, you can never be too thin or too rich*. But they also gave us paradigm-shifting wisdom: *The personal is the political*. We younger women need to find answers to our most crucial questions by facing up to and rewriting the seemingly intractable myths with which we have grown up—that girls have to be perfect, effortlessly beautiful, accomplished. In our hearts we need to get to the truth that tells us, with each slow and steady beat, that speed and skinniness are not the ultimate joys of a life well lived.

———————

Somehow the women of my generation learned to chase perfection and feel perpetually unsatisfied. Our first teachers were, of course, our mothers. But our second teachers are often mistakenly left out of this story: They are our fathers—often absent, usually joyful, and always powerful.

3

The Male Mirror: Her Father's Eyes

Weight preoccupation and the sources of young girls' shame about their bodies are usually blamed on mothers because of the powerful role that most mothers play in their children's lives. In the majority of stories young women have told me, their mothers' influence is apparent. Sometimes their mothers are beacons of unconditional love, natural beauty, fierce protection. Sometimes their mothers are well intentioned but unhealthy themselves. Sometimes their mothers are downright cruel. Mothers are never—or at least not in a single story I have heard—neutral.

Fathers, by contrast, are largely under the radar in the ongoing conversation about young women and eating disorders. Their influence on the way their daughters think about beauty and their bodies is often overlooked in the never-ending push and pull between daughters and mothers. Through their absence or presence, fathers teach us about relationships, attractiveness, and love. They are our first experience of being seen by a man—their fear, avoidance, or protection of our bodies (or our mothers') affect how we see ourselves and our relationships with men.

Our fathers' lives are often free from the restrictions and complications that our mothers have endured. Fathers cook family meals on holidays. They tend to say no with far less guilt. They swing by Wendy's without commenting on the calorie count of a Frosty. Fathers often become their daughters' only models of shirking responsibility, for better or worse.

My relationship with my mother veers from one extreme emotion to another; I can cry huge tears at the drop of a hat just thinking about how amazing and generous she is, but I can also feel like screaming into a pillow. I can feel myself reenacting some of her frustrating behaviors in unconscious ways. When I ask my boyfriend to repeat a funny story for one of our friends, he needs only to raise one eyebrow to remind me that I am doing exactly what I hate coming from my mom. My relationship with my mom is all frustration and profound admiration.

By contrast, the relationship I have with my dad is more playful irritation and unwavering respect. He is sweetly absentminded, easily impressed by my mom's cooking and my bad poetry, a history and geography buff who can supply Civil War battle dates or capital cities of foreign countries on cue. Very successful in his field, he is well respected and generally consistent and chill at home. There is more emotionally complex "stuff" going on underneath, but most of the time he shares that with my mom, not me, and his signature one-line e-mails, if not about taxes or flights, are almost always heartfelt praise: "I am so proud of you. I love you so much." He resigned from the prestigious men-only social club in my hometown when I was just eleven years old because, as he wrote in his resignation letter, "I cannot, in good conscience, belong to a club that my son can someday join, but my daughter will be barred from." I remember feeling ten feet tall when I read it.

But my intimacy with my father most often dwells in the heat of political discussions, the celebration of public successes, the safety of having a dad who I know will always take care of me when I need him. My adult friendship with my mother is an intense jungle hike, punctuated by unparalleled views and requiring great endurance, but friendship with my dad is now and has always been a stroll in the park.

To some extent, I chalk this up to our shared nature—concrete, reflective, sensitive, easily overwhelmed. I am grateful for the steadiness of our bond, relieved by the simplicity. But I know we have to keep striving to maintain a connection that includes some of the messy stuff. I have to ask my dad's advice after fights with my boyfriend. He has to reveal his fears about retirement. This is the stuff that keeps us honest and real.

Too many daughters and fathers settle for relationships with shallow intimacy. We stick to what's safe—the sweet little girl and invincible father routine, the intellectual debates that sidestep emotional messes. When it comes to the teeming underbelly of girls' lives at thirteen or seventeen, or even twenty-three—sex, insecurity, cellulite—we naturally turn to our mothers. Girls' issues with their bodies are about so much more than plumbing and primping. I think we need to have candid conversations with our fathers as well as our mothers about them. We need our dads' perspectives, since they are free from some of the hang-ups our moms carry around about their own weight, which could be a source of healing.

This happens, though it is rare. One fifteen-year-old from Detroit, Michigan, described an interaction with her father, a divorcé: "He had just been on a date with this new woman and he was telling me about her. I noticed that the way he described her started with how smart and funny she was, and ended with the fact that he thought she was really beautiful—but 'not in a conventional way.' Even though my dad was talking about another woman, that stuck with me as something I could think about myself." Sometimes an indirect communication, in which Dad isn't made uncomfortable talking about his daughter's looks, can have a lasting impact.

But at other times, being up front is critical. Dana,* a twenty-one-year-old from Savannah, Georgia, recounts that when she was at her thinnest in high school, her dad invited her to the movies. Waiting for the show with a big bucket of popcorn and a giant soda, she remembers that he casually interjected: "Honey, you seem really thin. I won't worry about you if you honestly tell me that you're feeling okay about yourself." Dana remembers being pleasantly surprised. "Thanks, Dad."

"I'm not complimenting you. I think you look great with a little more meat on your bones," he responded, in classic Dad terminology. "But you know I'm here if you want to talk about it." Though Dana didn't take him up on the offer, she remembered it. When she got home that night, she took off her shirt and looked in the mirror. Her collarbones, previously a source of pride, jutted in a way that now struck her as unattractive. "It was as if I could see myself through his eyes," she remembers. She would continue to struggle with yo-yo dieting through college, but she never transgressed into eating-disordered behavior. She says, "It was like my dad's words had built a border keeping me from getting really bad."

Fathers send messages about power, beauty, and pleasure to daughters. My father's life was a template of maleness; his success in the world was calculated in dollars and cents, unlike my mom's, and his familial attentiveness seen as a bonus prize, not a given. Friends' mothers would frequently comment on how extraordinary it was that my father came to all of my basketball games or showed up at an academic awards ceremony, with no similar mention of my mother, who was also always there.

My father's power was straightforward and universally understood, my mother's deep and unquantifiable. My dad told me once, on our sunny porch over omelets—his specialty—that he thought Sophia Loren was the most beautiful movie star. I did not ask, "Do I look like her, Daddy? Will I look like her?" But I filed it away as research in a lifelong search to understand the male definition of beauty.

Many fathers' messages are communicated in code: a derogatory term flung at a fat woman on the street, a subtle side comment and a pinch of Mom's waist, the suburban superhero Lester Burnham ogling his daughter's best friend in *American Beauty*. One of my friends in high school read her parents' marriage—its absence of sensuality and excess of bitterness—like the coffee grounds left in the bottom of a cup, a harbinger of things to come if she was not careful. Another friend saw her dad trampled by her teeth-clenching, controlling mother and learned that femaleness was about passive aggression and maleness about escape. One friend's father grabbed a brownie out of her hand at her brother's high school graduation party and threw it in the trash without a word. One of my students told me, "Daddy wasn't a big, direct influence on me, really," then paused, head tilted to the side, and added, "But I did find him watching South American beauty pageants on Telemundo all the time. Seeing that while I was growing up did make me think that men liked certain kinds of bodies."

These subliminal messages cause a lot of pain. Dads may be men of few words, but their lives speak loud and clear.

The Good Guy

Tanya's* mother and father got divorced when she was five years old. She was disturbed by watching her dad carry boxes from the house to the car, one after the other—the march of her family breaking apart. Her big brother, Sam,* the pleaser in the family, held her hand and told her everything would be okay. Tanya scoffed. Even at five, she knew that everything had changed.

She was right, but couldn't have possibly understood the depth to which she was wise at that moment. Her father, a teacher in Omaha, moved into a little house ten miles away, where she and Sam would spend every other weekend with him. At first there was some-thing vacationlike about their time with him—he would feed them foods that their mother banned, such as peanut M&M's and McDon-ald's Happy Meals. He would throw them in the air and sing songs for them and generally make them feel like the two most special kids in the whole world.

But when they returned home, to the house over which their mother ruled like a military chief, it was torture. They loved their mother, but she restricted everything they did—especially what they ate. Both Tanya and Sam were chubby kids, teased by cruel class-mates, their full cheeks pinched by fat aunts. Both were subject to their mother's rules—no opening new boxes or bags of anything unless given permission, no snacks before dinner, no eating after dinner. Eventually she would force them both to get on the scale once a week to track their weight. Because of the pounds added by their father's "fun weekends," the scale would climb higher and their mother would grow angrier.

Fathers feign innocence and get away with it. Men like Tanya's dad, desperate to show love to their children but incapable of doing it in words, often resort to food. His steaming pots of Kraft macaroni and cheese and bags of Lay's potato chips were a guilty father's attempt to indulge his kids, to show them that he still adored them even though he had moved out. Dr. Brad Sachs, a family psychologist, has seen many similar cases in his practice and explains: "A lot of fathers feel such guilt about not being available in a day-to-day way, yet they hesitate to take on the hard work of strong, effective parenting." The result can often be more severe than a few extra indulgence pounds. Dr. Sachs goes on: "Sometimes the daughters will develop an eating disorder as a way to elicit active, firm involvement from their fathers that they can't elicit in other ways." As with all unspoken guilt, this one festers and mutates, as it sickens both children and parents.

In addition to guilt, the psychologist and feminist author Robin Stern argues, many fathers had little aptitude for parenting: "Many of the men who raised your generation had no role models of involved and authentic fathering to rely on," she told me. "They were forced to invent the wheel, so to speak, and many of them failed. They were 'good daddies' and 'ineffective fathers.'" Most of our fathers did not know how to manifest what they wanted in their own adult, family lives—especially with the complications of divorce. Advocacy organizations such as Dads and Daughters, founded in 1999, cropped up to try to fill this gap, producing a newsletter and providing workshops for committed fathers. Unfortunately, not all dads recognize their own value to their girls' lives. In a recent poll conducted by Dads and Daughters, two-thirds don't believe that "their active involvement is vital to their daughters' well-being."

Tanya's story proves otherwise. When she started therapy, ten years after this indulge-and-deprive pattern began, she would point the finger of blame at her mother, who restricted and chastised her, made her feel bad about her weight every day, tried to control and curtail everything "large" about her. Tanya's mother had plenty of blame to shoulder, but it took Tanya much longer to point the finger in her father's direction as well. It took much longer for her to make the connection between the care packages of cookies and cakes that he sent, substitutes for his increasing absence, and her lifelong struggle with her weight. It took much longer for her to see that, as damaging as her mother's overzealous restrictions had been, her father's one-note act as "the good guy" was just as demoralizing for a little girl who wanted only to be loved for who she was.

Even among parents who stay together—which is actually the minority case these days—fathers often play the role of risk taker and rule bender. "Don't tell Mom" is a playful instruction thrown around by workaholic fathers who want to bond with their children without putting in real time. The father of a friend of mine would fill the house with junk food when her mom went away on business, allowing the kids to indulge in everything they wanted. He disbanded mealtimes and instituted a new house rule: "There are no rules!" The kids shrieked with joy, ate cartons of rocky road ice cream while staying up late on school nights and watching *Terminator 2*. Dad was the best. When Mom came home, the fun came to an end. She was grumpy and mean.

This may be many fathers' method for livening up houses where rules and responsibilities get too heavy, but the burden of figuring out what it all means ultimately falls on the children. Mom puts in the time, but she also restricts and restrains. Dad is rarely around, but when he is, it is a laugh a minute, a real party time. As a result, femaleness is equated with restriction in many little girls' minds. Maleness is about wild abandon, sweetness, fun.

These days Tanya can hear her mother and father speaking in her mind whenever she faces down a refrigerator of possibilities. She eats a sensible dinner—chicken, spinach, a little rice. The mother voice inside her mind is pleased, impressed with the sensibility of the meal, holding her breath that Tanya won't do anything to ruin the proper restraint of her dinner choice. She sits down to watch TV by herself. Her roommates still aren't home from work. Tanya begins to get antsy. She gets up at commercials and wanders around the kitchen. Sits back down. Wanders again. She gets the ice cream out of the freezer, her father's voice growing stronger, drowning out the angry, high-pitched whispers of her desperate mother. She heaps a bowl with vanilla ice cream, goes back to the living room, and shovels it in, not even tasting the rich sweetness. Then she gets a couple cookies, eats them quickly, and lies back on the couch, taking in the brief moment of contentment that she knows will fade quickly. She is indulged. She is filled. She is her father.

A sitcom later, she will be her mother again. When she kneels in the bathroom, finger down her throat, and tries—unsuccessfully—to purge her father out of her, she will hear her mother reading a diet book aloud at the dinner table, saying things like "I just don't want you to struggle with your weight the way I have."

As she lies in bed, trying to fall asleep, hands pressed on her bloated stomach, she will cry, still the little girl torn between two houses.

Daddy's Little Girl

In so many ways, the girls I have spoken with retain a part of their little-girl neediness beneath a veneer of security and savvy, the characteristic I have named the starving daughter. Girls like Tanya are not completely paralyzed by the parental voices inside their heads; the perfect-girl parts of them succeed in keeping prestigious jobs, having boyfriends, going out on the weekends looking nonchalantly hip—which is why these kinds of partial-syndrome eating disorders are so rarely treated. Tanya binges and purges a few times a month maximum—not the clinical definition of bulimia. She rarely talks about her tendency with her friends, never with her family. In fact, she is irritated beyond measure when either of her parents treats her as if she is still a child.

So many fathers seem to relate to their daughters in a *Father Knows Best* time warp—where a daddy called his daughters Princess and Kitten well past their adolescence. These retro fathers delude themselves that their daughters are still six and enamored with their daddies, even when, in fact, they are sixteen and painfully aware of their fathers' shortcomings. Many fathers seem adept at filtering out the cacophony of adolescent angst, boyfriends, complex friendships, hearing only what they want to hear—the straight A's or the marching band at the homecoming game. Parenting sons seems straightforward. Fathers expect a little rough-and-tumble rebellion from their growing guys, but their daughters' coming-of-age seems so emotional and conflicted that they prefer to avoid it altogether.

On my sixteenth birthday, my dad exclaimed, "Happy fifteenth birthday, Courtney! You must be so excited to be able to drive next year." He was joking, as he has on every single one of my birthdays, about his own discomfort with seeing me grow older. Each year we laugh and trade jabs about his increasing senility and my decreasing dependence, but there is a seriousness underlying our jokes. It is hard on my dad to watch me grow older. It makes him proud but uncomfortable, because he knows that being a woman and having a woman's body include a lot of dangerous terrain.

Many fathers would like to keep their daughters frozen in time. They resist their daughters growing up and becoming more complex, more pained, more independent women. They adore their "little girls" and want to keep them safe. Unconsciously, they must reason that keeping their daughters small, if only in their own minds, will ensure that safety. But daughters' bodies demand otherwise. In fact, Dads and Daughters was started by a father, Joe Kelly, when a friend told him a disheartening though common story: His nine-year-old daughter asked him if she looked too fat.

When nine-year-old girls are taking on womanly worries, not even the most sentimental dads can pretend nothing is happening. Mr. Kelly explains, "We came to the idea that it was significant that she asked him and not her mother. A girl is going to want to know how to get the attention of members of the opposite sex. The first one she knows is Dad. How he responds to her and reflects back to her is incredibly important." Today Dads and Daughters, based in Duluth, Minnesota, has only sixteen hundred members nationwide.

Most fathers are still in the dark about how to deal with their daughters' changing bodies. Silvia* grew up in the Bronx in one of those rare families that had a mother and a father both living at home. When her body started developing, at age ten, her mother made her wear a girdle to, as Silvia put it, "hold in my blossoming body." She says of her father's outlook on her early maturation: "He didn't say anything, but I knew he wasn't too happy. I don't think my father could deal with it. He would have been happy if I had stayed underdeveloped or wore a huge burlap sack at all times." Silvia internalized her father's fears, hiding her body in baggy clothes until she was sixteen.

Foremost in this effort to keep daughters little girls is the denial of puberty, and all the horrifying surprises that go with it, which is Mom's domain. Fathers often pretend to be oblivious to growing pains and late-night phone calls, the boxes of tampons and acne wash in the grocery cart. The changing body can seem a hidden, dangerous secret to the daughter whose father refuses to acknowledge its existence.

Silvia, now twenty-nine and a human resources coordinator at a law firm in Manhattan, continues to struggle with her body image. She says, "I do experience guilt, especially when I am shopping for clothes. I immediately feel like I have to lose weight." Silvia has also considered getting plastic surgery: "Truthfully, I think that my legs are too big. However, one of my aunts, who I was very close to, died in the process of receiving a tummy tuck. This experience opened my eyes."

Many women realize, in retrospect, that they developed anorexia just as their bodies were changing. They include the author of *The Beauty Myth,* Naomi Wolf: "Anorexia was the only way I could see to keep the dignity in my body that I had had as a kid, and that I would lose as a woman." Womanly bodies seem fraught with complexity, sites of service, starvation, submission. When fathers ignore changing bodies, they contribute to the cultural messaging that surrounds girls and young women: Ignore your bodies' wisdom, tame your bodies' hungers, they will only get you in trouble. A girl's ability to speak the emotional language of her aches and pains—differentiating, for example, between hunger for company and physical hunger—fades away. Taught to fear, ignore, and control her own body, she loses essential attunement to her unique appetite.

With the onset of girls' puberty occuring at younger and younger ages—one in seven Caucasian girls now start developing breasts or pubic hair by the age of eight, and one in two African American girls do—this split between "the girl" and "the body" can happen very early. Eating disorders now occur fairly commonly in nine-year-olds, and there are clinics throughout the country that devote themselves entirely to treating eating disorders in tweens, ages eight to twelve.

Some girls dive into the risks their developing bodies bring. "Easy," they are called by the guys at school. "A handful," they are called by a group of neighborhood dads standing around the barbe-cue. Emily White, a young journalist intrigued by the seemingly universal "myth of the slut," wrote *Fast Girls,* a dramatic narrative of teenage reputations ruined. She captures the "fast girl" at home beautifully: "The invasion of hormones turns the child into a stranger, and the stranger in the house forces the adults to ask questions: What happens behind the closed door? What dreams live behind the half-closed eyes? What does the body need, and furthermore, why does the body suddenly seem so urgent, angry, maybe transgressively beautiful?"

These girls who enjoy their new bodies scare fathers the most. The fathers are afraid of the choices their teenage daughters might have to make, afraid of the looks they will receive, afraid of the world their daughters are entering, which doesn't seem any kinder than when they were young men, especially not to young girls with women's bodies.

As their daughters inevitably stretch and strain against "little-girl" idealizations, fathers cling. So many relationships between young women and their fathers seem stunted—as if the father never truly saw the daughter after she turned twelve. This dynamic makes for cute nicknames and lots of coddling but little authenticity.

———————

For all of his teasing, my dad made a gallant effort to acknowledge my transition into adulthood. When my mom was tearing through *Reviving Ophelia* by Mary Pipher, he was reading *How to Father a Successful Daughter* by Nicky Marone. Like a lot of baby-boomer fathers, exposed to men's groups and feminism, he was into being a father. His intention has always been to be a part of every aspect of my life, even those that were once relegated to bathroom chats with aunties and moms. Even though his job prevented his full involvement, when it counted, he showed up.

When I first got my period, despite my best attempts to keep my dad away entirely, he tried to be a part of the conversation. I sat in the front passenger seat in our suburban-staple minivan with my lanky legs bent and my feet resting on the dashboard in front of me, my flip-flops thrown in the backseat with the groceries. He drove, humming along to the '50s music on the radio, his hands at ten and two, as always. When he reached to turn down the radio, I knew something was up. He cleared his throat and said, "You know, your mom told me about you getting your period, and I just want to say how wonderful I think that is. This is such an important time in your life, and I am very proud of you."

I was horrified. Proud? What could he possibly be proud of? I'd spent two hours in tears, bathroom door shut, as my mom shouted tampon insertion instructions through the keyhole. I didn't feel like it was an important time. I felt like it was an introduction to gross fluids and unpredictability, one more thing to feel insecure about, as if my chicken legs and lopsided breasts weren't enough.

I turned to look out the window in the opposite direction and said, "Thanks, Dad. I don't really want to talk about it," effectively cutting off the father-daughter bonding opportunity. We didn't speak the rest of the way home, only listened to the bubblegum sounds of Lesley Gore singing, "It's my party and I'll cry if I want to," lyrics that were stupidly simplistic compared with the complexities we both knew I was just beginning to face.

In retrospect, I am so thankful my dad took that risk. Even though it embarrassed me at the time, even though we didn't talk further about this rite of passage, it was somehow comforting that he'd broken the ice. He had said the word *period* out loud. He had admitted that my body and its strange new functions were not secrets or shameful. Even though I refused his attempt to have a dialogue, his words lived on in my mind. They were important at that important time.

A lot of father-daughter pairs are intimidated by the enormity of the task of creating a relationship in which they can talk about these kinds of things, but in reality, it takes only a two-second exchange. It takes only this kind of brief acknowledgment to open the door. Whether you walk through it or not is another matter entirely. My dad and I usually chose not to—or, more accurately, I usually chose not to. But that was okay. We didn't need the heart-wrenching, soul-baring relationship I had with my mom—we only needed to be us, with a dash of healthy discomfort thrown in.

My mother, bless her heart, had pushed us in this direction, sometimes to my horror. Once when I was home from college for a little vacation, she pulled up in front of the supermarket and said, "Ronnie, do you want to run inside and pick up Courtney's birth control from the pharmacy?" When she looked around and saw that both my father and I had turned ten shades of red and were shaking our heads at her infamous tactlessness, she persevered, saying, "Oh, come on, we're all adults here."

As much as I wanted to throw a toddler tantrum at that moment, I recognized that my mom was right. We *were* all adults. If I have learned anything from my mom's shocking and sometimes painful exposures, it is that a little awkwardness goes a long way in service of an authentic relationship. I didn't want to sit down and have a heart-to-heart with my dad about my sexual history, but it was important to me that he have an accurate picture of who I was. Though I retained some of my childhood spunk and stubbornness, I was not the same little girl Dad had coached in YMCA basketball, although sometimes it feels comfortable to act as if I am. I still hold my dad's hand, still curl up under his arm on the couch if we are watching a movie, still complain to him in my smallest girl voice if I want a reassuring fatherly fix (taxi money, ice cream cones, tax information). Then we talk about my health, my struggles in romantic relationships or complex friendships. I also look to him for authentic adult connection, as uncomfortable as it might feel at first. It usually ends up feeling just right. My dad gives great advice about how to be patient with my boyfriend or address underlying tension with a girlfriend. He gets outraged along with me at the rising price of birth control and my unending search for health insurance. Even if neither of us goes there intuitively, as my mother and I do, we are happy once we arrive. We are closer. We are friends.

My relationship with my dad, and the effort that we continue to make to be real with each other, is one of the layers of protection that stands between me and a full-blown eating disorder. He may not be as observant as my mom, but I know that my dad sees my body and that he would notice if it shrank. I know that he thinks I'm pretty now, and that he would still think I was pretty with ten more pounds. I know that he makes a concerted effort to be a part of my life, even the messiest parts, and that he will endure some embarrassment for the sake of that goal. And as he and I have learned, awkwardness often leads to authenticity.

The Switzerland of Parenthood

So many father-daughter pairs avoid being uncomfortable around each other, and thereby sacrifice their capacity for authenticity. It is a dance, of course—daughters must take responsibility when they waltz right past their dads as times get tough. But it is the fathers, as the hormone-neutral adults, who must let their daughters know that they are open to being embarrassed, that they want to share even the tough stuff, and that they choose not to father as their own fathers did.

Instead, so many fathers claim to be neutral third parties. There is no such thing in a family. These dads spend most of their hours at the office and come home to the aftermath of fights, steering clear of the storm. Many don't initiate uncomfortable conversations about girl-friends or crushes. Granted, most girls are relieved to have one less third degree each day—moms sometimes make their daughters feel perpetually cross-examined. But in the long run, this policy of moms delving in and dads opting out is not good for anyone. It sets the expectation that fathers, and other men, don't have to deal with the messiness of life—that mothers and other women do. It says that fathers don't have insight into the complexities of human relation-ships, bruised egos, love interests; fathers aren't interested in their daughters' daily travails, their struggles with the weight and acne that come with puberty. Mothers are sensitive and involved; fathers are strong and silent. This is the still-clinging residue, like burnt rice on the bottom of an old pot, of the traditional family model—the Cleavers, the Bradys, the Cunninghams.

Often still today the only time a red-blooded American father gets riled up about something having to do with his daughter is when she brings home a boyfriend. Then he bristles like an agitated porcupine and gives the young man a talk about respect and curfew. The lesson for the daughter is that her father's role is to protect her pristine body from being violated, not to empower her to protect herself or make choices that prevent her from having to worry about protecting her-self. The message is that men are either violators or protectors of

women's bodies; they are not involved in the process of understanding, politicizing, or healing those bodies.

The myth of neutrality is especially ridiculous and potentially
damaging during adolescence. When a girl is coming to understand
her body and its meaning in the world, she is drawing on every
resource possible. Her mother's thwarted diets and self-criticism
hurled at the mirror, her big sister's one hundred sit-ups a night, her
health teacher's brush over the female reproductive system are all part
of this understanding. And yes, even her father's avoidance of everything to do with what femaleness is coming to mean—menstruation
and bra shopping, food restriction and fitness—is a message. For an
adolescent, an adult's inaction is an action. Silence is a speech.

––––––––––

Alexandra* immigrated from Armenia to the American South when
she was just four years old. Her parents manifested the American
Dream, clawing their way up from poverty to provide a relatively
comfortable life for their three daughters, and Alexandra, for her part,
adopted a truly American mentality: "Everything has to be perfect. I
know I will never have the perfect body, and that really angers me."

She recognized how hard her father worked. Her family did not
have a BMW or a Lexus, like their neighbors in the small, wealthy
town in North Carolina, but they were definitely middle-class until
her father lost his job and their financial hardships started. Her sister
dropped out of high school at sixteen and started working at a day-
care center to contribute to the household. Her father, already quiet
and uninvolved in his daughters' lives, became even more withdrawn.
The family kept their financial insecurity secret from others.

Alexandra's perfectionism was intensified by her family's
struggles. She didn't want to end up like her sister, so she worked
obsessively in school. This obsessive behavior bled into her body
image. She read about the latest diets on the Internet and bought all
the best sellers. She tried every fitness fad that came around—yoga,
Pilates, kickboxing, spinning. She spent all her graduation money on
a personal trainer.

Now she is putting herself through college with loans, a part-time job, and a few precious scholarships. She is still close to her mother and her sister, though thousands of miles away, but feels as distant from her dad as ever. She says, "My dad is hard to talk to. He only cares about how I am doing in school and issues of that nature. We've never had a relationship beyond that. He doesn't know how to deal with girls and what they go through."

All the stress of being financially independent and so hard on herself—"My grades have to be perfect or I will freak out"—has caused Alexandra to eat more than usual. "I think about food 24/7," she admits. "It gives me comfort, and I guess I really feel like I need comfort right now." Alexandra estimates that she has gained twenty pounds since she started school. She explains, "I am always looking in the mirror and feeling disgusted with myself. Although I didn't think so at the time, I used to look really good in high school. Now I have love handles, cellulite on my thighs, and countless other imperfections." Alexandra doesn't have an eating disorder—"I would feel too disgusted to stick my finger down my throat"—but she feels deeply ashamed. She won't let her new boyfriend touch her waist.

When she calls home and her dad answers the phone, they don't discuss any of this. Instead, he asks how her studying is going, and she tells him about her latest A paper. She doesn't ask about his job search for fear it will make him feel bad. After an awkward silence, he hands the phone to her mom, and she can finally burst into tears.

Fathers like Alexandra's surely see their daughters in three dimensions but treat them as if they see only one—school. Grades are finite and simple, leading to concrete discussions about college or career aspirations. Girls should be encouraged to study hard, achieve excellence, look forward to college and beyond. Fathers stick their flags resolutely in this even ground of grades and goals, claiming it as their jurisdiction. It is a noble commitment, but there is another country closer to home that they neglect to explore.

This is the country where girls' self-esteem lies, where they struggle with their identities, where they wrestle with the meaning of their changing bodies. If fathers pretend none of that is happening, they essentially shut out a critical dimension of their daughters' development. Turning a blind eye to Alexandra's unhealthy obsession with working out or getting perfect grades, her father teaches her that she is invisible unless accomplished, that no price (including her mental health) is too high. His silence, now that she is in college and gaining weight, sends a clear message that her swelling body is shameful, something he cannot talk about because it embarrasses him.

Alexandra uses this word, *shame*, repeatedly. And shame, as we have learned from our mothers' movement, is intertwined with silence. In the coded language spoken between daughter and father, shame and silence are often interpreted as one and the same.

On a visit home for her twentieth birthday, May* had a bunch of friends over for her mom's famous homemade cake and real English tea—her mother is a wealthy anorectic woman obsessed with feeding others. Her stacks of cookbooks filled whole shelves in their San Francisco town house, and she had killed forests of trees since she discovered how to print recipes off the Internet. For college, May had relocated to Chicago, far away from her mom, her eternally empty refrigerator, and piles of pictures of food, recognizing that it all contributed to her own tendency to be self-loathing in spite of her gorgeous looks.

As her mother fretted about the right forks, the temperature of the tea, the consistency of the cake, May assured her that everything was perfect, teasing her about being such a meticulous hostess. They giggled together, hugged frequently, recounted old birthdays in vivid detail.

May's physician father was in his office, checking his e-mail.

Her brother lay on the couch, reading a philosophy text for school.

There was a complete and total division between the world of the women—homemade cake and loving jabs—and the world of the men—business correspondence and philosophy. The women were worrying that everyone would have a good time, that the cake's hint of lemon had been maintained in the baking, that they each took only the tiniest, most demure taste. The men were involved in things, apparently, more urgent than cake or celebrating May's birthday.

This separation illustrates a complete and total incapacity on the part of May's father to engage in the real life of his daughter. This is about his total ignorance of her total obsession with the size of her thighs. This is about the thousands of hours May's father has missed of her childhood because he was in surgery, saving someone else's life. This is about the check he writes every month to pay her exorbitant psychotherapy bills—the specious relief he gets from signing his name on that check and feeling like he is "fixing" the problem of his daughter.

May's father would come to Chicago to take her out to dinner at expensive restaurants. She listened as he held forth on the latest PBS documentary or political controversy. She smiled and tried to fit in a smart, ironic word here and there to show that she was informed. As they left the restaurant, he would slip a hundred-dollar bill into her coat pocket. She would shake her head, say, "Oh, Daddy!" but not return it. As they parted, he would kiss her on both cheeks, and she would thank him. Then they would walk in opposite directions like two strangers after a first date.

May never spent much time with her father outside these formal dinners and carefully planned vacations. She had a strong sense of her parents' political views, their philosophical leanings, the musicals they loved, and the classic movies they adored. But she knew nothing of her father's soul. She knew nothing of what made him tick, what drove him, what scared him. She knew nothing of what he loved most.

And he knew just as little about her. He didn't know that she went through wildly different diet phases: one week eating only grapefruit and cottage cheese, the next only drinking coffee and smoking cigarettes, the next consuming everything in sight. He didn't know that she despised her own body, saw it is as the seat of her inability to take control of her life. He didn't know that she jumped from adoring guy to adoring guy, searching for some affirmation to fill up the hole inside where self-love was supposed to be.

Or worse yet, maybe he did.

"Father Hunger"

Nearly a quarter of young women were raised by no father at all. According to the U.S. Census Bureau, whereas 77 percent of kids lived with two married parents in 1980, that proportion has continued to drop—now holding steady at 68 percent. Twenty-three percent of children lived with only their mothers in 2004. Much has been written about the characteristics of a largely "fatherless" generation, which psychologists claim is especially bad for boys, who have no partners for playing catch, no sense of security, no male role models. Less has been written about the fallout for fatherless girls.

Dr. Margo Maine, a psychologist specializing in eating disorders, is convinced that missing fathers are among the major contributing factors to eating disorders among young women today. Either an absent father or a deficient relationship with a present father, she argues, contributes to the pangs of a gnawing feeling called "father hunger." She defines it as "a deep, persistent desire for emotional connection with the father." When that connection doesn't happen naturally, girls often try to force it.

When daughters don't feel seen, they sometimes try to make themselves impossible to ignore. Some girls get fixated on being thin and beautiful in order to win their fathers' praise and, they hope, their overdue attention. Some girls eat to fill the hollow place where their fathers' love should be and in the process get bodies that their fathers can't help but see because they are big and getting bigger. Some girls become obsessed with sports, convinced that they can win their fathers' love by beating them at their own game. Some girls, like Delilah,* get pissed.

As a tween growing up in a working-class family in a suburb of Boston, Delilah brooded over pretty average concerns; she thought that she was disproportionate, her nose too big, her waist too thick. The truth was that Delilah, like her mom, was a petite, pretty girl with a smattering of freckles across her pale Irish skin. But she wasn't convinced, especially not once puberty hit. "We never talked about puberty in my house," Delilah remembers, "so I wanted to pretend it wasn't happening."

Denial is a family trait. Delilah's dad was often verbally and emotionally abusive while she was growing up. She remembers, "My mother covered for my father really well, so I thought he was a terrible, terrible man. I didn't realize that he was a terrible, terrible *drunk* until I was in my midteens."

At fourteen Delilah was caught drinking and punished severely. She was enraged at being grounded for a month for something her father did nightly. After a week stuck in her tense home, she started trying to make herself throw up. Strangely enough, she didn't associate this behavior with her mother, who she knew had suffered in her twenties from bulimia so severe that she had been hospitalized. Delilah's mom, frightened by the resemblance to herself she saw sprouting in her headstrong, self-critical daughter, had deliberately told Delilah about her affliction.

"It didn't feel like I was throwing up to lose weight like my mom," Delilah explains. "It felt like I was throwing up because I was angry about something. I remember hovering over the toilet, crying hysterically, blood vessels breaking on my face."

Eventually Delilah's friends took notice and told on her. Her mother was crushed, her father angry. The drives home from her weekly therapy appointments, she remembers, were hell: "He was scared I was telling the therapist it was his fault, so he would harangue me afterwards. 'What did you talk about?' When I said nothing, he would scream at me, 'You're fucking lying to me. I'm paying for these appointments!' "

Delilah stopped throwing up because it was too easy for others to detect, and started starving herself. She would avoid breakfast altogether, drink a glass of juice for lunch, then eat a bowl of Raisin Bran for dinner. As she shrank, her brother and her mother grew more desperate and her father drunker and angrier. She would arrive home from babysitting, and he would wake up from his drunken stupor on the couch and scream at her, "You selfish bitch, waking me up! You think you're the only one who lives in this house!" and then drag himself upstairs.

At some point his rage got so bad that he crossed the line and physically pushed Delilah's mother. She filed for a divorce the next day, and he moved out. Delilah would visit him in his childhood home, which was located in an old graveyard, and leave depressed at both his condition and his criticism. "My father was always very tough on me," she says in an obvious understatement. "He told me how chubby I was, that I had tree-trunk legs, that I was selfish. I have a lot of faults, but being selfish is not one of them." Unfortunately, Delilah wasn't able to convince herself that the other criticisms weren't valid either.

Her father's peace offering to drive her to Duke University, where she would attend college, got ugly when he packed a cooler full of beer in the car. She was grateful to be rid of him finally when he took one last teetering turn into the campus parking lot, shadowed by tall and impressive buildings so unlike where she had come from. When the last of her things were unpacked and her father drove out of the lot, it felt like a new beginning.

But it wasn't long into her first college year before Delilah started purging again. She remembers, "I was throwing up constantly. It was actually breaking the toilet in our dorm sometimes. I was having to do minor toilet repairs." She memorized the least populated bathrooms on campus and started frequenting them between classes. Her junior year she tried ipecac for the first time—an over-the-counter syrup made from plant extract designed only for people who have ingested poison.[†]

†According to Rader Programs, a private company providing clinical programs for eating-disordered patients for over twenty years: "The misuse of ipecac syrup can cause significant and severe medical complications and even result in death. Karen Carpenter, the recording artist who suffered from an eating disorder, actually died from the misuse of ipecac syrup. The alkaloid emetine from the ipecac syrup had caused severe damage to her heart, which eventually led to her going into cardiac arrest and subsequently dying. Complications of the misuse of ipecac include but are not limited to cardiac arrhythmias, irreversible damage to the muscles of the heart, seizures, shock, hemorrhaging, blackouts, high blood pressure, respiratory complications, dehydration, electrolyte abnormalities, or death."

Delilah packed it in her bag when she went home for the summer, and her mom found it, immediately sending her back to therapy. This time Delilah wanted nothing more than to stop purging. She finally started to make the connection between the anger she felt about her dad's behavior and her disease, but it didn't mean automatic healing. Her father hunger ran deep.

She continued to throw up off and on through her senior year. Her dad continued to make drunken phone calls to her cell phone, blaming her for her parents' breakup in slurring epithets: "You put too much fucking pressure on the relationship, Delilah. You always were selfish!" But Delilah's future was bright, her mother was doing well on her own, and she had created healthy relationships with her brother and younger sister.

A month after she graduated from Duke, Delilah had relocated to Chicago. Her friends surprised her for her birthday. She remembers, "We had this beautiful meal out in the city; we were all dressed up and everything. Then I went to the bathroom and started throwing up." Her voice shifts here, taking on the tone she uses when disciplining the first-graders she now teaches on Chicago's South Side. "I looked at myself in the mirror and said, 'You have to be kidding me. You have all of these wonderful friends. They flew in from all over the country. Get out of the bathroom, now.'"

She hasn't purged since.

Delilah continues to try to create a relationship with her father, whom she describes as "a total drunk." On a recent visit, she recounted for him some of the things he had said to her, and he broke down in tears. "I don't remember," he kept repeating. "I don't remember."

But his tears didn't endear him to her. On the contrary, Delilah explains, "My father is especially unforgivable because he had been with my mother when she was hospitalized. He has lost everything. He has no excuse not to try to get better."

Recently he said something to Delilah's younger sister, just sixteen, about "getting big," and Delilah immediately called and in her tersest, scariest tone told him, "You ever say that to her again and I'll fucking kill you."

"I meant it," she tells me.

She breathes deeply and concludes with dignified finality: "I'm twenty-two, and I've got my shit together. I can support myself. My father is forty-six, and he lives in a house with practically no furniture on a cemetery with his alcoholic brother. The IRS is after him. His liver's got to be shot to hell. He's going to die soon."

She pauses, then continues in a gentler voice: "I love him, but I hate him. I just wish he would apologize."

Daddy's Little Clone

Delilah has the insight to see that her dad's life holds no promise, but many young women are under the impression that following their fathers' paths is the only way to go.

Kay,* a teenager from Atlanta, tells me in a whisper: "My mom works full-time, comes home, makes dinner, does laundry or whatever needs to be done for the family, talks to my grandmother on the phone, solves her friends' problems, helps me with a paper or something, then collapses. My dad works full-time, comes home, and hangs out." Tilting her head and raising her eyebrows, she playfully asks, "Come on, which would you choose?"

Jane,* a twenty-five-year-old from a Connecticut family, describes a wealthier retro version: "In my family there were two choices. One was to be like my mom—stay at home and clean, be cozy, that kind of thing. The other was to be like my dad, who is adventurous and active. It was very clear that my dad's thing was better. I got this perfectionist drive from trying to travel his path instead of my mom's."

The retro-homemaker role can induce loneliness and listlessness; the supermom role induces stress. Either path is less inviting than girls' fathers'. One might also argue that a traditional father's path is less rewarding than the mother's connection with her children, but that's hard to see at sixteen or even twenty-six. What is crystal-clear is the supermom-induced exhaustion of a hardworking mother and the fake-smile desperation of a stay-at-home mom. Thinking our vision is

20/20, we daughters prefer the inviting mix of seriousness and playfulness that our fathers have the luxury of generating.

Just as our mothers' bodies predict our adult forms, our parents' lives serve as holograms for our futures. When your father shouted "You be anything, do anything you want" as he ran out the door, he left more than your overworked mother behind. He left an echoing contradiction rather than a ringing endorsement. To fill that void, many girls empty their bellies, thinking that doing so will free them up to follow an easier, less encumbered path.

Naomi Wolf's anorexia was an effort to reject her mother's life. "The things we saw women doing for beauty looked crazy," she writes. "I wanted to travel, but I saw that beauty led women in circles. My mother, a beautiful woman, got too little of the pleasures that I could understand. I saw that her beauty hurt her: teeth-gritting abstinence at celebration dinners, fury on the scale, angry rubdowns, self-accusing photographs posted over the refrigerator." Wolf chose to starve the new curves out of her twelve-year-old body and, in so doing, avoid the narrowing of her world. "It was the only choice that really looked like one: By refusing to put on a woman's body and receive a rating, I chose not to have all my future choices confined to small things."

Wolf, like so many young women on the brink of the world, wanted to do "big things"—such as mentally bitch-slapping know-it-all boys in Ivy League classrooms, getting prestigious scholarships, and flying around the world, making lots of money. These are considered grand in our society, while the "small things"—birth, death, heartache, nourishment, family, spirit, just to name a few—are classified as women's overlooked good works. Taut and hidden bodies get to fly to exciting places, get to house incredible minds that think big-picture. Mothers are buried in details, usually immobile with so much responsibility, putting out fires all the time. Curvy and substantial bodies are relegated to the home and never-ending caretaking to be done.

For years, my mom encouraged me to read Marion Woodman, and for years, I brushed her off. My persistent mother explains, "She writes about archetypes"—*oh, nope, not reading that one*—"and the imbalance of feminine and masculine qualities"—*oh, okay, reductionist*—"and how this imbalance has led women to reject their bodies"—*yeah, not going to happen.* "Sounds interesting, Mom," I would say and then turn back to my dog-eared book by some dead white philosopher.

But lo and behold, after all these years, I found myself sitting next to my mother in a packed conference hall in New York City listening to Marion Woodman. My mom had flown all the way from Colorado to visit me and attend this lecture.

Woodman spoke of her own near-fatal battle with anorexia. She talked about the radical power of simply *seeing* someone else, truly and nakedly, without judgment. By the end, I was a tearful mess and willingly produced an admission to my mother: "You told me so." Woodman writes about perfectionism, about achievement, about bodies inhumanely cut off from souls. She also writes about the delusion that progress means accomplishments: "If we look at modern Athenas sprung from their fathers' foreheads, we do not necessarily see liberated women."

In other words, Athena—the Greek goddess of wisdom, efficiency, achievement, justice—is not a free and happy chick. She is, like so many of us who chase after our fathers' dreams, disconnected from her own body, self-hating, frustrated, and anxious about what feels like the ultimate and incessant distraction from work: soul. The perfect girl is Athena, marching on, checking items off of her to-do list, making Dad proud with her grades and her vocabulary, without listening a lick to the starving daughter inside. We are so overwhelmed by the voices of our mothers that we try to tune them out entirely—listening only to the incessant drumbeat of the march of our fathers' measured lives.

Jane Fonda, a big Woodman fan, wrote the following in her autobiography: "All my life I had been a father's daughter, trapped in a Greek drama, like Athena, who sprang fully formed from the head of her father, Zeus—disciplined, driven. Starting in childhood, I learned that love was earned through perfection. In adolescence, my feelings of imperfection centered on my physical being, and I abandoned the poor, loyal body and took up residence in my head." So while she was scissor-kicking those legs in the air, it was our mothers she was leading but her father she was channeling.

When we dwell only in our "dad's mind," we become alienated from the irrational and fantastic cravings of our "mother's body." We forget that the bleeding and the lusting and the swelling of adolescence and womanhood contain complex if painful wisdom. These two parts of ourselves—the rational striver and the intuitive wanderer— need not be so cleaved. Even when we neglect one, try to starve it or bury it, both are always there.

My generation of young women has repeatedly chosen the path of our fathers, the one we believed led to textbook achievement and less mess, but we are continually drawn across the field, to the winding path of our mothers. Woodman writes: "Often she is caught between two conflicting points of view: the rational, goal-oriented and just, versus the irrational, cyclic, relating. Her task is not to choose one or the other, but to hold the tension between them." But we have no parental models for holding such tension. Too often, men are still afraid to cry in public, unable to stay home with their kids, and unwilling to talk to their daughters about their bodies; women are afraid to insist on equal parenting, admit that they are angry, or realize their deferred dreams. Their legacy of fear is our conflicted fate.

4

(Perfect) Girl Talk: Inside Today's Teenagers' Minds and Stomachs

Raya* is sitting at a crowded Starbucks on the Upper East Side. She sets aside the outline for her paper on imperialism in Africa when she sees me come in. At just fourteen, she is an intellectual. A July spent in France convinced her she wants to be a linguist. She is taking French, Italian, and Spanish simultaneously; composing an original score for the winter concert; and vying for editor in chief of her school's newspaper—a quintessential perfect girl.

"Can I get you anything?" I ask. "A tea, a bagel?"

She laughs and replies, "I actually love bagels, but my friends think they are, like, the devil." She pronounces *devil* slowly, emphasizing both syllables with equal drama, then goes on. "We basically have a pact to keep each other away from bagels . . . at any cost."

The soap opera of female adolescence is an old show. In 1982 Carol Gilligan argued that young women coming of age are discounted because the language they speak is one of attachment rather than independence. Mary Pipher picked up the gauntlet and ran with it in her best seller *Reviving Ophelia,* in which she described teenage girls becoming "'female impersonators' who fit their whole selves into small, crowded spaces. Vibrant, confident girls become shy, doubting young women. Girls stop thinking, 'Who am I? What do I want?' and start thinking, 'What must I do to please others?'"

My generation was raised by mothers who spoke Pipher-ese: "preadolescent authenticity," "self-denial," "emotional nourishment." In fact, I recently discovered my mom's old copy of *Reviving Ophelia* buried in the familiar bookshelves of my childhood home, and was amused to see all the anxious underlining and exclamation points throughout the yellowing text. I imagined her reading it feverishly when I returned home from summer camp right before eighth grade, my newly shaved legs cut by the cheap razor borrowed from a bunkmate.

The idea that girls standing at the edge of adolescence were in danger of falling into confusion, frustration, and depression spread like wildfire in the 1980s and '90s—leading to the hipification of the Girl Scouts, the founding of *New Moon* magazine, and other "for girls, by girls" empowerment projects across America. Eating disorders were a quiet part of this danger. Pipher mentioned them briefly, Gilligan not at all. Both still clung to the outdated "good-girl" archetype.

Our understanding of the breadth and depth of teenage-girl hell has expanded now that researchers and writers, theorists and psychologists are riffing on that dangerous terrain covering the land mines of sexuality, the trashy trail of fashion magazines, the mountain of expectations. Numerous books have emerged on the vicious alchemy of girl culture, most notably the 2002 best seller *Odd Girl Out* by Rachel Simmons. Even comedians, such as the *Saturday Night Live* genius Tina Fey, have gotten into the mix with films like 2004's *Mean Girls,* with a screenplay from another book about girl culture: *Queen Bees and Wannabes* by Rosalind Wiseman.

Despite this wealth of developmental literature and sidesplitting satire, being a girl doesn't appear to have gotten any easier. My mom had thoroughly educated me on the complexity of female friendships, but when I heard Tania Bittington* vomit violently in the bathroom after a sleepover pizza binge in seventh grade, I really did not know what to make of it.

Tweens still seem to lock themselves in their rooms on their twelfth birthdays and basically stay in there until they hit eighteen. Girlfriends still communicate through a rapidly spoken foreign language made up of a string of the undying *like* and initialisms impenetrable by the average adult (FYI, IM = Instant Messenger, BFF = Best Friends Forever, BOGO = Buy One Get One). To investigate the secret social world of teenagers and how it influences the way girls feel about their bodies, I knocked on the proverbial bedroom door and slipped right in. Looking too young to buy a beer finally paid off for me.

Raya recruits her six best friends, all students at an elite private institution, to meet me for a dish session after school. The girls tumble into the office, giggling and yelling, a tangle of expensively shampooed hair and trendy clothes. They have come from dance rehearsals and volleyball practice, after-school study groups and frozen-yogurt binges. They practically smell like ninth grade. My stomach turns as I immediately remember what it was like to possess teenage hyperawareness—to hear, see, smell, feel, even taste with superhuman intensity at all times.

One of them plops down on a leather chair. The girl has long, spindly legs and a flat stomach. Her ribbed white tank top pulls taut against her large breasts, covered only by a thin cotton hoodie. Her bright red curly hair is tangled in big silver hoop earrings. She wears designer jeans, a Tiffany bangle bracelet, dark eyeliner that stands out against her pale skin and its freckles. Her name-plate necklace, a style borrowed from another borough, reads "Kaya."*

She reaches for a carrot from the snacks I've brought and preempts an answer to a question I haven't yet asked, as if trying to impress the teacher: "Sometimes I think about what I ate the day before and I won't eat anything the next day." Then, turning to her friends, she adds, "You guys always yell at me for that, but, whatever." Raya had, in fact, confided in me that Kaya often eats on alternative days, her own personal diet plan.

Ella,* a tall, scowling girl with long, straight auburn hair, reveals, "I have these weird tics. Like at the movies today I got popcorn . . . so I ran home."

"I'm always thinking I'm going to start eating right on Monday. Or, like, now that it's the end of the year, I think, I'm going to lose weight when school is out," explains Rachel,* a girl with long dark hair and a pink velour hoodie over a pink tank top. The other girls immediately start clapping and shrieking—"Me too!"

Kaya laughs with her head back and yells, "We're all on diets!"

Going into this meeting of the minds (or midriffs, from the looks of things), I knew that I was in for an experience of the wealthiest and perhaps most neurotic teenage girls in America. These girls knew a thing or two about dieting, fitness, and cosmetic surgery, and I wanted to understand how bad it had gotten. I wanted a sense of the resources that the most privileged girls in America were throwing at their "body projects."

But I also wanted an insider's view of the way girls on the other end of the economic spectrum are experiencing their bodies, girls who don't have nutritionists or expensive health food, girls of color educated in public schools, girls who don't have the luxury or the curse of mothers watching over their every move. Some experts would still have us believe that eating disorders are a white, wealthy problem only, and much of the research on adolescence and eating disorders is on girls with high-earning parents (in part because most of the research takes place in colleges). Girls who aren't white or well-off are usually mentioned as part of the obesity epidemic. Maybe mostly white girls had eating disorders back in the 1980s and early '90s, but the obsession with food and fitness has become an equal-opportunity destroyer.

Two thousand miles away from Manhattan, I walk into a renovated garage with big, ancient computers piled on top of hand-me-down desks, and a dozen Latina, Native American, and mixed-race teenage girls snuggled into weathered couches immediately fall silent. They are from the Girls Inc. Santa Fe summer program—a group of mostly low-income fourteen- and fifteen-year-old girls destined to spend the hot desert days learning about digital photography, swimming at the pool, braiding one another's hair, making friendship bracelets, and, I later learn, analyzing the fat content of each and every lunch they are served.

The first to shatter any naïve hope that less money corresponds with less obsession is Gina,* a gorgeous fifteen-year-old Latina with dark eyeliner, a tank top with, of course, NEW YORK CITY emblazoned across the front in big red letters, and tight, flared jeans. After I explain what my book is about, she volunteers: "Practically every single one of my friends starves herself. I don't do that, but I do check the calories in everything I put in my mouth."

Lori,* another Latina teen, has a short, hip haircut and black cat's-eye glasses. She adds: "I used to be bigger, but then I learned I had a thyroid problem and started taking medication. That helped me eat less. I'm a lot happier now. People are a lot nicer to me."

Julie,* half black, half Latina, pulls her yellow tank top down so that it covers her belly button, starts playing with the two glittery bracelets on her arm, and adds: "Yeah, actually, me too. I used to be chubbier, but I stopped eating emotionally and started exercising more. I still don't like how I look, but at least I'm not fat." She is fourteen.

Mean Girls for Real

When the seven Manhattan girls have settled into the various couches and chairs around the room, I ask them to fill out a quick survey with their biographical information and answers to a few questions. After a search for pens and pencils "that don't suck," they begin to discuss the meaning of ethnic background. When they collectively decide that they are all Caucasians, with the exception of Rosa,* who is half Puerto Rican and has two moms, they write their answers in the slots. Rachel asks: "Can I abbreviate?"

Before I can respond, Kaya laughs at her. "You can't spell it, can you?"

Everyone else laughs along with Rachel, and she wonders aloud: "Why do I say really stupid things?"

"Yeah, why do you talk?" Kaya, definitively emerging as the queen bee, echoes. After a few moments, perhaps realizing how harsh she sounds, Kaya adds, "Whatever. Don't listen to me. I'm dumb too."

No one even looks up from her survey. Rosa puts the earbuds of her pink iPod into her ears. Raya plays with Rosa's long, curly hair. Rachel flops down to sit on the floor so she can write on the coffee table, crosses out "cauc" and writes "white" and "jewish." To the next question—How often do you think about food and fitness?—she writes, "All the time . . . I'm constantly thinking about how I look and what I can do to meet expectations."

In Santa Fe, things are a bit more civil, at least on the surface. The eight girls in the room don't go to the same schools during the year, so they seem to have less resentment toward one another, less fuel to throw on the fire. They have even renamed themselves the "Skittles." Despite the fact that some of them are far more sophisticated—hoodies, cool sneakers, and highlights seem to be the markers—everyone is included in the conversation. In fact, they have taken over one of the walls of the garage and written their group name in big bubble letters, and their individual names all around it with stars, hearts, and emphatic underlining by the most enthusiastic members.

But the harmony is just on the surface; stories about underlying tension quickly emerge. Lori, the one with the cat's-eye glasses, gets the other girls thinking when she tells a story about the way her "friends" used to treat her: "Nobody liked me because I was fat. Seriously. Every time I would say hi to someone who was a friend of mine, or someone I thought was my friend, they would be like 'Who's that?' It sucked."

"And it changed," I probe, "when you lost the weight?"

"Yeah, all the sudden these people are being nice to me again. It made me so mad. I mean, these girls think it is easy to be skinny or something. Do they think fat girls don't have feelings?"

This strikes a chord with Gina, who brings the conversation closer to home: "I don't mean to talk bad about people, but one of the girls in this group"—she pauses and then reassures everyone—"she's not here right now. Anyway, if I do look at the nutrition information on something we're eating, she will throw it out of my hands and be like 'You're dumb.'"

A few of the others let out little gasps. One girl, an uncombed, dirty-shirted twelve-year-old, seemingly content listening in while untangling different colors of yarn from a big knotted ball, says quietly, as if to herself, "That's mean."

Gina continues, "Sure, *she* has a nice body. She doesn't have to worry. It makes me feel self-conscious standing next to her." I'd actually seen this conspicuously absent "mean girl" when I came to visit the center earlier. She had the quintessential "stick legs"—long and thin but still unshaped, spaghetti-string arms, a flat chest. Clearly the body that Gina is coveting has not even endured the aches and pains of puberty. Gina goes on: "People tell me I'm big-boned. I have to worry about these things."

Gina looks like she would weigh about 110 pounds soaking wet. Her tiny arms and legs look dense, like they are made of pure muscle.

"You're not big-boned," Lori reassures her.

"You're built!" another girl chimes in. "Like Madonna!"

Julie adds to Gina's story: "Yeah, that same girl says stuff to me too. She's like 'You think you should really eat that?'"

More gasps escape from the Skittles. Julie goes on: "See, we always go swimming on Tuesdays, and I never like to go swimming, because I'm self-conscious of being in a bathing suit. So I'm there, right? And I was eating in the snack bar area, and she's like, 'Should you really eat that?' She's running around in her little bikini, and I just feel like she's screaming, 'I'm skinnier than you!'"

The specifically female cruelty of these girls and their stories reminds me of myself at fourteen. Sitting in a ceremonial circle, the light cast from a candle painting ominous shadows on my best friends' cheeks at midnight on a Saturday. Time for our weekly "truth talk," where we would masochistically revel in telling one another brutal, entirely unnecessary truths—"The shirt you wore on Monday was so 'sixth grade.'" "Jay told me he doesn't actually like you." "Your mom told my mom that your parents aren't doing very well."

I don't know exactly when or how truth talks were invented, but they took on a destructive life of their own among my girlfriends starting in junior high. Slumber parties, once marked by playful games of truth or dare that led to the flashes of little white butts running through the backyard, became ominous. We sat, cross-legged, face-to-face, and tore one another apart—dissected every clothing choice, flirtatious fumble, lapse in hygiene, or uncool transgression.

Girlhood friendships quickly morph into adolescent power struggles. Relationships that once shared soaring joy and delicious secrets become more like indentured servitude. If you're not on top, you have to pay your dues in snide comments and backstabs. If you are on top, you cling to your authority desperately, ever aware of how far the fall to the bottom really is. Everyone is watching everything that everyone does, always. It is a grueling performance that seems unending.

The body is a critical part of the act. Tween girls are afraid that their forms don't fit the mold. They have seen the social deaths of girls who are too big or dressed wrong. When they go through the big double doors of middle school, they learn the math of self-hate—pounds, calories, and carbs—and the language of body critique—*fat, chubby, gross, nasty*. They pepper conversations with these words and measurements to show that they too are cool enough to participate in the female ritual of weight obsession. They establish their distance from their kid selves through skimpy lunches, public self-deprecation, and girl bonding over the dreaded bathing-suit season.

Eating disorders and their extensive knowledge of them are a common topic in this constant effort to appear savvy. Raya confides in me that the Manhattan girls have their own abbreviations—"a-rex" for anorexia and "b-mic" for bulimic—which they throw around, mostly in reference to others. Raya explains, "Like someone might warn me, 'You can't even eat around her. She is totally a-rex.'" Her admission reminds me of the recent uproar over the Gossip Girl series, risqué fiction for girls Raya's age. In *I Like It Like That,* the characters—all teenagers much like the ones I'm interviewing, growing up in the lap of luxury in Manhattan—dismissively refer to bulimia as "stress-induced vomiting." Apparently "art" does mirror life when it comes to eating disorder–normalizing tween lit.

The teen body is on display at all times. Teens know that they are being watched, because they are also watching. A fourteen-year-old is trained, it seems, in the merciless observation of even the most minute imperfection. If she is casting this eye on others, she rightly reasons, certainly her own thick thighs and little belly are being noted by the judges. I had evidence in our ritualized truth talks. Teen girls, especially those who live in Manhattan, seem to have a running dialogue of brutal truths.

They see their bodies as enemies conspiring against them, plotting to leak, explode, bloat at all the wrong times. And like self-fulfilling prophecies, they inevitably do. On Halloween, a dark red spot seeps through tight bell-bottoms, revealing exactly what the thirteen-year-old sought to hide. She aches for the wrong boys, has legs too chubby to be cute, gets pimples on the most important days. One breast grows before the other. Her miniskirt sticks out on the sides because she has no hips to fill out the built-in cotton curves.

All of these imperfections, so big and looming in private, can be overshadowed in public by associating with the coolest, most desirable girls in school. But being in that shadow is never comfortable; these girls are living examples that the closer you get to popularity, the further away you get from feeling like you belong there.

Best Friends, Fiercest Rivals

After a few reenactments of the day's bloopers and a dishing session about how hot one of their teachers is, the Manhattan girls start to delve into their experiences of food, friendship, and the inevitable competition.

Ella, who wears a cut-up Knicks shirt over a white wife beater and designer jeans, launches in. "I have friends who have eating disorders, and they seem proud of them. It's like a competition. I ask them to explain it to me, and they're like, 'If I go out to eat with someone, I try to eat half as much as they do.'"

Kaya laughs nervously and says, "I sort of was like that. You guys know how I eat. I get a bowl of pasta and throw half of it away so that I don't eat it." She pauses for a moment and then squeals, "I'm so hungry right now!"

"But who are you doing it for?" I ask. "Is it for you, for guys, for other girls?"

Heather,* a girl with long highlighted hair, a gray Champion hoodie, and eyelashes covered in mascara, holds a cell phone in her lap but pauses from text messaging long enough to jump in: "I feel very self-conscious a lot of the time, and a lot of that has to do with the girls who are around me. Girls don't try to impress guys; they try to impress girls. When I get up in the morning and get dressed, I am not trying to look good for girls, but I *am* trying to be accepted by them. If I'm at school around older girls or girls who have a higher social status, I want them to look at me and approve of me."

Rachel affirms, "When you walk down the street and pass another group of girls, you look each other up and down. It's as if you are all asking, 'Who can wear more money?' I hate girls."

"Yeah, girls are such bitches," says Rosa.

Ella, emerging as the voice of tough truths, counters, "It's not as if *we* are really nice to everyone, guys."

"Sure," Rosa replies, "but it wouldn't change anything if we were. There is this girl in our grade who is so nice that you don't want to be around her. We're not mean people." She pauses, pushed by her friends' skeptical looks to justify further: "I mean, I think her new haircut is awesome."

"Seriously?" Heather balks. "What the hell died on her head?"

Everyone laughs, and Ella screams, exasperated, "You guys!"

While each girl from Manhattan seems to have developed a customized method of diet madness designed to outdo the others, the girls Gina describes from her Santa Fe public school have created a climate of collaboration, tinged with a competitive spirit—a sort of cooperative self-hate.

She reports, "We'll be at lunch, and my friends will see something and be like, 'Oh, that looks good.' So they'll all eat, and then right after, one of them will be like, 'That was gross. I need to get rid of that.' And the other ones will be like, 'Oh, yeah, me too.' And then they all just follow, one by one, into the bathroom."

"They all go in there and throw up together?" I ask, hoping that I've misunderstood her.

"Yeah, all together. Like a big party. I think it is so stupid. I really do."

"So you don't join them?" I ask, trying to keep the emotion out of my tone.

"No, I think it's pathetic. I mean, I really want to be skinnier, don't get me wrong, but I'm not going to go make myself throw up to get there." She stops for a moment, takes a breath, and then launches in, louder than before. "Also, it's like I've seen them doing this, and they do get skinnier and everything, but they never think they are skinny enough. They always want to look like someone else. They're like, 'I hate that I am three pounds overweight.' Or 'I want her hair, it's so pretty—'"

Julie steps on the end of Gina's sentence. "Actually, Gina, I *do* want your hair. I was just thinking that. It is so pretty."

Gina blushes, and everyone laughs.

The habit of comparing yourself mercilessly to others first forms at this age, and it proves central to the development and continuation of eating disorders and eating-disordered behavior. One teacher at an all-girls, private school tells me that, out of her fifty seventh-grade students, twenty are in constant competition to eat less. Some of them make pacts—pinkie swearing that they won't eat anything but vegetables for two weeks. If one girl slips and breaks the pact, she is thought of as an untrustworthy friend, a girl with a lack of dedication. "I am disgusted by the gap between most of these girls' thighs," the teacher tells me, "but there is nothing I can do. If I call attention to it, I will just exacerbate the problem." When she has informed parents, she explains, it usually results in her students feeling punished, not cared for. "Honestly, the mothers are usually worse than the daughters," she admits with a sigh.

Multiple studies have analyzed the effects of this bitter competition among teenage girls. A recent study found that 44.8 percent of girls look to their friends for advice on "how to get a good body." In the same study, 55.3 percent of girls thought that their friends would choose an ideal weight smaller than their own. In another study, researchers found that girls were more likely to worry about their bodies because of the pressure they sensed from their friends rather than their actual weight deviation from their ideal. In other words, it is the pressure, not the pounds, that weighs most heavily on a teenage girl's mind.

Some girls seem to swallow this pressure hook, line, and sinker and have some sense that they deserve it or even like it. These girls answered my questions with shocking declarations in that trademark teenage language of extremes—"Yeah, I diet all the time. I eat nothing"—and then shrugged. They looked at me with skeptical fourteen-year-old eyes, almost amused at the concern of this girl in her twenties. "Thanks for talking with us," one of the Manhattan girls said to me with a sticky sweetness. "I'm sure this isn't how you normally spend your Friday evenings. Don't you want to be out on a date or something?"

But a few of the girls who were not prematurely cynical seemed to have the eyes of trapped wild animals. These girls expressed an underlying outrage at the world around them, confiding in me about their extreme behavior and then clenching their teeth, stiffening their jaws, holding back tears as they looked off into corners. One of the Manhattanites said, "Yeah, we're a bunch of the most blessed girls you will ever meet, and we spend all of our time feeling not blessed. Sometimes I wonder if I would be happier if I were poor and went to some terrible public school." There was an undercurrent of anger when these girls talked that was absent from their friends' commentary. They felt indignant and disgusted with the way things are but, at the same time, unable to escape.

On the one hand, most teenage girls recognize that the competition, cruelty, and judgment that saturate their friendships are wrong. They are fully capable of critiquing these attitudes from both moral and philosophical bird's-eye views. On the other hand, they feel helpless to break out of this behavior. At fourteen, these girls can wax poetic about the injustice of gossip and fake friends and, in the next breath, crack a joke about a girl's skirt being way too short. "She's a cheerleader," one tells me by way of justifying their cruelty. "She's not even smart or anything."

Not participating in the culture of observation and judgment seems like a choice that doesn't even exist; it would lead to social obliteration. A girl who can't sass or throw out a biting comment here or there is boring—relegated to the back of the class, the lonely table in the lunchroom, Saturday nights with Mom and Dad. Raya tells me that her group of friends interacts almost entirely in sarcasm and criticism cloaked in jest: "If you get mad, the girl will inevitably be like, 'Whoa, chill out. I was just joking. Why do you have to take everything so seriously?'" Raya's friends tell her that she acts uncool around guys. They roll their eyes and assure the shaggy-haired rich boys from the neighboring prep school that "Raya is just weird, ignore her." Raya has no recourse.

The only way to evade the sting of a joke, these tween girls believe, is to provide no material, to be, in essence, perfect. The constant sense of being watched, the merciless critique, the competition over body, boys, brand names, and everything else, lead them to strive for perfection and avoid vulnerability. Being vulnerable in a middle school is dangerous. So they swing their own punches to become part of the machine of judgment and criticism, two more observing eyes in the audience. This is one of the sickest parts of the teenage girls' twisted version of the "crew"—it feels so damn good when you are on top.

Megan Hinton, her perfect dark hair lying in layers around her shoulders, didn't say anything outright, but when we would go to the movies with boys, she would always make sure we had extra time beforehand so she could do my hair and makeup. I reveled in those moments, sitting on top of her washing machine, feeling the soft brush of the eye shadow applicator across my eyelids, Megan's breath on my cheek as she leaned in close to make a perfect corkscrew curl with her state-of-the-art curling iron. I felt taken care of, comforted, loved.

I had fantasies about being the awkward girl in *The Breakfast Club,* the one with beauty potential that would be miraculously unleashed when her hipper best friend gave her a makeover. I imagined walking into the movie theater to a soundtrack, all the boys turning and gasping at the suddenly transformed Courtney—whereas I had once been a bookworm with knock-knees, I would suddenly be a newly discovered beauty.

It is funny, now, to reflect on how intensely powerful this fantasy was to me; but it is even funnier to realize that, ten years later, this is still my self-image. Despite the men I've seduced, the inches I've grown, the awards I've won, the compliments I've garnered, I still feel, in the deepest parts of who I am, like frizzy-haired Courtney Martin, sitting on Megan Hinton's washing machine wishing for silky locks. Perhaps at the center of so many women's body hatred are their still-lingering thirteen-year-old selves. Beneath the corporate CEO and the talented pianist, deep within the supermom and the super-model, is the teenage girl, still hating her own body after all these years.

For the Boys

Apparently some girls are waiting to be discovered, just as I was a decade ago. The girls in both Manhattan and Santa Fe repeatedly bring up specific incidents when guys at their schools made comments. Sometimes you want these comments—"If they call you fat," Raya explains, "then you know you're *not* fat. So if they don't call you fat, you worry that you actually are." Sometimes you don't want these comments. The Santa Fean Gina explains the less ironic situation at her school: "If a boy calls a girl fat and tells her she needs to lose weight, she will seriously go straight to the bathroom and throw up. That's how stupid the girls at my school are." Either way, boys are dictating who gets the stamp of approval and who is socially defective. Through their casual commentary about what is hot and what is not, they perhaps unknowingly set the standard to which these girls strive.

When I ask the Santa Fe crew if they care what boys think, an instinctual chorus of nos follows. Girls Inc., though a 140-year-old organization, feeds its contemporary gals a constant diet of "go-girl empowerment," so they can be "smart, strong, and bold." To the camp counselors' credit, these girls have a Pavlovian response to *boys,* as if the word itself recalls afternoons spent listening to inspirational speeches they have sweated through about independence and feminism. "So you really don't care?" I ask.

"I mean we don't *want* to care," Gina clarifies. "I mean I don't care as much as some of the girls I know. They will do absolutely anything a guy tells them to."

Julie agrees: "Yeah, I know girls like that. Whatever their boyfriend says is cute, they will wear. If he doesn't like an outfit, they'll throw it away."

"Okay, honestly," Gina confesses, "I once had a boyfriend who told me, to my face, that he thought I was fat. I was so crushed. At the time my self-esteem was so low that I just stayed with him and tried to lose more weight." She brushes her hair out of her face, looks up, and lets out a guttural sound. "God, I hate thinking about that. I hate how weak I was."

Julie comforts her: "A lot of people have stuff like that, Gina, I did. It was my birthday, and my boyfriend bought me something, like, thirty sizes too small and then said I should lose weight until I could fit into it. I broke up with him, but that made me depressed for a while. It made me really upset, and it shouldn't have because he was such a jerk. It was one of the most painful times of my life."

As the sun starts to set over the skyscrapers outside, I ask the Manhattan girls the same question: "So do you care what the guys think?"

Ella gets real: "I notice that people who go to Josh's* house every Friday or Saturday night"—she pauses for a few seconds, considering how blatant to be, then continues with a fuck-it sensibility. "Okay, Heather and Kaya . . . you both are so skinny and so freakin' hot and whatever, and I don't usually go. I'm never invited . . ." She trails off and then sarcastically adds, "Whatever, I like doing homework."

The air in the room gets thick. Everyone shifts in her chair and readjusts the pillows on the couches. Heather unbraids and braids her hair nervously. Kaya plays with the rubber LIVE FREE bracelet around her wrist.

Rosa reassures Ella, "People invite themselves to Josh's house, Ella."

Ella's not buying it. The volume of her voice rises as she slips into second person: "You try to be thin. You feel like you might be accepted in some way, like it might change who you are, what crowd you are with, who likes you. But nothing changes."

"Ella, it's not like that," insists Rosa again.

"Yeah, right," Ella spits back with an acidic tone.

Thinness is desirable, not just because it is the standard presented on the cover of the Victoria's Secret catalog (which these girls already receive in the mail and order from with their own credit cards) but because it translates into party invites and boyfriends—tangible markers of ninth-grade popularity.

Though these girls have been raised on Spice Girls feminism, they can't pretend that their self-images aren't drawn partly by the boys whom they crush on. The girls in Santa Fe seem especially in tune with what boys want, even if they are clear that they think these boys are scum. The girls in Manhattan take a more nuanced approach to guys—talking about some as genuine friends, others as enviable competitors, just a few (many of whom turn out to be teachers) as "cute."

Boys certainly have power in influencing girls' friendships. If Heather and Kaya get invites to Josh's house on a Saturday night, their friendship will be strengthened by the experience. They will have inside jokes on Monday about the stupid kid who puked in the bathroom or the surprise kiss. It is here, in their ability to influence girls' bonds with one another, that boys matter most.

Even if Josh doesn't make his party list based on whom he finds attractive, it is Ella's theory, not the reality, that keeps her running home from the movies after eating popcorn or working out before school five days a week. In fact, Ella's drive to exercise has gotten so obsessive that her parents took away her gym membership as punishment. They have no idea that, in her mind, they are also taking away the one way she knows how to work toward those Saturday-night invites in her desperate grab for attention.

Perfection Projection

The Santa Fe crew has a bit more sober outlook on the popular clique, probably because they aren't in it.

Gina breaks it down: "To be popular, you have to wear tight jeans with nice shoes—like something from Foot Locker or Hollister. You can't get your clothes at Ross." (I'm in trouble. I love Ross.)

Julie confirms. "Yeah, if you want to be popular, you wear short skirts, tiny tank tops. There is a certain group of girls at school who wear the skimpiest clothes and show their thongs and stuff. Then there are a bunch of us who just wear jeans and long shirts. Those girls, the thong ones, will be like, 'You're ugly, why don't you do anything for your looks?'"

"Yeah," Gina agrees, "those kind of girls are at my school too. They think they're perfect. They think everyone should try to look like them."

Julie wisely explains, "Sometimes I do wish I looked more like those girls, honestly, but I also know that their lives aren't so wonderful either. Even the people that you think are perfect have their flaws and things that they're not happy about with themselves."

Back in Manhattan, Ella isn't done breaking it down. She is brave, but she again uses the second person to soften the blow: "You really do want to go to those parties. You really do want to be accepted by the pretty, skinny girls, and they look like they don't give a shit. They look like they can be who they are—effortlessly gorgeous."

"Ella, you're hot," Heather counters.

But Ella will not be placated that easily. "Nothing anyone says is going to change how I feel about it. It is so hard because I feel like no one understands it. It seems like everyone else is accepted."

This pushes Heather, clearly one of Ella's "effortlessly gorgeous" friends, to set the record straight. "I think that everyone has their own opinion on everyone else. They evaluate other people according to how they live, but really, maybe they have the same issues. If I were to look at Kaya, I might think, *Oh, she has the perfect world,* but meanwhile she's looking at everyone else and thinking they have the perfect world."

This age is the beginning of the giant, deadly delusion that perfection is just out of reach for you and effortlessly possessed by the next girl. At fourteen, you are always one step away from being cooler, prettier, smarter, and more athletic, but that step turns out to be nothing less than a leap, your insecurity an insurmountable hurdle in your own mind. Despite a teenage girl's best intentions, perfection is impossible, and even self-confidence will not be accomplished by buying one more pair of shoes, spending one more hour at the gym, eating one fewer meal. It requires work far more internal and difficult than simple deprivation or drive, but at fourteen, in an instant-extreme-makeover culture, that kind of work seems irrelevant. What *is* relevant is your best friend, Kaya, whose calves are long and spindly, tiny but muscular in platform sandals. Ella swears, "I will never show anyone my calves. Not even my husband." The two centimeters that she would like to cut off of her calves with a knife, so they could look like Kaya's, define her entire self-image.

I am struck by the way this group of Manhattan girls has clearly identified who is perfect among them and written it in stone. When I look around the room, I see girls with varied forms of beauty. Kaya has a nymphlike quality to her, a flitty, fun, and loud presence. Rosa reminds me of a grasshopper, long-armed and spunky. Raya has a small-bear quality to her, a round face that suggests sweetness. Rachel has a striking nose, a mane of long, cascading hair. Heather looks pulled out of the seventies. Ella is, in fact, the one I find most beautiful. Her anger intrigues me but, even more, her stately face and style. She stands out in a way that Kaya and Heather, her perfect idols, don't.

These girls see themselves not through kind eyes but through the lens of perfection, a hungry, unsatisfied view built up from years of biting at one another's heels, surviving the neuroses of their own mothers, trying just to make it through an elite adolescence. Self-confidence, like love, cannot be bought. These girls are some of the most privileged in the nation—in fact, some of the most privileged in the world—yet they all have stories to tell me about their own intimate oppressions, their daily battles to feel good about the women they are becoming and the girls they have been.

There could be no more apt candidate for "perfection projection" than Heather. Beautiful, with professionally highlighted, long, straight hair, soft, clear skin, and striking blue eyes, she is the daughter of one of the most powerful women in the advertising industry. She lives in a fabulous penthouse on Park Avenue, has a cook to make all her meals, a driver to chauffeur her to school, autographs from all of the stars who have gone through her mom's corner office. But beneath the appearance of a calm surface is a murky underwater world where Heather holds her breath.

———

"I started going to a nutritionist when I was eleven years old," Heather explains. "I had to have surgery on my collarbone. My mom wanted me to go so I wouldn't gain weight while I wasn't as active. My mom has to look really good. She works with a trainer and stuff. My dad is really muscular, and so I got the man body from him.

"When my mom loses weight, she'll ask me, 'How much do you weigh now?' And I'll be like, 'Oh, I weigh 112.' She weighs 109 now. She's not trying to rub it in my face, but she's trying to show me how it works when you really stick to your plan and work out and stuff."

Heather goes on: "I go to my nutritionist once a week for an hour, and she helps me through my family issues or anything that's bugging me, anything that can make me eat more. We're not close, but I can tell her stuff. I told her stuff about my mom and how she is always watching me." Heather morphs into her mother, doing what I can only imagine is a dead-on impression: " 'Heather, are you sure? That's your second Tasti D-Lite of the week.' "

Back in her own skin: "It made me want to not eat at all or eat in her face—ha! I brought home Tasti D-Lite after dinner one time, and my dad was like 'You need to watch this sweet tooth.' I was just like 'Fine, I'll have it in my room.'

"When I went downstairs afterwards, my mom was waiting for me, and she was like 'Your dad told me what you did.' I was like 'I didn't *do* anything!'

"I told my nutritionist, and she talked to my mom, and my mom is no longer allowed to say anything, but I still feel her watching me and judging me as I eat.

"I can't eat in the same room as her. I was a vegetarian for a while. Because I wasn't having chicken, I could eat by myself. I enjoyed that so much because I wasn't being watched."

Ella corroborates. "Yeah, I don't like eating in front of a lot of people because they judge. Like 'Why aren't you eating?' You are suffocating me! Get away from me! Oh my God! That's how I feel 95.7 percent of the time. I want to be able to eat in front of all of you guys because I love you"—she motions toward the group—"but I just can't do it. It's annoying that people assume that you have an eating disorder because you have a salad for lunch. Fine. You don't want me to eat, I won't."

Just Being a Girl

As most of the Girls Inc. campers head home, I am hoping for some kind of high note to finish off my time with these revealing, fascinating, and sensitive girls, but I will have no such thing.

"So is there anything else you want to say? Anything else you want me to understand?" I ask.

After a bit of reflective silence, Julie sighs and says, "Look, I'm saying all of this. I'm saying you don't have to be like the popular girls, you don't have to want to be skinny or whatever, but am I like that? No. I'm not self-confident. I have absolutely no self-respect for myself. I'm ugly. I just want to go in the corner. I don't want people to see me. I want it to be like that—feel good about myself and all that. I tell myself, 'Oh my gosh, I wish I liked myself for who I am.' I hope I do one day, but right now, I just don't."

"It sounds like the voice inside of your head is really critical," I respond.

"You know, you're verbally saying, 'I'm skinny. I'm beautiful. Look at me.' Inside, you're like, 'I'm fat, I'm ugly.'"

"Is there any way to change that voice inside your head?" I ask.

Julie shrugs, suddenly looking forty-five instead of fifteen. "I tried. It's not working. It's just life." She looks down at the glittery bangle on her wrist and adds, "A girl's life, at least."

The New York City girls start to gather up their things and put their Diet Cokes and Bic pens into trendy purses and messenger bags—apparently backpacks are no longer cool. Moms start to arrive in cabs, cell phones start ringing incessantly. It is clearly time to bring this conversation to a close.

"So when will all this stop?" I ask them. "Will it get easier as you get older?"

Kaya shakes her head and says simply, "Freshman fifteen."

Rachel hasn't heard of it. "What? What's that?"

Ella explains, "It is this thing where every freshman girl in college gains fifteen pounds because of all the cafeteria food. I've honestly cried thinking about it."

"So it never stops?" I ask, still trying to understand how they see their obsession playing out in the long run.

Ella levels with me. "If I'm not thinking about my body or calories, I'm probably sleeping or dead. I don't see that changing anytime soon."

"Nope," Kaya concludes, "this is just being a girl."

5

Sex as a Cookie: Growing Up Hungry

Something happens to some girls at a certain age, a kind of madness, as if their own bodies were too powerful or too busy or too change-able; they are appalled. They indulge peculiar hungers; they want to stick their noses, their tongues into the filth of the world, maybe to reassure themselves that it doesn't all come from themselves.

—Mary Gordon

All of these are about emptiness, about misdirected attempts to fill internal voids, and all of them tend to spring from the same dark pool of feeling: a suspicion among many women that hungers them-selves are somehow invalid or wrong, that indulgences must be earned and paid for, that the satisfaction of appetites often comes with a bill.

—Caroline Knapp

Entering the current world of teenage angst prompted a flood of memories of my own tumultuous years "behind the bedroom door." Our bodies had the capacity to attract the attention we were all so desperate for. In this way, they were our weapons against medioc-rity, against invisibility. But when one of my acquaintances got preg-nant at seventeen, my worst suspicions were confirmed—our bodies

were also capable of great betrayal. In this way, they were our enemies. I felt like my own body was about to explode at any moment—
like it was a time bomb waiting to go off.

Sex, like food, was infused with wildly inflated meaning. Our
struggles with one mirrored our struggles with the other: *I should, I
shouldn't, I should, I shouldn't.* We were equally naïve and unin-
formed about both—miseducated by the alarmist sex Q&As in teen
magazines and the manipulative diet ads beside them. Aspiring perfect girls spent much energy trying to curb and manipulate physical
hunger and sexual drive to our advantage.

In retrospect, I realize that my friends and I were on an alarmingly
fast track when it came to sex and all its adult consequences. No one
was on a faster track than Jen, my best friend since sixth grade.

I walk through the automatic doors leading to the passenger pickup at
Denver International Airport and nervously look around at the cars
parked along the curb. I don't even know what kind of car Jen drives
anymore, whether her hair will be long or short, natural brown or
bottle blond, whether she will be frail, as she was the last time I saw
her, a couple of years ago at a neighborhood Christmas party, or the
way I remember her from high school—scarred shins, strong, thick
thighs, big breasts, and all.

As if on cue, a white Acura pulls up, and though there is a glare on
the windshield, I can see Jen's narrow face beaming inside. She bounds
out and skips around to my side of the car, giving me a big hug before
I can even put down my bag. I breathe deeply as I wrap my arms
around her waist—she is herself again: flat, wide stomach perched
atop strong soccer-player thighs, breasts spilling out of her skimpy
tank top, long, tangled hair.

As we wind our way around the airport exit roads and head for
I-25, we launch into a feverish exchange about the impending wedding of our other childhood best friend. We will be on the road to
Utah, where Katie is tying the knot, for eight hours, long enough to
reminisce about who we were and tell each other about who we have

become. As we drifted apart after high school, the space between us became more than the miles that separate Boulder, Colorado, where she lives, and New York City, where I do.

Wild Horses

As a little girl, Jen was madly in love with horses. She had miniatures all over her room, calendars, posters, stickers, T-shirts, and books all covered with the Arabians and mustangs she adored so much. When I would come over to her house, she would beg me to play horses with her. Though I preferred Barbies, I would sometimes humor her for a few minutes, pushing the plastic horses through the yellow and orange shag rug, "neighing" occasionally. Eventually I would try to slip a Barbie or two into the story line. "They have to have owners, Jen!" I would rationalize. "No they don't," she would stubbornly reply. "The best horses are the wild ones."

When she was old enough, Jen convinced her parents to get her some riding lessons so she could mount and ride the real things. Unfortunately, severe asthma left her coughing and wheezing for days after her weekly trail rides. The minute she stepped off the horse, any bare skin would be swollen and red in a giant hive. She resorted to steroid inhalers and wore layers of clothing even in the hot sun, but nothing kept her lungs from rebelling against her deepest love. She raged when her mom would suggest she stop riding, slamming her bedroom door so that the little horses perched all around her room shook on their tiny plastic legs.

All the way through sixth grade, her uniform was a white Hanes T-shirt, a pair of jeans, and a little silver horse that dangled around her neck.

———————

But all that changed as soon as Jen hit thirteen. Seventh grade marked the moment when childhood faded away and adolescence came rushing in. As we drive through the farmland before the Wyoming border, grown-up Jen remembers. "Breasts were what changed things for me. I loved them, and I realized that everyone else loved them . . . that there was a real power there. I could tell that my new body scared my parents and excited the guys I had always been friends with."

Whereas Jen had once been a tomboy, notoriously muddy and fast on her bike, she now became a guys' girl. She quoted *Point Break* and *Dazed and Confused* exhaustively, cursed expertly, and didn't even blush when guys asked her sexual questions. Her uniform changed from those white T-shirts and her little horse pendant to skintight bodysuits (yeah, remember bodysuits?) and mall bangs. Jen purposefully wore her baggy jeans so low that boys could see where the bodysuit hugged her widening hips. It was a brazen invitation, a declaration that she had chosen to be a certain kind of girl and was not ashamed.

I ask her about this as we head past a herd of bison and a few shaggy llamas. She doesn't even need to think before responding: "I had hung out with guys enough to know the way they talked about girls, and I knew that you were either coy and pretty—like you were—or sexy and slutty. There was no in-between. Since I was already feeling sexual and realizing the power of that, I chose the second. I remember deciding very early on that I was just going to disregard people's judgment and do what I wanted to do."

And she did. At fourteen years old, Jen lost her virginity to her older, more experienced boyfriend. "I remember being so relieved," Jen says in retrospect. "I really wanted to have sex before I turned fifteen."

Despite the free-love movement, Erica Jong, female condoms, and Foxy Brown, teenage girls still have only two choices: prude or slut, uptight or loose, worried or carefree, smart or fun, pretty or sexy, girlfriend material or a good hookup, respectable or adventurous. Adult women have a bit more gray area to play in, but when you are an adolescent, things are still painfully and artificially black and white.

One teenager from Texas explained, "You can't be too prudish or else you aren't considered cool, but you can't flaunt that you've been promiscuous either or else you'll be considered a slut. You also need to be casually sexy, but not overtly so or you'll be considered cheap. This, for me, results in a very complicated system of rules and systems with boys that disallows me from being genuine with anyone I decide to be close to in the sense of 'dating' them."

I was the prude, the innocent, the brain, the snob, the tease. Boys liked me, but usually out of a strange fascination with my moldy virginity, my stubbornly clinging fears of sex and its implications; pain and pregnancy were the two that most often raced through my brain when I heard the war stories of other girls having sex with older boys in the basement, blood on the couch, fog in their brains, awkward appendages, and the absence of pleasure. Our bodies really were battlegrounds. Pain, I understood early on from Judy Blume novels, was part of the territory. And at thirteen, I could still hear President Reagan's voice, absent of emotion, full of blame, decrying teenage mothers. It seemed like my body had to be controlled. Pleasure was about the last thing on my mind.

And it was all Jen could think about. She dressed like she was eighteen and talked like she was twenty-five. Like the horses she once rode, she was an untamable, fiery animal—constantly trying to break free. She went after trouble at top speed. She flirted mercilessly, talked big, and more often than not, followed through. She gravitated toward the bad boys—the strong and silent types with questionable pasts. She hooked up. She made out. She got off. She earned her reputation.

This is where the bottom drops out of our so-called postfeminist scenario.

Both my mother and Jen's did all the right things—nonchalantly put books about menstruation on our bookshelves, told us that they were always there "to talk," continued to check in intermittently to see if we had any new questions. Jen's mom even told stories about her own wild days, when she had a motorcycle, a boyish short haircut, and a bad boy of her own (hard to believe coming from Mrs. Clark, the computer engineer with a passion for bird-watching). My mom described her own inadequate sex education for our mutual amusement over coffee ice cream and *Designing Women* reruns. She told me about a great gynecologist to whom I could go at any time with questions. She was genuinely open. Most radically, she pretended that one of the nonprofits she consulted with happened to give her a big bag of condoms—"Don't know what else to do with these but throw 'em in the hall closet," she hollered to no one in particular as she stuffed the brown paper sack in between the linens and the aspirin.

In spite of our mothers' best efforts to demystify sex, it had found a flashing neon home in our brains. None of the books, however candid and well intentioned, explained how to handle a body with so many powers and vulnerabilities. We didn't feel compelled to discuss the complexity of social implications with our mothers. I certainly didn't want to explore my fears about the mechanics or pain with my mom (again, pleasure wasn't even on the radar).

We had seen films of the sexually revolutionary seventies on television—beautiful girls with long, straight hair illuminated by a kind of foggy sunlight dancing in tiny tank tops and bell-bottom jeans to bad music. We had even seen pictures of our own parents, looking swollen and high, smiling the biggest, simplest smiles on earth in that foggy sunlight. We knew, in theory, that women were supposed to have the same ability as men to choose who, when, where, and how without incurring devastating labels. It was a lovely theory.

But in 1995 hip-hop reigned, and boys in puffy jackets and jeans falling off their asses wanted to have sex with girls who knew what to do but hadn't had a lot of experience. The captain of the team also wanted to have sex, but he wanted to have it with a sweet girl from a good family who hadn't had sex with anyone before (despite his own history). On Monday morning in the echoing hallways of Palmer High School, your weekend's adventures were fair game, and consequently, your reputation always hung perilously in the balance. I played the game—smiled coyly at the boys who thought of me as desirable and untouchable, kissed only in committed relationships, and then only with boys who pledged their undying love in notes left on my car and public declarations worked into party freestyles.

Jen had a full-force sex drive by the time she hit seventh grade. She wanted to try everything, anything, with anyone. As she put it, "It was like uncharted territory for me. I got a thrill out of every new thing I tried." While my uppity, intimidating thing worked for some guys, Jen's free-spirit style was hypnotizing. In Mr. Wolf's biology class, the guys followed Jen with their eyes as she entered the room. Her exposed hips and spandex bodysuit changed everything.

Jen laughs when I recall this memory on our road trip. "Do you know I actually talked to Josh a few weeks ago, and he still remembers those bodysuits? It was a power trip. I realized I could hook up with guys and play with them sexually. But I was also totally aware that afterwards they were going to lose respect for me, so it was a really tough duality. I adopted this mentality really young: Well, fuck it. I'm going to do whatever I want and not give a fuck what people think. Which is pretty much impossible at that age. I think that shame must have ended up somewhere inside of me, even if I thought it was a bullshit double standard."

Body as Currency

Jen and I were good "North end" girls doing bad-girl things—drinking forties with our Hispanic boyfriends, quietly slipping into the house as the newspaper hit the porch, dressing up and going to the one underage club—the Metro—that was part of a strip mall and had shootings once a month or so.

But we were also perfect girls. We both got nearly straight A's, both took all of the AP classes that were offered at our big, under-funded public school, and were both on the newspaper staff. "Remember when you wrote that column with the lead line 'I am a virgin' in tenth grade and totally blew your boyfriend's spot because he'd told everyone on the football team that you guys had sex?" Jen shrieks. How could I forget? His friends followed him around for days, laughing. I had only meant, in my righteous, fifteen-year-old way, to declare publicly that it was okay to be a prude (of course I was speaking to myself as much as to our readers).

Jen and I had both figured out that the female body was currency. If withheld, it could have tremendous power over big-eyed boys with small-town dreams (cute girl, baseball scholarship, nice truck) or the ones from the east side of town whose parents smoked pot and didn't care how late they got in. Withholding was my specialty.

But Jen had figured out that by being one of the guys and advertising her undeniable sex drive, she garnered a different kind of respect. She wasn't girlfriend material, per se, but she was "down." She had special relationships with all kinds of guys, proselytized about the clitoris, shot the shit about porn, and unabashedly recounted her best and worst sexual experiences so they could avoid similar pitfalls. They adored her for this—a girl with a guy's mouth, a big-breasted woman with a dude mentality.

"I left high school feeling on top of the world," Jen explained as we entered Laramie. "I saw myself as this well-liked free spirit who liked to have sex and did it on her own terms."

I had spent much of high school defending Jen to those who didn't know her well, those who hadn't benefited from her sage advice or potty mouth. "She's not a slut. She's sexually liberated. She says when, she says with who, she says how much," I would explain to a guy at a party who made an offhand comment. But even as I was spouting off borrowed Hollywood rhetoric (*Pretty Woman*), I had my own doubts. There was something aching and self-destructive under Jen's bravado, something desperate in her insatiable appetite for physical intimacy. I didn't understand enough about the subtleties of sexuality to distinguish Jen's authentic desire from her bad-girl, attention-seeking act. Problem was, Jen couldn't either.

Sex Ed 1-0-Nothing

Poor excuses for sex ed curriculums unfold in cramped classrooms reeking of sweat and Taco Bell. An over-the-hill male gym teacher does a speed-reading of the section of the outdated health text on sexuality, quickly pointing out the gruesome sexually transmitted disease photos, and then looks down at his Big Gulp as he asks, "Any questions?" After three seconds, he moves the hell on.

In the 2005 documentary *The Education of Shelby Knox*, a spirited teenager rallies her peers and tries to fight the sex ed policy in her town of Lubbock, Texas, to no avail. When teachers in her school are asked any question whatsoever about sexuality, they are mandated to respond: "The only way to ensure the prevention of pregnancy and STDs is abstinence." Like broken pull-string dolls, they parrot the same reply over and over again.

These are the tools that Jen and I and Shelby, that virtually every young, hormone-flooded kid in an American high school, are given to navigate the chaotic and confusing terrain of developing sexuality: a few rotting-beaver shots and a mandate. So what are we left with? Experimentation. That's it.

By 1990 the average girl lost her virginity by the age of fifteen. A teenage girl today is twice as likely as was her mother to have multiple sex partners by the age of eighteen. Eighty-four percent of college-educated single women agreed in a recent poll that "it is common these days for people my age to have sex just for fun and not expect any commitment beyond the encounter itself." Another study found that 60 percent of high school juniors had sex with someone who was no more than a friend.

Jen tried it and told the rest of us how painful, messy, enjoyable, frightening, exciting, and seductive we could be. No sex education class or admonition is going to prevent kids from exploring their own sexualities, a necessary and healthy part of getting older. But with something other than a thirty-minute speed-read from Coach, we could have made somewhat educated decisions about what to try when. Maybe we could have had a stronger sense of how to interpret our many growing hungers (for attention, for love, for sex). Maybe I could have indulged my quiet desires with a sense of self-determination, as opposed to feeling like I was "giving in." Maybe Jen could have walked her talk, said "fuck it," and actually internalized a sense of self-respect.

Abstinence-only education (a $1 billion effort since 1996) is built around the unrealistic assumption that you can convince kids not to experiment by pretending there is nothing to be curious about. Studies by well-respected and politically neutral authorities have officially proven that this assumption is false.[†] And it takes only a look around to see how contradictory a teenager's informal sex education is to the one that comes from the classroom. Ariel Levy of *New York* magazine writes in her book, *Female Chauvinist Pigs*: "What teens have to work with are two wildly divergent messages. They live in a candyland of sex . . . every magazine stand is a gumdrop castle of breasts, every reality show is a bootylicious Tootsie Roll tree. But at school, the line given to the majority of them about sex is just say no."

Jen's and my adolescence illustrates the point. We were two wide-eyed teens embarking on the journey of female adolescence, of which sexual foreplay, if not sex, is an integral, exciting, and terrifying part. On these matters, our mothers were cautiously open, our school was definitively closed, and every rap video, Hollywood movie, horny teenage boy, and rumor mill was haphazardly bombarding. We had no accurate information on variable sex drives or the mechanics of healthy sexual encounters (communication, condoms, clear boundaries). We had no models for authentic sensuality or embracing our bodies. Every form of mass media told us that sex was where we could fly or crash.

We needed someone to illuminate and discuss the idea that human beings have infinitely different and complicated sexual desires and needs. We needed someone to explain that part of our teens and twenties would be devoted to the potentially delightful and difficult exploration to figure out ours. Sure, we needed to know about the danger and likelihood of STDs, and abstinence as a viable option, but we also needed to know about masturbation and foreplay and the wide variety of sexual practices.

†According to the Centers for Disease Control, the majority of Americans don't walk across the graduation stage with their virginity intact regardless of the abstinence-only educators' profoundly naïve efforts. The Alan Guttmacher Institute (AGI), further, reports that the United States has more than 80 teen pregnancies per 1,000 girls, far higher than most Western European countries ("Teenagers' Sexual and Reproductive Health: Developed Countries," www.agi-usa.org/pubs/fb_teens.html). As Ariel Levy reports in *Female Chauvinist Pigs* (p. 161), AGI's website reads: "The primary reasons why U.S. teenagers have the highest rates of pregnancy, childbearing and abortion among developed countries is less overall contraceptive use and less use of the pill."

Studies show that the more dissatisfied a teenage girl is with her body, the less in control she feels in sexual relationships. Girls with body-image issues are less likely to use condoms, fearing "abandonment as a result of negotiating condom use." We teens needed to practice communicating while experimenting. We needed to reflect on our own, personal definitions of trust, safety, and spirituality in relation to sex. We needed to know that our bodies were the sources of the sexual feelings we were experiencing, and that the feelings were okay. Then maybe our bodies would have seemed more okay too.

By not talking about sex, or its infinite variations and complexities, the educators in our lives only infused it with a more potent power. The neon flashing place in my brain shone brighter and more fluorescent: SEX! SEX! SEX! We were thinking about it anyway. The idea that if adults pretend sex doesn't exist, teenagers won't think or talk about—or, gasp, do it—is ludicrous. If I had known that my sheepish and still-developing desires were normal and that not all of sex led instantly down the path of lecherousness and pregnancy, I would have had a lot more fun and a lot less anxiety throughout my teen years. Likewise, if Jen had known that her potent and high-speed sex drive was not something to be ashamed of, but something to be aware of and deliberate about, she may not have felt such a compulsion to live up to her reputation. Hell, maybe she wouldn't even have had to contend with that reputation. If guys and girls alike learned about the wide variety of sexual drives, maybe neither would be so pigeonholed.

But we all learned that sex was forbidden, exciting, one-dimensional, and dangerous. We learned that it could get you sick, grounded, pregnant, or sad. We learned that guys wanted it and girls shouldn't. Most important, we learned that sex was the most powerful thing a girl possessed.

Sex as a Cookie

I am grateful for the calming, unchanging Wyoming landscape out the window as Jen starts telling me the uncensored version of her college days. She went to the University of Colorado in Boulder, a school notorious for its rich out-of-state kids, loose sexual mores, and lots of drugs and alcohol to make it all easier. Students there don't seem overwhelmingly motivated by school. Instead, they get excited about building waterslides from truck beds on the lawns of frat houses, burning couches in the streets, and doing sake bombs at sushi restaurants on their parents' credit cards.

Jen, initially, felt she fit in just fine. She liked to party, and though she was basically middle-class, she managed to find lots of rich kids with unlimited bank accounts to support the lifestyle. She probably liked school more than the next kid—she immediately fell in love with sociology—but she managed to go out on most weeknights and still drag into class the next morning.

But what first appeared to be a place practically designed for Jen's hedonistic lifestyle quickly backfired. Jen was hooking up. A lot. She understood that this was part of the college scene, a built-in bonus of going to a big party school where she was no longer the only sexually charged, compulsive kid around. But what on the surface seemed simple and socially acceptable—casual hookups without emotional attachments—had unforeseen complications.

Jen explains, "I was devastated in college because I really went thinking that guys loved me and I had no problem getting whoever I wanted, that I could hook up and still have a great relationship with them and earn their respect. It was completely opposite. The guys would change the second you hooked up with them and be convinced that you were obsessed with them.

"I had all these ideas internalized—I'm just a free spirit, free-loving, like to sleep with people because I love it and I have fun with it. But in college, nobody knew that about me, so all of a sudden, I was just that dirty slut who must not have any self-respect."

Guys with whom Jen had hooked up on the weekend pretended they didn't know her by Monday. Some of them told their friends all about their nights with her, insisting that now she wanted to date regardless of her actual lack of interest. Jen, and every girl like her who indulged in a one-night stand, became a stereotype—her three-dimensional flesh the night before suddenly deflated to one dimension in the morning. It didn't matter if Jen went into these hookups with a sense of feminist agency. She was in a time warp, an inherently sexist social scene. What started under the pretense of a modern flirtation—dancing to hip-hop at a packed house party, drinking Red Bull and vodka, smoking some weed out back—was reduced to an old-fashioned dichotomy as soon as it was over: conqueror and conquered, stud and slut, free agent and desperate girlfriend, boy and girl.

———

In most colleges across America, a Jen is flailing at the center of this sexism. Some are better—the Ivy Leagues and the small liberal arts schools tend to dress up their misogyny in intellect; some are worse, particularly where the Saturday football game or the fraternity party that night are the be-all and end-all. Most play by a largely unspoken but quickly understood set of rules that allow guys to conquest to their hearts' desires and elevate their reputations, and allow girls the opportunity to be conquered. There is a reason that college kids call making out, for those of you who were raised with drive-in movie theaters, "giving it up"—a girl *is* giving something up, and that mysterious "it" is her control over her identity.

Lots of guys in college who hooked up with lots of girls were still known for other things: their premed rigidness, their interest in the Middle East conflict, their brilliant sarcasm. But the girls I knew who hooked up a lot became known mostly for that quality alone. A guy can be a "slut" and a sweetie, a jock, a dreamer, a joker. When a girl is labeled a "slut," the rest of her identity seems to fall away. When that happens, her entire worth gets tied up in her ability to hook up with guys and, therefore, her ability to look beautiful, thin, and desirable, to be fun, to dance on the bar. She doesn't have the opportunity to be taken seriously once she has garnered the "easy" label.

These girls' sexuality becomes their project. They cultivate it, sculpt their bodies into it, dress in order to show it off, master subtle and not-so-subtle flirtation, seek the right parties, spot the right men, go after them with the kind of ambition required for an A in organic chemistry. They seek this experience with a vengeance, going after the goal—an ultimately unsatisfying hookup with an unknown dude—as if their lives depend on it. In some ways, they become their own conquerors.

———————————

Jen realized pretty quickly what was going on but felt powerless to disengage. She tells me, "I didn't know how to turn off that feeling of wanting to hook up, and it became absolutely devastating to me." She continued to find cute boys at parties, bring them home with high hopes that she could have a fun, painless hookup, and then be blind-sided by the hangover—a result not of too much alcohol but of too much faith. The guys didn't respect her in the morning. In fact, they pretended not even to know her name.

It was truly a case of her mind and her body at war. Her mind knew that things were not what they seemed, that if she hooked up with this guy tonight, tomorrow he would make her feel cheap. But her body, her potent sex drive, her deeper, inexplicable hunger for attention were always dragging her into situations regardless of the consequences. It was as if her mind were the warden, guarding the cell of her wild and out-of-control impulses. A few shots of tequila, Jen's signature poison, and the warden went to sleep.

Twin Hungers

The compulsion to hook up soon joined forces with a compulsion to overeat—plunging Jen into oblivion. She says, "I started compulsive eating, because I was so frustrated and out of control and I hated my body. I didn't love my body in high school, but it was kind of like playful power struggles. Completely manageable stuff. When I got to college, it was out of control, absolute hatred for my body."

Jen would start with one bowl of cereal and then justify having another and another and another until she was bloated, kneeling over the toilet, trying to make herself throw up to no avail.† She ate all of

———————————

†Many women, like Jen, tell me that the only reason they aren't bulimic is that they are physically incapable of making themselves throw up.

her roommates' food, drank all their milk, and felt silently guilty. She explains, "It breaks my heart to think about how much I hated myself. I would yell at myself, call myself a fat bitch. I would be so, so mad after overeating. I would come home and compulsively eat and cry myself to sleep. I couldn't control it."

Jen quiets down and taps the steering wheel distractedly. "There was so much to be sad about," she says. Then she turns to me, takes her eyes off the endless road in front of us, and asks, "How do you let yourself feel that big of an emotion?" I think it is rhetorical until she answers herself a few moments later: "You don't."

Sex and food became twin struggles in Jen's life. Just as she was starting to understand that her desires for sexual pleasure and male attention were leading her into self-loathing, an insatiable hunger for carbs and sugar crept up on her. She craved not one-night stands but cookies, cereal, and ice cream bars. And the hunger was overwhelming. There weren't enough frat boys or Fig Newtons to fill the hole inside her.

In *Eating, Drinking, Overthinking,* the psychologist Susan Nolen-Hoeksema writes at length about the kind of reaction Jen had to the chaos of the college scene. Food, alcohol, and depression, she argues, are "the toxic triangle" that often push women over the edge. She writes: "Whereas men tend to externalize stress—blaming other people for their negative feelings and difficult circumstances—women tend to internalize it, holding it in their bodies and minds." Instead of relying on her sharp sociological mind to critique the double standard under which she was suffering, Jen internalized the pain and blamed herself.

Sex and food are the two most loaded issues of our time, the Pandora's box of our culture, universal and forbidden simultaneously. We even use the same language when it comes to both: *temptation, pleasure, crave.* Just as we are surrounded by advertisements for food that we "shouldn't" eat, invited to indulge because we deserve it, we are told, in the next thirty-second spot, that we should get back to the gym if we want to work off some guilt and make ourselves worthy of a bikini this summer. Sexual images are all around us, and pornography is accessible at the touch of a button, but any teenage girl who wants to protect her reputation must exercise absolute restraint, wait for a committed relationship to explore her sexuality, and keep quiet about masturbation.

How can anyone, under these conditions, be expected to know her true desires? How can anyone navigate the dangerous terrain of reputation and expectation on the road toward her authentic sexuality? How can an eighteen-year-old woman excited about life emerge without hating the body that leads her into temptation?

The Mind-Body Standoff

One night the vicious cycle that Jen engaged in—go out and party, hook up, feel bad, overeat, feel even worse, rev up, and do it all over again—got her into a situation she couldn't muster the strength to get out of.

It started like any other kind of hookup—Jen thought he was cute, he thought she was sexy, she invited him back to her room, and he happily followed. But once they started hooking up, Jen realized that she had trouble on her hands: "I wanted to have sex with him, but I knew it wasn't a good idea because he was going to be an asshole afterwards. I knew this guy, and he was a real jerk." Her mind, in other words, saw the trap; her body wanted to step into it anyway.

She remembers: "I just was so insecure that I kept saying no and he just didn't listen. He just started having sex with me, and I was like, 'No, no, no. Please don't,' but he didn't listen . . . so I just lay there." Jen estimates that "he had sex" for about fifteen minutes.

The entire time, she remembers, she just lay there feeling resigned. "I just thought, *Oh, well, my body isn't going to do anything about it.*"

Jen is quick to clarify: "He wasn't a big guy; it's not like I couldn't have thrown him off me. I was so mad at myself for so long about that. I didn't tell anyone about it, or think about it, or process it."

Months later, her compulsive sex and compulsive eating both raging out of control, Jen had a wake-up call in sociology class. As she listened to her professor, a woman she respected and identified with, talk about rape and its variable definitions, that night hit her like a ten-ton truck. *I was raped*, she sat in the packed lecture hall thinking. *I was raped*.

She went home that afternoon and bawled for hours, finally feeling the depth of her sadness and anger over the ignored no's she had muttered that night. She cried for all the times she had been disappointed by guys, for all the times she had been disappointed by herself. She mourned the loss of her high school self—the one who could flirt and fuck with the knowledge that people understood her. She raged about the double standard, the injustice, the ignorance. Ultimately, she prayed for a healing. She prayed that her mind and her body might again be one.

Now, years after the experience, Jen looks at it through a more nuanced lens: "After it first happened, I knew that I had a battle in my own head and I lost. I had done something that I didn't want to do. All I knew was that I had fucked up.

"When I sat in that class and called it rape, I thought he fucked up because he should have stopped. Now that I'm a few years out, I understand that *we* fucked up.

"Neither of us had enough of a sense of ourselves to handle the adult situation we were in." Jen moves from the personal to the political with ease: "That's why I think sex education is so important. Not just 'This is how you have babies' but 'This is the complicated shit that is going to come up because you've been socialized as a girl your whole life and you've been socialized as a boy your whole life and the things you've both been taught when you come together are going to fuck you both over.' "

———————

Here's where that complete lack of sex education comes back to haunt us. We have never learned to communicate about sex, and the drunken throes of passion aren't a great time to learn. Those same high school kids who suffered through the gym teachers' five-minute muttering and the crotch-rot pictures are now free to run around with their exploding hormones and their miseducated minds on a college campus. When they come colliding into one another under the usual circumstances—alcohol, celebration, desperation—the damage is often done quickly and foggily. This common experience of being mixed up in a sexual encounter where the boundaries are unclear and the talk sloppy is at the center of so many date rapes on college campuses and the regret, self-hatred, and eating disorders that often follow.

Despite the fact that Take Back the Night marches and rape crisis centers are standard on just about every campus, sexual encounters in college continue to be notoriously brief, unsatisfying, and sometimes even violating. In a study of six thousand students at thirty-two U.S. colleges, one in four women reported being victims of rape or attempted rape, and in another, 13 percent of college women indicated they had been forced to have sex in a dating situation. In a study of 477 male students, mostly freshmen and sophomores, 56 percent reported using "non-assaultive coercion"—i.e., threats, teasing, manipulation—to obtain sex.

These numbers remain so high in part because we haven't been able to revise the notion of "rape" in our minds—violent, straightforward, intentional, evil. In fact, it is a slippery slope from the "non-assaultive" stuff to the more serious violations. Much of the rape that goes on in the privacy of dorm rooms is initially mutual and playful and leads into something confusing and painful—a direct result of our lack of practice communicating about and understanding the complexities of sex.[†]

Recovery from one of these encounters is often brutal and can be more painful than the rape itself. Women wade through a cesspool of self-doubt—they replay the event, or what they can remember of it, in their heads and blame themselves for not being more assertive. Eventually they find some anger buried deep inside and try to climb on it to get out of their self-hate. Sometimes they take self-defense classes and

---

[†]This is not to say, of course, that violent, straightforward rapes do not go on, or that the victim is at fault. It is simply to point out that rape can be as confusing for the rapist as it is for the victim and, further, that the confusion often stems from a lack of education, preparation, and sobriety.

punch padded assailants until their grief goes quiet. Sometimes their own bodies become their punching bags.

In a recent study, 80 percent of patients with eating disorders reported they had a history of abuse. It doesn't take a Ph.D. in clinical psychology to understand the relationship between sexual assault and eating disorders. When a girl like Jen endures rape, she feels as if her body betrayed her. When she cannot confront the real enemy of that betrayal, she focuses her energy on the most immediate substitute. By starving and/or purging, she finds a tangible way to seize control and punish. By bingeing, she feeds her pain and protects herself from other, future violations. She has a place to put that energy, a conduit for all that anger and sadness, a simple distraction from the confusing reality.

Dr. Karen A. Duncan, an expert in sexual abuse recovery, has worked with almost thirteen hundred women—the majority of them exhibiting eating-disordered behaviors. She explains that female victims of sexual abuse often "blame their bodies for the sexual abuse. They say things like 'If I didn't have breasts, if I didn't look like this, then things would have been different.'"

Dr. Duncan remembers a thirty-two-year-old patient who had been sexually abused by both her father and a male cousin. She also came in with an eighteen-year history of eating disorders. Though weighing only 115 pounds (at five feet eight) at the time, she informed Dr. Duncan that she was scheduled to have a liposuction procedure the following week. It would be her fourth in a year. "She was self-injuring," Dr. Duncan explains, "in order to feel in control of her own pain. And each time she caused herself that pain, it was, in a sense, a reenactment of the abuse she so long endured."

Freak

Things didn't get easier for Jen. In fact, they got much, much harder. When she came home after her first year, she told her parents that she felt in danger of getting an eating disorder. They made an appointment for her with one of the psychologists in the network for their health insurance, and Jen, relieved, went to her first session. She remembers, "This woman, who had known me for fifteen minutes, told me that she thought I had been molested as a kid. And all I could think was *Here's the fucking shame again. I'm telling you with my whole heart, I am a sexual person. I don't know why, but I know that from the time I was really young, I've enjoyed sex.* And she's saying, 'That's not possible. No, you've been molested.' That was horrible for me, another person, more reassurance that you're not normal. You're fucked up. There's no way that you were born with those desires." Despite great need, Jen has never been back to therapy.

The hits kept coming. During her sophomore year, Jen noticed a suspicious red bump on her vagina. When she was diagnosed with HPV,[†] she wasn't surprised. But she was crushed nonetheless: "I felt like I was being punished for being a slut. Everything that was central to my identity—the crazy sexual experiences, the spontaneity, the fun—I wasn't allowed to do anymore. I thought my life was over." Her body not only remained the enemy but became even more explosive, even more out of control and unworthy of love in Jen's mind. Her binge eating increased. Her self-loathing grew so large she couldn't contain it.

She trusted one of her closest friends with her diagnosis, then quickly learned that this friend had shouted, while standing on a bar in a drunken rage: "My slut friend Jen has warts! She's dirty!" Jen basically shut down. She remembers, "I felt like such a freak. I pretty much decided no more girlfriends."

That decision was immediately painful as Jen had to go through the medical process of having her warts removed alone. The clinic waiting room was filled with repentant boys with their heads down,

---

†According to the Centers for Disease Control, at least 50 percent of sexually active men and women acquire genital HPV infection at some point in their lives. HPV, short for human papillomavirus, is the name of a group of viruses that includes more than one hundred strains or types, some of which can cause cancer. An HPV vaccine has been developed.

waiting for their girlfriends to emerge; nervous mothers; big sisters; steadfast friends. But Jen cried through her entire procedure and then left the clinic alone, got in her car alone, drove home alone. Sat in her bedroom and wondered, alone, if she would ever feel okay again.

For months Jen wallowed in this despondent, isolated space. She ate sporadically and compulsively, not consuming anything until late in the night and then gorging herself on ice cream and cookies. She didn't phone anyone, go anywhere, or enjoy anything.

I feel a knot of guilt in my guts. "This is the time," I remember as we drive west on I-80, "when you just stopped calling me back, right?"

"Yeah," Jen confirms. "I didn't pick up a phone for months. Literally. I didn't do anything."

As I sit next to Jen through the last miles of Wyoming, a silence possible only between intimates sets in. I gnaw on some beef jerky and ask myself, *Why wasn't I there for her?* I reflect on what happened to our friendship.

In high school, we shared the kind of bond that only hormonal, confused, and bright girls do—it was messy, scattered with shared boyfriends, secrets, jealousies, complete and utter adoration. Jen was everything I was not. I was everything she was not. And somehow, we still shared the same sensibility about the world. When college hit, we cried buckets and swore our allegiance to each other, swore we wouldn't forget. Jen wrote me beautiful letters, made me mix CDs, called me weekly, and told me gory stories about making out with lacrosse players in frat house bathrooms. I was grateful. I had, as of yet, no stories of my own. I spent most of my freshman year huddled over astronomy textbooks and *The New York Times Book Review,* wishing I had gone to a school where the parties didn't take place in private apartments inhabited by much cooler, much more cynical juniors and seniors.

When I came back home that summer, I had gained the requisite "freshman fifteen," and so had Jen, but we still recognized each other's bodies—I was tall and dark, she was small and had dyed her hair a dramatic blond. Everything was as it should be.

But as college wore on, we separated physically, mentally, and morally. We talked less on the phone. She stopped sending me letters or mix CDs. I didn't go to Boulder and visit. When we did see each other at the neighborhood Christmas party, it was like running into a stranger who wore a mask of my former best friend. By junior year, Jen had shrunk. She was a fraction of her former size, manic, inauthentic. I would ask her how she was doing, how she was *really* doing, and she would bounce around and shriek, "Awesome! Jack* and I are moving to Minnesota! Everything's awesome!"

And I hated her. I hated this wisp of a girl who had taken over the strong, explosive body of my best friend. I hated that she was syrupy and sweet. I hated that I knew she was lying, even if she didn't. I hated . . .

Jen breaks the silence by launching into her story again. "So let's just get this over with, shall we?" she asks playfully.

"Shoot."

Running Away

"I stopped being depressed because I fell in love with Jack . . . and Adderall," she launches in.

Jack was a happy-go-lucky, athletic kid from a wealthy background. He had an Elmo key chain, an adorable puppy, and he had adored Jen since first meeting her. When she felt at her worst, Jack made her forget, because of both his optimistic nature and his access to the prescription drug Adderall.†

Jack had been diagnosed with attention deficit hyperactivity disorder (ADHD). Jen had not. Both realized that if they took the drug he had been prescribed by the CU Health Center before going out, and

†According to the FDA, Adderall is a central nervous system stimulant (amphetamine) designed to treat attention deficit hyperactivity disorder (ADHD). The FDA now warns that Adderall, like all amphetamines, has high abuse potential. http://www.fda.gov/cder/drug/InfoSheets/patient/AdderallPatientSheet.pdf.

again in the morning, they could party all night and still go to school the next day. They started spending hours in the library together, popping pills and discussing each other's readings. Jen was so absorbed in Jack that she did his reading instead of her own most days. They would take smoke breaks every half hour to mull over his latest assignment, talking a million miles a minute, congratulating each other on how brilliant they sounded.

The drug helped Jen forget about a lot of things—the friends she no longer spoke to, her ambition to go to graduate school, the HPV, the rape. It also helped her forget to eat. She was no longer hungry, physically or otherwise. She had what she needed—acceptance, distraction, maybe even love. She would go for days at a time eating only what Jack insisted on—cheese and crackers at midnight, a shared burrito on the way home from drinking. When they did eat real meals, Jen didn't worry, because she knew that as soon as she popped another pill, she could make up for it by abstaining for as long as she needed to feel empty again.

In essence, Adderall put Jen in control again. Her mind was no longer the slave to her erratic and compulsive tyrant of a body. Instead, she was intellectually overstimulated and corporeally mute. She had no hunger pangs, no more sex drive, no exhaustion. She was a satisfying blend between an Energizer and a Playboy bunny—hot, thin, and unstoppable.

But of course, all was not well. In the middle of Jack's finals, he ran out of Adderall because Jen had been taking so much. He decided to fake a prescription to get more. Jen remembers sitting outside the health center waiting for him to appear with the new bottle: "I'm sitting there in his car, and all of a sudden I see the place get surrounded by police and I know Jack is getting arrested."

Jack's parents, a venture capitalist and a doctor from Minnesota, got him a good lawyer, and he was released with a slap on the wrist. In retrospect, Jen can't believe that she and Jack didn't realize how serious it was: "The ironic thing is that, in order to get him off with a lesser sentence, the lawyer claimed that Jack was addicted. We thought it was hilarious at the time—we still didn't get that we both *needed* the drug."

When Jack's parents offered to help them both settle in Minnesota after graduation, they jumped at the chance to get out of Boulder—romanticizing their new life far away. They bought a house they couldn't afford. Jack started working in his dad's company. Jen languished all day in bed, taking Adderall, admiring her body in the mirror, painting the rooms in colors to match her moods: deep purples and pinks, greens, blues, yellows, and oranges. She remembers, "That's when I really stopped eating. I started to be very, very conscious of the fact that I wasn't eating, and it became a big game. How long can you go, how little can you eat, how much weight can you lose?" She got so thin that she couldn't lift the groceries out of the car and carry them into the house.

Eventually Jack decided enough was enough. He realized that he couldn't get through a workday without taking an excessive amount of Adderall and that Jen was totally incapacitated and addicted. (At her worst, Jen was taking sixty to eighty milligrams a day. The average person with diagnosed ADHD takes five to twenty.) "We have to stop," he told her. They had two days' worth left.

"Then we have to move back to Colorado," Jen answered. "I hate it here."

"Agreed," he said.

Jen was scared shitless. All she could think about was gaining weight—she was afraid that without Adderall, she would spin completely out of control, start bingeing again. At the time, she could imagine nothing worse.

Jack and Jen got themselves off Adderall without telling anyone about their addiction. Sometimes it was frightening—like when Jack abandoned his car on the highway and started running, fueled by a manic sense that he had to go somewhere as fast as he possibly could. Jen weaned herself off more slowly, pleasantly surprised that her appetite didn't come back, at least not right away. What did return was her ability to experience emotions. She remembers: "I literally hadn't felt anything for over a year. The first time I cried, I was so happy."

They did make it back to Boulder eventually and decided to go their separate ways. Jack moved to Chicago and started working for a Web-design company. Jen bartends at Chili's—she drinks often, hooks up less, and is in the process of piecing her life back together. "It feels like I am just completely rebuilding my life," she explains, "one puzzle piece at a time. First I got off the drug. Now I am trying to develop a healthy relationship with my body again."

Her appetite did come back, and it scared the hell out of Jen. She hadn't made choices about eating sober for so many months that at first she wasn't sure she remembered how. But now she tries to eat whatever she feels like eating—which includes a lot of fattening Chili's cheese dip and milk shakes—and stay very active. She also journals frequently and pays a lot of attention to her self-talk.

"I used to look in the mirror and think, *Oh my God, I'm gross. I need to lose some weight,* and then drop it," Jen explains. "But now if I catch myself saying something like that, I counter it with *Whoa, clear your plate for the night, because you have some work to do. Start writing. Go for a walk. You know where this leads.*"

As we pull into Salt Lake, I am feeling overwhelmed and a bit hopeless. I am struck by how little I understood, at thirteen and seventeen and even twenty-one, about the wide variability of sex drive—that neither my lack of it nor Jen's abundance should have been cause for such shame. This business of growing up a girl—developing a woman's body and interpreting what it means, its capacity to give pleasure followed by such pain, its vulnerability to pregnancy, to disease, to violation, to self-hate—is so incredibly complicated. It feels like a ten-ton weight is handed to every girl at the age of twelve, and then she is invited to mount the tightrope of adolescence. It is as if we look at these spindly-legged, ponytailed girls, fresh out of sixth grade, and say, "Now you will be grown. You will be watched. You will fight every day of your life to be respected—by yourself and others. You will have to read between the lines, protect your reputation, be wary of your best friends. You will have myriad hungers. You will need to control these constantly."

It's too much for any one girl, and yet it never changes. I ask Jen if there is anything she feels she could have done differently, anything her friends or her family could have done to prevent all the pain she endured growing up. "I needed someone to help me internalize self-respect," she reflects. "No one ever told me that you could do what you wanted sexually and still respect yourself. If there was someone I could have talked to who was more like me, someone who could have said, 'I know everyone in your whole life worries about you—your parents, your friends—everyone wants to know why you are doing this with so many guys. But this is okay. It doesn't mean you're bad, and it doesn't mean you hate yourself. It might . . . but it doesn't have to.'"

As Jen says this, her voice lowers a bit, her eyes darken, and she transforms into the woman that she needed—a roughshod, experienced, wiser, and softer her. She is taking the GREs soon, and I secretly wish that she will apply to become a social worker or a sex educator, that she won't forget.

I turn off the voice recorder I've clipped to Jen's collar, lean back in my seat, and sigh. As we get further away from adolescence, the cacophony between our minds and bodies quiets, but we still try to understand who we are as sexual people. It is amazing to me that I am still, at twenty-five, filled with so many questions. When the judgment of the outside world and the assumptions about what is normal and abnormal are turned down, what do we hear? When the layers of fear and loneliness are stripped away, what do we truly crave underneath? How can we accept our bodies, even appreciate them, as the seats of this craving?

————

Katie, our third musketeer, gets married against the backdrop of a breathtaking mountain. A creek runs nearby, the late-afternoon sun burns the bare shoulders of spaghetti-strap-dress-wearing friends and family. Jen and I sit side by side. Jen wears a skimpy tank top that shows off her reclaimed breasts and a short skirt with tall heels. I am in a more modest calf-length halter dress that shows off my upper back, one of the only parts of my body I feel unequivocally good about. We turn to see as the music indicates Katie's descent from the ski lodge stairs above and squeeze each other's hands.

And there she is in a white strapless dress with a train, a string of pearls, hair coiffed underneath a traditional gauzy veil—the works. I flash back to a night in her dad's Suburban, shouting out the lyrics to the Lost Boyz, making dinner in her parents' house for our boyfriends before homecoming (or, technically, picking up steaks from Outback), skidding away in my Accord when a house party got violent, defending at a school board meeting our right to publish a story about a lesbian alumna in our campus newspaper, drinking too much, laughing too loud, loving so desperately.

I feel like Katie is playing dress-up, like we are back in my attic, trunk top hanging off, red polyester dress and boas spilling over the sides. Part of me wants to shout, "Take that off before people take you seriously!" The other part is awed by how much more mature she seems than teary-eyed Jen and me. Jen leans over to me and whispers, "Wow."

"I know, wow," I respond, then squeeze Jen's hand.

6

The Revolution *Still* Will Not Be Televised: Pop, Hip-hop, Race, and the Media

The body has become the primary canvas on which girls express their identities, insecurities, ambitions, and struggles.

—Lauren Greenfield

Anyone naïve enough to believe that the Madonna-whore dynamic Jen and I played out in our teenage years has run its course need only look at the career of one Britney Spears to be convinced otherwise. She is the virgin-slut myth personified, a swinging pendulum of virtue and vice. She began her career in pigtails and a Catholic school uniform, complete with public promises about her sacred virginity. Just three years later, she gyrated and sweated her way back into the spotlight with songs such as "I'm a Slave 4 U," in which she confirmed that she was, after all, sexual and not prudish. Before long she was swinging back in the other direction: making babies and putting on her best—okay, not that convincing—performance of a virtuous mother. A couple kids, a divorce, and multiple hospitalizations later, she's become the media's favorite punching bag.

On MTV and BET, every pop icon flips the script before today's watchers get a chance to read it. For us eighties and nineties gals, Madonna was just a slut, straight up, no take-backs. She was *like* a virgin, very clearly not one. (That, of course, was before she and Britney kissed on the 2003 MTV Video Music Awards—confirming every teenage girl's lurking suspicion that, unless she kissed girls for boys' enjoyment, she was uptight.)

In the wasteland of corporate rap, a teenage girl can also find a virtual smorgasbord of female archetypes: video ho (bad girl), boo (good girl), or momma. Fall down the slippery slope from rap to porn—thanks to BET After Dark and Snoop Dogg's pair of porn videos—and there is a gaggle of naked, submissive, and horny women with fake tits and incessant moans to emulate. The visual variety of female bodies to which the average girl is exposed through television, movies, the Internet, and music is, to put it mildly, severely limited.

The thin, gyrating female body is the visual standard; the aural standard is silence. Older women may have carved out a little space in the public sphere to chat (all-knowing, all-seeing Oprah, tell-it-like-it-is Meredith Vieira, classy Diane Sawyer, barrier-breaking Katie Couric), but young women continue to be largely mute on any and all subjects beyond fashion and their fiancés. We are not featured on panels or interviewed about political issues. We rarely get serious news anchor positions or the chance to smirk and sass on faux-news shows.

Instead, you can find young women paying homage to their dress designers on the runway, blushing about their latest flings, or singing clichéd lyrics on entertainment television. Even if a token young woman does get a minute of airtime, you can bet that she will be rail-thin, undeniably attractive, and usually horrifically unhealthy. Case in point: The seventeenth season of *The Real World* featured twenty-four-year-old Paula Meronek, who not only suffered from anorexia and bulimia but also had an abusive boyfriend and an addiction to alcohol. The show tried to paint a "happily ever after" picture of Paula's "recovery"—supposedly thanks to the support of her roommates—but to date she admits to still taking diet pills as she travels the country hitting bars for paid appearances at a gaunt size. She is back together with the boy who beat her so badly she had to be hospitalized.

Girls learn that, while their voices may not be heard, their bodies speak volumes.

Icon Dolls

Let me just admit this up front: I love Christina Aguilera. When I first saw her video about being stuck in a bottle—containable, waiting, passive—I wasn't impressed. That stick-thin blonde with bad hair, writhing on the beach, struck me as horribly ordinary and pathetic. But once Christina changed from those saddlebacks to some serious stilettos, she changed my mind. Her tiny little body was made fierce in black chaps, and I liked that she reclaimed the idea of being "dirty." Once the mean-spirited whisper in a junior high hallway, it seemed powerful and proud when she screamed the word, ass in the air, boxing gloves ready. When she did the video where she stood in a big line with a bunch of girls from her crew and pointed a water hose between her legs at some disrespectful guys, I was way past smitten.

For a few months I pruned in the shower while belting out her song "Beautiful" at the top of my lungs. Christina doesn't seem savvy, necessarily, but she seems real. Quirky, raw, and unapologetic, Christina thinks that we all deserve to feel beautiful.

I have the same secret love for Kelly Clarkson. She didn't "disappear" the moment she became famous, and she continues to act surprisingly human and endearingly excited about her career. When she rocks out, she isn't worried about a little belly sticking out or a bump in her ponytail. Her hit single "Since You've Been Gone" is the jump-with-fist-in-the-air-inducing "I Will Survive" of my generation.

I don't get the same feeling from the other leading ladies on the Top 40. Whereas Christina is using her sappy but touching lyrics, her hose, her crazy voice, and her little body as tools of her own fierce expression, her counterparts seem unarmed and horrifically mute. Whereas Kelly has an authentic personality and a refreshingly "average" physique, other young stars seem like automatons without fault. They may be toned and expensively dressed, and sometimes they even sing words out of their painted lips, but for all intents and purposes, they are mute. Their power comes not from their sassy declarations in nine octaves but from their toothpick necks and good hair.

The Olsen twins appear repeatedly dumbstruck on the streets of the West Village, with coffee cups and layers of ill-fitting skirts to hide their disappearing bodies. Once full-cheeked, Lindsay Lohan completely denied that her overnight transformation into a skeleton was the result of an eating disorder. She evaded questions about her lifestyle, preferring to puff on her cigarette. Multiple hospitalizations and a *Saturday Night Live* intervention later, she admitted to *Vanity Fair* that she struggled with bulimia (though she has yet to turn her struggle into any sort of treatment). The miraculously disappearing Nicole Richie became a fashion icon overnight, thanks in large part to Rachel Zoe, the stylist who also aided Lohan's career boost. The *Los Angeles Times* reports, "Fashion insiders have whispered privately that she [Zoe] is single-handedly bringing anorexia back." Like it was ever out.

Benny Medina, talent agent, talked about Richie to *Vanity Fair* in June 2006: "I think she's motivated to be scary-little. . . . There's an aspirational look; the younger generation has become obsessed with thinness that pushes it to the point of concern. It's a style. I personally think everyone in California has an eating disorder."

When today's pop girls aren't totally mute or quipping in dangerous contradictions, they are completely vacuous. An interview with Britney Spears is like listening to pink static. She giggles, blushes, coos, and every once in a great while, tries to take a stand—but it mostly sounds like a child throwing a tantrum. Paris Hilton's only contribution is her favorite phrase: "That's hot."

One refreshing exception is the *American Idol* runner-up Katharine McPhee, who admitted to *People* in June 2006 that she struggled with bulimia for five years before seeking treatment right before her stint on the show. She admitted throwing up seven times a day at her worst, which she described as "putting a sledgehammer to your vocal cords." After a three-month hospitalization, she claims to have made peace with her appetite. She now uses the "intuitive eating approach," which entails—gasp!—actually paying attention to your authentic hungers and satisfying them rather than living by dogmatic rules about "good" and "bad" foods.

It is rare that a star such as McPhee is so up-front about the ugliness of trying to be beautiful in our cookie-cutter culture. The majority of pop stars today are living, breathing, gyrating icon dolls or, as Pink brazenly calls them in her hilarious 2006 video, "Stupid Girls." They have nothing to contribute outside the realms of fashion and conspicuous consumption. Most dolls come with accessories such as a yippy dog with a diamond collar worth more than a semester's college tuition and a line of noxious perfume. Pull one of their strings and they will squeak vapid lyrics.

In fact, one of the major sensations of 2004 was actually called the Pussycat Dolls by the Los Angeles choreographer and creator Robin Antin, whose dream was to make "everyone look like a real, living doll."

It wasn't always this way. There was a time when female musicians were actually musicians, when they had a message beyond their midriffs, when their bodies were not their only claims to fame. Thirty years ago female singers were icons with personality: Janis Joplin, Aretha Franklin, the still-raging and amazing Bonnie Raitt. These women's lives had not been molded for celebrity from birth with Disney mouse ears, talent scouts, and personal trainers. Janis Joplin, while certainly not a healthy role model, spoke her mind and lived the hell out of her short life. Aretha Franklin became the "Queen of Soul" after having two babies and a dream in Detroit in her teens. Bonnie Raitt left Harvard to ride the highways of the South with old blues musicians.

Nancy Sinatra's boots were made for walking. Gloria Gaynor knew she would survive. Fergie, from the Black Eyed Peas, just wants to tell you about her "humps." Today's pop stars' bodies, not their songwriting or singing abilities (most appear to have none), make them famous.

Today's young pop icons don't have to drop out of school to get famous because they don't go in the first place. They are anti-intellectual and apolitical, asserting opinions on nothing besides the latest "in" Las Vegas clubs and designer shoes. They spend money, party, and starve. Their biggest statements are official announcements of breakups and engagements. Their reality shows, rather than revealing that there is more than meets the eye, confirm that we have seen all there is to see. These women are spoiled brats in undernourished bodies, unaware of the world outside of their Hummers and high-rise apartments.

Media-Literacy Fatigue

Most young people are hip to the fact that the news is often subjective, stardom is sometimes bought with cold, hard cash, and fashion spreads are Photoshopped to death. We barely batted an eye when Ashlee Simpson came up lip-synching. We know Julia Roberts has body doubles. We have seen airbrushing transform a textured face into a smooth polish on *America's Next Top Model*.

My generation grew up with a healthy dose of cynicism about most Hollywood stars, whose bodies must be groomed and toned and tightened and plucked into submission. We know that all of this takes a lot of time and money that most of us don't have. We know that models actually look strange and giraffelike in person, that they couldn't get prom dates because they were so tall and awkward. The concept of "media literacy" was born about the same time most of us were.

But for all our twentieth-century savvy, we are still swooning, celebrity-entranced teenagers and twenty-somethings with subscriptions, sometimes justified entirely by the "Stars Are Just Like Us" section and hipster irony, to *Us Weekly*. Pop stars are part and parcel of American culture, and now that we are exporting MTV and the tabloids along with McDonald's and Coke, part and parcel of everyone else's culture too. Even if we intellectually think they are full of shit, pop stars still capture our collective imagination. We like to make fun of them. We like to critique their clothes and their dance moves. And unfortunately, yes, sometimes we still like to emulate them.

It is not that a football stadium's worth of fourteen-year-old girls saw Lindsay Lohan's shrinking body on *Access Hollywood* and promptly decided to starve themselves, just as she did. We are not so directly affected or so hopelessly naïve. We have sat in high school and college classrooms and watched Jean Kilbourne's series of feminist films about the tyranny of skinny images infiltrating our brains; *Killing Us Softly,* her first, was created the same year I was: 1979. We don't buy the theory that mean male media executives have a vendetta against easily influenced teenage girls. The executive directors of most women's magazines are women. Though there isn't sexual equality in the leadership of most entertainment corporations, there are females in top positions at Sony, Universal, CBS, ABC, Paramount, Fox, and the most popular kid in school, MTV.

We can be mercilessly critical of any and all fluff that is thrown our way, but we remain incapable of intelligently processing *all* these media messages *all* the time. The onslaught is paralyzing, the magnitude mind-numbing. And frankly, intellectualizing with every turn of the glossy page isn't all that much fun either. Unlike our foremothers, we aren't convinced that high heels are made in the devil's workshop or that fashion can't be fun *and* smart. We have media literacy fatigue.

The sum total of all of these thin-is-in images *does* have an impact on the way we see our own bodies, not because we are impressionable or naïve but because we are human. It is exhausting to be constantly critiquing and filtering the contradictory media and advertising messaging through a media-literate lens. As one fourteen-year-old Manhattanite, who sounded and looked like she was twenty-four, told me: "Sure, *Us Weekly* asks 'Is Lindsay too thin?' on the cover, but inside they publish her entire diet—total mixed messages. If I'm feeling bad, I may not think outright, *I'm going to be thin like her,* but I do read the diet and take a mental note. I do feel jealous. That must translate into some behavior even if I'm not, like, totally aware of it."

These constant images have stretched the definition of what is "too thin." We are accustomed to seeing collarbones jutting out of designer dresses, hips pressing against size-0 pants, tiny waists in cinched belts. These tiny bodies are normalized—the icon dolls that perfect girls play with when we grow out of Barbie. We reject the formless dresses and Chico's-a-go-go of our mothers and explain away the thin figures on the runway as an unavoidable part of high fashion. Many of us believe that fashion's fun, creative elements outweigh its skeletal models.

These skinny, one-dimensional women march through our lives so incessantly that we barely notice their comings and goings. As media literate as we are, they still affect the way we feel about our own bodies. I can feel the creep in my own casual consumption—my brother and I flip through a stolen copy of our landlord's *Us Weekly* like two twelve-year-old boys hiding in a tree house with a father's stolen *Playboy*. "You mean Tom Cruise walks through doors, just like us?" we scream in mock shock. In the "Who Looks Hotter?" section, I start rooting for the "bigger" girls, convinced that if Kate Winslet looks better in that Versace dress, then I too have a chance of being attractive. Suddenly what began as an ironic, gut-busting media critique becomes a statement about my own self-worth.

The result of all this unconscious exposure to tiny, toned bodies is a new ideal. We may brush aside women such as Lara Flynn Boyle or Calista Flockhart—too thin for us. But if these women are the extreme, the acceptable alternative is not much fleshier. We feel better admiring Maggie Gyllenhaal or Claire Danes, though both are very thin, because they do indie movies and wear hipper clothes—the politically correct waifs. We feel progressive when we compliment the bodies of curvier ladies such as Beyoncé and J. Lo, even if they too are airbrushed, dieted, and boot-camped into perfection.

Many of the girls I interviewed talked about how the Kate Moss days were long gone. They didn't want to be that thin, they told me, but they *did* want one of those "in" bodies that men lust after—big tits and a shapely ass, a flat stomach and a small waist, perfect skin, great hair. "Pop culture has definitely shaped the way I think about my body now," nineteen-year-old Roxanne, a Filipina from New Jersey, explains. "Beautiful, I learned, means the right size breasts—pretty big but not too big; the right size waist—small; and the right size ass—kinda big but very fit."

Even if the shape is slightly bigger, there is still a "right size." Even if the standard you ascribe to is a little fleshier, the strategic placement and toning of that flesh is a tall order. (There are even jeans made with "butt boosters" to enhance size and shape for those born with smaller or flatter asses.) It is still tied up in the everyday push and pull of willpower, the agony of constant comparisons, the effect of expectations according to ethnicity. The everyday margin for success is still very narrow, even if the models are a little wider.

"Fat in the Right Places"

Bonita,* a seventeen-year-old Dominican from the Bronx, leans over the table a little and lowers her voice as she tells me, "The reason I was going to the gym was to try to get a bigger butt. I did mad lunges for the longest time. Latinas are supposed to have asses, you know. I mean, that's the stereotype."

When the size of her butt barely changed, Bonita was disappointed. "You're supposed to be skinny but have the curves. You are supposed to have a butt and breasts but be thin all at the same time." She leans back and rolls her eyes. "Crazy, right?"

I met Bonita through a program for young leaders where I worked one summer and was immediately struck by her insight, her quiet power, her humility. She is strikingly beautiful—big, deep brown eyes and a small, taut body that looks like it could carry her through just about anything. She immediately caused some acute crushes among the male participants, though she seemed entirely unaware of her effect on them. We kept in touch after that summer—I would invite her to film screenings or book readings, and she would update me on her love life or her college search. When I told her about the subject of my book, she laughed—her signature response to discomfort—and said, "You know that's not just a white-girl thing, right?"

Eating disorders don't discriminate, though white women are still the most likely to develop them. Women of color dance along the spectrum in the same neurotic and obsessive range as their white counterparts. When I began researching this book, I interviewed Tiffany, a powerhouse in a compact Chinese-American body who admitted that she was hoping to lose some weight before heading back to the London School of Economics. Felice, a statuesque Caribbean-American, laughed when I asked her if she had ever felt too preoccupied by food and fitness. I would be reading someone's answer to my e-mail survey, noting all of the classic responses, and then stop short when I realized that the respondent was biracial or East Asian or Mexican-American. By the third month of this continuous surprise, the novelty wore off.

Researchers confirm my anecdotal findings. In a study conducted in urban public schools in Minnesota of five thousand teenagers, it was found that Hispanic, Asian-American, and Native American girls tended to report similar or more concern with the size of their bodies and as much eating disorder–like behavior as their white peers, if not more.

In her 2000 study, Dr. Ruth Striegel-Moore, professor and chairwoman of the psychology department at Wesleyan University, also found that black women were as likely as white women to binge and purge, and were more likely to fast and abuse laxatives or diuretics. Other studies she has conducted have supported her theory that women of color who are in close association with white culture, sometimes called "upwardly mobile," are more often affected by eating disorders. Striegel-Moore told NPR: "What we think drives some of the binge eating is stress-related, and so if you're talking about someone who is upwardly mobile or who is in a context where they're, you know, a token person, they may experience a considerable amount of stress and that may, in part, contribute to their eating problem."

The numbers confirm that women of color commonly have eating disorders, but they are not getting much formal treatment. Striegel-Moore says these women are "unrecognized by the health-care system." News stories on the issue rarely feature blacks, Latinas, or women of other minority groups, wrongly implying that eating disorders remain a disease of the white and wealthy. In a recent Florida State University study, researchers showed fictional diaries of a sixteen-year-old girl with weight preoccupation to 150 random people. When these people were told that the writer of the confessions was white, most said that she appeared to have an eating disorder. When they were told she was black, people didn't see cause for alarm.

If a woman of color seeks help, she will most likely be speaking with a white therapist, doctor, or nutritionist—not a comfortable situation for some young women who feel that their problems are better understood by someone who shares their culture.

A twenty-one-year-old Puerto Rican woman, Stephanie,* bravely stood up in front of the women's studies course I teach, despite the fact that she had not previously participated in class discussions, and told the class about her struggle with anorexia throughout high school. She ate so little each day that she developed acid reflux disease, forcing her to go to the hospital and admit to her mother that she wasn't eating breakfast or lunch at school, as she had claimed for months. Stephanie started eating three meals a day again but did not get counseling; a year later, when she switched schools and felt the pressure to develop curves in the right places instead of feeling fat all over, she went back to her dangerous eating habits. This time she was worse. She remembered, "I had bad stomach pains, my chest hurt, I was short of breath, and I wanted to throw up. I thought I was going to die.

"I feel that pop culture had a lot do with how I viewed my body," she theorizes. "All I saw were these women with flawless, built, but skinny bodies. I started to believe that my body would only be okay if it looked like that too." Though I respect her analysis, I don't trust her past tense. She has never gotten counseling, a necessary part of any recovery from an eating disorder. Like many families unaccustomed to dealing with this kind of problem, Stephanie's didn't insist on it. They felt that their family was strong enough to be the support she needed. Maybe they're right. But she is still so quiet in class, sits in the back, looks gaunt in the face. What if they're wrong?

Bonita, unlike Stephanie, focused on fitness on her road to the "fat in the right places" body. In addition to doing wall sits and squats, she was eating chopped-up celery with vinegar poured over it for dinner, a trick she learned from her cousin. In fact, all of the women in Bonita's family are obsessed with their body size. Her older sister has a personal trainer. At the time of our first interview, despite the fact that money was tight, Bonita's mother planned on getting a tummy tuck.

"By the time I was eleven," Bonita reflects, "I was worrying about my weight. When I went through puberty and gained a few pounds, I remember deciding not to eat any more bread because I'd heard my sisters talking about that diet. I would say to myself, 'You ate already, you're not going to eat again for the rest of the day.'"

When I hear Bonita talk like this, I get nervous. Is there something she's not telling me? Does she, or did she, have a partial or full-blown eating disorder? "Do you ever not eat for a long time? Do you ever make yourself throw up?" I ask her, point-blank.

"Naw," she responds immediately, shaking her head. "Sometimes I feel disgusted and I want to throw up, but I've been told that you don't do that. I've watched *Oprah*. I don't know . . ." Her resolution fades and then she admits, "Honestly, I've tried, but it doesn't feel right." Bonita can't name a female friend or family member who isn't obsessed with her weight; she also can't name one with an eating disorder.

This vague wisdom that making herself throw up just "doesn't feel right" is actually a profound protection—a layer of discomfort that separates Bonita from the full-blown hell so many other girls experience. Young women of color frequently expressed a point past which they wouldn't go in their quest for the "fat in the right places" ideal. In part they may be resisting adopting behavior they know is associated with white girls; by refusing to go down that road, they stay loyal to their culture.

A few months after I had last seen Bonita, we met at a coffee shop and she started telling me about her latest adventure. She is writing spoken-word poetry and performing it in a café on the Lower East Side. She says, not a bit shy, that she thinks she might be pretty good. Her eyes seem even bigger than the last time we met, her future even brighter as she looks ahead to college.

When we get around to talking about her family, she laughs and then sheepishly admits that her mom did get that tummy tuck, with some liposuction thrown in. "If that didn't make me never want to get plastic surgery, I don't know what would," she reports. "The recovery was gross."

We try to narrow down Bonita's prospective colleges, and I promise to write her a glowing recommendation. Right before she is about to leave, she leans in and this time doesn't laugh at all. "The weird thing—about the tummy tuck, I mean—is that it made the scar on my mom's belly disappear. That was the scar she got when she had me, 'cause I was a cesarean section. *That* just doesn't feel right."

The Young Boy's Club

In the attic of my childhood home are rows and rows of records that my parents kept from their high school and college days: the Beatles, the Four Seasons, the Rolling Stones, all gathering dust. Every once in a while my dad will go up there and dig around for something, put it on the record player, and reminisce about what he was doing when he first heard a particular song. He puts on Herman's Hermits and describes his first high school homecoming, how the girls stood on one side, straightening their itchy skirts and repinning stray hairs into their beehive hairdos, and the boys stood on the other, bragging about what they wanted but realistically wouldn't do with their dates after the dance. Despite my dad's silver hair and laugh lines, he looks young again, lit from the inside.

I try to imagine myself at his age, digging around in the dusty CDs of my youth and uncovering my high school classics. I might put Common's "I Used to Love H.E.R." in the ancient CD player— surely everything will be completely digitized—and talk about the first time I heard it, sitting in my boyfriend's white boat of a Cadillac in front of my house at fifteen years old. I might play some of the Roots' early stuff or Black Star, reminisce about how frequently I saw them both perform at little clubs around New York my first year in college. I might put Snoop Dogg or Dr. Dre on and go even further back, to the days in junior high when we would find a parentless house and have our first house parties. The girls would sit on one side of the room giggling and looking up adoringly at their boyfriends, who stood in a self-conscious circle, freestyling (rapping unwritten lyrics spontaneously).

Our greatest hope was to be woven into one of the rhymes.

Hip-hop is the music of my generation, no doubt. It is the sound that, like the Beatles for my parents' generation, or U2 for the one between us, makes us feel alive. It is the soundtrack of our adolescence, the background music of the most defining moments of our teenage lives. It is a reflection of our tepid political consciousness—the distrust we feel for traditional government, the nuanced way in which we approach race and class issues, our obsession with consumption. Hip-hop is what moves our bodies and defines our expression.

Though it was born in the inner-city neighborhoods of the 1970s, it was not until the late eighties that hip-hop made its way to suburbia. For kids in the cities, especially those from working-class families, hip-hop was part of their lives as early as elementary school. My boyfriend remembers listening to Slick Rick's "La-Di-Da-Di" and doing head spins on the living room floor with his brother and sister in Brooklyn circa 1985. For those of us raised farther inland, among sprawling, paler suburbs, hip-hop was generally a junior high–era epiphany. I can easily recall my brother's obsession with the Beastie Boys circa 1993; he and his two best friends each claimed the persona of one of the members of the rap group and performed their songs at summer camp talent shows.

I was in love with hip-hop at first sound. Though a writer myself, I never thought to join the cipher (the group of people standing in a circle and taking turns freestyling). My girlfriends and I did everything we could to identify ourselves as part of the hip-hop culture—we took photographs at hip-hop shows, dressed in baggy jeans and hoodies, dated boys who signaled our legitimacy. But we never, for a second, considered trying to write or perform our own raps. Looking back, I realize that we never thought of the music of our generation as *our* music. It was always borrowed, always impenetrable, always male.

When my mom was moved by Joan Baez, she could have picked up a guitar and learned to create her own music. She could have agonized over the lyrics, expressed something truly her own, communicated it to the world (okay, maybe just a living room of stoned hippies). Girls of my generation couldn't interact with the music that moved and defined us in the same way; we couldn't add our voices to the raw and real mix that so appealed to our teenage angst and outrage. Instead, we dressed, danced, waited on the sidelines of house parties, cultivating an image of hip-hop rather than contributing to it.

The almost complete absence of female MCs (masters of ceremonies, those who write and perform raps) from hip-hop music indicates that its boys'-club mentality goes far beyond its sexist lyrics or its pornographic video visuals. Women are not encouraged, nor are they inclined, to put their own voices into the mix. Instead, they learn early that their place, in either corporate rap or conscious hip-hop, to a lesser extent, is as silent partners.†

Young women's voicelessness is even more disturbing when you consider the nature of hip-hop. It is a music, a culture really, built on the idea of grassroots participation. It was intended to be an ongoing dialogue in which performers become audience and audience becomes performers. Drawing from far older African oral traditions, hip-hop is predicated on the idea of liberation through storytelling.

But if you look at the average roster of MCs, it would appear that

---

†The difference between "corporate rap" and "conscious hip-hop" may be subtle to an outsider but is fairly distinct for fans of the music. Conscious rappers, such as Mos Def and Talib Kweli, write more thoughtfully and critically of political and social issues than do 50 Cent or Cameron, for example. Conscious rappers usually have smaller releases of their albums, make less money, produce videos with story lines or a cinematic feel. Some artists cross over between the two subgenres, but that is more the exception than the rule.

women have no stories to tell. Women griots offered their voices to the West African tradition that hip-hop echoes; but in the era of commercialized rap, most young women speak only with their bodies. Some exceptional women choose to break-dance, write graffiti, or DJ, but more often than not, these choices are greatly shaped by the safety of silence—none of these expressions requires the risk of speaking.

––––––––––––

When I first saw Mariana* walk into Elementary, an extracurricular hip-hop club at Columbia University, I was mesmerized by her. She seemed to weave in and out of the nerd rappers and big-bellied hip-hop drummers with ease, laughing with them, touching them lightly on the shoulders. She seemed to have none of the self-consciousness that I did about being white and privileged and totally entranced by hip-hop but unable to participate in any meaningful way.

I would later learn that part of her confidence stemmed from the fact that she actually had figured out a way to be a part of the culture. At sixteen years old, she got a couple of turntables and started practicing DJing from her Austin home. By the time she got to college, she was adept at doing some of the difficult skills that real DJs must master: scratching, blending, and beat matching. She had the respect of the guys in that club, in part because she had done something that few girls would do.

Mariana is now one of my best friends and continues to DJ in clubs throughout New York City and beyond. We sat down on a recent Friday night in her apartment and talked about her brave choice, her continuing frustrations, and the way her body is an often overlooked subtext of the larger story.

––––––––––––

Mariana remembers a time when she was unafraid to rap. Six years old, shoveling the snow with her big brother in New Jersey, freestyling to her heart's content: "My mom used to read this book, *Tales from the Arabian Nights,* to us, and we would rhyme about Ali Baba and the Forty Thieves, Sinbad the Sailor, all the characters in that book." The brother-sister duo even recorded a rap for their grandparents' wedding anniversary. They wore out their Run-D.M.C. record, fought over the mix tape with "The Humpty Dance" on it. Mariana goes on: "It was such a natural thing to do—rhyme off the top of my head for five minutes. It was probably awful, but I never felt ashamed or embarrassed. I don't understand why I never felt embarrassed when I was little and then, just a few years later . . ."

She trails off, stumped at the shape of her own history. Mariana's story, though about a modern music, sounds like an old tale. Carol Gilligan's idea about girls losing their authentic voices, along with their innocence, at adolescence fits eerily well here. "I turned twelve," Mariana remembers, "and suddenly I just stopped being able to freestyle. My brother didn't want to hang out with his little sister. I became a cheerleader. Everything was different."

How does a shoveling, rapping, carefree Mariana turn into a self-conscious perfect girl come junior high? Mariana doesn't have an explanation she's satisfied with, but she can't help thinking it had something to do with her need to "look good": "Girls feel we have to look good and perform well, not look silly or dumb. I think that's part of the perfectionism—maintaining an image." Rapping requires a modicum of playfulness, a sense of humor about oneself, the security to risk screwing up, and the resiliency to pick yourself up if it happens. Girls, especially thirteen-year-old insecure, self-conscious, type A girls, aren't adept at any of the above. Expressing yourself in that way means being watched and evaluated, losing some control, being the center of attention. Mariana also reflects: "Rap involved posturing, competition, machismo. What twelve-year-old girl wants to risk being typecast as boyish or masculine? Instead, we want to conform, generally, and do things that won't call negative attention to ourselves."

The culture of machismo was inextricable from the culture of rap in Mariana's public junior high school: the Starter jackets that seemed to swallow up still-developing boys, the usually empty threats of violent revenge for stolen girlfriends, the gangsta-lean swaggers tried on like hand-me-down, ill-fitting coats. Mariana reflects: "I stopped rapping because it was no longer part of my culture. When I finally started going to parties, I would see a cipher, all guys, and I was intimidated.

The girls were with the girls, looking cute and doing whatever. The guys were with the guys." Looking cute is the innocent first phase of letting your body do the talking.

What sounds innocuous in Mariana's reminiscence is the crux of the hip-hop problem for women. The girls are looking cute. The guys are expressing themselves, developing a sense of spontaneous voice, practicing making mistakes and learning from them, generally being seen *and* heard. Looking cute means losing out.

As Mariana got older, she didn't find it any easier to join in the cipher, but she found other ways to be involved in hip-hop. Many hip-hop acts came through her new hometown, Austin, and Mariana was in the front row for most of their shows. She started taking note of the DJs; she liked the idea that they got to participate fully without putting themselves smack-dab in the center of attention. She explains: "[As a DJ,] you play other people's music. If you are an MC, everyone is staring at you and listening to your music. [As a DJ,] you can fade into the background a little if you want to. DJing is a little more removed, a little safer." She got some turntables and started practicing.

Around the same time, Mariana was going through a lot in her relationships with boys and with her own body. She was full of an inextinguishable angst, fed by her attraction to fiery guys, risk takers, artists, druggies, wannabe thugs. Though on paper she was every parent's dream—the perfect girl with nearly perfect grades, a place on the cross-country team and in student government—in real life she was testing all kinds of limits.

While she was discovering DJing, she met her older boyfriend, Brad.* He cut and burned himself when he was overwhelmed or anxious, and Mariana started to as well. She remembers, "I was so confused, so tormented. When you are a teenager, you are just so affected by everything, so affected by the world. For a few months, anyway, cutting became my way of dealing with it." During the week, Mariana was getting nearly perfect grades and running cross-country. On the weekends, she was sneaking into clubs and experimenting with ecstasy, cocaine, and mushrooms. Just before her sixteenth birthday, she took unlabeled drugs at a party and blacked out. When she came to, she realized that she had had sex for the first time.

In retrospect, Mariana realizes that her weekday self and her weekend self were not as different as they appeared. "In both cases, I felt like my body didn't really matter, like I could beat it up in service of my larger goals—whether that was numbing my angst or getting the A. In fact, it was really in cross-country that I learned that ethos of working through the pain. I decided early on that I needed to ignore what I actually felt so that I could be this person I thought I wanted to be: the good DJ, the good student, the good runner." One of the trademark perfect-girl talents is this ability to ignore and overcome the body's weakness in pursuit of a goal. We quickly condition ourselves to tune out our own internal signals, our aches and pains, our hungers, and tune up our plans, our determination, our control. What works in the short term, however, eventually leads to burnout. Many of us, so expert at overcoming our own pain on the road to success, end up crossing the finish line, but not without disease and heartbreak.

The ultimate sign that Mariana knew how to ignore her body came her senior year. She had sex that she describes as "confusing. I couldn't tell whether I was forced or not, but I definitely remember saying that we shouldn't because I knew I wasn't on birth control at the time." Soon after, she realized she was pregnant. Mariana reflects, "It seems like you hear so much about how not to get pregnant when you are a teenager, but then when it happens, you are so secretive about it, you don't know what to do with yourself." She told no one. It was almost as if she didn't even tell herself, instead continuing to drink and do drugs at parties, run races, look forward to college.

Not long after, she had a miscarriage. Once at the hospital, she refused to tell the doctors any of her family's information, opting to pay the two-thousand-dollar bill with the money she had saved for college from her after-school job. At home, she got two hours of sleep, woke up at 4:00 A.M., and started on her psychology presentation, due that afternoon.

Mariana felt like her body was something outside herself, uncontrollable and dangerous. It attracted attention. It got sick and hungover.

It got pregnant. It bled. The only way for her to deal with it was to ignore it. Pain became a passing nuisance, something to overcome on the way to achievement, or master in order to keep up appearances. Mariana's body was weak and her determination to bypass it strong.

DJing was and still is an outlet in which Mariana's body takes a backseat. She explains, "DJing is a way to hide your body. I like to hide behind these two huge, hunking pieces of metal [the turntables] and play around with funky equipment. In essence, I get to hide my femininity for a second." She describes the effort as mechanical and technical—words usually associated with masculine pursuits.

Ironically, just as Mariana is using the turntables as an escape from the spotlight, many women have chosen to use them as the way in. Mariana can't hide her disappointment with women who use their looks to get gigs and publicity. Other female DJs who are far more expert, such as Cuttin' Candy, Mariana's mentor, get less recognition because "they flaunt their skills, not their bodies." Some female DJs even play clubs topless—"the ones and twos" that their audiences are paying attention to are certainly not the turntables. Mariana resents women who use their bodies instead of their skills because what they do undermines women's already vulnerable place in the culture.

Spinning was a safe way for Mariana to be part of hip-hop culture not only because it hid her body but also because it hid her privilege. Here was a white upper-middle-class girl, a next-door type going to an expensive college prep school—perfect on paper—who felt anything but ordinary. She swooned at the life stories she heard slip from her favorite rappers' lips. They described a world she thought was tragic and beautiful in equal parts. She wanted to be part of a community more raw and real than the liberal lip service and fake smiles of her classmates' mothers and fathers. This is part of why she was attracted to dangerous men, part of why she drank and crossed the lines of her own square upbringing, part of why she got behind the turntables despite every indication that it was a man's place. Mariana wanted a place of her own that allowed her to contribute to hip-hop culture but still feel "safe."

By DJing, she could participate in the music she loved without the risk of exposing herself. Paradoxically, she could win the respect of those around her while in retreat from them. Hidden behind the booth, she was no longer a growing girl with an exploding body or a privileged white chick. She was a music connoisseur, a hip-hop aficionado, an artist. She joined the collective scream of her generation without ever opening her mouth. "DJing," she explains, "can be a way of expressing myself without ever feeling too vulnerable . . . without ever truly expressing myself."

Shut Up and Bling

After we talk for a while, Mariana and I reminisce about all of the female MCs of the eighties—fierce women with brazen tongues who seemed to predict a future that never happened. She doesn't have to search long among her hundreds of records before locating some of her favorite oldies: Roxanne Chante, Queen Latifah, MC Lyte.

She laughs as she takes the vinyl out of a weathered sleeve and puts it on one of her turntables. As a commanding but playful female voice starts rapping, she holds out the jacket to me: "1998," she tells me. "So fly." The three solidly built girl members of Salt-N-Pepa grace the cover in spandex, head to toe. Their gold chains and African-print hats look to be making their heads too heavy to hold up. The song is appropriately called "Spinderella's Not a Fella (But a Girl D.J.)."

Mariana pulls out another sleeve, this one with Monie Love on the front in an orange coat, big white socks, black Timberlands, and a giant pink bow in her natural black hair. It is her 1993 Prince-produced *Born 2 B.R.E.E.D.* Lest you worry that the title indicates a barbaric message, she translates the righteous acronym for you: "Build relationships where education and enlightenment dominate."

Mariana and I bemoan the contrast between these fierce women and the skinnier, objectified tokens we have today. Foxy Brown is not much more than a glorified video ho, delivering uninteresting and depersonalized lyrics when she's not defending herself in court for assault charges. Lil' Kim, after what appears to be way too much plastic surgery, looks as white and objectified as your average boy-band backup dancer. Even Lauryn Hill, the great hope for girls in hip-hop, went down in a blaze of preaching and politicking. There are still a few reasons to cling to the dream that hip-hop could be a home for female fast-talkers: Lady Sovereign, Medusa, Jean Grae, but these women tend to stay outside of mainstream hip-hop.[†]

Corporate rap, as entertaining as it may be, isn't much more than a succession of macho braggarts throwing clichés over hot beats while being gyrated upon by practically naked women. Women are objectified not just in the videos but often in the lyrics as well. The notorious R. Kelly, for example, compares his female prospect to a car in one of his recent songs. I'd quote the lyrics, but I don't want to pay R. Kelly so I can publicize his already overexposed misogyny.

Not exactly the enlightenment that Monie Love, or the rest of hip-hop's female fan base, was hoping for. Today's rap voice has gotten even more misogynistic and less creative than it was when I was leaning an ear toward the high school house-party ciphers. R. Kelly's car metaphor looks almost charming next to some of his other lines, such as "I like the crotch on you." Others are just flat-out offensive. Obie Trice, a Detroit rapper signed to Eminem's Shady Records, urges fat women to hide their "blubber" so as not to offend him while he scours the crowd for thin girls.

Women around my age have learned that our place in hip-hop is as comic relief or status symbols. We are encouraged to buy the albums, laugh off the offensive lyrics, and dance to the good beats in the club. The most accessible and least risky way to be involved in the culture of hip-hop is to cultivate the image of a female fan. Shell out hard-earned money on the music's favorite brands or imitations, and keep your mouth shut. Rely on your body and the requisite leather bags, designer shoes, gold chains as your only forms of expression.

The message is being sent to young women rap fans that their role is to consume and costume: Nelly swipes a credit card down the ass

---

[†]Lady Sovereign, a quick-tongued and side-ponytailed Brit from a working-class background, signed with Jay-Z's Def Jam Recordings, one of the largest labels in the business, in 2006.

crack of one of his dancers, White Chocolate, in the video for his hit song "Tip Drill." (Don't worry, because of the video's nearly X-rated content, it is played only on after-hours programs in America, such as *BET Uncut,* when all of the parents have gone to bed.) The video was the last straw for black feminists at Spelman College, who hosted a series of public discussions on corporate rap and misogyny in March 2006, followed by a promise that they would boycott Nelly's pre-arranged appearance there in April. Nelly made no apologies to his outraged female fans; instead, he told *FHM*: "It's acting. Halle Berry can go on film and get the dog shit freaked out of her, and she wins an Oscar. I swipe a credit card down the crack of a girl's butt, and I'm demoralizing women?"†

Well, yes, Nelly dear. There is a difference between reveling in the objectification of women and creating a piece of art that explores the meaning of loneliness.

Nelly is obviously a few gold teeth short of a mouthful, but when speaking with MSNBC.com about female complicity, he made a little more sense: "This is a grown woman that told me, 'Go ahead, do it.' I never forced any of these girls to do anything. This is a job, they agreed to do it, they knew everything that was into it and these girls would be doing it whether Nelly was shooting a video or not."

He's got a point. What about the women in these videos? Aren't they willingly contributing to a culture that emphasizes only their capacity to buy and bootie-dance? Don't they have a message? Don't they want their voices to be heard? In fact, White Chocolate has made a cottage industry out of her swipe of fame and now hosts parties where attendees are invited to swipe their own credit cards down her infamous crack. So apparently there *is* a new role for women in hip-hop—that of hired-out ass crack. White Chocolate told *The Atlanta Journal-Constitution:* "I'm not representing anybody but myself. No one is exploiting me. No one is making me do anything I don't want to do. . . . I've been in about twenty-seven music videos doing my thing.

†Nelly was referring to Halle Berry's role in the 2001 film *Monster's Ball,* where she plays a widow who gets involved with her late husband's executioner.

I've got a five-bedroom house on a half-acre of land. Drive a Jag. If anything, hip-hop has been very, very good to this woman right here."

The bottom line, as so many rappers tell us, is "the Benjamins." Corporate rap is based on hot beats and Nelly-style objectification, and women such as White Chocolate make good money buying in. Akiba Solomon, a hip-hop critic and feminist, explains: "These girls are smart entrepreneurs. They are capitalists." Hip-hop may have begun as a free-form cultural expression with liberating potential for all, but it has become an industry made up of generic hit factories—built on the bodies of women, mostly black.

Unfortunately, money also flows in the other direction. A Gucci bag, a gym membership, a new CD all drain already paltry bank accounts. Debt is rampant among the underemployed and overenthused female fan base of hip-hop. Even if they can't rap, they want to look like they could dance for the rapper. Even if they can't afford the name brands in the latest videos, they want to appear as if they can. As Anya Kamenetz, the *Village Voice* writer behind the Generation Debt series, writes: "Hip-hop culture is the 800-pound gorilla of youth marketing."

Girls like Mariana, like Bonita, like White Chocolate learn early on that they are welcome to consume hip-hop to their hearts' content, but their contributions will be limited. Mariana found a loophole. Bonita is hitting the gym and gathering diet tips from female family members. White Chocolate decided that her chances of carving out a hip-hop identity with her clothes on were slim to none.

Where the answer is money, the question is usually power.

Naked Power

In *Female Chauvinist Pigs,* Ariel Levy argues that girls today have misconstrued the feminist message about power through liberation. Instead of understanding the previous generation's conviction that power and freedom come through critiquing society's rigid sexual stereotypes, we show our tits. Female chauvinist pigs (FCPs), she argues, essentially equate promiscuity with power. Despite what the

Girls Gone Wild empire or *Maxim* would have us believe, Levy maintains, acting like horny dudes does not liberated women make.

But in a world that communicates through every click on the remote and every turn of the page that female bodies get attention and money (and words do not), is it any wonder that girls willingly shed their clothes and pose in the pursuit of power? Is it any wonder that we obsess over every little thing we put in our mouths in anticipation of this future unveiling—whether it be for a video camera or just for a cute boy? Is it any wonder that we are a generation dead set on carving our bodies into monuments of the power we so want to possess?

The answer, of course, is no, and Levy recognizes it: "Adolescents are not inventing this culture of exhibitionism and conformity with their own fledgling creative powers. Teens are reflecting back our slobbering culture in miniature." FCPs watch the latest music videos where the woman topping the charts is the same one mounting a greasy male dancer. They watch America's richest twenty-somethings gallivanting off to lavish parties in a poverty of clothing. They don't hear these women asserting liberation philosophy; they listen to their moans and giggles in leaked sex tapes. Feigning stupidity and starving, not feminism, seems to be the most direct route to fame and fortune.

Levy hints at her understanding that beneath the bare breasts of the average FCP is a girl with a heart hungry for attention (the juvenile version of power): "Proving that you are hot, worthy of lust, and necessarily that you seek to provoke lust is still exclusively women's work. It is not enough to be successful, rich, and accomplished." It is not enough to get straight A's or win a national debate award. It is not enough to devote your Saturdays to the soup kitchen and your Sundays to planting trees. It is not enough to be a great artist or a great scientist or a great writer. All of these things may make you successful, but power is another matter entirely.

Popularity is powerful. Beauty is powerful. Confidence is powerful. Being smart, outspoken, dedicated, and/or college-bound is potentially powerful but also potentially disempowering in the slick social world of high school. If you are considered tense, for example, you lose power. If you talk too much, become too emotional, or "take things too seriously," you lose power. If you "make a big deal" out of age-old traditions of female objectification, you lose power. As Levy writes, "Raunch culture, then, isn't an entertainment option, it's a litmus test of female uptightness."

In Spanish class in eighth grade, a boy whose attention I coveted used to throw his pencil a few feet in front of his desk and ask me to retrieve it. I knew what was going on. I'd heard my hip-hop-culture-inspired nickname—"Ghetto booty. Hey, bend over, ghetto booty"—whispered as I made my way down the hallway with a gaggle of girl-friends. I had seen the quizzes scrawled in bad-boy handwriting on notes passed in class: "Who has the best butt in the 8th grade?" There was no question about it: It wasn't my straight A's or my big heart that the boys noticed, it was my shapely butt.

Most of the time I would tell this dark-eyed boy to go get his own pencil, that I wasn't his servant, but I would be sure to punctuate my go-girl message with a coquettish laugh. Every few times, I would summon up the courage to get up from my desk, saunter over to the chewed pencil, bend over, and pick it up with a flourish. The boy in question would swoon. I felt a little bad, but I also felt undeniably powerful.

In that same year, I won the schoolwide spelling bee. I remember being horrified when my name was announced over the loud-speaker—as if the small bit of coolness I had collected through months of self-conscious nonchalance and detached ambivalence had suddenly morphed into a steaming, stinking pile of lame. I picked up the pencil with exaggerated flair twice that day, trying to make my crush forget my p's and q's.

I have heard this sentiment repeated by the women I have inter-viewed. Smart, accomplished, and thoughtful, they know that none of this is as instantaneously powerful as their appearances. They make an effort to resist this truth by cultivating their minds, bulking up their bank accounts, saving the world at every turn, but it is thrown in their faces over and over again. Flirtation, a hot bod, and sultry sophistication are all immediately powerful. The rest is slow redemption. Our frustration with this situation seems to do nothing but make us less effective at dealing with it.

Truth is, many perfect girls indulge the power we possess through our looks—we may flirt with the boss, take a free drink, ask for a higher grade with a low-cut shirt on. We chase away the guilt with the excuse that we are just taking advantage of our disadvantage, subverting the system, reclaiming our right to equality. But deep inside, we know it is an act of desperation—a flailing grab for a log in level-five rapids. We bet on our bodies in the exchange of power because we fear we have no more powerful currency in the real world. Sadly, we are often right.

7

What Men Want: The Truth About Attraction, Porn, and the Pursuit

It is 2:00 A.M. at one of those "it" bars in the Meatpacking District of Manhattan. The place is packed wall to wall with women who are too little and men who are too much. Thin blondes in backless, sleeveless, braless outfits wobble on knee-high stiletto boots and hold pink cosmopolitans precariously balanced between two dainty fingers. Men lean in toward their tiny necks, trying too hard over the loud music, their one extra spray of cologne making the women cough as they giggle. The men's tabs will be left open too long, the women will hobble around on those three-inch heels all night despite blisters—symbols of their twin determination.

I go outside to get a breath of fresh air and huddle near the giant heat lamp by the heavy metal doors. The wind comes off the Hudson River in violent bursts, sending a wave of foot stomping and arm rubbing through the long line of those waiting impatiently to get in. They remain steadfast, imagining a utopia of beautiful people free from hang-ups and loaded with cash inside.

The bouncer fulfills every stereotype—linebacker body, black, gruff, and unimpressed with the twiggy women who bat their eyelashes at him, dropping the names of bartenders who no longer work there. At one point, he reaches for the velvet rope to let in a busboy who went on an emergency lime run, and a couple of girls in miniskirts and faux fur coats lunge for the inside. The busboy slips in, and the bouncer replaces the velvet rope just in time for the two girls to clothesline themselves. Some guys in tight sweaters and designer jeans smoking next to me barely muffle their laughter and holler, "Oh, poor ladies! I'd let you in." One of the girls smooths her hair back into place and tilts her head to the side, as if to say, "Aren't I cute and helpless?" while the other reapplies her lipstick. I feel like puking, and it's not because I'm drunk.

Just an average Friday night between the sexes.

The dating scene is a meat market—still the hunters and the hunted, the stalkers and the prey, the fine pieces of flesh and those who want to "kill it." Sure, men and women now trade roles more freely— sometimes the hunted is a doe-eyed guy and the hunter a fierce woman ready to lead—but the dance is still the same. The only reason I can get into this particular spot, given that I am physically incapable of three-inch heels and am a disaster with a mascara wand, is that my friend Pete really is the bartender. He is the one who mixes the strong drinks for the hopeful young lads and lasses early in the night and mixes the weak ones two hours later, when they are drunk with disappointment and debt, or sloppily licking each other's faces in momentary triumph, hoping like hell that the gin doesn't wear off.

So why, night after night, tab after tab, blister after blister, do we repeat this strange and usually unsatisfying mating ritual?

We want to have fun. We want to dance. We want to relieve stress. We want to be young and reckless. We want to meet people who don't bore us with the same predictable stories. We want to believe in the magic of chemistry. We want to earn bragging rights about the posh club we got into. We want to feel lusted after and to lust. We want to numb, forget, fuck.

The truest answer is that we want to be seen and we want to be loved.

To Be Seen

All of that TV watching and magazine reading provides us with a dangerously narrow and boring definition of "hot" when we are young, and little material to broaden that definition as we get older. The yesteryear posters of teenage heartthrobs tacked on bedroom walls from Sacramento to St. Louis—Alyssa Milano, Jason Priestley—and those of today—Jessica Alba, Chad Michael Murray—are emblematic of what both boys and girls think beauty will look like when they are old enough to embody or entrap it. Twenty-eight-year-old Brian of Colorado Springs, Colorado, believes his apple-pie definition of beauty was born in front of the "almighty MTV" and hasn't changed much since. He lists his favorite attributes: "Pretty face, small ass, little body fat. Blond or brown hair. Give me head cheerleader over exotic beauty any day." The color of the hair seems to be the only element up for interpretation.

Dimitriy, a Russian-born twenty-year-old, unemotionally explains: "Pornography, pop music, and hip-hop videos influence me to look at every single imperfection of a female." In the next breath, he expresses that he thinks girls should "be taught to love their bodies by parents and through school." What role could he play in this? I ask. He just shakes his head. "I don't know what I can personally do, because I am not affected." But when I push him to consider whether he feels pressured to look a certain way, he answers, "Girls are just as shallow as guys, so there is a constant need to look your best."

Another of my students, twenty-two and Dominican, admits, "I feel pressure to be fit, and it comes from going to clubs and other social gatherings where a lot of men obviously spend a lot of time on their bodies, as far as working out. Because of this, I allot an hour a day for four days a week. That way I don't go overboard with the pressure."

Sadly, the only thing modern about the modern meat-market scene, besides the occasional reversal of roles, is that men are starting to feel as pressured as women to conform to a cookie-cutter mold of what is attractive. Every guy who responded to my official survey and every guy I informally surveyed over a beer or a long walk confirmed that he feels pressure to be fit. Brian admits to caring a lot about looking good. He explains, "If I'm not having sex with quality girls, I start to feel pressure." He adds without a hint of sarcasm, "Sometimes I wish I could have an eating disorder that I could control. It would be great to be able to puke after eating too much pizza some night or not eat at all for a couple of days. My genetics fucked me. I work hard just to be in average shape."

Part of this new pressure can be attributed to the popularization of magazines—sometimes called "lad mags"—such as *Maxim, FHM, Stuff, Details, GQ,* and *Men's Health.* Though they are notorious for featuring half-naked women with thin, taut bodies—an old story— they also introduce a modern message: six-pack-abs exercises, fashion trends, and sex tips for guys. *Men's Health* is filled from cover to cover with ways to make men as neurotic as women about their bodies: "Flip the Fat Switch," "Transform Yourself," and "Lose a Pound Per Week!" On the fleeting—thank God—FX sitcom *Starved,* which made light of eating disorders for a few laughs, three of the four afflicted main characters were men.

So in this increasingly level playing field of airbrushed abs and steel thighs, both young women *and* young men are being pressured to fit a form. The mass media don't run just one loop anymore but two—Barbie *and* Ken. In fact, recent research indicates that there is a rise in men suffering not just from obsessive working out or the taste of those godawful muscle-building shakes but from full-blown eating disorders. In America alone, 1 million men have eating disorders, a 30 percent increase since 1972. The age at which men develop eating disorders appears to be a few years older than women, whose average onset is seventeen. The eating-disorder specialist Margot Maine reports on the unique nature of some men's suffering: "New terms such as 'muscle dysmorphia' and 'reverse anorexia' have been coined to describe their eating disorders, reflecting society's emphasis on strength and power and the changing ideals for men's bodies." None of these terms, however, appears in the psychological diagnostic manual at this time.

Like minorities, many men may be undiagnosed because of the misconception that eating disorders are only a female disease. While we may not have gotten hip as a society to the fact that men are suffering from such disorders, it would be hard to deny that they are suffering for beauty (as women have since the first eyebrow tweezer was invented). The beauty industry has taken note of men's anxiety about their bodies and created cosmetics lines and hair removal products for them. Nail and hair salons are no longer women's country—now men get manicures, pedicures, and professional waxes. Men are just learning what women have known all too well for far too long—that there is a slippery slope from beauty regimen to straight-up tyranny.

———

One twenty-year-old guy who described himself as "lower-middle-class and fatherless" wrote this in reluctant answer to my question "Have you ever struggled with an eating disorder?":

Okay. Well, I guess so. Back in high school I used to be heavier, by a lot. I'm six foot, and I'd say I weighed in at 240 pounds, and not the captain of the football team kind of 240. I never had a good opinion about the way I looked, so I did what any fat person does to be accepted, be funny. At the end of my senior year, my way too much beloved girlfriend broke up with me. I was an emotional wreck, if ever a guy in a potentially published statement could admit to being one. I didn't eat for three weeks, and if I did, it was quickly vomited in a fit of distress soon after. I survived solely on a diet of Nestea Cool.

Family tried to get me to eat, but I wasn't really in a state to hear them, it was all one big depressed blur. I dropped 40 pounds in those three weeks, and even after I still didn't eat much. In the following two months, I lost 40 more. It certainly was a far cry from healthy, and I burned away a lot of muscle mass. Even so, afterwards, once the overdramatic emotional issues were resolved, I found myself feeling a lot better. A lot of aspects of my personality changed, much of it in a way that, a year earlier, I would have considered a lot shallower.

Any natural affinity we, as individuals, might have for more flesh or crooked teeth or short stature is washed away in a flood of airbrushed images. When you are young and trying to fit in, taking the time and energy to notice what you really crave would be like resisting a force feeding day in and day out. Holding on to your mother's love of your unique beauty practically requires growing up in a cabin in the middle of nowhere. With no electricity. Alone.

Making one narrow standard of beauty is the aim of corporate culture; if we acknowledged a variety of beauties, women would spend far less money on diet books and miracle pills, and men wouldn't be shelling out for designer labels and Rogaine. A huge business is built on making us feel unattractive. The marketing of inadequacy also undermines our view of ourselves and how we understand our worth in the world. Instead of relying on our own perception, we look outside ourselves for constant affirmation.

Every little girl, at one point or another, whether secretly or openly, wishes she could be a model in order to make her beauty official. Megan Hinton and I were walking around the Citadel mall in Colorado Springs aimlessly one average twelve-year-old's afternoon when a "scout" from a modeling agency approached us and told us that we were both "raw beauties that needed to be cultivated." Neither of us knew what *cultivated* meant, but we were sure this was our chance to prove, once and for all (mostly to ourselves, of course), that we were pretty. We begged our parents to let us pay the exorbitant fee for the start-up classes, but they wisely refused. I remember stomping up to my room and staring at myself in the sticker-covered mirror nailed to the back of my bedroom door. Was it real? Could I be pretty?

A lot of guys, whether they admit it or not, get involved in sports or join a band, in part, for the same reason. Coolness is certified by a captain spot on the basketball team or a drum set in the garage. Just as girls dream that the walk down a fashion runway would lead them to the end of their wondering—*Am I beautiful? Will I ever be?*—boys hold fast to the football and their delusion that if they score a touchdown, they will finally end the game and their own insecurities. At school talent nights, they freestyle a trail of clichéd, machismo rhymes, hoping that some girl will follow them. Both sexes wish for a quick fix for their self-image.

We walk around wondering what we look like through most of adolescence and, with less urgency, for the rest of our lives. Our inability to really see ourselves imbues the judgments of strangers with tremendous and undue value. When I get catcalled on the street—"Hey, beautiful. Hey, smile, beautiful. You're too pretty to worry"—I am slightly annoyed but also oddly swayed. *I hate when people tell me to smile. Huh, a stranger thinks I'm beautiful today. That's nice. I knew this shirt looked good.* A man I have never met can instantly put a little swing in my step.

Unfortunately, it works in the other direction as well. When I go to the bar feeling a little proud of myself for getting the mascara on my lashes instead of my eyelids, and wearing that new shirt I'm not totally sure about, and no one offers to buy me a drink, I sometimes go home feeling deflated. *This shirt really isn't that cute. I need to pluck my eyebrows. Who would buy a drink for a girl with hair as frizzy as mine?* Again, a bar full of half-drunk strangers has the power to make me hang my head.

We are dependent on the kindness of strangers because of the onslaught of skinny-and-fit female or tall-and-toned male images that we suffer daily. We become unsure of our own sight so early on, convinced that the only accurate view of ourselves is outside ourselves. We search for signs that we resemble the mold—an invite to homecoming from a football player, a wink in the elevator from a cute coworker, admission into an exclusive downtown club. We feel, in these brief, usually fruitless encounters, like we are being seen when really we are just being noticed. The difference is significant.

Being noticed is ordinary, fleeting, and impersonal. Being seen is extraordinary, lasting, and intimate. Being noticed is common and only skin-deep. Being seen is rare and profound. It is what happens when you stay up all night talking in a stranger's car because the conversation is so good you forget to reach for the door handle. Suddenly it is dusk outside and your stomach is growling and your future feels as if it is laid out in front of you like a highway in the desert. Being seen is when your boyfriend knows that the horseshoe scar on your knee was from when you fell in the gravel of the playground in fourth grade playing flag football, and he adores it. Being seen is a hand on the small of your back as you walk through a doorway, a glass of water when you are coughing in the middle of the night, his making a passing reference to something you said so long ago *you* barely remember it. Being seen is when your girlfriend asks, "Why do you seem sad?" before you have realized that you are, indeed, sad. Being seen is rarely about physical beauty. Being seen is never about being buff or thin.

Being noticed, by contrast, is easy. It is par for the course for most women, especially young, to be noticed, a deeply engrained ritual of our culture. Men watch. Women are watched. In our reality-TV culture, ordinary girls, as well as models and actresses, become accustomed to being objectified. The most significant example of this, of course, is the Girls Gone Wild empire, now estimated to be worth $100 million, built entirely on the naked breasts of spring-breakers, sorority girls, and brainiacs losing their minds and shirts on a bender. These women are compelled to take it off by their own bottomless hunger for attention—which, on a deeper level, is a sign of feeling fundamentally unseen.

Maxim has a section specifically for the "girl next door," where "readers put their girls on display for us"; one (supposed) girlfriend, half-naked against a wall of wooden slats, is accompanied by the disturbing title "Trapped in a Sauna," and the boys at *Maxim* have written the caption "The background and the subject force the intrinsic question: Why the hell get married?" In other words, why create a relationship with a woman when you can just trap her in your local sauna or ogle her in your favorite lad mag? Perhaps the more disturbing part of this equation is not the drooling *Maxim* followers but the girls who misinterpret the drool as a sign that they are finally being seen. *Cosmopolitan* magazine, the U.K. edition, ran a recent article to convince women that their objectification is their responsibility: "23 ways to get bare-faced confidence: If stripping off is an instant no-no rather than a yes, yes, yes, you need a body confidence makeover." It seems we are all supposed to be after the same goal: getting women naked and on display.

Ben, twenty-seven, of Minneapolis, explains, "I think the first messages I ever got about women's bodies and attractiveness came from magazines and TV. The messages I got from those sources were, in my memory, less about which specific body types constituted attractiveness (although I think I recognized that big breasts were pretty significant and sexual) and more the general objectification and sexualization of women's bodies that goes on in most media. Despite my parents' constant critique of those images, that way of seeing women stuck with me for a while."

The Porn Question

The elephant in the room during any conversation about attraction, of course, is pornography. Men, while around women, usually pretend it doesn't exist unless the women bring it up, and women, for their part, rarely bring it up. As a result, it festers in both of their minds, a telling silence in an otherwise candid conversation, a pretend game in an otherwise authentic intimacy. Neither is sure he or she can handle where the conversation might lead, namely to the question "But how does that change the way you see *my* body?"

Most of the men I have talked to about this critical element in the alchemy of attraction supply me with the standard "separation-of-porn-and-real-life theory"—that the bodies they choose to look at on the Internet or in videos (magazines aren't interactive enough these days) have absolutely nothing to do with the bodies they choose to love in real life. On a purely rational level, this makes no sense. The brain stores information and recalls it when similar circumstances arise. It is why you recognize a cheeseburger when you see one, even if you haven't eaten one in months. Seeing a naked woman in the flesh again, even if you haven't seen one in months, is going to remind you of other naked women you have encountered—whether in the digital or the real world. We can hope that your brain's ability to recall allows you to react appropriately to familiar stimuli, biting the cheeseburger and not the naked woman, for example. (Or whatever floats her boat.)

Porn is not evil. I am no *Hustler*-burning prude. Porn plays a role in a lot of people's sexual lives, couples' and women's included. Sexual arousal is multidimensional (visual, sensual, emotional). I wish I had access to some kind of mood-altering URL that could instantaneously transport me to an imaginary land of sexy, fleshy real women and men whose sensuality was so powerful it could push the deadlines, appointments, and errands from my mind. (A Google search for "feminist porn" surfaces *Dragon Lady: The Dungeon Mistress* and other disturbingly funny titles.)

Having said that, I feel very uncomfortable considering the implications of dudes everywhere spending even half an hour a day staring at girls' bodies that have been, more often than not, surgically enhanced, covered in makeup, and airbrushed practically into animation. The days of finding big brothers' *Playboys*, filled with tan lines and fan bangs, are long gone. Those big-haired women look pudgy and blemished compared with their faker, thinner turn-of-the-century equivalents. One guy told me that he actually remembers hiding in the attic next to his father's stash and kissing a centerfold square on her two-dimensional lips. She was overwhelmingly womanly to him, round in the right places, lusciously intimidating. He understates, "Nowadays porn seems pretty different." A little boy logging on to his dad's favorite porn site today might feel like he is looking at a picture of a body strangely similar to his own, with the exception of the Photoshopped giant fake tits.

Even if men's porn viewing is constantly counterbalanced by a social critique—most guys I know are hip to the fact that they are supporting a less than feminist business—they can't control the way these images affect their sexual preferences over time. Sex drive, like hunger, is not easily circumscribed. Preference is shaped by biology *and* conditioning. A guy can't make himself like a round belly if all he's stared at for months on end is flat-as-a-board tummies. He can't convince himself, no matter how politically conscious he is, to prefer small breasts if massive breasts are what he has conditioned himself to get turned on to.

Guy after guy has told me that he feels as if he possesses two totally separate sexualities, the one in front of the screen and the one in front of the girlfriend. I'm skeptical. I know that when I get a pop-up ad for Häagen-Dazs while checking my bank account balance, I end up craving ice cream, not the frozen yogurt already sitting in my freezer.

On an emotional level, of course, it is more complicated than that. How much association is there really? One guy puts a twist on the old separation-of-porn-and-real-life theory: "Pornography plays no role in what I am looking for in real life. When I'm looking at porn, I'm looking at porn. I'm not thinking about work, not worrying about my health, and I'm sure as shit not wondering if the girl being sexed up by a German scientist and his evil Frankenshlong creation would make a good girlfriend. That's silly. Don't worry about the porn."

Doesn't the flesh-and-blood version kick the digital version's ass any day, simply by virtue of being real and unpredictable? Another guy confirms, "Porn made me hate fake tits, I'll tell you that much." Since the first women were hunting down dinner and the first men were gathering the sticks to cook it, we have all loved the chase. It is not the ready and waiting that really turns us on; it is the real and unsure, the surprising and rewarding, the four-dimensional and hard to get.

With the wide variety of images available nowadays—women of all ethnicities and sizes in all kinds of strange situations—could porn actually serve as a force that widens the definition of beauty, unlike mainstream magazines, which show only one brand of pretty? A dude theorizes: "Whatever you are into, there is a site out there for you. This could either be considered positive or negative based on your values when it comes to sex, but I think for some it's positive because you don't have to look at rib cages if you don't want to. I find it a lot more attractive to see naturally lit, not-too-glammed-up people together, rather than some posed shit."

That's all the *good* news. The bad news was explored in Pamela Paul's recent book, *Pornified,* which contains exhaustive interviews with men, mostly young, talking about the huge force fake women have played in their real lives. Paul discovers that many men *do* make connections between the porn they favor and the women they seek out when they turn off the video or close the window on the screen. In fact, some men's lives have been destroyed by their dissatisfaction with life (i.e., women) outside porn.

Harrison, one of the men Paul interviews, reports difficulty even being intimate with real women because his sexual imagination was so bound up with perfect porn-star bodies. He worries: "Had I ruined my sex life permanently?" He was also showing up late for appointments, staying at home on weekend nights, and having trouble finding or keeping a job because he would lose track of time looking at online porn. Eventually he cut back on his browsing time, explaining that he felt like he was "losing control" when "porn began affecting [his] thoughts with regard to [his] day-to-day life." He still struggles to keep his mind from wandering to a two-dimensional porn star when he is with a woman in the flesh.

I heard the same thing, rarely but strongly expressed, from a few men I interviewed. Usually these men worried about their expectations, not about the size or shape of women's bodies but about behavior: "It causes me to have unrealistic expectations for what my sexual experiences should be like," confessed one guy. And another reflected, "In general, I'd have to say that pornography affects what I view as sexy or hot in a behavioral way much more than a visual attractiveness sort of way." And finally, one young man confessed, "Watching submissive women indulge every fantasy of the dominant male in a porno is, at the same time, arousing and horrifying. I hate myself for watching and being turned on by a submissive, weak-willed woman, but perhaps it's that vulnerability that I'm attracted to. It's just arousing to see a woman be dominated sometimes."

Perhaps men's pornography preferences are a fun-house mirror of their real-life desires, for a female personality rather than a female body. Or as one guy put it, "Pornography is the carnival sideshow of attractiveness." Guys who seek out vulnerable women off the screen want submissive porn on it. Guys who seek out authoritative women in life want leather and whips on their websites. One thing is for sure: Men who are worth a damn generally do not see porn stars as physical templates for finding women they want to have relationships with. If a man's penchant for women with big tits and tiny waists disqualifies you from dating him, that's a little gift from your old friend Cindy Margolis, the most downloaded woman in history.

Just as mainstream media affect people differently—holding sway on some impressionable minds and being strongly rejected by others—porn is surely only as influential as a man (or woman) allows it to be. Porn doesn't shape attraction. People using and producing porn shape attraction. If women and men were given more access to porn that spoke to their unique desires, featured women and men of various shapes and ethnicities, and highlighted personalities instead of, well, you fill in the blank, then maybe it could turn us all on to the power of bodies that don't fit a boring, unachievable mold.

"Hot Girls": Bingeing for Boys

I call one of my guy friends from happy hour and tell him he should stop by after he finishes work for the day. "Are there any hot girls there?" he asks, a question I have heard perhaps five, maybe ten thousand times since puberty.

"Well, I don't know," I sass. "None of them have pulled out state-issued ID cards certifying their official 'hotness.' Could be fakes."

He chuckles good-naturedly, but I know his decision about whether to come really depends on the number of women he would find attractive and potentially want to have sex with (keep in mind it is only 5:00 P.M. on a frickin' Wednesday). And I have learned from experience that when guys say this, it isn't that they don't want also to hang out with me or the rest of their old, familiar crew. It isn't even, strangely enough, that they actually plan on approaching any of these so-called hot girls and trying to make a connection. It is more like a reflexive scratch for a Darwinian itch. The more I think about it, the more I come to believe that it isn't about the hot girls at all. It is about self-worth.

I have decided that "Are there any hot girls there?" is shorthand for "I need to fill an existential hole in the center of my soul." I am only half kidding. I believe that, in the same way my girlfriends and I have often felt black holes at our centers, my guy friends have felt something dark and insatiable. Instead of trying to fill it up with food, or starve it out entirely, guys are convinced beautiful women and lots of money will make them feel full. (Much of the time it appears that making the money is also, ultimately, about getting the women.)

Even at five years old, my brother and his best friend's favorite pretend game was that they were gun-toting heroes who traveled all over our treacherous backyard and throughout the imaginary enemy–filled house looking for "Mrs. Sexy Woman," who, of course, needed saving. Those little guys were convinced that the most exciting thing they could do was find a sexy woman. While we, the perfect girls, try to numb the pain of imperfection with chocolate cake or proud defiance of it, men are searching every city and suburban town for a woman who will symbolize their worth. In this culture of women's bodies plastered on billboards, popping up on computer screens, selling every imaginable product, we all learn the lesson that beauty is the most universal symbol of success. Women seek to turn themselves into that symbol. Men seek to find a woman to serve as the symbol for them.

Guys search for the bar with the hot girls on a Saturday night and empty their wallets for the cover charge once they find it as if possessed. *Could the sex be that good?* I used to wonder, but then I realized they weren't actually having that much sex, and their stories sounded more like comedy than like ecstasy. In fact, most of the time, the stories from the night before include the crew of boys who already know one another standing around and making fun of the one guy brave enough to hit on a woman who isn't vying for their tips ("hot girl" bartenders are the coward's favorite ego boost).

In this ritual, packs of broad-shouldered young men wander the streets in search of "hot girls," with something strangely familiar in their glazed-over stares and desperate, hungry searches. They can never get enough. There is always some other bar that is supposed to have even "hotter girls." And even when they find a "hot girl" willing to entertain their attention for a time, their eyes dart about, wondering if they are missing out on the "hotter hot girl" across the dance floor. They are eternally unsatisfied.

While women are trying to be the perfect girls, these guys are out trying to find them. But the perfect girl doesn't exist. We are all chasing after an imaginary woman. A witty guy friend of mine explains it this way: "What's tough is when you go out with a bunch of guys, all of whom presumably/supposedly like the same thing (busty, skinny, slutty), and then you find this little gem in the corner who has glasses and busted teeth and a book bag (three things that you find attractive). This gem has a few flaws which you find endearing, but to the group, she's a fallback option if nothing better comes along. I usually don't care and will talk it up, but even I have stopped myself thinking, *Maybe Barbie will be next.*"

The never-ending search for "hot girls" is not just about sex but about ego, the compulsion to find a woman who will make a guy's friends and family and fragile sense of self shout, "You are *the* man!" The search stems from deep insecurity and a fundamental fear that the world will not provide a decent partner alongside whom he can ride off into the sunset. As a friend, Jim,* explains, "If anything, guys are attracted to the prospect of someone enjoying their company, which I am sure is a mutual feeling between the sexes. The guys I hang out with love the idea of possibilities. We know that not all women are attracted to the same type; therefore, the more women there are in a place, the greater the chance one would be crazy enough to dig one of our dumb asses."

As in playing the lotto, guys figure that the more opportunities they play, the more chances they have of winning the jackpot. Their fate seems to rest on the slim chance of picking the right numbers, on the right night, in the right bar. As Brian puts it, "It's not like baseball, where one out of three is a good average. There are so many variables, besides her reciprocated attraction, that go into a successful night (if she's single, who she's there with, her angry, less-attractive friend who's been watching guys talk to her all night). Meeting at a bar and actually sleeping with a truly 'hot girl' is a rare occasion. It's the holy grail."

It does seem as if guys are searching for something divine, grasping in a dimly lit bar for a soft hand that makes them feel like the world is a place of possibilities, like they too are worthy of enjoying beauty and wonder. It isn't usually a casual search but a concerted, dogged effort. Another guy in his twenties reflects, "Whenever I was successful at a bar (hookup, phone number, intense ball-blueing flirting) was when I could not care less about picking anybody up. The hungry, wolf-eyed look isn't attractive."

Just like a woman scanning her refrigerator on a night home alone, searching for something, anything, that will make her feel less lonely, the man scans the crowd at the bar restlessly, never full. Even when he rests his eyes on someone who will do, and makes a reluctant choice—the chocolate-fudge ice cream or the tall brunette with the long legs—he already knows that he will still feel empty when the connection fizzles. He hardly tastes it, hardly enjoys the experience. It was all in the thrill of the possibility that something would satisfy his cravings, and now it is over and confirmed—there is no food sweet enough and no girl "hot" enough to make him feel complete.

Women sometimes choose boys over a binge too. A Carrie Bradshaw devotee gets dolled up to go out on a Saturday night when the buzz in the air is palpable and the possibilities endless; she drinks to take the nervous edge off, waits hopefully or pursues bravely, and usually lands a guy who wants to take her home—making her feel, if only for the last few hours of the night, chosen.

When the sun comes up, she turns over and is rudely awakened to the reality that the guy is sort of an asshole or really kind of stupid. Being chosen doesn't feel like an honor as she slinks back to her own house, changes into her dad's old shirt and some sweatpants, curls up in her own messy sheets. They both linger in their separate beds, in their separate, lonely mornings—the "hot girl" and the boy who beat the odds. Eventually they will purge the night from their memories, but the emptiness will come back, even stronger and more aching than the weekend before.

Four-Dimensional Attraction

Women worry that, unless they have perfect bodies, they will never be able to attract the hypercritical male sex. Tania, a striking twenty-year-old Haitian-American with beautiful skin, remembers having trouble getting a date in high school: "I decided that the reason I did not have a boyfriend was because I was ugly. From that point on, I literally stopped eating. Food disgusted me. I drank liquids but skipped all meals. This continued for a few months, until my parents noticed my massive weight loss and started forcing me to eat. I still rebelled, and so eventually they sent me to my aunt's house, where she would sit next to me holding a belt. I eat now, but I still do not eat too much. Food is more my enemy than my friend."

Tania's real enemies are her own misperceptions about her beauty, specifically, and the nature of attraction in general. Guys sell themselves short when they dumbly repeat this Cro-Magnon-man mantra: "Must find hot girls, need sex." I have asked them, when they return to our more evolved *Homo sapiens* level (I'm talking opposable thumbs, the wheel, the whole works): "What do you honestly find attractive? Don't give me your politically correct answer. Lay it on me."

And almost every one of them answers in some form or another: confidence and a sense of humor.

In truth, if you are worrying about snagging a man, you would be better off spending your time taking an improv comedy class than running on the treadmill; watching *The Daily Show* instead of *Desperate Housewives;* and reading Amy Sedaris instead of the latest diet book. Guys don't want disappearing women. In direct contrast, they actually want women who are present, strong, and ambitious. Guys don't want women who maintain a tiny size if it isn't their natural weight. They want women who carry their size with grace. Guys don't want women who are obsessed with every little thing they put in their mouths. They want girls who can put back a few beers, eat a burger, get an ice cream if the weather is hot and life is good.

More than big tits and a small waist, or expensive clothes and a trendy haircut, guys want girls who can make them laugh their asses off. They want women who challenge them, mystify them, make them go on spontaneous adventures. Guys want someone who makes them feel totally comfortable and seen on the one hand, and pushes them to be uncomfortable on the other: keeps them on their toes, makes sweet fun of them, inspires them to be even more authentic to who they truly are, even if it means taking a few risks.

Here is some more straight dope from their honest and always entertaining e-mails:

> I'm usually more interested in image than a specific body type, I think. Chuck Taylors, a rock T-shirt, and jeans are sexier than blondes in lingerie.

> I like women who smile and laugh, are not strangers to sarcasm, who are effervescent, unpredictable, willing to delve into a variety of topics, willing to question their assumptions, willing to make themselves vulnerable and expose weakness, and are not consumed by self-consciousness. A girl who loves herself is very attractive. If they're convinced, I'm convinced. Physically, voluptuousness is attractive, as is a nice round, full ass. Large breasts are a great bonus feature. Across the board, a good personality makes any woman who is physically mediocre more attractive, while a physically attractive woman with a garbage personality is just that, garbage.

> Physically: pretty, mostly tall, athletically built, yet curvy, dark hair, nice butt. Not attracted to very skinny or very big. Basically, if you are not a

rail and I can pick you up, I am good to go. More about the ass than I am the breast, but both are great. I say that because most ass men don't mind a couple rolls for a nice ass. Maybe that's why all these white women are with black dudes [written by a black dude]. Personality: smart in a way that I am not (which is not too hard), similar but not the same. I need to learn something and feel like I can teach as well. I tend not to like the loud, popular ones. All my previous girlfriends from high school were never the ones that other people sought after.

Seriously, I like all types. I've hooked up with all types too. Tall and skinny, tall and fat, fat and short, petite. Flatties, busties, no bodies. In fact, I'd say the only type I haven't are uglies (but that is purely subjective) and maybe jocks. If I can find two or three sexy things about a girl (one, if she is hilarious), then it's a go. I think a lot of men are like that. No one expects the total package, but there have to be a few components that make her desirable to you.

Dark hair, tall, great body, smart, sarcastic, educated.

I like women with big noses. Otherwise I'm generally attracted to women who make me laugh and will challenge me. I find competence and confidence attractive also. I think, like a lot of men, that I am also instinctually attracted to women that I can't have.

Intelligent, humble, creative, caring, confident, full-bodied. I'm not attracted to extremes usually, so that includes both emaciated and overweight. I like it when a girl looks like she feels comfortable in her own skin.

I am most attracted to girls who are very funny and charismatic, can talk intellectually about art and politics, have pretty smiles and smart, unconventional senses of style.

Notice that not one of these guys mentioned lusting after the kind of woman who vomits her dinner up in the bathroom or pushes away her plate with three-fourths of her lunch left untouched and cold. Not one mentioned liking women who spend the bulk of their free time obsessing over the size of their thighs and taking aerobics classes. In one recent study, girls and boys as young as five years old already differed in what they thought was "the nicest shape for a lady to be." Girls selected an ideal female figure that was significantly thinner than that chosen by boys. Even at five, the girls also aspired to thinner figures for themselves.

Of course looks matter. You can't see sarcasm, intellect, or kindness from across the room. But after about three seconds, the first impression becomes about more than your bust or butt size. It becomes about chemistry, conversation, values, interests, and passions. As the *Family Guy* creator, Seth MacFarlane, sarcastically quips about Paris Hilton, "Who wouldn't want to have sex with a grasshopper?" These guys aren't looking for women who initially attract them and then quickly bore the hell out of them or seem like they might break from a spontaneous wrestle for the remote. They are looking for a whole package—someone they find physically intriguing (not necessarily thin) in the first glance and mentally, emotionally, spiritually, and, yes, sexually fascinating from there on out.

Most of the guys I just quoted are in their twenties and a few of them in their late teens. In-the-thick-of-puberty teenage boys tend to speak only in a borrowed language of grunts and degrading slang that they learn while clicking on Internet porn sites and taking notes in the locker room. They are new to, and therefore inordinately fascinated by, breasts. They sometimes make smart, lovely teenage girls feel like inanimate objects.

Screw 'em. If you are fifteen and sick of being objectified by the boys in the hallway, go out with the girls, play sports, and write scathing commentaries about the jerks in the school newspaper. Don't overlook the nerds—they usually end up being the most humanlike of the high school male species (and the most successful). Bide a little time. Some of them will get smarter and way less annoying later on.

If you are adult and still dating guys who can't imagine anything more titillating than, well, tits, you might want to reconsider your own taste in men. These men don't deserve you. And you don't deserve them.

Does This Make Me Look Fat?

When I asked guys to articulate what kinds of women they were attracted to, they were usually (a) frightened of how I might respond to their answers and (b) stumped at what their answers might actually be. Men are afraid to be honest about their ideas or desires when it comes to body shape and size because they recognize how incredibly sensitive women are about the subject. In fact, they seem afraid even to articulate their ideas and desires for themselves; many of them said my survey was the first time they had reflected on, rather than reacted to, their own desires. Ever. Women shy away from these conversations for fear of the brutal truth.

As one woman explains, "I've gone there at different points in different relationships, and I usually end up hearing something that I pretended was fine with me at the time, but it reverberates in my head forever. Like once a guy I was dating told me that he looked at porn stars that resembled me. So then I started thinking I was just a type, that he didn't really love me because of me. Of course if he had said he looked at porn stars that didn't look like me, that would have provoked a ton of insecurity too. I'm starting to think it is best just to avoid the topic entirely."

And a guy echoes her: "I feel like my girlfriend would look way too far into everything I said if we talked about attraction. She takes everything so personally and interprets it in such weird ways. It would just be a really bad idea." After a quick pause he adds, "Which sucks because I actually am really physically attracted to her and I wish she could get some kind of security out of that."

This silence does a disservice to both sexes, stunting our intimacy and letting our worst fears fester. Unfortunately, most women bring the issue up with their boyfriends at moments of knee-jerk vulnerability—getting ready to go out for the night, dressing for a wedding, or fifteen minutes before a job interview—by asking the quintessential question: "Does this make me look fat?"

There is no good answer, no way out. A string of deep and unspoken concerns is snagged on that one tiny question mark. "Does this make me look fat?" is sometimes female code for "Are you attracted to me?" or "Will I be as beautiful as the other women there? Will I be the most beautiful?" or "Have you noticed that I put on weight? I'm ashamed" or the mother lode, "Do you still love me?"

Even if the answer is "You look great, are you crazy?," only fleeting appeasement is possible. These are not moments conducive to what we really need—confirmation of our whole and lasting beauty. For that night, you may feel okay again, maybe even beautiful, but the nagging feeling that you are inadequate will come back, and you will have no deeper answer to fall back on.

Men and women, like fathers and daughters, need to strain to have genuine conversations about bodies and beauty. Talk about your fears on days when you feel most safe. Bring up your worries when you are carefree and capable of going wherever that conversation might lead.

One young woman, just about to graduate from high school, told me the following story:

I dated my boyfriend almost all of high school, and we had never had a real balls-to-the-wall conversation about my body insecurities or his preferred body types or anything like that. I was paranoid because the one girl he dated before me was skinnier and just looked totally different. I used to think about that and wonder which of us was his *real* type, but I would never say anything because I was afraid of what the answer might be.

Finally, right near prom, I just blurted out this question: "Do you think I'm pretty?" I felt stupid right away. I mean, I knew he thought I was pretty, at least to a point, or he wouldn't be with me. But then he just started talking about how beautiful he thought I was, not in a fake way but, like, real, important things about me that he noticed that, like, no one else would notice. I felt great, so I asked him to tell me, honestly, what guys say about their girlfriends' bodies or the girls' bodies that they hook up with. He said that there was pressure to be funny and that usually meant being critical, and that he had, honestly, fallen into that sometimes just because he wasn't thinking. But he also said that he was sick of it, just focusing on certain parts or whatever, and that one of the things he was looking forward to about college was hoping that guys might be cooler about girls. I felt so relieved, like a ten-ton weight had been lifted from my shoulders.

By speaking honestly about his attractions and experiences, her boyfriend provides a counterexample to the usual "don't ask, don't tell" policy of most young couples. By contrast, the story he tells about his interactions with other guys about women's bodies is, sadly, quite common; in the traditional men's world—sports bars, locker rooms, corporate bathrooms—the significance of women's weight is overemphasized, perhaps as much as it is avoided in coed conversations. As Colin, a sound engineer and DJ from Oakland, wisely explains, "Men are taught to avoid speaking about women's weight with women and then taught to overexaggerate women's weight with men. I think it's important to do neither . . . and instead just try to be thoughtful and honest on the issue."

We cannot expect men to be truthful if we communicate, even nonverbally, that we don't really want their truth. Yet we will never trust them if they aren't truthful; we are too smart to believe their half-hearted reassurances. We will never destroy our inaccurate assumptions about physical attraction if we don't have the heavy blunt objects of truth to knock them out.

———————

When Todd* started dating Mary,* he was totally enchanted by her— physically and otherwise. She was in law school, loved the same kind of music he did, challenged him intellectually, and talked about how stupid she thought it was that girls obsessed about their weight. Todd had dated his share of weight-obsessed women and was really ready to have a relationship in which he wasn't forced to reassure his girlfriend that she wasn't fat ten times a day. Mary seemed perfect because it seemed like she understood the futility of trying to be perfect.

But as their relationship grew, so did her honesty about her own body issues. It turned out that Mary had battled bulimia in high school and still clung to some of her "diseased" thinking. Todd first noticed it when they would go out drinking and Mary would insist on stopping by their favorite all-night diner on the way home. She would order pancakes, milk shakes, french fries, bacon, and donuts all at one sitting and then look exhausted and act really unhappy by the time her food came, eating feverishly or not at all. At first Todd thought it was kind of fun—that Mary really was spontaneous and completely unlike the restricting women he had dated previously. But the more he experienced the poorly hidden battle inside her brain, the less he felt at ease. He realized that what had seemed like spontaneity was actually residual self-hate.

It wasn't that she was throwing up. In fact, she never relapsed even once during their yearlong relationship. But the ghost of her disease haunted them both. Todd remembers, "It didn't matter that she wasn't technically bulimic, she still thought about herself in a really critical way, and that was enough to make her severely unhappy." Six months into the relationship, Mary started talking more candidly with Todd about her self-image. She thought she was fat, ugly, unworthy of his love. In truth, all of her self-confidence was a surface-level act. Deep down she was convinced that she was still unacceptable.

Todd did everything he could to convince her otherwise. He patiently talked her through hard times, outlining her irrationality step by step until she was laughing at herself. He paid careful attention to the way he complimented her, focusing on what he found unconventionally gorgeous about her. He talked to his mom and sisters about Mary's struggle, asking them for advice on how he could convince her of her beauty.

Eventually, though, Todd's efforts exhausted him. He was sick of spending the first two hours of every Friday night convincing her that she looked great so they could go out with friends. It was like their relationship was a broken record, and he finally refused to put the needle on the vinyl ever again. They broke up, despite their otherwise rich connection. Both were devastated. Mary felt incapable of believing Todd's words, and Todd felt incapable of using them any longer. In the end, it was Mary's disbelief in the beauty of her body, not her body itself, that held her back from love.

Guys are seriously affected by their "better halves'" body issues. Almost every time I told a man—young or old—that I was exploring these issues in my writing, he would immediately respond with a knowing look and a story about a woman he had loved who suffered from an eating disorder. In almost all these cases, the disorder became a force too great for the relationship to survive. These men spoke the words *bulimia* and *anorexia* as if they were the names of cruel and devious men who had stolen their love away. They looked so powerless during the telling of these stories, so abandoned. It was as if each man had a picture in his mind of how beautiful this woman was, a picture that she refused to look at, and he was left feeling betrayed, overlooked, beaten.

These men could not have cured their girlfriends' eating disorders with their words, but their honest affection does have real power. If women and men could speak more freely more often about the nature of physical attraction, the truth might be hard, but the results could be liberating.

To Be Loved

Despite the Venus and Mars psychobabble, we are both, women and men, from the same lonely planet. We are not, in truth, the hunters and the hunted; we are all just sweet, big-eyed animals looking for someone to love and be loved by. Underneath our worries about our boyfriends' porn consumption or our misguided notion that if we were thinner, we'd have more dates is a fundamental insecurity that we aren't worthy of love. Underneath his hot-girl hedonism and his hesitation to talk with you about attraction is his desire to find something that makes him feel full. We all need connection that fortifies us, that makes us feel that we belong somewhere with someone, that we are more beautiful and important than we ever imagined.

I'm not talking about romance or the diamond big enough to require its own airplane seat or the trip to Aruba. I'm not talking about the perfect couple with the perfect relationship and the perfect little house in the perfect neighborhood, decorated floor to ceiling in Crate & Barrel. I'm talking about love—messy, raw, frightening, hilarious, hard, and deeply satisfying.

We have been duped into thinking that love is a logical extension of animal attraction, when really it is more closely related to friendship. We have been misled to put such emphasis on our looks, to consider our ability to attract a guy or a girl in a bar as a predictor of the rest of our lives—happily ever after or very much alone. The truth is that your ability to attract a guy or a girl in a bar predicts nothing but your ability to attract a guy or a girl in a bar. The classic stories of falling in love amid the chaos of this crazy world feature two strangers stuck somewhere as a result of a freak snowstorm more often than they do straight-up hotness. How many happily married couples do you know who first met at a bar? I rest my case.

Being thin may get you noticed, but it will not get you seen, and it will never get you truly, fiercely loved. Only all four dimensions of your beauty—spirit, soul, mind, and, yes, body—will get you that. Both men and women are trapped in this maze of self-scrutiny, weight or shape preoccupation, preening and primping, searching and spending. But love doesn't dwell at the end of this maze, even if you do find your way through. Love can't be won like the lottery or hunted down like an animal. Love is much more elusive and complex. In fact, it is not something outside of us, waiting for us to find it. It is already inside, sometimes taking long, languid naps, sometimes watching, all the time waiting to be woken up by a resonant voice.

There is no one-size-fits-all beauty, no perfect girl, no ideal guy. There is only a fit, plain and simple and miraculous.

8

All-or-Nothing Nation: Diets, Extreme Makeovers, and the Obesity Epidemic

The slender girl in our culture is not the healthy antithesis of the pathological fat woman, but is in fact her sister—the kinship forged by the emotional attitudes that find expression through the body but remain otherwise mute, unknown and unexamined.

—Kim Chernin

This is a culture where we seesaw madly, hair flying and eyes alight, between crazed and constant consumption, where the insatiable hunger is near universal, as is the fanatical belief in the moral superiority of self-denial and self-control. Culturally, we would be diagnosed as bulimic not anorexic, daily veering back and forth between two extreme points, bingeing and purging. The frenzied adoration of the anorexic body, and the violent hatred of fat, on ourselves and on others, reveals not that anorexia is beautiful, nor that fat is particularly despicable, but that we ourselves are intolerably torn.

—Marya Hornbacher

Susan* drags herself out of bed, despite a serious urge to stay buried under the covers, and pulls on her tights and fleece jacket. She quietly slips out the front door of her shared house and heads to the park, where she will walk the loop—three miles—as she does every morning. Her latest alt-country infatuation blares in her earphones and helps her keep pace.

When she gets home, she showers quickly, inhales some instant oatmeal, and rushes to her car so she can get to work at her usual fifteen-minutes-late mark. As she pulls into the parking lot, she sees her boss wrestling with the sun visor on her windshield. Susan rushes in and plops down at her desk just in time.

The day passes as most days do at the marketing firm where she works, uneventfully. She is still in a lower-level position, so she doesn't get much responsibility. She spends most of her time instant messaging coworkers, "window-shopping" online, and doing the occasional faxing, copying, collating job.

Lunch hour is in the corporate cafeteria, where stir-fry with brown rice is her unbroken routine. She refuses the cookies that her coworker brings in to share—giving the excuse that she is allergic to walnuts. She isn't, but ever since college she has been trying hard not to eat sweets. She knows she will think about the cookie for the rest of the day.

The afternoon actually moves fairly quickly because she is invited into a brainstorming meeting for a new account. She snacks on some carrots, trying to remind herself that the more small meals you eat throughout the day, the more weight you can lose. It feels nonsensical, like she is cheating.

On her way home, she stops by the grocery store to pick up some fresh ingredients for the chili she wants to make that night. She loves cooking, is constantly thumbing through the latest cookbook, drooling over the eight-by-ten glossies of her favorite recipes as if they were porn centerfolds. The chili turns out well, and she begs her roommate to eat some with her. She hates eating alone.

They spoon up the black beans and spicy corn as they sit in front of their favorite TV show, *Gilmore Girls*. Susan, too tired to clean up afterward, puts the dishes in the sink and crawls into bed. She recounts everything she ate that day—the oatmeal, the stir-fry, the carrots, the chili—and feels satisfied. Then she recounts everything she didn't eat—the cookie, the candy bar she saw as she was waiting in the checkout line, the cupcakes someone brought to the marketing meeting, her roommate's ice cream, calling to her in the freezer. The thought of those foods makes her stomach feel hollow and her heart deprived. She turns over on her side and curls up into a little ball, reminding herself that this feeling is far preferable to the gluttonous bloat she used to experience.

Gareth wakes up at 6:00 A.M., drags herself out of bed, pulls on her sweats, sports bra, and a tank top, and heads to the YMCA just a few blocks from her house. After offering her membership card and a smile at the door, she heads upstairs and gets on one of the last available elliptical machines. She puts her iPod buds in her ears and starts rocking out.

After a solid forty-five minutes of churning away, she goes back home, showers, throws on some new duds from Old Navy, drinks an ungodly amount of coffee, and grabs a Luna bar as she heads out the door. She rides the subway with a coworker. They share dreams from the night before, laugh about their supervisors' incompetence, answer hipster boys' winks with a few of their own.

Work flies by because Gareth is insanely busy. She files briefs, makes a mountain of copies, exchanges the occasional inside joke with a cubicle mate over IM, checks her e-mail a thousand and one times, until finally it is lunch and she heads outside.

She is practically blinded by the sun as she goes to a nearby park. She sits on a bench, cracks open her signature Diet Coke and a Tupperware filled with egg noodles, broccoli, and chicken—leftovers from the night before—and sings to herself quietly. The meal is good. The sun is too hot. She heads in after buying an apple from her favorite fruit vendor.

The rest of the day is a bit sluggish. Sometimes Gareth wonders if she isn't too efficient in the mornings. She can't stand being bored. She passes the time updating her profile on Facebook (she has a new boyfriend she met online), writing an entry in a private blog she shares with three friends, and researching graduate schools; she wants to go back to school for a master's in social work. She walks by the receptionist's bowl of candies a few times and each time successfully resists her urge to grab a few. She is trying not to eat sweets.

Five o'clock hits none too soon. She heads back onto the subway, busying herself during the trip home with her latest crochet project, a scarf for her cousin's new baby.

After climbing the five flights of stairs to her apartment, she is greeted by squeals and shrieks when she walks in the door. Her two roommates—one an elementary school teacher, the other a nursing student—are laughing at a sitcom on UPN. She plops down next to one of them on the hand-me-down couch and lets out a sigh. After agonizing a bit over what she should eat for dinner—*I've been so good all day; I wish I had the energy to make a big salad*—she succumbs to ordering in. She eats her favorite Thai dish, panang, while cracking up over her roommates' impressions of Lorelai and Rory on *Gilmore Girls*.

Afterward she feels the urge to go into the bathroom, to do what she never believed she would do, but she resists by distracting herself with a long phone call with her best friend—an investment banker who is constantly seeking her advice on his love life—then crashes into bed. After reading some Tom Robbins, one of her favorite authors, she turns off the light and lies awake, composing her meals for the next day. Eventually she drifts off to sleep.

So which one of these perfect girls is fat and which one is thin?

———————

The obesity and eating disorder epidemics are not separate issues but, in fact, flip sides of the same coin. Both conditions stem from our inability to think of health and well-being in terms of balance, what Buddhists call "the middle path." Just as we are a white and black society, a rich and poor society, an us and them society, we are a thin and fat society. There is no middle ground. There is all and there is nothing.

We are also a society of extreme makeovers and fantastical notions of physical transformation. We have no sense of body types or what health professionals call the "set point." Dr. Susan Albers, author of *Eating Mindfully: How to End Mindless Eating and Enjoy a Balanced Relationship with Food,* explains: "According to the 'set point' theory . . . your body has a genetically predetermined weight range. Your body tries to keep your weight within that range and will automatically adjust your metabolism and food storage capacity to keep you from losing or gaining weight outside of that range or set point." Far from having a set point, most of the girls I spoke with have a cut-and-paste idea of their own bodies—as if they could transform themselves into anything if they had enough time, money, and self-control.

In my mother's day, you could be "stringy" or "pear-shaped" or "sturdy." Now you are either thin or fat. Perfect or not. Worthy of praise or deserving of scorn. In more than one hundred interviews, I met few women who actually had a realistic sense of what their bodies were capable of. In the age of extreme makeover, it is no surprise when a young woman weighing 250 pounds at five feet nine leans over her cup of coffee and says in a furtive whisper, "I've always thought I would eventually be a size five."

Another describes how her college roommate would slip out of their dorm room in the wee hours of the morning, then, later in the afternoon, nonchalantly ask, "Do you want to go to the gym? I haven't been yet." This deceptive, Herculean effort (because let's face it, getting up that early in college is nothing short of Herculean) wasn't about losing a few pounds or toning her triceps. "She wanted to change her entire body type," her roommate explains. "She was short and stocky, and dreamed of being sinewy and tall. She really believed that could happen if she just went to the gym enough." Even sadder than her delusion was her misplaced time and energy.

Willpower, fastidiousness, dedication—all qualities spuriously associated with being thin—are lauded, while powerlessness, laziness, weakness—all qualities spuriously associated with being fat—are detested. All of this is socially constructed, a symbology of our own making. In fact, obesity[†] results from numerous factors, just as anorexia does. Some of these are obvious: Scientists continue to identify genes associated with obesity. Some are harder to pin down: a family culture of celebration through fattening foods, a mother who teaches her daughter that food is associated with guilt and shame, layers of fat added to ward off sexual abuse. According to the *Clinical Guidelines on the Identification, Evaluation, and Treatment of Overweight and Obesity in Adults,* "Our understanding of how and why obesity develops is incomplete, but involves the integration of social, behavioral, cultural, physiological, metabolic and genetic factors."

Susie Orbach, author of the groundbreaking book *Fat Is a Feminist Issue,* was in 1978 the first to publicize the idea that there was an undeniable psychological component to the female struggle with fat. She wrote: "Fat is a social disease, and fat is a feminist issue. Fat is not about lack of self-control or lack of willpower. Fat *is* about protection, sex, nurturance, strength, boundaries, mothering, substance, assertion and rage." Nearly three decades have passed, yet very little progress seems to have been made in the way people understand this issue. It is easier to blame individual women than to tease out complex causes or hold amorphous institutions, such as the fashion and diet industries, accountable.

Our lifestyle seems to perpetuate both obesity and our ignorance of its causes. We are a society, an economic system, even, based on excess, a nation of addicts in one form or another (TV addict, alcoholic, cokehead, nymphomaniac, workaholic). We drive our cars to work through smog-clouded traffic jams and vie for the best parking spots so we don't have to walk too far to the office, then spend our lunch hours cooped up in an airless workout room, spinning in

†According to the Centers for Disease Control, obesity is defined as a body mass index (BMI) of more than 30.0 kilograms divided by meter of height over your recommended weight, and anything between 25.0 and 29.9 over means you are overweight. The BMI's validity, however, is questioned by many authorities. As the critic Steven Shapin writes, "The BMI net catches some surprising fish. At 6'6" and a playing weight of 216 pounds, Michael Jordan was 'overweight' (with a BMI of 25)" (in "Eat and Run: Why We're So Fat," *New Yorker,* January 16, 2005).

circles. We stay up late at night watching bad television and then drink a quart of coffee the next day, rinse, and repeat. We drink Diet Coke with our Big Mac and fries, consume massive quantities of low-fat, low-calorie, wheat-free, fake cookies hoping that one will taste like the real thing. We barter with ourselves—the denial of dessert brings self-worth, the consumption of calories is a loss of control. The contradictions are thick.

The Ignorance Epidemic

Gareth looks up from her crochet project just as the train pulls into the Brooklyn Jay Street station, where she must get off and switch across the platform to the A train to Manhattan. She stuffs the yarn into her new orange leather clutch—her guilty pleasure is purses—and positions herself in front of the door, waiting for it to open.

"Yeah, that's right, get off the train, you fat bitch!" yells a man sitting nearby. He looks to be in his forties or fifties, dressed in jeans and a leather coat, possibly drunk but not obviously so. His words hang in the air like a noxious gas. A woman nearby gasps, clearly offended. An older man with white hair and a friendly, wrinkled face shakes his head silently. Two schoolkids in puffy jackets muffle their giggles with their hands.

It feels like the doors take a year to open. Gareth stands there, staring straight ahead, humiliated and silent, unsurprised. She has heard this kind of thing before. In fact, she has heard it so often that the effect is dulled at first. Later she will relive this moment in her head many times over, articulating the multitude of sassy responses she could have spat back, but ultimately this reflection will do nothing except give her the sharp stab of familiar pain. It is loneliness so deep that she must turn it into anger in order to survive.

Gareth is my best friend, and yes, she is obese by clinical standards. She is also brilliant, kind, popular, magnetic, and in a loving relationship. She dresses up to go out on Saturday nights, dances her ass off, gets the occasional free drink from a hopeful guy. She is a powerhouse at the office, blazing through her daily tasks with efficiency and conscientiousness. She is an activist and an actor—mentoring a little girl with AIDS, marching in pro-choice rallies, writing and performing monologues in off-Broadway productions.

This is not a woman who has "checked out," contrary to what so many thin people assume about those who are fat. She doesn't sit at home and lament her size. She isn't passive or embarrassed. She certainly isn't lazy. In fact, she is the quintessential perfect girl; she puts a tremendous amount of pressure on herself to excel in everything. In college, she was so overextended that she basically stopped sleeping; She had to get to her job in the college activities office, attend her a cappella group meeting, ace all of her sociology classes, memorize her lines for her part in *The Vagina Monologues,* and still have time to party with friends.

There is nothing atypical about Gareth's biography. In fact, even at her present size, she is certainly not unusual—64.5 percent of U.S. adults age twenty years and older are overweight, and 30.5 percent are obese. She grew up in Connecticut in a divorced, middle-class family, made it to New York City as soon as she could, excelled in college, moved to Brooklyn, and got an administrative job at a nonprofit. She spends her time trying to make the world a better place and figuring out how the hell she fits into it. On paper, she is a perfect girl. To the ignorant, naked eye, she is flawed.

Sizeism, in fact, remains the only truly socially acceptable form of discrimination on the planet. We see living in a fat body as an insurmountable disability. The feminist therapist Mary Pipher wrote "Fat is the leprosy of the 1990s" almost a decade ago. Today fat is the death penalty of the twenty-first century. Skinny girls, counting their carrot sticks for lunch, can't imagine being lovable at *that* size, applying for a job at *that* size, even living at *that* size. In their minds, fatness is a social death sentence. When I asked the fourteen-year-old Manhattanites how their lives would be different if they were fat, they were struck silent. After a few moments, one responded, "I would be dead."

Paradoxically, we as a society catastrophize the state of being fat for a woman like Gareth, but we have little awareness of the pain of her internal world. We dramatize fatness through news segments on the obesity epidemic and Morgan Spurlock, of the 2004 documentary *Super Size Me*, stuffing his face with McDonald's fries, thanks to which the general public's awareness of this health-economic crisis has skyrocketed in recent years. Yet our awareness of the emotional and psychological pain of fatness remains virtually nonexistent.

We are deathly afraid of fat. In some ways, we should be. According to the World Health Organization, there are 1 billion overweight and 300 million obese adults across the globe. Fatness is linked to an increased risk for heart attack, stroke, type 2 diabetes, and some forms of cancer. According to the National Institutes of Health (NIH), health care costs for treating diseases caused by obesity are estimated at $100 billion a year and rising, just within the United States (inexplicably, the NIH spends less than 1 percent of its annual budget on obesity research). The physical, psychological, and economic implications of widespread obesity are undeniably frightening.

These figures call for increased scientific investigation, programs that teach children how to eat nutritious food and exercise, and large-scale reeducation of medical professionals. We all indulge in something—too much sitting in front of the computer and TV, too much eating out, too much smothering of bitter feelings with sweet desserts. The obesity epidemic does not, however, call for mass hysteria—pumping more money into the already bloated diet industry.

There is evidence that our approach to fatness is about as unhealthy as fatness itself. In a recent poll by *ELLEgirl* of ten thousand readers, 30 percent said they would rather be thin than healthy. Dieting is ineffective 95 percent of the time. That means, in America alone, we pump $40 billion a year into a crapshoot industry with only a 5 percent chance of payoff. Besides being hard on our pocketbooks, dieting is hard on our bodies and hard on our psyches. Many women are pushed to use diet pills that damage their organs, such as twenty-three-year-old Janet, who admits, "Even after my friend had a ministroke from taking ephedra, I sometimes wonder if I can search the Internet and find some on the black market. Crazy, right?'"

Thirty-five percent of those who diet go on to yo-yo diet, dragging their bodies through a cycle of weight gains and losses; 25 percent of those who diet develop partial- or full-syndrome eating disorders. As the mindfulness expert Susan Albers writes: "The dieting mindset is akin to taking a knife and cutting the connection that is your body's only line of communication with your head." There is little hope for long-term health improvement with this vital line severed.

In fact, studies show that prolonged weight loss is more often the result of psychological work. In a two-year study by nutrition researchers at the University of California, Davis, behavior change and self-acceptance were far more effective in achieving long-term health improvements in obese women than America's most lucrative scam: dieting.

Although obesity is generally unhealthy, some smart people are saying we should focus on fitness, not fatness. J. Eric Oliver, an expert in obesity and a political scientist, argues in his 2005 book, *Fat Politics: The Real Story Behind America's Obesity Epidemic,* that the health risks of obesity have been grossly exaggerated. Being fat, he maintains, is not equivalent to being unfit. The latter is actually the most accurate measure of a person's health and life expectancy, not weight. In fact, being underweight actually kills more than thirty thousand Americans a year. Equating weight loss, instead of lifestyle changes, with improved health, Oliver argues, is "like saying 'whiter teeth produced by the elimination of smoking reduces the incidence of lung cancer.'" Even a group of researchers at the Centers for Disease Control admits, "Evidence that weight loss improves survival is limited."

Conflating obesity with laziness or stupidity is an inaccurate habit of linking a physical trait, in this case fatness, with personality, in this case slovenliness. This is equivalent to believing that all smokers or anorectics are incompetent. Just the fact that someone is genetically predisposed to fatness and struggles with the complex psychological implications of food and body image does not disqualify her from being brilliant, talented, and effective. As obvious as this sounds, many of the health professionals I spoke to about this issue aired an unmistakable tone of disdain for fat patients. While they were able to empathize with women who undereat, the idea of overeating sent them into a dispassionate laundry list of how to decrease input and increase output—as if people were machines.

Another reason that we chalk fatness up to lack of willpower and neglect a variety of other causes, as the writer, comedian, and fat activist Wendy Shanker points out, is jealousy: "The perception is that fat folks are just lolling around their living rooms like Jabba the Hutt, bathing themselves in tubs of ice cream and candy. Not true. But I think the fantasy of 'eat whatever you want, fuck everyone else' is really appealing, scarily appealing, so a good way to stamp that fantasy out is to get all willpower-y on some fat ass."

While talk of the obesity epidemic is everywhere, honest conversation about our knee-jerk disdain for fat people is nowhere. A small community of brave women and men, like Wendy, have raised their voices in the past decade, calling for an end to fat discrimination, but they are fat themselves—distrusted by the majority of Americans, who are either disgusted by them or fearful of being associated with them.[†] Fat people remain the butts of jokes, even in our politically correct climate. They are ridiculed and belittled in school, singled out in shopping malls, bombarded with diet tips from strangers and family members. Susie Orbach writes: "Above all, the fat woman wants to hide. Paradoxically, her lot in life is to be perpetually noticed."

Weighing the Blame

Gareth remembers, "Weight was an ever-present fixation in my family's house." Both of her parents were big, though her mom fought her size constantly. She even opened up a Gloria Stevens, a chain gym for women in the eighties (like Curves today). Gareth remembers sitting on the carpeted floor of her mom's office, doing her math homework and listening to the women pounding away on the floor. "Grapevine now, ladies!" her mom would shout. "No pain, no gain!"

Gareth's then-single mom (her parents divorced when she was young) started bringing her to Weight Watchers when Gareth was still

†For a list of fat-activist resources, see the Resource Guide.

in grade school. The experience of fidgeting in her seat in the waiting room until the woman in the white coat came in and weighed her in front of everyone is indelibly burned in her brain: "I can still hear that woman's voice, announcing my weight. I can still see the look of disappointment on my mom's face, on the faces of all the women in the room."

At the dinner table, her grandfather would say, "You can have more of these vegetables, Gareth. These vegetables won't hurt you." He would add, "Look, it's not our fault." Gareth's grandmother would nod and tell her that fatness had genetic roots.

All this made Gareth feel torn in two. Was she naturally fat, as her grandparents attested? Or, as her mom seemed to believe, was her weight in her control and, therefore, a sign that she wasn't trying hard enough? Though she didn't realize it at the time, these questions would deeply affect her entire life. In fact, these questions are some of the most pressing medical-psychological-social preoccupations of our time.

As a society, we seek answers—black-and-white declarations, either-or cures. But fatness is not simply a medical issue. Gareth is fat not *only* because of genetics. Just as she is fat not *only* because of a lack of willpower. She is fat because she has a genetic predisposition to fat, because she grew up with a father who sells chocolate for a living and often showed his affection through tarts and candy bars, because her mother—however well intentioned—restricted her food and, as a result, made love feel conditional. She is fat because she is fascinated by food, generously cooks for others, and enjoys a good hamburger. She is fat because she refuses to live a watered-down life—cutting out carbs or sugars or meat, becoming one of those difficult dinner guests or boring picnic companions—so that she can be thin. She is fat because, like so many of the rest of us, she sometimes uses food to fill an emotional void. She is fat because she lives in an advertising age when every potential craving, insecurity, and discomfort is preyed upon.

Most programs designed to curb obesity neglect the complicated causes of fat. Dr. Janell Lynn Mensinger, an expert on both eating disorders and obesity in women, has been continually frustrated by the culturally ignorant, gender-blind, and usually unsuccessful interventions by medical doctors to reduce obesity. She explains, "There is such an emphasis on the body as this biological organism that must be controlled in a completely medical way. Emotions get completely pushed aside because most physicians have very little psychological training."

At a recent conference on pediatric obesity, Dr. Mensinger sat next to a tiny exercise physiologist who was lamenting the low success rate of programs to teach children to maintain a healthy weight. Dr. Mensinger remembers, "She segued right into talking about how she used to be a size nine and now she is a size five, thanks to two hours a day of rigorous exercise. She acted like size nine was an atrocity! And this is who obese children from poor, minority backgrounds are supposed to identify with?"

If we admit that obesity is linked to poverty, then we have to look at classism, perhaps the only issue we are less willing to discuss than sizeism. If we admit that obesity is linked to culture, then we have to look at race, an issue still tolerable only in bite-size, politically correct portions. As the health expert Natalie Angier writes: "Despite the nondenominational nature of fat . . . in many cases, obesity is inversely proportional to socioeconomic status—that is, the higher your station in life, the lower your weight." If we admit that obesity is linked to incest, then we have to look at a long-standing taboo discussed only on *Oprah* and in banned books. Dr. Michael Myers, a physician who has been treating obese women for over twenty-five years, estimates that 40 percent of his patients have been sexually abused. If we admit that obesity is linked to our culture of extremes, then we have to talk about advertising—the crooked backbone of our economic system.

There is only one rational reason to fear fatness: health risks. The other reasons, which play unconscious and insidious roles in our negative perception of fat people, are profoundly American. Obesity is rampant in the heartland of America—the sprawling suburbs of the

Midwest and the South, the farm towns throughout Texas. But it is rarely admitted that our struggle over the meaning of fat is at the heart of our national identity.

Fat Inside

Twenty-eight-year-old Felice is a woman who changes the air that she walks through. She is tall, big-hipped, dark-skinned, has a laugh that can turn around a no-good day. She is so striking, in fact, that she intimidates men. They can imagine asking her for advice, lavishing her with compliments, respecting her as much as they do their beloved mothers, but they would have no idea what to do with a woman so powerful in form and spirit.

Felice wasn't always so intimidating. There was a time, back in her middle-class, Episcopalian youth in Mount Vernon, New York, when she was nerdy and shy, teased by her family about being chubby. Her mother was a nutritionist and her next-door neighbor her pediatrician—a nasty combination when you are twelve and still carrying around baby fat. She suffered Sunday weigh-ins, where her adherence to her imposed twelve-hundred-calorie-a-day diet was assessed. Usually she failed these tests. Felice sneaked off to the candy store with her friends after school in secret protest. She ate a sandwich with real mayonnaise for the first time on a class field trip and remembers turning to her bus buddy and asking with wide eyes, "What is this magical thing?" She liked to run around the neighborhood with the bottom of her shirt pulled up through the middle and back around—every little girl's sweet misinterpretation of sexy in the eighties.

Felice resisted her Sunday weigh-ins as she got older and her relationship with her mother got more complicated. She spent hours in the basement of her house, making dance routines that she thought worthy of *The Grind* on MTV. Black girls, she understood, were supposed to have big asses, small waists, and big breasts. One dancer, in particular, symbolized her ideal body—"She was in a lot of the early nineties videos, like the one for 'Around the Way Girl,'" Felice reminisced, laughing heartily.

Felice was happy being a "geek," playing in the marching band and excelling in her science and math classes. Going to engineering school at Columbia and getting out of Mount Vernon—and away from her mother's careful eye—seemed logical.

College was an initiation into "geek as chic." Suddenly Felice wasn't just a nerd without any sex appeal, she was a beautiful, big woman who happened to be adept at calculating sine curves, designing unbreakable bridges, *and* writing poetry and autobiographical plays. She started to perform all over the city. She started to believe that she had the capacity to be pretty.

She still secretly longed to be as sexy as the ladies popping and locking in rap videos. Too many guys thought of her as great friend material. She felt smart, brilliant, even; now she wanted to feel hot. After a long Sunday at church on a visit home, her mother told Felice about a fellow parishioner who had recently lost a lot of weight on something called the Atkins diet (this was 1996, long before Atkins took over the world and then crawled away in bankruptcy). No bread, no sugars, plenty of protein—Felice was committed. Her mother was thrilled.

In the first two weeks, Felice lost nine pounds. Within a year, she had lost fifty. As the pounds dropped off, her fantasies added up— being toned and tightened, in her mind, was tantamount to happiness. She had always had everything going for her, except this one thing. Now that she would have it, she figured, there would be nothing standing between her and true bliss. Whenever she felt depressed or inadequate, it was always easy to blame her weight. Now that she would be smaller, there would be nothing to weigh her down. "I imagined the life that thin women led," she explained, "to be easy, carefree. Everything just fits."

It didn't quite work out that way. As with any diet, eventually Felice hit a plateau. She was buying Dolce & Gabbana dresses at Filene's Basement, feeling fine, but she still wanted to lose thirty more pounds, which just didn't seem to be coming off. Atkins was hell to keep up, and her willpower was growing thin. When she sneaked a piece of bread, she felt guilty. Even fifty pounds lighter, she felt harassed by the voices of the perfect girl and the starving daughter in her head. She was exhausted by the effort to deny herself ten times a day. Even after all that effort, she felt perpetually unsatisfied. Looking back at photos of that time, Felice is shocked by how thin she was: "If I would have lost thirty more pounds, I would have been emaciated."

Eventually Felice realized that there would be no "true bliss" moment, no matter how thin she got. Her life, from the outside, wasn't that different. She got compliments at her thinnest weight, but not many more than she had at her heaviest. Guys were interested in her, as they had been when she was overweight, at about the same rate. Her spirit, after all, remained full-figured; guys were still intimidated by the heft of her intellect. Her job, her apartment, her lifestyle, all felt the same, if not a bit more restrictive, a little less spontaneous and fun.

But even more surprising, her interior life hadn't changed either. Felice spoke of this profound understanding: "I realized that my weight had so little to do with my weight. If I'm skinny and tell myself I'm fat every day, it doesn't matter what I look like. My experience of myself in the world is still unsatisfying."

―――――――

Our all-or-nothing nation is built on foundations of fantasy. Our imagination is harnessed to America's favorite adolescent fantasy—how much prettier, thinner, richer, and more successful we will be one day. When Felice was sweating away in the basement of her childhood home, painstakingly imitating the dancer in her favorite video, she was rehearsing for a lifetime of longing: *Someday I will be thin like her and my whole life will feel different. Someday I will fit into those clothes and get the attention of those boys. Someday my mom will be proud of how I look.*

This perpetual American daydream is written in the language of "somedays." "Someday" whispers us to sleep at night, gets us through a boring workday, makes our little lives bearable. The 250 ads the average American sees a day brainwash us into believing that we need more shiny, new things and, of course, food—glorious piles

of chocolate chip cookies, decadent ice cream, burgers the size of ele-
phants. "Someday" soothes insecurities, and numbs discomfort, and
keeps perfect girls running obediently in the hamster wheel of weight
preoccupation. Someday we will be thin. Translation: Someday we
will be happy, loved, and powerful.

I asked Gareth, "How would your life be different if you lost
weight?"

She answered immediately. "I think of the thin me as the better
me, as a me with self-control and a me without health risks. Maybe
my acting career would have taken off. Maybe I would just be happy."

But even those precious few who get to this "someday" destination, as Felice did, aren't happy or better. In fact, Felice was less joyful
and interesting because she was expending so much energy denying
herself the foods that didn't fit into her diet plan. Felice wasn't even
healthier, because she was avoiding whole food groups and loading up
on fats that raised her cholesterol. She may have been better at saying
no, but true self-control would have allowed her to say yes sometimes
too, without the fear of losing her resolve completely.

Dr. Sharron Dalton, nutritionist and author of *Our Overweight
Children,* explains, "Many people believe that having personal control is 'just saying no.' In fact, saying no to food works for some
people for short periods of time. For others, it becomes an unhealthy
end in itself. For most of us, to maintain a balance between 'yes' and
'no' requires multiple skills in this food-laden, anxiety-enmeshed,
sleep-and-time-starved environment that makes healthy living a big
challenge."

If you live fat in your head, then you are. If you believe you are
unattractive, you will experience the world as an unattractive woman.
If you hound yourself about everything you put in your mouth, you
won't enjoy eating. Regardless of the number on the scale, if the number inside your head is large, insurmountable, and loaded with meaning, then you will feel weighted down by its implications.

After publishing *The Fat Girl's Guide to Life* in 2004, Wendy
Shanker traveled the nation doing readings, signing books, and talking to fans. She reflects, "The best lesson that I learned touring is that

every woman, no matter how heavy or how skinny, feels fat. When you're thin, you're never thin enough. When you're fat, it's not permanent—'I'm a size eight stuck in a size eighteen body.' When I used to see some hot-bodied girl saunter down the street, I'd give her a dirty look, sure that she had a perfect life. Now I know better. I know that she may look different on the outside, but inside she feels the same way I do. So instead of a dirty look, I throw a little mini-vibe of compassion her way."

This is the heart of the matter: A perfect girl can rule just as tyrannically, and a starving daughter can ache just as deeply, inside a thin body. Our dissatisfaction is never, at its deepest, about our bodies. This is why fat women and thin women often experience the world in similar ways. If a thin woman feels inadequate and "thinks fat," she may endure less hate coming from the outside in than a fat woman but just as much criticism and sadness from the inside out. Likewise, if a woman of any size is able to stop her negative self-talk and accept herself, she may experience the world with a little peace of mind.

The Swinging Pendulum

Tracing the blue veins visible under the pale skin of Susan's* upper arms until they disappear under her microscopic tank top is evidence that you can be too thin, just as you can be too fat. Susan has inhabited both extremes.

Susan, though in her twenties, looks twelve. Her skin appears to be stretched over her tiny frame, her nose and eyes look too large for her head, everything about her reminds me of prepubescence, that time before hips and breasts and everything messy that comes after. When Susan was actually twelve, she was rudely introduced to womanhood through a pair of unignorable breasts. She remembers, "The boys stared at them, my aunts commented on them, my friends admired them. I hated them. I felt like they had taken over my identity."

Susan cowered under the power of her new identity as a "blossoming woman." For years she hid under big hooded sweatshirts and her father's hand-me-down flannels. She sat on the sidelines of gym class, refused to go bra shopping in her hometown, gave her mom the evil eye anytime she mentioned Susan's body to one of her sisters.

But when high school started, Susan tired of her wallflower routine and hungered for a special place in the crowded halls of her big public school. She flirted with the power of her body—shedding her baggy, ironic T-shirts for a tighter, clingier fabric—only to feel guilty afterward for garnering the attention of older boys. She learned to joke about her breasts, to make self-effacing comments that she knew would lead to compliments. She called her breasts by silly nicknames before her ogling boyfriends could. It somehow felt less embarrassing coming out of her mouth first. She coped but never felt comfortable, never got over the sense that her breasts and curvy body were foreign invaders. In fact, the more she joked about her size and became outwardly easygoing about her voluptuous breasts, the less powerful she felt—as if she were betraying her true self, accepting this form that never felt like hers.

Eventually the discrepancy between Susan's behavior on the outside—witty, easygoing, playful—and her feelings on the inside—vulnerable, tired of being watched, powerless—developed into a pretty serious case of self-hate and weight gain. Her self-effacing humor grew even more bitter and frequent. The attention she drew from boys was no longer sexual but shaming. She became the fat girl who told the funny jokes, the best friend, the overlooked. In some ways, with more weight, she had gotten freedom from being watched, talked about, leered at. But she didn't feel vindicated, she felt victimized. She realized that she did want attention. She wanted out of her folds of flesh and out of her misery.

She discovered veganism and running, and her life started anew. She passed on family dinners, instead preparing stir-fry and slow-cooked brown rice. She drank herbal tea instead of coffee, worked out at least once a day, went to yoga and Pilates classes religiously. She went out with new friends on weekends, but instead of resorting to the late-night pizza slice as she once had, she stuck to a strict rule about not eating after 9:00 P.M. Her veganism provided a sound excuse for not indulging in friends' birthday cakes or her mother's Thanksgiving pumpkin pie.

In just six months, Susan lost forty pounds. Since she was five foot four, this changed her appearance entirely, astounding old friends and family. Boys were starting to look at her again, even though, along with the stomach and the love handles, she had shed her breasts. Her chest wasn't flat, but it was certainly not the center of attention any longer. Susan felt triumphant, healthy, even a little righteous.

But what had begun as a mission to lose excessive weight became an unstoppable process of paring down. Friends started to worry, inviting her out for coffee and nervously bringing up her dwindling weight as they drained the last gulp: "Are you sure you're okay?" Susan insisted that she was fine, that she was eating three meals a day, that she felt better than ever. And she wasn't lying; she still believed it herself.

When she lost her period, she started to suspect that her friends' worry was warranted. She said nothing to anybody—afraid that they would watch her even more closely than they already seemed to be doing. Her mom looked worried and kept offering seconds. Her dad teased her about being so light she might blow away in the wind. Neither communicated their fears about her health in a direct way.

Now, still thin but trying to incorporate a wider variety of foods—including a few fattening ones—into her diet, Susan is struggling over the meaning of her own shrinking. "I don't think I'm anorexic," she tells me firmly. "It doesn't feel problematic. It feels good. But I recognize that it looks problematic to some of those who know me best. I understand that I am worrying people, and I take that seriously."

I believe her when she says this. Susan can't lie. I believe that she is as confused as the rest of us about the way to lead a balanced life. It is as if she once dragged her extra weight across a land of minefields and now floats through the air, weightless and far from the ground. The latter feels better, I understand; it just doesn't engage you with earth.

Susan's journey from one end of the spectrum to the other is a battle for control. This word spills out of the mouth of almost every woman with whom I speak about food and fitness, no matter where she sits on the spectrum. It is the zombie mantra of a generation of perfect girls: *control, control, control.* Their eyes glaze over, their authentic hungers dissipate, their unique notions of beauty or health or quality of life fade into a guilt-producing, impossibly rigid refrain. Bodies on either end of the spectrum seem to become public property, though of course the larger the body is, the more cruelly it is treated.

Being thin doesn't prevent self-hate. Susan struggled to put almonds in her mouth not because she wasn't hungry for them or detested their taste but because they symbolized a terrifying slip down the slide of self-control that she had so carefully avoided with her rules and regulations, with her life-strangling refusal to be sponta-neous, indulgent, or silly. Authentic hunger had become anathema.

Gareth experiences stints of fierce self-control punctuated by devastating falls out of control—bingeing and purging. Her cycle of deprivation and indulgence, followed by shame and then more depri-vation, can complete a full revolution in just hours. Sometimes she doesn't even binge, just feels a swell of anxiety about her size and how she fits into the world, and purges even the most sensible meal. Susan has stretched her own process over a decade. For now she is thin and in control. But of course, as her anxiety over the small stuff indicates, she already knows that it is only a matter of time before a big fall.

Susan Nolen-Hoeksema, author of *Eating, Drinking, Overthink-ing,* writes about this cycle: "Here's where the all-or-nothing thinking kicks in and sabotages us. . . . In the scientific literature, this is called the abstinence violation effect—we've violated our diet (our absti-nence from food) and our all-or-nothing thinking leads us to eat far more than we need to quell our hunger and need for nourishment." Where there is no balance, there is only saturation or starvation. Feast or famine. Gluttony or deprivation.

True health is "the middle path," along which control is some-times lost, sometimes won, without much fanfare. There are unex-pected and delightful detours along the way. There is no "good" or "bad," only "right now"—tastes, moods, the occasional craving, like different kinds of weather, all welcomed and satisfied without judgment. True health is balance. Balance is freedom.

Fat Bitch

Gareth is onstage, the shadow of her voluptuous silhouette on the wall behind her. I am watching it, instead of her, as she gives her monologue, because it feels too hard to look her in the eye when she is speaking such brave and brutal truths. Her words start celebratory but quickly become accusatory:

> In a way it is easy to be proud of my body. I'm proud of what it does for me and what it can do for other people. But every time I get dressed I think about how other people will see my body and I can't help but hear the words *fat bitch* in my head. I've been hearing them most of my life. It's as if people feel the need to make judgment on my character as well as my body all at once. And it works. It makes me feel huge and obtrusive and grotesque, deformed.
>
> It's true. I am fat. I am not attractive to most people. Most of the time, I am not attractive to myself. Where does that leave me? Angry with myself? Yes. Angry with society? No.
>
> I think that's a cop-out, and it's not a cop-out for me. It's a cop-out for the people that judge my size. It's like, at this point, we all know that the media, old white men, corporations, the fashion industry, and all sorts of bad people or things out there shape the way we view ourselves and others. Okay, I get it. But don't you think, at some point, knowing all this, we should start taking some responsibility for our thoughts and words? I mean, isn't that the point of all this higher education, all this enlightenment?

As she reaches the end, she starts screaming her questions at the stunned audience: "So what's going on, people? Why do I still feel like crap? Huh? Who can tell me? Do you know? Can someone please explain it to me?"

I can almost hear the audience members' brains buzzing with rationalizations:

> *But fat is unhealthy.*
> *I don't date fat women, but I have nothing against them.*
> *Why is she complaining? She's one of those beautiful fat women.*
> *When is this going to be over? It's torture.*

Gareth pulls herself together, takes a deep breath, and says calmly, "I know what you are all thinking, and it's okay," then ends, cool as ice, "You want the fat bitch to shut up," and struts out of the spotlight and off the stage.

Gareth is beautiful, especially tonight. She's dressed in a knee-length black skirt, cut in uneven triangles on the bottom. Her shirt is a rainbow of reds, oranges, and yellows—as fiery as her monologue—cut low, revealing the tops of her breasts, freckled with beauty marks. Her eyes are outlined in dark pencil, making them seem even bigger, even more striking. The spotlight bathes her in an ethereal light.

But most of the audience members instead focus on her anger. They are not used to being called on the carpet for their judgment of obesity. They feel attacked, misunderstood, perhaps defensive. They have fat friends. They aren't narrow-minded, just concerned about the obesity epidemic. They thought that was the right way to be. They feel unmoored, the first phase of a new consciousness.

Gareth's monologue provokes a storm of self-reflection. I would never say anything rude to a fat man or woman about his or her weight, but would I think it? I preach tolerance, but would I ever consider dating someone who is overweight? When I compliment Gareth on her new haircut, is there a part of me that feels relieved she is undeniably beautiful *despite* being fat? Do I identify her anger more quickly than I would a thinner friend's? Do I patronize by complimenting her eyes, her sense of humor, her determination—as if the rest of her doesn't exist?

Just as racism is not primarily about frightened white women clutching their purses but about the seemingly mundane, unconscious voices in our heads—*Why do black girls have to be so loud? That Latina woman is probably a great nanny. This new Asian guy is probably really smart*—sizeism is not about the drunken man who screams "fat bitch" at Gareth on the subway as much as it is about the march of hateful inner monologues she doesn't hear, but she senses: *That girl would be so pretty if she would just lose some weight. I wonder what is wrong with her, must be lazy. This fat bitch is taking up more than her share of the bus seat.*

When I started to pay attention to the voices in my own head, I was frankly horrified. It wasn't only fat women on whom I unconsciously commented in my own head, it was thin women too: *That skinny girl looks like such a bitch. I bet she's vacuous and vain. That woman shouldn't be eating that muffin. I feel sorry for that little girl. She is going to be lonely if she doesn't lose some weight.*

Seriously humbled by my own judgmental nature, I realized that thinking this way about other people creates an inner climate of suspicion. *If I think this way about her, what is she thinking about me?* Like a chronic gossip suddenly aware that other people probably talk about her behind her back too, I woke up to the fact that I was sealing my own fate of mercilessly judging and being judged, even if my participation was unspoken.

That understanding is Gareth's gift to me. It is a daily struggle not to listen to the voices—the furtive whispers, the outdated instincts—that try to slip under the radar. But it makes me feel more generous in general. It makes me feel less scrutinized myself. Sometimes I sit on a subway car and look at every woman purposefully and lovingly—as if she were my mother or best friend. It is breathtaking how beautiful they all are when I see like this. It makes the entire world seem as if it is spilling over with humble loveliness instead of paralyzed with hate.

Gareth shook me out of complacency again when she danced in a burlesque show on a small stage in New York's West Village.† In only a purple teddy and fishnet stockings, she shimmied before a packed room of onlookers sipping glass jars of whiskey, hooting and hollering good-naturedly. In the scene, she was the object of desire. A wiry black woman with short dreads, dressed in a tuxedo, sang Bessie Smith's old classic "Need a Little Sugar in My Bowl" as she gazed at Gareth adoringly.

Seeing women of all different sizes, not just Gareth but others, dance in near-naked shamelessness, shaking their pockmarked thighs and generous booties, I felt suddenly comfortable in my own skin. It was a revelation to see my own body, in all its imperfections, reflected in the women dancing before me. I understood something different about sexuality as well—that it doesn't have to be pumped full of collagen, taut, narrow, high-pitched. This sexuality was generous, sometimes large, idiosyncratic, very real. For me, it was a paradigm shift—from perfection to playfulness. For Gareth, it was a sacrifice.

"After opening night," she explains, "I had this weird mixture of pride and shame in what I'd done. I mean, how could I ever put *this* body out there? How could I ever show it to everyone, in a scenario where it was supposed to be attractive and sexy?" Despite her conflicting feelings, Gareth geared up to do the show two more times. Each night she strutted onstage, did what she had to do, and breathed a giant sigh of relief afterward. Gareth is a talented actor; she looked empowered through and through to the audience that cheered her on. She remembers, "People kept telling me that they were happy to see someone with some flesh on their bones up there."

"And what did you think about that?" I ask, eager to understand the dissonance between the way she was received and how she felt inside.

†Burlesque, a form of live entertainment usually including music, comedy, and sexuality on display, originated in the 1840s but has experienced a recent renaissance among young, mostly urban feminists.

"I think they're trying to make me feel better," she quickly answers. "They want to support this even if they don't really want to see it."

"Just as you want them to see it even if you don't really want to do it?" I ask.

Gareth laughs. "Yeah, I guess you're right. When I talk about the burlesque with people, I say, 'Yeah, it was really empowering,' but it hasn't had any real effects on how I feel about myself." Gareth pauses thoughtfully, then goes on: "I do feel two-faced about it. I mean, I lied about my confidence and my empowerment because I thought that it was important for people to see. I still do."

Even though Gareth exudes an air of comfort with herself, she has never been able to shed her own perfect girl, starving daughter dichotomy. Susie Orbach calls this enduring self-hate "inevitable. The cultural pressure is internalized and hard to evacuate. One tries through political activism, but the forces pressing in visually and commercially are such that the pain of being fat in this society and the pain of observing others' struggles with their bodies cannot simply be met with activism."

Gareth still feels flawed, even though she advocates that others stop seeing her that way. She still feels weak, even though she appears the epitome of strength. She still punishes herself ten times a day, even though she asks others not to. She still suffers the echo of her weight being announced in a public waiting room. Even if she can stand onstage and urge the world to get comfortable with her weight, she cannot assuage her own decades-long discomfort.

———————

A tiny, noiseless tear builds up in the corner of Gareth's black-lined right eye and spills onto the dirty floor. She is lying on her side, gripping my hand with the strength of a woman in labor, clenching her perfect teeth. Looming over her is a tall beanpole of a man with multiple piercings. He is concentrating, but not enough. Over the buzz of his tool, he asks me in a thick Australian accent: "So do you have any tattoos?"

I take a swig of the beer I smuggled into his shop on St. Marks with the hand that isn't being smashed and answer, "No."

"So you are her uptight friend?" he asks, a smirk spreading on his face. Gareth laughs through her grimace.

"I guess you could say that," I answer, and then immediately regret it. Surely this will only encourage him.

Indeed: "So why don't you get a tattoo? You think your body is too precious?"

I take a deep breath. Look down at Gareth's face, growing pale, feel our hands, stuck together with sweat in addition to the force of her grip. "No, probably just scared," I reply, though I know that he hit the nail on the head. I do think of myself as too precious. The small of my back too smooth for the interruption of a clichéd butterfly, the tiny bump of my anklebone too endearing for a Chinese symbol. I also worry, of course, that my stomach is not flat enough for a flower, my upper arm not toned enough for a band of vines.

When he is finally done, little traces of blood are bubbling up from Gareth's armpit to her hip bone. He wipes them away with a damp cloth, stands back to admire his work. I stare at it too, impressed, mesmerized, honestly, a little bit horrified. There is a zipper, at least two feet long, etched into her pale skin in black ink made even darker by the blood seeping from its lines. At the top, it appears to be pulled a few inches open, as if Gareth is just aching to crawl out of her own skin.

9

Past the Dedication Is Disease: Athletic Obsession

Just as perfect girls tend to operate in either feast or famine mode, they are extreme in their fitness regimens. We buy expensive gym memberships with high hopes of sticking to our no-excuses get-in-shape plans, only weeks later to stop going altogether. Instead of just walking more, we pledge to run marathons; two months down the road, our expensive running gear goes to waste when we lose enthusiasm. We spend hours at the gym or no time at all. We are fitness nuts or sedentary TV watchers.

The benefits of my generation's involvement in organized school sports from a very young age are indisputable, but the costs have been largely overlooked. My own dad reflects: "I thought that succeeding in sports would be good for your self-esteem, that it would make you really competent." He had no idea that my involvement in sports was also my first exposure to young women with the perfect-girl mentality.

_____

"This is what we've been practicing all season for, girls. This is what we got up early on Saturday for, what we went home early on Friday night for, this is why we have been running and lifting and busting our

asses up and down that floor. Don't let this pass you by. Leave everything out on that floor."

A few minutes before it was time to run out for our warm-up,
Wendy,* the best junior on our basketball team, would gather us all
around for a pep talk, something short and sweet but meant to make
us understand the gravity of the moment. The rest of us would nod
eagerly, some stretching or bouncing up and down with nervousness,
fueled and focused by Wendy's gurulike energy.

That Wendy was the best player on the team was no small feat.
Our big public school (two thousand students) in suburban America
teemed with aspiring athletes and women raised on Title IX. Every
year after tryouts, as many girls left the gym in tears as in triumph,
and some of those in tears ended up relieved; we practiced, lifted, and
had team meetings until 7:00 P.M. on weekdays and often had to come
in for two-a-days on Saturdays. I wasn't raised in a religious family,
but when I was in high school, Sundays had an undeniably sacred feeling for me—Coach simply couldn't ask us to come in for practice. If it
wasn't illegal, he might have. He did ask us to condition over winter
break, which none of us but Wendy did. Most of us had to run to
throw up from the intensity of the third hour of practice on January 2,
but Wendy continued charging up and down the court. We would
rinse out our mouths, wipe our faces, and get back in line beside her.

Wendy was five feet nine, with long, straight black hair held in a
French braid, beautifully svelte, strong calves, collarbones that stuck
out of the top of her sports bra, a mischievous smile, a killer jump
shot. Wendy was consumed with getting a college athletic scholarship.
But by her junior year, it looked to me like her dedication had taken
an ugly turn; she was shrinking.

"Now everyone get together," she shouted. We would huddle
close, arms around one another in a big circle of shiny brown and
white polyester, and do our final cheer before heading out on that
floor. I was always next to Wendy, her tiny body pressed against me.
She would scream, "Palmer High, what time is it?" And we would
answer, "It's time to get rough! It's time to get live!" Louder and
louder we would answer until we were all worked up into a frenzy of

smiles and screams, and then Wendy would throw the locker room door open, and our intro music—something from OutKast—would begin, and we would wind our way around the gym to the cheers of our families, friends, and crushes filling the stands. It felt, absolutely, like being a rock star.

———————

"See Jane run" took on new meaning in 1972, when the landmark legislation Title IX was adopted, guaranteeing girls equality in access to sports, to playing fields, to school stadiums, and to funding for sports in educational institutions. No longer was our overwhelming choice between cheer squad and spectator. Title IX states: "No person in the U.S. shall, on the basis of sex, be excluded from participation in, or denied the benefits of, or be subjected to discrimination under any educational program or activity receiving federal aid."

Title IX was the air I breathed. In my blissfully ignorant, go-girl upbringing, no one ever put a limit on my physical activity. If I could run faster, I ran faster. If I beat the boys in kickball, I did so happily. When I wanted to be a serious high school athlete, my desire was as encouraged and admired as my brother's aspirations.

A lot of us girls have athletic leanings. One in 27 high school girls played sports in 1972, but today 1 in 2.5 does. In a recent story touting the health and hipness of girls today, based on interviews with more than one hundred, *O: The Oprah Magazine* reports: "Across socioeconomic lines, girls today feel entitled to do what they want professionally, to have what they want materially, and to be who they want to be emotionally. After talking to dozens, I came to believe that a good deal of their empowerment came into being on the athletic fields."

But this "you-go-girl" sentiment is, unfortunately, only half the story. Dr. Craig Johnson reports that 13 percent of female athletes suffer from full-blown eating disorders, and another 16 percent have a drive for thinness so severe that it warrants diagnosis, even though they don't exhibit all of the symptoms. According to his recent

National Collegiate Athletic Association survey of female college athletes, 70 percent aspired to get their body fat lower than the percentage required to menstruate. A leading organization on anorexia reports that out of 695 male and female athlete respondents to a recent study, a third were preoccupied with food and a quarter binged at least once a week. Twelve percent fasted for twenty-four hours or more after a binge.

A commitment to and passion for a sport provide a foolproof disguise for many girls today; underneath the dedication is disease. Women martyr their bodies in the name of conditioning and competition. Encouraged by overzealous coaches and parents, many women overexercise and undereat. Clearly, not all female athletes have diagnosable eating disorders, but many fall somewhere on the spectrum of unhealthy eating to exercise that should alarm their families and teammates. After all, deprivation is not empowerment. As female athletes fade away, their stamina grows thin too, but as long as they can dig deep and perform, they and others feel, nothing is wrong. Sports are a performance.

The Performance

Our entire warm-up was choreographed. First layups, right then left, then pull-up jump shots, right then left. As we waited in line for our turn to lay it in off the glass, we tried to shake out the nerves or go through the motions of stretching to distract us from the other team, now taking their own shots on the other side of the court. They were inevitably bigger, but we were usually faster. Wendy was always faster.

She stood at the top of the shooting line, folding her leg and grabbing her ankle behind her, stretching her quads, staring down the other team. Most of us might steal a glance, but Wendy had no problem looking the other team dead in the eye before a game. With her long white skinny legs and her spindly arms sticking out of her jersey, that stare made her look really hungry, ravenous for the win.

The power of this kind of performance is palpable. Even when warming up for the game, we had the scary and wonderful feeling of being watched. Getting noticed is coveted in the complex social matrix of high school; being in front of that crowd was special, a moment apart at sixteen when the whole school was looking at you. At a time in most girls' lives when the quest to get noticed can take a nasty turn—drugs, sex, dropping out—sports are a constructive high. You perform with a crew, gaining the coolness of an affiliation. Playing sports let me be down with all kinds of kids who otherwise would have written me off as a snob from the north end. Jasmine* was six feet tall, black, full of badass attitude. She couldn't deal with the authoritarian style of our junior high coach, stormed out of the gym one day never to return, but when I went to parties in her neighborhood and spotted her there, we would embrace—old friends, bonded by our love of the game. I was seen by her on that court in a way that I never would have been seen otherwise. With a ball in my hand, I could transcend the label of "just another white girl."

When you play well, there is glory. I once got slammed by a girl twice my size as I was shooting a three-pointer. I heard the crowd gasp as I fell to the ground . . . hard. When I got up, my vision was blurry, but I sank my three free throws anyway—to the crowd's delight—only afterward realizing that a blood vessel in my eye had popped. I looked like a roughed-up boxer the next Monday at school, the white of my eye an ominous red. I got so many props it transformed the swelling into a badge of honor.

The flip side of this visibility is that, when you have an off game, everyone knows. When you miss a jump shot at the buzzer, it is recorded in the collective consciousness of your entire class—at least for the next week. And a week can be an eternity in high school time.

There were layers to our performance that had nothing to do with our actual athletic performance. Before the game, we combed and recombed our hair into perfect ponytails; fretted over pimples, makeup, and dirty shoes; asked one another for help braiding and rebraiding our hair. Many a girls' locker room is coated in a hard-to-remove film of glitter that doesn't come from just the cheerleaders.

As female athletes have gotten more press in the media and more playtime on major TV channels, more than their talent and skill has been exposed. Their bodies, not immune to the values of the culture at large, have come to be scrutinized. Nike ads or ESPN vignettes may emphasize how strong and powerful an Olympic runner or swimmer is, but just as often a female athlete is publicly pressured to prove that she is first female, i.e., pretty, sexy, sweet, and only secondarily athletic. As the *Village Voice* writer Joanna Cagan writes, "They're everywhere, these proud offspring of Title IX—strong, competitive, and practically naked."

To date, Olympic and professional athletes from America, Canada, and Australia have posed naked or nearly naked in *Sports Illustrated, Maxim, Playboy,* and their own pinup calendars. Some trace this trend back to Brandi Chastain's dramatic reaction to the U.S. Women's Soccer Team victory in the 1999 World Cup, when she surprised fans by ripping off her jersey to reveal the black sports bra underneath. Shortly afterward, she posed nude for *Gear Magazine,* "crouching," as one reporter put it, "like a question mark over a soccer ball."

The questions Chastain and her fellow athletes/sex symbols pose are complex: Are these playful attempts at reminding the public that female athletes don't have to play "like men"? Or are these naked sportswomen being exploited? Most important, how are young women reading these images? A study in the *Journal of Sport & Social Issues* recently reported that a group of fourteen- to eighteen-year-olds felt overwhelmingly negative about their own bodies after seeing such pictures.

The athlete's body is now another difficult-to-replicate form being dangled in front of adolescent girls. Although girls may be liberated by the emphasis on strength rather than thinness, the road to the Olympian's body can look strangely similar to an eating disorder: overexercising, undereating, a reluctance to listen to the body's signals that it's tired, hurt, hungry. And the destination—the thin, muscular, perfect body—of the parade of scantily clad athletes also looks strangely similar. Athleticism was supposed to empower us, and in so many cases, it has; but in others, it has created another giant cover-up.

"Empowerment"

When the buzzer sounds to end warm-up, we run back to our bench, pull off our side-button pants with a resounding chorus of snaps, and sit side by side, prepared for the announcer to call our names. As he does, each of us leaps up from the bench, runs onto the court, and shakes hands with an opposing team member.

It is always thrilling to hear it—the sound of my own name over the microphone. As I run by the line of seated teammates, I feel their encouraging pats on my calves, my ass, my back, and I know that I am a part of something, that they believe in me. When I reach that opponent in the center of the floor, I shake her hand amicably, but inside my belly is raging with a fierce determination to beat her.

When the buzzer sounds to mark the beginning of the game, ten girls run out onto the floor, each with a pounding heart and a surging hope.

———————

My brother insisted that I be good at sports. I have many fond memories of being dragged out to the alley, where he would force me to make ten free throws before dinner. By the time I'd made those free throws, I was sweaty and tearful, and Chris, triumphant and authoritative, would sink one more long-range jump shot before granting me permission to go inside. As we headed back to the house, he would say, half joking, half serious, "You know, I'll kill you if you ever get an eating disorder."

Chris was always a force that countered my adolescent black hole of self-hate. I bemoaned his hard-nosed methods but secretly loved our predinner ritual. It was evidence of the bond between us, but even more, it was proof that I too was strong and promising, that someday I would grace a basketball court as he did, run up and down for a whole hour without stopping once, have teammates who depended on me and taught me their secret handshakes. Someday I would be as coordinated and cool as my big brother.

I would do all he had, *but* I would also have teammates who refused to eat lunch or dinner on game days because it made them "too nervous." I would have friends who withered away into shadows of their former selves over summer conditioning sprees, coming back in September with leathery, tanned skin and visible shoulder blades like folded wings. I heard the cross-country runners brag about losing their periods, clearly marking it as a tribute to their dedication.

Nonetheless, sports are empowering for girls. My teammates were among my closest friends. We shared bonds far more resolute and unencumbered by gossip than my other girlfriends throughout adolescence. Some moments after practice or a game, I felt completely and totally happy—my teenage angst soothed by the dance of our one-three-one defense or the almost psychic connections we shared as we passed the ball down the floor. Sometimes the anxiety I felt about my body during the school day totally dissolved in the sweat of a hard practice—calories or fat thighs made irrelevant when the only question was: Can you box that girl out for the rebound? This was when empowerment still felt like empowerment.

But beneath the surface is a darker, more nuanced story about teenage girls and the drive toward perfection. Feminists have used the word *empowerment* as if it were a wall that they could build between girls and the culture they grow up in, but confusion, self-doubt, competition, and pressure all creep in, one way or another.

Deprivation as Dedication

Our team is losing at halftime as we jog, heads down, back into the locker room. The team sprawls around the center aisle of the lockers; some of us straddle the wooden benches; others sit on the floor, backs against the cold metal doors, heads between knees. We wait for Coach in silence, knowing he is checking on the stats with his assistant before berating us about our unconscionably bad first half. The bubble has burst.

Though he can't be more than five feet five, he has the wrath of a giant when he walks in and takes a deep breath, his voice growing louder as he recounts our foibles. "I don't know who that team out there was. I really don't. I have seen you in practice this week hitting the boards, running the plays, ready for today, but the team I saw out there looked like a bunch of losers. I could have put the freshman team out there and they would have stood up better against that team! At this point, I don't know if you even deserve to go back out there!"

I lift my head long enough to peek at Wendy, who is sitting closest to Coach on one of the splintery benches. Unlike the rest of us, who have that adolescent knee-jerk reaction against authority, she is nodding in agreement, eyes closed, rocking back and forth, as if she finds comfort in being chastised by our coach, loud and humiliating as an angry priest. While the rest of us feel angry and resentful toward him, she feels better. Her penance for being imperfect is self-flagellation. I can already see the plan forming in her head—a thousand baskets shot tomorrow morning, a ten-mile run on no breakfast, deprivation as dedication.

Young women generally don't take lightly their involvement in sports. Ask a serious female athlete, even one who didn't play in college, and she will tell you she stayed up late after practice to get homework done, ran that last mile with a sprained ankle, went to swim practice even earlier than the rest of the team to get in some extra strokes.

Athletics are predicated on this anything-for-my-sport attitude, but somehow it seems to pervert itself in the minds of eager young women. The guys I knew in high school who played sports were dedicated, sure, but when they left the football field or the basketball court, they didn't talk about a training regimen to make them improve, they gloated about how good they were. When they sat around Friday nights with a few friends, they glorified their own performance in the last game and talked about professional athletes whose physical ability they admired and tried to emulate. They had bravado—sometimes to a fault. No self-flagellation crept into their bragging monologues.

By contrast, girls feel strangely at home punishing themselves, as if we inherit some uniquely female gene for sacrifice and hard work that allowed our great-great-grandmothers to have babies in the middle of nowhere. We feel comfortable being hard on ourselves, justified in our self-criticisms, redeemed by our often outlandish dedication. We seem to crave the exhaustion of pressing to our physical limit, as if we thrive on unreasonable challenges. "Going the extra mile" is not above and beyond for female athletes; it is a must.

Girls take commitment to the extreme in their quest for perfection, often going past definitions of "healthy" in order to look or feel fully engaged in their sport. The trainer may recommend three miles of running a day for adequate conditioning, but the perfect girl decides that she will run five, then seven, then ten—all in honor of the game. Knowing that a healthy breakfast doesn't include too much fat or meat, she decides that means breakfast should be only a banana.

Teenage girls can be as dramatic about their sports as about their relationships. They want to be the best, whatever self-control or pain that requires of them. Megan, a nineteen-year-old Ultimate Frisbee junkie at Carleton College, explains: "I think that it pushes me towards excellence and finding the limits of my body, because I love having worked so hard I puke, or having taken such a beating on the pitch that I can't move the next day."

The girls with a drive for thinness and beauty used to be the ones in leg warmers heading to the local gym for an aerobics class, the ones who tried the latest diet and flipped obsessively through fashion magazines. But Jane Fonda, scissor-kicking her legs in the air, is no longer the paragon of the perfect athletic body; Mia Hamm is. In a 2001 study reported in the *Journal of Sport Behavior,* investigators found that perfectionism was significantly higher in Division I female athletes from the Midwest than in female aerobic exercisers. Thirteen percent of the exercisers worked out 450 minutes a week; that's equivalent to five times a week for an hour and a half. The Centers for

Disease Control recommend 30 minutes of moderate physical activity, five times a week. Even more excessive, 44.6 percent of the athletes surveyed exercised outside regular team practices. When you account for the fact that most Division I athletes have formal practice for at least three hours a day—with lifting and conditioning—that is equivalent to at least eight times more exercise than the government recommends.

I would guess that almost all female athletes have flirted with disordered eating, run a few miles on too little and realized they couldn't compete without real fuel, practiced too long without drinking enough water and grown dehydrated and shaky. Being involved in sports automatically makes you think more about the way your body works, looks, endures. Sportswomen test the boundaries of how much they need to eat and how long their bodies can go.

An athlete who cuts back on her food intake for a week in order to be more svelte for an upcoming swim meet is certainly not anorectic, but she has taken the mental first step toward making fasting normal. In multiple studies seeking to isolate the risk factors for eating disorders among athletes, many were found to have dieted at some point to improve performance or because a coach recommended they lose weight.

Some girls drive straight past their dream of athletic achievement into the dangerous territory of overexercising, undereating, overtraining. They may exhibit the signs for months—the protruding collarbones, the loss of menstruation, the plate left untouched—before anyone calls them on it and tries to get them help for something that is no longer called dedication; it is called a disease.

———

Kimberly, a highly competitive high school athlete from the Boston area, was recruited to play college field hockey, but what she really wanted to do was play lacrosse. When she arrived at Hobart, a liberal arts school in upstate New York, she was determined to be one of the two (of twenty-eight) first-year walk-ons who would make the lacrosse team. Known for her willingness to take on a challenge and her ability to set a goal and reach it, she was thought of by friends and family as a perfectionist. Coaches and teammates recall her as a player who always "left everything out on the field."

Adjusting to college was a bigger deal than Kim had anticipated. She went out to bars on the weekends and didn't get attention from many of the guys. Next to her disappointed reports in her diary, she began to log her weight. Looking back at these diaries years later, Kim was surprised to see that the two sprang up at the same time. "I didn't realize how much of my desire to lose weight was tied in to my desire to attract attention."

She stayed late after practice to condition more, she threw her entire heart into drills, she was ferocious and unintimidated during scrimmages. She ate carefully and nutritiously, never foods that would weigh her down at practice. She won her spot on the team and felt vindicated, but the struggle of her life was just beginning.

By October, things were going well—Kim was part of a tight-knit group of girls, she was losing weight rapidly and toning her suddenly visible muscles, and she was attracting the attention of a lot of guys around campus. She was playing well on the lacrosse team, though there were times when she felt light-headed and had to pretend otherwise. Her body was tired, but she was good at digging deep, used to calling on some hidden resource of strength when she needed a boost. By Christmas break, she was noticeably thinner. By Easter, she was emaciated. At five feet two, Kim weighed just seventy pounds.

Looking back, she acknowledges, "I know that it happened so fast, and that is pretty abnormal for anorexia. I really think that the only explanation is that I just got so caught up in my determination to 'beat the odds' in making this team, and I knew I had to go above and beyond my call of duty with how hard I trained."

How did Kim's original commitment so rapidly and unconsciously slip into disease? Where was her community? Where was the intervention? She recalls that her coach complimented her on her dedication to training. Friends at school didn't know her very well, so the rapid weight loss wasn't a red flag to them.

Her family knew better. They were so alarmed when they saw her in the spring that they immediately hospitalized her against her will. Though she didn't know it at the time, she would never go back to Hobart. She would also never play lacrosse again, but the competitive spirit was deeply engrained in her. "In the beginning," she recalls, "the anorexia felt empowering because I constantly needed to win. I won when I resisted food. I won when I worked out more. I won when I convinced people that I was okay. Eventually it became a very sick and twisted game."

Kim played this twisted game with all of her waning energy. She would feign a commitment to recovery just long enough to get out of the hospital and home, where she could control how little she ate once again. Her parents would go to work and she would exercise, against doctor's orders, and skip meals until they returned. When her parents caught on, she would go back to the hospital. Again and again and again . . . She was hospitalized a total of eight times before recovering.

Kim's revolving-door history is not unusual among anorectics. About 80 percent of the girls and women who get some kind of care for their eating disorders do not get the intensity of treatment they need to stay in recovery—they are often sent home weeks earlier than the recommended stay. In large part, this happens because inpatient services can cost as much as $30,000 a month. At Mirasol, a cutting-edge treatment program in Arizona, teenagers are required to stay for two months at a total cost of $57,000 (this includes a family program and continuing care). Ninety-six percent of eating-disorder professionals believe their anorectic patients are put in life-threatening situations because their health insurance policies mandate early discharge.

When Kim came home, she was barely able to think and was totally devoid of emotion, unattached to how she was making people around her feel—her family said it was like living with a "walking zombie." "When I got deeper and deeper into anorexia," Kim explains, "I truly did not feel like myself anymore. I literally was somebody else. I was not Kimberly for two and a half years."

Her last hospitalization was at a residential home, a growing trend in treating young women with eating disorders, where Kim lived, ate, and attended group therapy most of the day with eight other women. This was supposed to be a supportive environment but was actually her worst nightmare. "The mind-set of every single one of us was based around competing. We would sit in a circle during group and just think: *Who is the skinniest? Does she have smaller arms than me?* Oddly enough, I would even analyze the way the other patients were sitting and see if I could contort myself into that same skeletal position." Sometimes the competition was even more overt: "The second we were away from supervision, we would ask one another: 'What did you get away with hiding at dinner?'"

The competitive and catastrophically toxic environment of group therapy for eating disorder patients is vividly documented in Lauren Greenfield's HBO documentary *THIN*. Grown women infantilized by their diseases make fast friends as if they were thirteen-year-olds on the first day of middle school instead of patients in clinics, and then trash one another just as quickly. The catty, jealous, melodramatic nature of their relationships seems only to feed their disorders.

It was not the residential facility but the therapist she saw afterward who finally pushed Kim down the path to recovery. Wisely appealing to Kim's steely determination and spirit of competition, her therapist told her, "Okay, so you've proven to yourself that you can do this. You're really good at this. In fact, you're awesome at this. Why not try seeing if you can gain some weight? You will still be in control. You were in control when you started this thing. You're in control now. You'll be in control when you gain weight. It is up to you."

Kim had never looked at her disease this way, never realized that it had become one more game she was trying to master, one more competition she was trying to win. As with earning a spot on that elite lacrosse team, losing weight had become a goal. But there was no finish line with anorexia, no foreseeable end. The only way to heal was to convince herself that she would still be in control if she started gaining weight, that she wouldn't be "giving up." She decided to "compete" with her anorexia.

Almost two years later, Kim is still winning this, the most important game of her life.

Pressure from the Sidelines

Before the buzzer starts to announce the second half, our team squeezes in some shooting practice. Balls fly everywhere, few of them going in. It is clearly an off night. I take a few jump shots from the elbow, hoping to regain some of my confidence. There is nothing like the sound of the net to revive you.

Wendy is hearing a different sound. Her father, a stern small-business owner, is giving her an earful behind the basket. I can't hear what he's saying, but the tightness in his face and the look on Wendy's can't mean anything good. Wendy nods like a dashboard doll and stares at her shoes.

When he finally walks away, she heads over to the bench to retie her shoes, and I see Coach approaching. He's got another earful for her; this one looks a little less harsh. She looks him in the eye, again nods, interjects here and there with what appear to be ideas about plays that might work against the other team's defense. The buzzer sounds, and as we head back to the bench for the second half, I hear Coach say one last thing while giving Wendy a slap on the back: "Remember, we're counting on you here."

Parents and coaches sometimes put even more pressure on the ego and, in turn, the body. Perfect girls, already dead set on the finish line, are given even more incentive to go to any length to achieve their goal by overzealous supporters. In fact, their goals can often be difficult to distinguish from those of their parents and coaches on the sidelines.

The relationship between a coach and a serious female athlete is necessarily intimate. The athlete depends on the coach for guidance and inspiration. She looks to her or, most often, him to create training expectations and reinforce behavior that meets those expectations. When a coach makes offhand comments about weight or articulates a training philosophy that values weight loss more than getting stronger, the athlete's drive for perfection can become desperate. Dr. Craig Johnson explains, "Training girls in a method that equates low body fat with peak performance can bring disastrous results. All of us need to understand the risk of weight loss and realize that girls' weight loss is not a benign behavior."

Girls are vulnerable to their coaches' appeals to achieve—they want to please them, make them proud, prove them right about the worth of all that hard work. Coaches can take on a mythic force in young athletes' lives and become mentors for whom girls go too far, carving their bodies into symbols of their devotion.

Some parents also go too far in encouraging their daughters, not recognizing how vulnerable they are to the pressure to be perfect in all things at all costs. Mothers who were unable to follow their own athletic dreams sometimes live through their daughters. When things start to look dangerous, they fall back on the comforting notion that sports are "empowering" and turn a blind eye to obvious signs of disorder.

Fathers, eager to find a place to connect with their complicated daughters, sometimes see sports as the one true thing. It may be difficult to discuss relationships with boys, friends at school, their interest in art or poetry, but Friday night's basketball rivalry is something concrete, contained, and familiar. It makes dads feel progressive to support their daughters as ardently as they do their sons. Fathers are usually convinced that sports will give their daughters necessary life skills.

Many girls seek attention from otherwise absent fathers through their achievement in sports. Dr. Margot Maine, who coined the term "father hunger," writes that many women seek their fathers' approval "by exercising excessively, with their dads or independently, pushing their bodies to the point of exhaustion. They strive for a hard, lean body, believing that their dads will accept them if they achieve this. Often they pursue sports hoping to please their father rather than to fulfill any personal desires of their own."

Athletic achievement can become the prerequisite for parental attention—a dangerous and conditional proposition. The pressure to be a perfect girl becomes even more intense. The starving daughter's need to take a rest or show weakness cannot be tolerated by the superathlete aiming to win not just first place, but her parents' attention.

Sisters and Rivals

The coach didn't put me in during the third quarter. *I can't blame him,* I thought. *I'm playing like shit.* I had missed three shots in the first half and been weak on the boards. I was considering chalking this one up to an off night, a game better spent on the bench, when he tapped my shoulder. "Shelley."

I quickly jumped up and headed to the scorers' table so they could record the number on the back of my jersey. When the next buzzer sounded, I ran over to Shelley,* slapped her five, and said, "Great job." Under her breath, she answered, "Bullshit," and headed back to the bench, head down, but not before I gave her a swat at the head (translation: shut that up).

Wendy looked over and shouted, "We're in one-three-one. You're baseline. Work your ass off down there." Her sternness energized me, and I did a couple of little jumps in place to get my body warm again. We were not going to go down without a fight. No one could get me pumped up like Wendy.

As she dribbled the ball down the court, I felt a surge of nostalgia. Wendy and I had been playing together since we were in fifth grade. Back then she had been taller than all the boys in our grade, and I had been obsessed with Magic Johnson. We would finish practice at Steele Elementary and ride our bikes home side by side, fantasizing about all the girls we were going to beat once the games started.

We had been through a lot together, on and off the court, which created the kind of bond unique to teammates. But as I watched her body shrink, I had to resist the temptation to shrink mine as well. We had always been side by side; it took resolution not to follow her down this path too. Wendy was the girl whose body was most like mine in my group of friends. It was comforting to look at her on "bad-body days" and reassure myself that we were similar—that if I thought her body was an acceptable size, mine was as well (no matter how much the image in the mirror led me to believe otherwise).

When she started losing weight, I felt deserted, as if her apparent choice to overexercise and undereat was a veiled comment about *my* body, as if Wendy were leaning over and whispering in my ear—*we're actually not good enough, you know?* Of course, I never spoke to her about any of this.

I knew she was going to swing the ball my way before she did. I caught it unconsciously and instinctually looked inside. There she was, doing her damnedest to get a body on her opponent. I bounce-passed it in to her, and she went up for a beautiful, easy layup. Two more points. Wendy and I quickly slapped five as we booked it to the other end of the court—reenergized.

Sisterhood is complicated among teammates. Many female athletes express tremendous gratitude and love for the women with whom they grew up playing sports. Inherent in teamwork is a dependence on one another. Older team members are models for those just coming up. Michelle, a twenty-four-year-old gymnast from Denver, counters stereotypes about her sport when she explains: "If you don't eat, or you eat and throw up, you're not only hurting yourself, you're hurting your teammates as well."

The bond between teammates has a physicality to it, an intimacy reminiscent of family. I can remember the bodies of my high school teammates as if I had been in that locker room with them yesterday, though it has been nearly ten years. In practice we threw our bodies against one another despite the sweat, did dog piles on the birthday girl, huddled close in vans to away games to tell the stories of our first kisses in whispers that Coach wouldn't hear.

Teams are the strongest kind of community because they are built on shared dreams, physical challenges, and a hopeful journey. Ultimately, hope held us most closely together. We began every season with our shoulders heavy with the weight of possibility—*What if we could win state?*—and our feet fresh enough to carry the load. As the season waned, our load grew lighter, our feet more tired, but we had one another.

But the bond between teammates—especially female—is fraught with both covert and overt displays of competition, which is largely good and constructive but can also reveal how sensitive, insecure, and deprived girls feel. The stereotype is true—many girls become destructive and manipulative when faced with competition. Even teammates sometimes resort to backstabbing, unhealthy comparisons, and yes, unspoken but understood competitions between girls to lose weight and work out harder.

One Division I tennis player told me the story of her team and how it was corroded from the inside:

We were all so unbelievably close, that when one of us wouldn't eat or started just thinking more conscientiously about her calorie intake, the rest of us would follow suit. I knew that one of my teammates had once been hospitalized for anorexia, and so did everyone else. When she stopped eating again, instead of calling her out on it and trying to help her in some way, I think we actually started competing with her. I did. Finally the coach brought in a nutritionist to talk to us about the appropriate diet for athletes as physically active as we were. We took everything she said and twisted it—got hints of how to eat even less and still be able to perform. That girl and I never talked about it, but we both knew what was going on. Eventually she had to leave again and be hospitalized for a second time.

Just as sisters can hold you up and encourage you, they can break you down. In an athletic context, this breaking down can be insidious, because teammates are often pitted against one another for coveted positions, a coach's attention, or even a scholarship. And even beyond this overt competition, girls are notorious for creating their own subtle contests—most notably the race to be slimmer, stronger, and more in control.

Slippery Slope

My team lost. We didn't always, but when we did, we were so deflated that it felt like we collectively had the wind knocked out of us. After customarily slapping five with the other team, we gathered our empty water bottles and headed back into the locker room one last time for the night. We complained about the referees, compared notes on the dirtiest players, and then circled around to our own responsibility. "Sorry, guys, I played like shit tonight"—to which a chorus of girls would supportively holler back, "Shut up, we all played like shit." That was the beauty of the team-sport loss: There were twelve others to share in your disappointment.

Each of us dealt with the loss in a different way. The youngest of us was notorious for breaking into tears. She seemed to feel that the world had lied to her when we lost. Shelley always took it really hard too—not crying but punching lockers, sometimes storming off without saying a word to the rest of us.

Wendy faced loss as if it were a challenge from God; it only strengthened her determination to be more focused and condition harder. As she unlaced her sneakers and peeled off her two layers of tube socks, she would often offer a plan of action. "Guys, it just means we need to practice harder. We weren't ready. We have to get out there tomorrow and show Coach that we mean it." She skated right past any feelings of helplessness by visualizing her next workout, her next run, her next chance for redemption.

It resembled a healthy reaction. Clearly she had the resilience thing down. She was courageous in spades. Undoubtedly Wendy got a lot of positive feedback from coaches and teachers for this never-say-die attitude. But there was something eerily detached about it all, as if she had crossed the line of determination and moved on to obsession. She didn't process our losses the way the rest of us did—with obvious disappointment, a slow but inevitable recovery of confidence, renewed hope for a better game next time after pep talks from boyfriends and brothers. Wendy was a one-woman army. She marched straight past loss on her way to fight that inevitably losing battle (with herself) to achieve absolute and total perfection.

———————

There was no talk of wellness or personal best on my basketball team. It was "Win, win, win!" or go home with your head hanging—and be prepared to come in Monday and do some serious push-ups so that you remember your failings in the ache of your biceps. A high school athlete from the Bay Area also remembers this emphasis on competition without any thought of well-being or balance: "I dreamed of being a professional runner someday, and part and parcel of that dream was losing my period. I knew that that was what happened to serious athletes, so I saw it as something to aim for, something that would prove my absolute dedication to my goal."

The female athletes who achieved on the highest level were those who sacrificed everything for their sport. One high school lacrosse player from West Hartford remembers that she and her teammates were asked to attend practice over spring break instead of taking vacations with their families. Others stopped eating the foods typical of teenage happy-go-lucky life—pizza, burgers, soda—in the name of their sport, their childhood cut short by the desire to compete on an adult level. One Ivy League cross-country star I spoke to talked about missing her entire college experience because she was running. Only after college did she discover the joy of lazy Saturdays, sitting around with friends in a neighborhood park, drinking beers without worrying about every extra calorie.

The competition inherent in athletics can teach girls to set a goal, practice in order to achieve it, and be resilient if it doesn't pan out, but it may also teach them to drive forward like crazy, tolerate real pain, compare themselves with others constantly. This mentality gives female athletes an excuse to forgo food; run harder, faster, longer; strive—under all circumstances—to be the best. Their bodies are transformed into machines, not living, breathing flesh and blood but a series of muscles coordinated to achieve a task. Many female athletes stop listening to their bodies' fatigue or hunger cries.

This slippery slope from dedication to disease is too often ignored. Female athletes sometimes develop what sports medicine doctors and nutrition experts have come to understand as the female athlete triad: disordered eating, amenorrhea (the cessation of menstruation), and osteoporosis. This disturbing set of symptoms shows up in practitioners of all sports but especially those based on appearance, judging, or individual performance, such as gymnastics, swimming, cheerleading, and track and cross-country. However rampant the female athlete triad may be in these sports, it is certainly not limited to them. Doctors report seeing teenage girls with these symptoms in a variety of traditional and nontraditional sports. Of the big team sports of my high school—basketball, lacrosse, soccer, volleyball—all had one or two girls exhibiting the triad to different degrees.

There is a type of anorexia associated specifically with athletes called "anorexia athletica." Women suffering from this particular disease share the symptoms of anorexia—weight loss, gastrointestinal complaints, excessive fear of becoming obese, loss of menstruation—but they also compulsively exercise.

I played organized team sports for fifteen years and was even recruited at the college level but never heard a thing about either of these diagnoses. The only name for the behaviors I saw—skipping meals, staying after practice to run more, getting up before school to run again—was dedication. There was no effort to educate me or my teammates about the dangers of overexertion or lack of nutrition. In a 2004 study that appeared in the *Journal of Athletic Training*, 93 percent of trainers felt that increased attention needs to be paid to preventing eating disorders among female athletes, but only one in four felt confident identifying a female athlete with one, and only one in three felt confident asking an athlete if she had one. Even so, 91 percent of those surveyed reported having dealt with a female athlete with an eating disorder.

———————

And when the game is truly over?

After women athletes stop playing their sport, they often channel their drive into other things. They are the last to go to bed after a night out dancing, the first to wake up. They are the most obsessive about their jobs, staying into the wee hours of the morning even when everyone else goes home. They often continue to see their bodies as projects, as opposed to parts of them, and aim to sculpt their bodies, deprive them, harness their wild urges. Fiona, a dedicated field hockey and lacrosse player in high school, noticed that her ability to think healthily about food diminished when sports were over: "After season ended each year, I became more focused on what I was eating, how I would continue to stay fit, and what my scale read."

It is hellishly hard to be a serious high school or college athlete and then stop playing your sport. You have never known your body under these circumstances, with unstructured hours and unwatched appetites. Suddenly you are left with questions: *When and in what way do I work out? What is normal to eat when I'm not conditioning a few hours a day? How much is too much? How much too little?*

I was recruited to play lacrosse for Columbia University, but when I realized that the practice required would cut into my overachieving time—no Friday internships, no newspaper meetings—I decided to quit. Instead, I woke up at 7:00 A.M. my entire first year of college to go running in the park, and ate only a piece of fruit, if that, for breakfast on my way to Italian class. I hated running. It hurt my knees and felt boring and rote, but I didn't know how else to carry over the familiarity of extreme physical conditioning. I would be stomping along Riverside Park, my joints aching, my breath heavy, thinking of what I wouldn't eat that day because, now that I wasn't playing a sport, I couldn't justify it. I missed my teammates, missed the rush of running out of that locker room before a game, missed, even, the feeling of shared loss as opposed to the solitary displacement I felt as a first-year.

I missed Wendy—her pale, fuzzy forearms, her long black braid swinging like a pendulum across her back, her hip bones sticking out of the top of her mesh shorts. I imagined her, somewhere back in Colorado, running just as I was running, footfalls in excruciating rhythm.

We kept in touch sporadically after high school, and then not at all. Wendy never showed up at the impromptu reunions at smoky bars during Christmastime, when the rest of our high school came out of the woodwork. She wasn't, as I had hoped, at Katie's wedding. She stopped e-mailing back. Stopped returning phone calls. I wonder if she just got tired of the raised eyebrows when people saw how skinny she had gotten over the years. I don't know if Wendy ever had an eating disorder. All I know is that she was my first intimate introduction to the determination and rabid willpower that can so easily slip into one.

Sometimes I still drive by her childhood home, a place where I spent a lot of time coming up with new plays or recapping the latest game. Last I heard—through the neighborhood grapevine—she was living with a boyfriend in a small town, thin as ever.

10

The College Years: Body Obsession Boot Camp

In Hewitt, the cafeteria affectionately labeled Spewitt by the Barnard first-years who went there three times daily, I fully understood the gruesome extent to which women hate their bodies. There girls hovered just above steaming trays of eggplant Parmesan or corn bread—seemingly paralyzed, their eyes glazed, their breath heavy. They wandered, back and forth, back and forth, among the sandwich station, the cereal bins, the salad bar, as if lost and frightened. Like little girls, they were wide-eyed, restless, incapable. Once in line, they watched one another intently, composing their meals by comparisons: *How much did she take?* The waiting, watching woman behind takes just that much, or less if feeling particularly insecure. *Yes, just a few leaves of lettuce, fewer grains of rice, fewer flakes of Raisin Bran.* She feels better than the next girl, less fat, undesirable, and out of control.

When friends finally sit down together at a table, they all have a moment of silent calculation. At one meal my best friend, Allison, looked at my plate and said scathingly, "God, Courtney, you're so healthy." It was then that I understood that my choices made her feel bad, that I was no longer eating or not eating for myself but for all the women who sat beside me. My self-control was a black mark in their books, my indulgence was permission.

This strange dance was even more disturbing after Columbia boys discovered the Barnard dining hall a few months into the school year and started to trek there for our larger, juicier hamburgers and peach cobbler. They strode into the north entrance with their baggy jeans and short-sleeve T-shirts over long-sleeve T-shirts, swiped their IDs, and went straight for the burger line. They laughed and hollered to one another, seemingly delighted that it was time to consume greasy food and share inside jokes with their friends. Each piled his tray with five glasses of soda, three dripping burgers, lots of sides, unself-consciously. I envied them their freewheeling laughter, their autonomy, their simplicity, their joy found in food. Any joy the women at my table felt was in frightened spurts, self-hating indulgences, recriminating losses of control.

We picked and picked and picked at our plates, tore apart slices of pizza one tiny yank of greasy cheese at a time, peeled the skin off the chicken, abandoned the top slices of bread off our tuna sandwiches, consumed slowly, methodically, piece by piece. Meanwhile, of course, we were describing the pretentious twits in our first-year seminars, laughing about our roommates' sleep-talking nonsense, getting riled up about Rousseau or Machiavelli, Derrida when we were at our most brave. But all the while, even when constructing beautiful arguments about the primacy of the text or the misogyny of Aristotle, we were carefully, silently calculating our daily intake of calories.

These women were not outwardly obsessed or shallow but smart, imaginative, optimistic, courageous, and loving. Underneath the buzz of our wonder at the world and the comfort of sisterhood, however, was an undeniable, ongoing negotiation. The inner scholar soberly reminded us, *Naomi Wolf was right—the beauty myth is preposterous and destructive.* The perfect girl warned, *Watch it. Careful. Don't lose control.* And the starving daughter, far from home and afraid, whispered, *I want dessert. I want dessert.*

Our bodies became a topic of volatile inner debate.

Colleges are breeding grounds for eating disorders and unhealthy obsession with food, since this kind of neurosis usually starts between the ages of seventeen and twenty. Girls lugging trunks and stereos from far away land in one place, then proceed to teach one another how to starve, binge, and purge. Ninety-one percent of women surveyed on a college campus had attempted to control their weight through dieting, 22 percent dieted "often" or "always." Even more frightening, 35 percent of "normal dieters" progress to pathological dieting. Of those, 20 to 25 percent progress to partial or full-blown eating disorders.

There are cafeterias in California, Ohio, North Carolina that look just like Hewitt, the only difference being the regional cuisine (one college girl's cheesecake is another's green tomato pie). And in every one, you will hear furtive whispers about the dreaded "freshman fifteen."

The freshman fifteen has been proved a myth by multiple studies—56 percent of college first-years do gain weight, but the average is only 4.6 pounds, and 36 percent actually lose weight. Still, it's a significant preoccupation of most college girls. Instead of exploring values, great ideas, sexuality, instead of learning to write and think critically, instead of composing an adult identity, too often girls are agonizing over which has fewer calories, the bagel sandwich or the muffin. This agonizing leads to some pretty bizarre behaviors.

Christina, a graduate of NYU and a current Ph.D. candidate at UCLA, remembers, "A friend of mine would want to smell the food I was eating—food she wouldn't allow herself to eat but often craved." A fellow Barnard alumna remembers: "Spring break my senior year, two of my friends and I ate a piece of fruit each for breakfast. We spent the day at the beach, and six hours later, starving, we went to a restaurant where all my friends complained about how they felt guilty for being hungry considering we had been lying down on the beach all day. Then, of course, they all ordered salads."

Spring break, as *The New York Times* noted in 2006, has

become a make-it-or-break-it moment for many of the young and body-obsessed, for whom "this annual weeklong bacchanalia, unfolding across Florida, Mexico, and the Caribbean during March and April, represents the summit of deprivation and denial." Whenever girls travel in gaggles, as is the tradition come spring, they spread eating-disorder ethos. Dr. Margo Maine deems the disease-inducing drive for the bikini-ready body "contagious."

Eating disorders back on campuses sometimes take on a far more serious, even life-threatening form. In fact, Stonehill College, located in Easton, Massachusetts, was sued by its former student Keri Krissik when they denied her readmission after she suffered a heart attack as a result of anorexia. Resuscitated and implanted with a defibrillator designed to shock her heart back into a normal rhythm if necessary, Keri wanted to return to her Roman Catholic college for her junior year in 2001. One of Stonehill's lawyers gruffly articulated their fear that she would "drop dead." She never went back.

How did this sad reality come to be—a world where girls smell food instead of eating it and get defibrillators instead of diplomas?

Little Miss Can't Be Wrong

In college a perfect girl can indulge every fantasy, take challenging courses, join an unlimited number of clubs and activities, and exercise around the clock. After she gets over the shock of being a little fish in a big pond, she sets out to grow fast. Hungry for honor and status, she becomes class and club president, summa cum laude superstar, sits in the front row of classes, studies incessantly. My best friend, Allison, didn't come home for three days once in the middle of a semester. I finally found her asleep on a pile of flash cards in the library with empty coffee cups and drained highlighters strewn about her.

There are the occasional go-get-'em men, but they are rarities among a sea of running, hand-raising, worried women. When my Columbia boyfriend or his friends crossed campuses to take a class at Barnard, they commented on how damn accountable all the female students were. "I don't take classes over there anymore because the Barnard girls are too uptight," one complained. "I mean, they actually do *all* of the reading," he scoffed. Eventually he admitted that he had never checked a book out of any of the libraries on campus. It was our junior year, and this guy is no slacker. Now in medical school, he is determined to serve an underprivileged community when he gets out.

There are more of these perfect girls around than ever; women have outnumbered men on college campuses since 1979, and on graduate school campuses since 1984. This drive might be a good thing in the long run—if it were just academic. Unfortunately, the insistence on perfection bleeds straight from the brain into the body: from perfect test scores and grades to perfect fitness and physique. Researchers and psychologists confirm that girls most likely to develop an eating disorder, or plain old obsession with fitness and food, are high achievers; many attend the best colleges in the nation. According to a 2004 study of eating disorders at the University of Pennsylvania, 60 percent of women were trying to lose pounds even though they were at a healthy weight. Since 2001 eating disorders have increased fourfold there. At Georgetown, as many as 25 percent of students suffer from eating disorders. In campus health centers across the nation, there are waiting lists to see eating-disorder specialists on staff: Support groups overflow into extra rooms.

Take twenty-three-year-old Jennifer Boevers—a dedicated art studio major and an honors student at Mills College. The director of the Mills College Arts Museum, Stephan Jost, explained that she "pushed the limits of what undergrads are capable of." A senior and classmate, Charity Tooze, described her ethic: "She was so ambitious. I thought she needed to take it easy. She would be in the museum for eighteen hours a day and up on scaffolding, and usually I would see her only drink milk." Jennifer graduated in May 2004, destined for a career in the art world, but the only public exhibition that would ever be mounted of her work was a memorial at her hometown city hall—she died of anorexia on September 15, 2004. The casket was small; she was five foot five and weighed only eighty pounds.

For every visible casualty such as Jennifer, there are thousands of college women holding themselves to an irrational standard of perfection. They meticulously choose their three hundred calories a meal, convince themselves that working out twice a day is okay because first it was the treadmill, then it was the StairMaster—different muscle groups, different delusions.

Their bodies become biology experiments, split off from their minds. As Kate, a Barnard alumna, puts it, "In college, like no other time in my life, I was just so in my head all the time. I could go two weeks at a time without really feeling like I occupied my own body." Christina agrees: "There was a classic split between body and soul—one was always waning while the other was growing." This nasty disassociation cuts a college girl in half—part perfect girl, part starving daughter. She is driving toward success with her brain while trying to monitor the wild appetites of her neglected body. Running on the treadmill becomes mechanical rather than a joyful surge of adrenaline. Emotions—real, bona fide loneliness, not tears over *Extreme Makeover Home Edition*— are so neglected that they show up as vicious hunger pains.

Young women know how to be savagely self-critical. As I lay in the dark of my first-year dorm room, listening to my roommate's sweet snore, I would recount everything I put in my mouth that day: Banana for breakfast—good. Chicken Caesar wrap for lunch—bad. Salad for dinner—good. Cookie for dessert—bad. Another cookie at the newspaper meeting—bad, bad, bad. Tomorrow—run before class, eat nothing until lunch.

A cookie can suddenly take on the gargantuan meaning of a grade—if you avoid the sweet, comforting taste in your mouth at a boring meeting, you pass. If you are lazy, out of control, undisciplined, and eat this wretched little concoction, you fail. There is nothing more disgusting to a perfect girl than the taste of failure.

Shaky Beginnings

As I sat down in the circle of cross-legged, wide-eyed women who made up my orientation group, I was shaking. A tall redhead with a severely thin, pointy nose was telling the girl next to her that she had chosen Barnard over Harvard. Others included a woman with frizzy hair intentionally uncombed, combat boots, fishnet stockings; a tiny woman drowning in a huge gray sweatshirt and baggy jeans, Timberland boots on her tiny feet; and Allison, who was everything I always heard a woman should be: petite, blond, smart, and wealthy. She wore a periwinkle-blue sweater set and khaki pants. I had never seen a sweater set before. Her hair was curly, like mine, but somehow had been trained to sit in perfect coils all around her face. It seemed magical to me after the seventeen years I had wrestled with, ironed, brushed, and sprayed my own mop.

Allison offered immediate intimacy. She told me about her boyfriend, an equally blond "Choate man." (I had no idea what a Choate man was at the time but nodded in fake recognition.) Allison was a ballerina back in Texas—the Ice Queen in *The Nutcracker,* no less. I had tried out for a local production of *The Nutcracker* three times, finally to be awarded the part of a shuffling angel with plastic wings and an itchy costume. Allison's magic deepened. I was mesmerized by her and her stories. I was mesmerized by her perfectly flat stomach, small feet, ribbed turtleneck sweaters, and Searle coat.

Before long Allison and I were best friends—bonded over being so far from home. I was terrifically afraid, and Allison was my guide. The first thing she taught me was that perfection is usually very ugly on the inside.

―――――――

The first months of college are like learning to walk and talk all over again. Your high school status as the smartest, prettiest, bitchiest, nicest, or sluttiest is washed away by new beginnings. You arrive ignorant of the rites and rituals of college life. Along with everyone else, you are fresh and clean, and totally, completely freaked out.

In this insecure state, it is common for young women to latch on to the first person who seems slightly more seasoned. Her guide may be the girl who taught her the differences among the various fraternities, let her borrow a two-hundred-dollar sweater, knew how to attract an endless string of newly pimpleless boys. She may also teach a thing or two about how to starve.

A college first-year is a veritable sponge, soaking up the civil rights movement and the details of the Atkins diet as she constructs her identity. Indeed, 42 percent of undergraduate women told the feminist author Kristin Rowe-Finkbeiner that their foremost concern is "self-identity." Some of this process is joyful—being young and experimental, kissing boys on fire escapes, watching a subtitled film and actually liking it, maybe even dancing at a downtown club until the wee hours of the morning, high on something your parents just watched a *Nightline* special about. Some of it is downright excruciating. You get a D on your first political science paper and have to camp out at the Writing Room for extra help. You have to go to that chemistry class even though the guy you made out with the night before sits two rows behind you. *I'm never doing that again* is a frequent mantra of the college first-year.

In the yearlong Women's Initiative study at Duke that revealed young women striving for "effortless perfection," women students reported a "social scene in which women feel pressed to conform to powerful social norms that are often at odds with their personal educational development, and with affirming themselves as strong and distinctive people." A first-year's self-image is completely insecure and hinges on the smallest feedback from other people—the guy who asked for your number Saturday night suddenly confirms your worth as a human being; the professor who wrote "an original and well-written essay" on the bottom of your midterm convinces you, at least for the moment, that you are destined for great and wonderful things. And as the Duke study also confirms, even in the most rigorous of university settings, "being 'cute' trumps being smart for women in the social environment."

Your friends hold a potent social power when you are in this amoebalike state. I looked down at my plate one Wednesday evening in late September and noticed that I had the exact same meal as Allison: one piece of dry toast and coffee with artificial sweetener. Six months earlier, I would have been quite clear that this didn't constitute a meal, but here, in this wild and wonderful place where all the rules were new and all the faces foreign, it looked safe. My instincts were rubbed raw from all the self-doubt; the shady guy at the party, my professor's lecture on Machiavelli, that girl on my floor who did ecstasy on weekdays all gave me stomachaches but were admired by others. I began chalking up my little surges of small-town fear to naïveté, pushing through the yelps of fight or flight and sticking to it.

Allison seemed unhappy a lot of the time, but she was smart and beautiful. I was awed by her size-two jeans and her ability to attract boys instantly. If eating dry toast and drinking coffee translated into attention from boys and a jealousy-inducing waistline, I would try it. In this way, a piece of unsatisfying dry toast becomes a membership card into the biggest, most active club on campus: the girls who choose food not to satisfy hunger or desire but to avoid it.

Caroline Knapp disappeared pound by pound while an undergrad at Brown University. In her memoir *Appetites,* she describes how it all began: "If I had to pinpoint a defining moment in my history, I'd go back twenty-three years, to an otherwise unmemorable November evening when I made an otherwise unmemorable purchase: a container of cottage cheese." This tiny choice was the pinprick that let in the flood of deprivation. After tasting the unsatisfying nuggets of white pasty goo for the first time and feeling adept at denial, she decided, somewhere deep in the recesses of her powerful brain, that she would stop eating. This became the cornerstone of her identity— smart, fun, and skeletal, or, as she put it, "The inner life—hunger, confusion, longings, unnamed and unmet, that whole overwhelming gamut—as a sculpture in bone."[†]

For most women in college (or high school, for the quick studies), there is a similar moment when they unconsciously choose to buy in. For some it is marked by a container of cottage cheese or a piece of dry toast and a cup of coffee, or a Diet Coke, or nonfat yogurt, or tofu. These seemingly simple, fleeting food choices are actually representative

---

[†]Knapp's *Appetites* is one of the books that influenced me the most on this subject. Tragically, she died of cancer right after she finished writing it in 2002.

Perfect Girls, Starving Daughters

of much larger decisions. They are not choices about food. They are choices about control. The first time you let deprivation feel good, you let in the possibility of disorder. What begins as just a flirtation with willpower can quickly become an obsessive love affair.

The Elephant in the Dorm Room

On the first really warm day in May, the students of Columbia and Barnard gather at the steps leading up to the luminous dome of Low Library at the center of campus and pretend that school is over, despite the reality of finals looming. Frat boys play Frisbee. A crew of black guys laugh over inside jokes. Three short, stocky girls with their sorority symbols displayed not so discreetly on the backs of their short shorts eat frozen yogurt out of minuscule foam cups. I sit with Allison and a couple other girls from my floor, watching the melee, and gossip:

"Those shorts are way too short. Who do those girls think they are?"

"I know," I chime in. "Why would you ever want to be in a sorority?"

"Yeah, they just remind me of the girls back home. Why would I want to pay dues to live in a house of gossipy girls who all have eating disorders?" Allison wonders aloud. I look around, silently counting how many of us have or are on our way to having eating disorders. Every last one.

An eerie silence follows.

We were not in an official sorority, but every girl everywhere who has a group of girlfriends can't claim to be far from the short shorts and the club dues. We didn't wear ribbons in our hair or have secret handshakes, but we certainly had our own unspoken rituals: the milling over the salad bar, the silent survey of plates at the table, the chorus of "shut up" when one of us admitted to feeling undesirable. And, of course, one of the most ingrained rituals of all—the slow walk back up to our dorm floor with requisite groans and regrets: *I can't believe I ate all that. Yeah, no kidding. I feel like I need to get on a treadmill for a week. Why didn't anyone stop me from getting that last cookie?* If you didn't express your disgust with yourself, you were smug. If you did, you felt bad, but at least you didn't feel alone.

All-female communities are both the best and the worst of college life. Whether they are composed of sorority social butterflies or the cynical and serious breed who vehemently reject sorority ethos, they are basically incubators for screwed-up ideas about food and fitness. In a recent study, women both in and outside of sororities showed equally disturbing levels of body dissatisfaction. Sororities put their body hatred right out on the table. Literally. In one University of Oregon sorority, a friend of mine told me, new recruits are forced to stand on tables in their underwear and let the older girls circle their "problem areas" with black permanent marker— reminders of what they need to work on in order to achieve the standards necessary to call themselves sisters.

My girlfriends did not circle girls' problem areas with black marker, but the shared agenda to be thin and perfect is evident in the raised eyebrows of a critical suitemate at dinnertime or the one-upmanship in subtle deprivation: *If Allison can be nonchalant about skipping meals, why can't I?* Christina's girlfriends at NYU wouldn't tell one another when they were going to the gym because "it was a way to get one up on the rest—sneak in a workout and avoid the possibility of encouraging another girlfriend, who you were in competition with, to burn some calories."

She also remembers: "The girls with the more discreet eating 'issues' would make fun of the girls with more flagrant 'in-your-face' eating disorders. Sometimes we would rag on the girls with anorexia because every once in a while they would listen to their screaming hunger and eat all of our food in the dorm kitchen. Like, 'Oh, great, Heather decided to eat tonight and devoured all of my pesto pasta. What a stupid bitch.'"

Eating disorders, or less severe weight obsessions, are often masked as diet restrictions or food preferences. Your roommate eats nothing but nonfat yogurts and Luna bars because she claims she just can't get enough of them. You haven't seen a morsel of solid food pass the lips of your best friend in days, but Diet Coke goes down fine. Another friend insists that she eat only a quarter of every dinner out so she can take home leftovers, but you have never seen her unearth a single foam container from her fridge. A University of Texas sophomore describes some of the most common excuses: "Girls feign lactose intolerance or pretend they have food allergies to avoid eating carbs, dairy, and sugar. Vegetarianism is also a common trend among those trying to shed a few pounds."

Hidden within the otherwise supportive and intellectually vibrant all-women's communities is the canker of acute competition over food, a constantly escalating drive to work out more, better, faster than the girl next to you at the gym. Like a monster, it lurks within the hearts of otherwise loving girlfriends, rearing its ugly head at mealtimes. It talks in furtive whispers, disguised as an inner voice: *She's skinnier than I am, I hate her. I can't eat tomorrow.* Or even worse: *I'm so relieved she's getting fat. Look at her, her stomach is getting really gross. I'm much prettier than she is.* It reverberates in my head during a yoga class, where, ironically, I am supposed to be breathing in self-love and light: *That girl is better at this than I am. I'm too fat and inflexible to look like that.*

The University of Pennsylvania junior Caroline Rothstein knows this voice all too well. She has suffered from bouts of anorexia and bulimia over the past ten years. Caroline told her campus newspaper that she feels like at least half the students at Penn, especially women, have some sort of issue with eating but laments that nobody will say it aloud: "The fact that nobody talks about it makes it more shameful. Everyone thinks that she's alone. People can keep everything inside their heads."

In a vibrant, verbal college community, young women share almost everything—test scores, literary theories, boyfriends, and makeup secrets—but when it comes to their own food and fitness regimens, they become mute. Naomi Wolf describes this silent breed of college girls as "walking question marks challenging—pleading—with schools, universities, and the other mouthpieces that transmit what is culturally acceptable in women, to tell them unequivocally: This is intolerable. This is unacceptable. We don't starve women here. We value women." But still, fifteen years after *The Beauty Myth* was published, there is no such transmission.

To speak about our disordered relationship with food, to externalize our most unwise inner voices, would confirm how sick we are. So we stay silent. We write about the theme of the body in *The Scarlet Letter.* We make fun of our mothers' fad diets. We sneak into a bathroom stall, wait for the last girl's slippers to go padding out, and then stick our fingers down our throats to dislodge the secret. Somehow retching our innermost fears and failures has become easier than saying them aloud. One woman remembers: "Hearing someone throw up for the first time in a public bathroom at school—and it's not like I hadn't thought about it before, but—that was what made purging a reality for me. It made it accessible." She would go on to purge a few times a month for years after college herself.

The silence is contagious. While it is socially appropriate to complain about gaining a few pounds—a little self-deprecation makes others feel you're nonthreatening—admitting to skipping meals or throwing up after them was generally taboo when I was in college. Today it seems more acceptable for college women to talk about it. We wanted to believe that we were smart enough to stay very thin but not stupid enough to get an eating disorder.

Too Smart to Be Sick

Serena speaks in a torrent of words. She is a brilliant, endearingly clumsy, hip, and self-effacing young woman who makes other people feel smarter just from being around her. She studied cultural anthropology at the University of Michigan, focusing on contemporary religion and society, and lived in a co-op filled with hippies, hip-hoppers, and indie rockers—all kids who thought of themselves as far more enlightened than those who blindly followed the sexist edicts of the dominant Greek system there.

But after one year of drinking beer, eating dining hall food, and getting side effects on a birth control pill, Serena suddenly felt fat. She didn't talk about it with her friends. It would have been horribly uncool and would have transformed her from a cool girl who knew a lot about indie rock and contemporary literature into a cliché. The last thing that Serena wanted was to be a cliché. Perfect girls pride ourselves on uniqueness as we are constructing our identities—*I need two more parts carefree drinker and a bit less bleeding heart, or maybe a little more Heidegger and a little less Toni Morrison.* We want to be seen as free from the lame hang-ups that other girls have. It is so suburban to be counting calories or reading diet books, so philistine.

But when we succumb to feeling fat, just like the next imperfect girl, we are hit with guilt. We develop a double consciousness, or what the British psychologists Helga Dittmar and Sarah Howard describe as a marked contrast between our "awareness of ideals versus our internalization." Serena, highly educated and bursting with conviction, despised the thin ideal that terrorized young women (her awareness of ideals), but in her heart she was never good enough (internalization). The contrast led her to keep silent, and she developed low-level anorexia.

Her disease was fed by the silence surrounding it. Because she was embarrassed that she was thinking and feeling like a "stupid girl" inside, she projected a blasé detachment on the outside. She was nonchalant about her weight loss with family and friends when she went home to New Jersey on vacations, and her friends at school largely ignored her disappearing flesh. It was as if no one addressing it out loud made it stay in the realm of smart-girl happenstance rather than become a very deliberate and restrictive stupid-girl obsession. In fact, educational attainment continues to prove one of the most predictive factors for eating disorders. A 2004 Canadian study confirms that "education appears to be more important than occupationally defined social class in explaining body dissatisfaction."

Another woman I interviewed, who prefers to stay anonymous, talks about losing weight after a breakup as a seemingly magical, spontaneous event. Suddenly she was fifteen pounds lighter and getting compliments from friends and family, but she remembers, "I wished people would stop talking about it, as if the more they mentioned it, the less real it would get. I actually felt like I was walking around on eggshells, so as not to scare the weight back on or something. It was like this precarious silence that I clung to while trying to look like I wasn't clinging at all."

Despite what carefully silent girls try to exude, the weight does not magically disappear, nor does it magically stay off. Serena was not, despite her performance for family and friends, "effortlessly perfecting" her body. She was keeping exhaustive lists of the foods that she succumbed to each day and the number of miles she ran. She remembers, "My best friend found the lists of what I'd eaten and freaked out at me. After I rebuffed her, she only made occasional joking comments."

Irony and humor are the ultimate weapons of the smart girl trying to evade her stupid-girl fate. We make fun of the calorie counters in the dining hall and then pick at our milkless cereal. We brush off the concern of our mothers with quips: "Afraid you'll lose good feminist points if your daughter loses a few pounds?" We mercilessly make fun of ourselves if we let a little self-consciousness about our weight spill out. It is a fine distinction: Looking in the mirror and whining, "I feel fat!" is lame, but smoking cigarettes and feigning disinterest in food is cool. Being Barbie-like is unoriginal, but resembling the actress Chloë Sevigny is hip. Churning away on treadmills is stupid, but going on long, meditative runs with your iPod blasting the latest Björk is smart. Though we make an effort to keep track of these fine distinctions, many of us slip up and reveal that we are as obsessive about our weight as the cheerleaders we so mercilessly made fun of.

About five years past anorexia and two years into medical school,

Serena recognizes that her perfectionist tendency is both the backbone of her success—she scored almost perfectly on her recent boards—and the bane of her existence—she continues to feel ravaged by critical thoughts about her body. The anorectic behavior has gone away, but much of the insidious, destructive thinking hasn't changed. She explains: "Despite a certain amount of insight that tells me such a view is unfair and masochistic, I have a tendency to believe that everything comes down to self-discipline—if I fail at something, be it not doing well on an exam or eating too much at a meal, then that represents a breakdown of self-control."

In the next breath she admits: "I hate being this way; I dislike that I am associating myself with the superficial, diet-obsessed women I scoff at. I am often shocked and frustrated with myself that, despite being an insightful, self-aware feminist, I feel bad when I eat a freaking bagel."

This double consciousness—being "an insightful, self-aware feminist" on the one hand and a guilty, obsessive sheep on the other—festers inside perfect girls. We end up not being liberated but enduring a double dose of guilt: the initial guilt over eating too much or skipping workouts, and the subsidiary guilt of feeling dumb for it. It is an ugly, silent spiral that seems to feed perfectionism and secrecy. The silence means that smart girls don't get help. Which, of course, is really stupid.

I spoke with a group of mostly first-year students at Colorado College after a screening of Jean Kilbourne's *Dying to Be Thin,* a documentary on the tyranny of the advertising industry. Twenty or so eighteen-year-olds poked fun at Kilbourne's conspiracy-theory take on the "evil gatekeepers" of the industry when so many of those with power are now women. I was impressed with their analysis of Dove's Real Beauty campaign—"Sure, it is awesome to see real bodies, but do you notice what they are selling? Thigh cream!"

However, when I brought up this idea—that college-age women often feel too smart to have eating disorders and, therefore, don't talk about their personal struggles—I was met with a silence so thick you could hear the buzz of the television behind me. The conversation sputtered to a revealing close.

Survivor Guilt

Pointing out to a friend that she seems to be too thin or is obsessing about her fitness and body is awkward and dangerous. Unless she admits to it—a rare case—you become insta-bitch, the girl who thinks she's better than everyone else, free from the disease that everyone knows (if not admits) is pretty much universal on some level, a meddler, a Pollyanna. If she does admit to it, chances are you will feel guilt anyway—over confronting her too late or not in the right way.

These kinds of interactions demolish otherwise vibrant friendships. Many girls in their late teens and twenties have suffered a lost friendship, the casualty of an eating disorder or related issue. I have stood in buffet lines at weddings listening to wet-eyed accounts of college roommates confronted and lost. Over coffee and drinks and in walks in the park, girls have told me of their undying regret that they didn't say something, anything, earlier to a friend who wasted away. Adult women, women with babies and even grandbabies, blurt the names of friends who used to "throw up after meals," though back then they didn't know the label for what was happening. It is now a typical female experience—identifying disordered behavior in a close friend, mulling over whether or not to say something, worrying about her reaction, nervously intervening, suffering the consequences.

My fear over offending or misinterpreting or prying kept me from saying anything to Allison for a very long time. It actually took me almost a year even to put it all together—the four helpings of peach cobbler in Hewitt followed by a sudden disappearance, the constant sore throats and lame excuses for skipping meals altogether. It was very real, but very hard to put my finger on. Certainly a part of me didn't want to shatter my own fragile illusion about Allison: the ideal, gracefully flawless blonde. I had made up a story in my mind about our friendship—two fiercely smart, effortlessly alluring girls taking on the world arm in arm, two Lois Lanes destined to be their own Super-men, two third-wave feminists, as smart as our moms but not afraid to be a little excited about being pretty.

The truth was ugly.

I listened to her vomiting in the bathroom of our ninth-floor apart-ment, the retching and the gagging, the small pause, and then more of it. The sound filled my ears, echoed inside me. I got up from the kitchen table, where we had just shared a lunch of Kraft macaroni and cheese, and stood at the door of the bathroom helplessly. I opened my mouth a few times, meaning to say something, to yell *stop*, to tell her how much I loved her, to ask "Are you okay?" and nothing came out.

Eventually I heard the sound of flushing, and she opened the door, running into me as she left the bathroom. We were standing so close, tears filling up my eyes, a look of blankness, of numbness on her face, as if the entire five minutes had never taken place. The tears in my eyes spilled over. Finally I found words: "How can I help you?"

She didn't respond then, didn't even change her facial expression. It scared the shit out of me. How could she see me crying, hear me ask this question, and not feel connected? Not respond? Where was my best friend?

We walked into her bedroom, just left of the bathroom, and both sat on her quilt-covered bed. After a minute of my tears, my helpless, aimless blubbering—"I want you to get help. I don't want you to be in so much pain. I hate this. How often do you do this? Don't you want to stop?"—she finally started to tear up too. Finally there was some energy in the room, some reciprocation, some trace of the best friend I had pajama-danced to Madonna with in our first-year dorm room, the one who had flushed our first weed purchase down the toilet in a frenzy of paranoia, my beautiful ex-cheerleader best friend.

We hugged desperately, clinging to each other, and then she finally spoke, barely audible, her words lost in my dirty-brown curls: "I want to stop." Then a sob escaped her.

Confrontation doesn't always go so well. One extremely thin history major told me a painful breakup story. After converting to the virtues of vegetarianism, yoga, and marathon running at twenty-one, Joey* lost a lot of weight fairly quickly. She felt wonderful, like she finally had some control over her impulses and some awareness of her emotional needs. She was getting interested in new ways to make elaborate vegetarian delicacies.

Joey went to visit her best friend in Los Angeles, excited to share her new insights and lifestyle changes. Because Joey had suffered from bulimia when she was younger, she figured her friend would be thrilled to see that she was finally finding a healthy way to lose weight. But when she arrived, her friend was anything but thrilled.

She seemed distant and preoccupied. Joey asked about her new boyfriend, and Beth shrugged and gave rote answers. Joey asked how her writing was going, if she was still thinking about applying for an MFA, and Beth* replied unemotionally, "Not really." Joey stopped trying so hard, and the silence grew thick. She left the next day confused and worried about her friend.

But a few days later, it was Beth who turned out to be most worried about her. She phoned and left a grave-sounding message on Joey's voice mail: "We really need to talk. Please call me back as soon as you can." Joey, thinking perhaps her friend was going to own up to whatever was making her depressed and disconnected, called back immediately.

"I don't know if we can be friends anymore," Beth began. "I can't see you like this. You look like a Holocaust victim. It's repulsive." Joey was stunned. She listened to her best friend since childhood express her concern, but in such a way that all Joey could feel was a full-on attack. Her friend was accusatory and scared, fearful that what she saw as Joey's unhealthy obsession would rub off on her (she too had suffered from bouts of disordered eating and excessive exercise). The Holocaust comment would be crushing for anyone but was especially painful given that the two best friends had grown up attending the same synagogue and danced at each other's bat mitzvahs.

It was the last exchange they have had in over a year. "I miss her," explains Joey, still thin but certainly not skeletal. "I just can't get over those words. They were so calculating, so unjustifiably cruel."

Eating-disorder clinics and associations offer recommendations on how to confront friends with eating disorders. Some of the tips are helpful—"Be a good role model in regard to sensible eating, exercise, and self-acceptance"—but most of them read like copy from a 1980s Girl Scout manual: "Compliment your friend's wonderful personality, successes, or accomplishments. Remind your friend that 'true beauty' is not simply skin deep." They might as well add: Sing your friend a few high-pitched notes of Whitney Houston's "I Will Always Love You."

Our drive to be beautiful is not about just a manicure and some makeup; it is about respect, power, and love. When we confront someone about her eating issues, we are also confronting her about her deepest hungers and insecurities. You confront with your best intentions and pray like hell—despite being otherwise agnostic or atheist or confused—that your friend sees your love through the fog of her own defenses.

Allison did get help, though her recovery was not clean or quick. She went to one-on-one therapy, group sessions, was an inpatient for a spell at a Manhattan hospital. But eventually her eating disorder would land her at a residential facility in Tampa, Florida. She remained in Tampa after completing her program and is now in the process of applying to law school. She isn't healed completely, but she is completely healing.

When we are together, I feel like I am back in the company of a long-lost sister—someone who has seen the best and worst of me, someone of whom I have seen the best and worst. She comes to New York fairly often, and we have brunch and go out dancing.

When we are apart, which is most of the time, she writes beautiful e-mails: "I know that my recovery is in my hands and I feel equipped to handle that responsibility. Most importantly, I know that I have a choice today. I can be ruled by a number on a scale or I can live my life. Those are really my two options." Despite her bravery, Allison says that sometimes it feels like she is still deciding after all these years.

Going Back

Some naïve part of me actually thought that if I went back to Hewitt, over five years after the first fateful swipe of my ID card, things would be different. Surely I had experienced the worst of the worst, the climax of unhealthy body obsession among Barnard women—some sort of strange meeting of social and psychological forces that made us, the class of 2002, the really screwed-up ones. I could sleep at night if I knew things weren't as bad today. I could stop talking about it if only I knew girls today weren't.

I was not comforted.

There were more leg warmers and fewer hooker boots, more blazers and fewer hoodies, more cropped sweaters and fewer cardigans, but besides that, things seemed to have stayed about the same. To my surprise and delight, the cafeteria had been remodeled and brightly painted; it no longer felt as if we were in a submarine. Now it was opened up, almost unrecognizable, but the ethos about eating had not undergone similar reconstruction.

A gaggle of girls, resembling my own first-year crew, piled in and waited patiently as their IDs were swiped. They giggled, running into one another as the line grew longer, swapping stories of the day's mishaps and epiphanies. I overheard two girls talking about my favorite old professor: "When he read that letter from a former student about regretting becoming a lawyer, I had to swallow back the tears. I mean, now I don't even know if I want to go to law school anymore!" Another pair, one tall and brunette, like me, the other petite and blond, like Allison, were singing the lyrics to Gwen Stefani's "Hollaback Girl" to themselves, laughing at their piss-poor rendition and searching for their IDs in oversize purses of neon hues.

The jovial, light mood became heavy as the girls entered the land of overwhelming choices, the cereal bins smashed up against the vegetarian options smashed up against the hot chocolate and the soda machines. The hot food steamed ominously from those same aluminum trays. I watched, this time overtly, as the Courtney and Allison look-alikes retraced our nervous path through the maze of options, almost as if they had learned the choreography, a dance passed down, one Barnard girl to the next. They first peered through the glass at the hot food options.

"That macaroni and cheese looks so good," said the blonde, squinting at the condensation-covered glass separating the drooling coeds from the food.

"I know, I hate that," said the other, sighing. "Are you going to get it?"

"I don't know."

They stood there for a few more seconds, as if they were still confirming whether, in fact, that pile of orange cheese and pale noodles was what they had first hypothesized. The blonde finally wandered away to survey the vegetarian options, eventually picking up one of the standard white plates and putting a few pieces of spongy tofu and overcooked squash on it. She looked at her friend, who had given in and was now standing in the hot-food line. "Going for it?" she asked as she brushed past. It was more recrimination than question, more gloat than inquiry. "Going for it?" hung in the air, an understanding between the two of them that one of them had failed.

Back at the crowded tables, women sat down one by one and started picking at their food. Most girls still didn't seem to know how to take a real bite. A girl in black-framed glasses and Converse All Stars, the hipster uniform, cut her grilled chicken into tiny strips, and then tinier strips, and then even tinier strips, until she had a mound of pale meat shredded to nothing. Her company, another hipster, this one more hip-hop than punk, with a Triple Five Soul sweatshirt and big hoop earrings, took three bites of a tuna fish sandwich and then pushed it aside, seemingly disgusted by the prospect of completing the task. At another table, a delicate black girl with a Caribbean accent shoveled half a bowl of Frosted Flakes into her mouth. In between bites she described an evil professor—"an angry man with some serious little-man syndrome"—to a girl with practically a mullet haircut who was gnawing on a tiny piece of cheese like a mouse on Ritalin. They abruptly stood up, took their trays to the conveyor belt, and walked away.

As their trays disappeared under the rubber curtain, I felt hopeless. That bowl, that half-cleaned plate, those sticky glasses, would be washed by the kitchen staff, piled up, filled with some other sorry excuse for a meal, consumed or half-consumed guiltily, put back on the belt to disappear again. Rinse, repeat. Just as it had happened when I was here. Just as it will continue to happen . . . unless we make it stop.

11

The Real World Ain't No MTV: How the Body Becomes the Punching Bag for Post-College Disappointment

All of us failed to match our dreams of perfection. So I rate us on the basis of our splendid failure to do the impossible.

—William Faulkner

After college, I tossed out everything that stank of the girl I had been before: a tattered poster of a Georgia O'Keeffe painting, platform shoes, Mardi Gras beads, a massive trunk that my parents had thought would be part and parcel of my East Coast experience. I was preparing to be someone new. Someone who carried a briefcase instead of a backpack. Someone who knew people who knew people. Someone who didn't have to watch her best friends pick at paltry meals and stare off into space in the common room or listen to the echo of gagging against bathroom tile.

Composing a Life

Getting your first job and moving into your first apartment or house is a second birth, a time for, as Mary Catherine Bateson puts it, "composing a life." A cultural anthropologist and daughter of Margaret Mead and Gregory Bateson, she knows what she's talking about. Her landmark book, *Composing a Life,* followed women of different persuasions and passions as they created their lives in the eighties.

Reading it right out of college, I was moved by the common threads—a drive born of a vision, detours that turn out to be destiny, a search for balance. I passed the book around to my crew of best friends and received it back with dog-eared pages, highlighted and underlined. One of the passages most decorated with stars and exclamation points was: "Ambition, we imply, should be focused, and young people worry about whether they are defining their goals and making the right decisions early enough to get on track. These assumptions have not been valid for many of history's most creative people, and they are increasingly inappropriate today." We each highlighted this passage, but none of us heeded its wisdom. Once again, the dissonance between what we knew in our heads and what we practiced in our lives proved significant.

As much as I was comforted by Bateson's words, I felt she had left out a piece: the body. None of the women she followed spoke about their bodies or about trying to see food in a different way (not as an indulgence but as a necessity, not as a foe but as a friend) or about exercising in a healthy way. Maybe their generation didn't share this preoccupation; or maybe they didn't talk about it.

Inherent in "composing a life," I believe, is developing an adult approach to a healthy body. Many young women dreamed that, along with our new apartments, we would inhabit new bodies: bodies that we didn't criticize so much, that were grown-up enough to want balance, that could finally step back and let our intellects and personalities step forward. That dream, unfortunately, is rarely realized.

The (Feminist) American Dream

Rolled up in a diploma, whether from Princeton University or Hazard Community College, is a lifetime of answers to the question "What do you want to be when you grow up?" My dad would videotape my brother and me on each birthday and ask us that proverbial question. Perched atop our hot tub back on Tejon Street at four years old, swinging my leg warmers happily in the air, side ponytail in full effect, I answered like a true inheritor of a confusing feminism: "I want to be part-time waitress, part-time doctor."

Legacy is also rolled up in that diploma. The go-girl parenting taught us to set goals and go after them, enter interviews with poise and purpose, believe that we deserved just as much money and just as many promotions as any guy. We girls were destined for big, important things, just like boys, and had an obligation to take ourselves seriously and have fancy titles. I wanted to make my mom proud. The hitch is this waitress thing.

My generation was raised on a steady diet of empowerment and equality, but we saw who was serving it up. Some moms were the CEOs, indeed, but also the caretakers, the washers, the cookers, the criers. They were obsessed with their weight, exhausted, bitter, self-sacrificing. The food for thought that we got as little girls didn't exactly constitute a balanced diet. The ambition wasn't tempered with wellness. The demand for excellence wasn't countered by a reasonable expectation for flaws here and there. The responsibility was still visibly and weightily on the shoulders of our mothers for most everything. Yet they were still expected to look "light as a feather" while carrying the load.

I wanted to be a waitress, in addition to being a doctor, because I thought that meant I would be pretty, thin, helpful, and witty. I wanted to take care of people. I wanted to make them feel good. I wanted to wear little skirts that showed off my perfect little legs.

Thus we have the paradox of the (feminist) American dream. The women of my generation are busting with ambition and fully believe in our capacity to take over/change the world. But we are not free from the notion that, to be successful, one must also be thin and pretty. Coupled with our ambition to lead is our ambition to disappear—two highly contradictory forces. We still don't want to take up space. We are still concerned with caretaking (not for ourselves, of course). We still want to look good while climbing our way to the top (and most of us are not particularly excited about stepping on anyone else's toes on the way up). We still believe that we will never be fulfilled until we are thin, never be complete until we are pretty.

"You can be anything" has become the (feminist) American dream—a beautiful theory without solid evidence, a cruel carrot dangling in front of young women. Although we may be able to land any job, hold any public office, direct any movie, most of us will never feel thin or pretty enough while doing it. Even our work, well known or award-winning or world-changing, won't make us feel beautiful. We can be well educated, creative, capable, experienced, and still not have the capacity to figure out how to free ourselves from guilt over every little thing that we put in our mouths.

Jane,* a Bellevue, Washington, native with a self-effacing sense of humor and a go-get-'em attitude, was big-city-bound. Upon graduating from Connecticut College, she packed her boxes and shipped them to the Big Apple, far away from her family. Jane wanted to distinguish herself. The plan: move to New York City, become a publishing diva, and lose the weight she had been struggling with for the past ten years.

A job listing on craigslist—every post-college girl's new best friend—led her to apply for a "junior account executive" position at a public relations firm that represented authors. In a bubbly cover letter, she wrote: "I am a professional spinner. I have been cultivating my skills since the days when I didn't push my sister down the stairs. I've used my skills to convince my parents to send me to Europe, to transfer to an almost top tier school, and to most recently convince my dad's tumor that it needed to be eviscerated. The doctors, who didn't initially believe, tell me that it was the drugs; I like to believe it was my power of persuasion."

She heard back the next morning, but when she went in for the interview, she was a little thrown off by the debris that littered the office. Her potential supervisor, Calvin,* assured her that they had so much business, there was no time to clean up. He was looking for a smart woman who wouldn't buckle under the pressure of coordinating key interviews for some of the nation's top-selling authors. He seemed instantly to fall in love with Jane as the woman for the job.

His unfettered enthusiasm was intoxicating. She was already signing on the dotted line when he mentioned a small caveat: She would be replacing someone else in the company who didn't yet know he was getting the boot, so her first task would be to come in after hours and download all the documents from his computer. Red flags waved aggressively in her head, but the image of shaking hands with Augusten Burroughs, one of her favorite writers, crowded out the warning.

One Rung at a Time

Perfect girls like to move full steam ahead, climb the ladder of success two rungs at a time, run rather than walk. Perfect girls are planners. Most like to set short-term goals and then take the appropriate steps to reach them as quickly and efficiently as possible. If there is a spot/boy/job at a team/bar/company that we desire, we are usually pretty adept at doing whatever it takes. This tendency—to stick to a goal under any and all duress—makes us especially vulnerable to eating disorders. Once we decide to lose weight, we can be tenacious about taking off the pounds. When that fails, as almost all diets inevitably do, we inflict a tremendous amount of guilt, shame, and disappointment on ourselves. If we succeed, well then, we usually just whet our appetites for more success.

Setting short-term goals and going after them works beautifully for perfect girls throughout high school and college. By being so productive, perfect girls get a lot of attention, encouragement, affirmation, even love from teachers, parents, and coaches. They have constant reinforcement that they are, in fact, destined for greatness. But short-term goals aren't as straightforward in tall buildings with matrices of five-by-five cubicles filled with other smart, ambitious people. Suddenly an onslaught of external forces—inaccessible supervisors, nasty coworkers, downturns in the economy, office policy, precedent—can derail a perfect girl from her path. Turns out that, unlike the design-your-own-major flexibility of college, the corporate hierarchy is pretty firmly set in its ways. Your boss does *not* intend to brainstorm a nontraditional career path for you that would allow you to bypass the coffee pouring and the collating on your way to real responsibility and prestige.

Perfect girls who are politically opposed (i.e., hate getting up early, dressing up, or taking orders) to the corporate work model, like me, are so convinced of our capacity to make it on our own that we pursue freelance journalism careers, start our own businesses, decide to dive into that abyss of freedom and, too often, poverty vaguely labeled "consulting." (This approach often leads to a feverish and compulsive graduate school application process.) We may not be trapped in a taupe cage, but we have the same obstacles keeping us from becoming well known for our brilliance and accountability and getting lots of gigs and spending cash. Unlike our corporate peers, the self-employed have absolutely no chance of affirmation or reinforcement, unless you count being offered an opportunity to write a two-thousand-word article "for the experience" (i.e., no money) as a pat on the back.

When we young women hit the real world, we aren't accustomed to the idea of climbing the career ladder one rung at a time. We don't plan on paying our dues in dead-end jobs. Perfect girls are impatient; we dream big and fall hard. Efficiency, not resiliency, is our strong suit. We're in the market for fireworks, record breakers, unprecedented success. We are running, full force, without time to consider where the finish line might be.

———————

Sara Shandler had more reason than most to believe that she would bypass the drudgery of assistant jobs and head straight to prestige when she graduated from Wesleyan. At just eighteen years old, she edited an angst-filled response to Mary Pipher's *Reviving Ophelia*, cleverly titled *Ophelia Speaks*, in which she recruited girls to write about their experiences of adolescence. By her first year in college, she was crisscrossing the country on speaking engagements. Suddenly, just after having crawled out of the cesspool of adolescence herself, she was scrawling on the inside of her book "It's hard and it gets better!" for thousands of teary-eyed teenagers who attended her book signings.

Three years after the real peak of her book's hype had died down, Sara was feeling confident as she moved to New York and started looking for senior jobs at magazines. The qualifications for some of the jobs she wanted were lofty: five years' experience minimum. No problem, she reasoned. She'd started her book at seventeen, so that should count as five years of writing-editing experience. So what if it wasn't with a big-name magazine? She even got a few interviews, all of which ended with a puzzled look and an admission: "You really are great, Sara, but you are just so young. You have virtually no experience."

Sara was crushed. After having bared her soul in her book, spoken at colleges across the country, appeared on talk shows, and been interviewed by journalists galore, she had no experience! It seemed that her age was *not* just a number, that the media world was just as tied to traditional notions of career development as other industries, that she would have to sit down at an assistant's desk just like everyone else. After some crying jags and a few calls home, Sara accepted a job at *Seventeen* magazine, where she would write some articles, although she would also be organizing the table of contents and handling the occasional package that needed to be messengered.

And thus began Sara's long journey with a condition she dubbed "Desk Ass." She explains, "I guess at the crux of it was this transition from my senior year of college, where I really had a handle on my whole life—good grades, professors who thought I was smart and interesting, terrific friends, and, yes, a body I felt good about—to living in New York and paying my dues, working long hours at my first real job for people who didn't think I was anything special . . . and then my reward was this new, bigger, wider, flatter, dimpled ass. The ass of inactivity. Desk Ass."

Sara's only solace was shopping at lunchtime and the occasional boredom-induced candy-bar run. When she got to leave the office and meet up with friends, she wanted to have lots of fun, indulge herself, taste something good if she couldn't feel something good. "Cellulite was like the irreversible icing on this new life that I felt like I had no control over," she jokes.

Sara had been moving through life, up until that point, with a goal always on the horizon—as she describes it, a mentality in which she always knew "I want X." First X was getting into a good college. She took the necessary steps to do that and got into Wesleyan. Then X became putting together *Ophelia Speaks*. She solicited writing tirelessly, edited, anthologized, and publicized. In college, when she wanted to lose a few pounds, she limited herself in the dining hall, cooked a couple of tofu dogs, and dipped them in some mustard for dinner. Done.

But now, sitting behind a desk all day, vulnerable to the commands of more senior editors and part of a world that generally believes in the virtue of "paying dues," she realized that she couldn't execute in the same way. Her life no longer fit into six-month spurts of goal setting, pursuing, and achieving. Her success as a journalist depended on her own efforts, but also on time, the whims of her supervisors, the economy—chance.

"Eventually," Sara reflects, "I accepted it [Desk Ass], or learned to overlook it, at least, which was huge, since that was about being okay with not being totally in control of everything in my life. All *sorts* of factors were getting in the way of my being as controlling as I like to be, but . . . so be it. My ass was bigger, my boss didn't fawn over me, my bank account balance was dismal. But oh well. Eventually I just sort of gave myself permission to figure those things out in time, and things slowly came together. Job, recognition, apartment. I even think my ass is better now. Not college-ass good, but totally respectable."

Sara's story points to an important lesson for perfect girls. There is a fine line between having outlandish, dangerous expectations and believing in your own capacity to do great things. Maintaining a healthy, steady self-image is based on achievable goals and states of being that are independent of the market or your managers. Sara came to understand that time and patience, not rapid tenacity, were what she needed in order to survive the inevitably rocky post-college period. She had to have faith in her goodness as a well-intentioned, intelligent, and kind person beyond the front-page bylines she had hoped for or the promotions she had thought her potential promised. It was not her thinness or her killer commitment that would make her happy, it was her acceptance of the present—albeit confusing, sometimes disappointing, and occasionally boring—moment.

Humble Pie, Anyone?

This giant slice of humble pie is served to the best of us. Girls across the country have told me still-painful stories about their falls from the precipice of post-college fantasy to the pit of unpaid bills, bad coffee, and uncomfortable shoes.

Jennifer, a minister's daughter from Houston, was an executive assistant at a Yiddish theater company right out of college. When she answered the phone her first day on the job—"Jennifer speaking"—an old man on the other end screamed, "Jennifer? Jennifer? That sounds like a shiksa name! You aren't Jewish, are you?" The daily abuse continued from there.

Lissa,* a New York native, actually abandoned her first job as a CBS page and headed west to fulfill her romantic dreams of doing hands-on film work. When she was hired by two documentary filmmakers in their forties, she was thrilled. They were energetic, passionate, and, it turned out, lesbian partners. Which was fine until one day when half of the partnership raised her eyebrow over a burrito and said, "Lissa, I've really enjoyed working with you. I am really attracted to you." It took Lissa five days to drive straight back to New York.

Lee* worked for a nonprofit that had UN contracts, a huge endowment, and a huge creep as the supervisor. On business trips, he would ask Lee to come to his room so he could dictate his reflections on the day's meetings. When she arrived, he would be wearing a spandex swimsuit and doing push-ups. In between action items, he told her about his Asian fetish and his recent Botox injections, and urged her to "loosen up."

Dawn* had to take an office job at a company she was morally opposed to, make copies and create spreadsheets late into the night, and then endure her supervisor's weekly freak-outs about her boyfriend's reluctance to get married. Sometimes the CEO would call Dawn to sit in on a board meeting, seemingly giving her an opportunity to learn something, only to call her "sweetie" and ask for coffee, light and sweet.

———————

Turns out, none of us is special. Yeah, yeah, we are all as unique as beautiful snowflakes. Each of us has a distinct blend of gifts to give the world. But when it is 9:00 P.M. and your boss still hasn't given you the fax he so desperately needs you to send before you leave (and God forbid he learn to use the fax machine himself), you feel a few meltdowns short of a beautiful snowflake. You feel like a what's-her-name. You feel, for all intents and purposes, invisible. Momma actually *didn't* say there would be days like this.

Dr. Robin Stern, psychologist and feminist author, has seen many women at this disappointing moment in their lives shuffle into her office dejected, tears welling up in their eyes. She says, "Sometimes there is so much disparity between what young women are told to expect and what actually happens that they get disillusioned. The ones who blame themselves tend to get depressed. If they aren't good at managing their tough feelings, sometimes they get stuck exercising massive amounts of control in order to just keep going, or worst-case scenario, they back off from the ladder altogether and give up the climb. It is all much worse if they grew up seeing themselves as special or precious."

Part of this attitude, of course, is about privilege. Plenty of perfect girls were raised in households where they didn't learn to delay gratification. We were conditioned to articulate our goals and then get help to make them happen. Sure, we had to do our schoolwork, and there is no shortcut around the track during practice. But in general, perfect girls have resources, networks, open doors, and encouragement—safety nets they never expected to fall into. Our whole lives, we leapt as high as we wanted and evaded sobering falls. When I didn't get the editor-in-chief position of my high school newspaper, I cried a little, then quickly convinced myself that I liked commentary better anyway. When I didn't get into Harvard or Yale, I cried a lot, then started spouting statistics about the value of an all-female college. But distraction is not so easy post-college. Hard work, patience, depersonalization, unwavering self-confidence, and resilience are all necessary skills to get to the top. There is no leaping, only radical humility. Turns out we must climb the ladder like mere mortals. This is a deflating realization, but accepting it is ultimately healthy for mind and body, and also can be a great relief.

———————

Jane's job at the agency was a complete disaster. Calvin turned out to be a nightmare—instantly confessing his deepest, darkest secrets to Jane despite the professional setting and vast difference in age. The office got messier and the work less intriguing—she was scheduling meetings not for Augusten Burroughs but for a security guard writing a trashy tell-all. She developed chronic migraines—at her worst four or five a week—and worked through the pain. When she thought about quitting, she could only imagine the disappointment on her mother's face, the endless hours of job searching, the potentially violent fit that Calvin would throw.

Jane started doing what so many young women do when they feel fooled and out of control—she started bingeing. She ate entire boxes of Entenmann's mini-cookies or pints of Ben & Jerry's. Sometimes she binged on healthy cereals, such as Kashi, somehow justifying bowls and bowls of it with the low calorie count. When she was feeling really hopeless and far from home, she made herself throw up afterward. "I've never had a full-blown eating disorder," Jane tells me during our first interview, "but I do have a bingeing and purging tendency. If I eat something that I consider unhealthy or bad, that has any sort of stigma to it, then I consider purging it. Usually I don't."

"What keeps you from doing it?" I ask.

"I have this one friend who can't get pregnant because she was bulimic, and for me having children is the greatest thing a woman has to look forward to. As much as I want to be thin and successful, I don't want to deprive myself of that. Had I not had a friend like that, I don't know . . ."

Eating disorders can greatly impair women's ability to have children. Dr. Brenda Woods of Remuda Ranch attests that "the medical community doesn't even consider eating disorders as a cause of infertility because patient lab work usually comes back normal," though one study showed that nearly one in five patients at an infertility clinic had eating disorders. Even if women with eating disorders manage to get pregnant, their disease can cause devastating consequences for their babies; pregnant women with eating disorders have a higher incidence of first-trimester miscarriages, stillbirths, low infant birth weights, breech babies, and congenital malformations. They are also more likely to suffer from postpartum depression and have more problems breast-feeding.

Though Jane scared herself out of vomiting with the threat of this kind of fate, she certainly wasn't freed from her body issues. She didn't have the energy to use her newly purchased gym membership. She didn't have time to prepare healthy foods. She was lonely, disappointed, and hungry for something, anything that would make her feel better. In a matter of months, she gained sixty pounds.

Grasping for Control

After one has swallowed the giant slice of humble pie, a stomachache and a sense of helplessness set in. The average post-college flunky has no control over her work and, therefore, no control over her time. She feels at the mercy of others—her landlord, her boss, the jerk buying her a drink at the bar. When the rest of the world feels chaotic, a diet is something finite and tidy. If your roommate, your coworker, or your best friend is insensitive, food feels comforting. You may not be able to choose what hours you work, what neighborhood you live in, or how much money you make, but at least you can determine what you eat for lunch. Your sphere of influence shrinks post-college, but your body is still at your mercy.

As a result, a lot of young women resort to rigid control of their appetites and their fitness regimens. Like children of divorce, many perfect girls experiencing the disappointment, chaos, and false promises of the real world blame themselves for what is happening. Refusing to indulge in foods they crave is a form of self-punishment. *I don't deserve that ice cream. I have nothing to show for myself. I don't make enough money to spend so frivolously.* Tiny portions at lunch make them feel superior to their coworkers who always claim to be on diets but don't have the self-control to avoid the leftover sandwiches from the board meeting.

Likewise, when a perfect girl can't excel in the boardroom, she can always excel in the weight room. *I will work out longer, faster, harder. I may have a meaningless job, but I'm not lazy. You sit around all day long, now move!* These girls are the ones who actually get their money's worth for their gym memberships, clinging to sleep-depriving routines of going before and after work to run on the treadmill, to take yoga, Pilates, aerobics, and spinning classes. They like the instructors who are the most maniacal, the ones who yell at them and call them lazy (matching the voices inside their heads). They try to outshine, outstretch, outspin the other girls in the class. Not surprisingly, a lot of the girls who go this route were once high school or college athletes. The dedication is familiar; the obsession takes hold quickly.

One recent college grad I spoke with worked as a paralegal in a law firm and had recently discovered that she had no interest in law. To cope with the monotony of the copying and collating, she started running eight miles a day, every day. She leaned over her cup of tea and admitted to me, "I've decided to train for a marathon because I think that will help me ease up a bit on the running. There are days when you are supposed to run just a few miles or not run at all. I think that would be good for me."

I responded calmly, but my inner radar was blaring. Run a marathon in order to run *less*? I could barely get myself around the three-mile loop at Prospect Park without Kanye West blaring in my ears and the temperature just right—too hot and I got tired, too cold and I got cranky.

After further investigation, I found out that she had indeed suffered from a bout of anorexia, what she called "a weird phase," while studying in London. After she shrank dramatically, her parents forced her to stay home before heading back to school to start her fall term. She would sneak out before they woke up to go on long runs in the dark. She recounted this time in her life as if it were a part of her distant past, a silly, childish phase like mall bangs or a belly button ring.

A few months later, still waiting for her response to some follow-up questions, I got back in touch. We shot a few quick e-mails back and forth:

Haven't head from you. Is everything okay?

Sorry, I'm working on getting back to you. Life has been pretty crazy—I got a stress fracture in my foot.

Oh no! Were you running? When is it supposed to be healed?

Yeah, I have no idea when it's going to be better. I'm totally freaking out about it, actually. I've been stripped of my vice! I feel like I have no way to deal with any sort of stress. I can't work out at all, which is impossibly hard for me, and I probably won't be able to run the marathon either . . .

She never responded to my follow-up questions.

Starving for Guidance

Perfect girls, flailing and fresh in the real world, need mentors. Women who have dealt with the uncertainty of a new career and navigated the maze of corporate cubicles all the way to the corner office should have insight on setting realistic expectations, striving but also self-protection, stamina in a slow-moving corporation. A mentor can offer positive feedback at a time when there is none, a shoulder to cry on when criticism creeps in, a free lunch now and again.

Perfect girls also need templates—women who have survived some years after college and become calmer and wiser in the process. During my senior year in college, I attended the Woodhull Institute for Ethical Leadership's Young Women's Retreat, an experience designed to give newbies necessary skills in negotiation, public speaking, and financial literacy, and a chance to reflect on their dreams. Far more life-changing than these skills was my exposure to women in their late twenties. Wide-eyed at twenty, I looked at Jessica—six years my senior—and thought, *I could be like that. I could be a journalist,* and at Robin, twenty-nine, and still composing her life, and thought, *Look at that. Robin is awesome, and she doesn't have every little thing figured out. She's creative and spontaneous, loving and open.* Kimmi, twenty-five at the time, was one of the most beautiful women I had ever seen, and she wasn't the size of a toothpick.

Calm surrounded me at that retreat, as if someone had put a heavy blanket over my tired body. There was none of the teenage angst I had become so used to, none of the frenetic energy of mealtimes, none of the self-absorbed rambling. The calm filled me with a great hope that one day, in the near future, I might be friends with women just like these, and what was more, be a woman just like these.

The problem is that I had to go on a retreat to get this kind of experience. Our society is not set up for intergenerational interaction. We run around in our little circles composed almost entirely of women just our age, and unfortunately, at twenty, these women are chickens with their heads cut off as cleanly as our own. We can confirm one another's experiences, be sisters in struggle, and speculate until we are blue in the face, but we can't provide that unparalleled calm or wisdom that a mentor or a "big sister" can. We can't comment on the water with radical insight because we are the guppies anxiously and erratically swimming in it.

Not only is our society not set up for intergenerational interaction but, in my experience and the experience of many other young women I know, when we do set our sights on a mentor, we are often disappointed. I have had a self-described feminist supervisor pull me aside and tell me that it was in my best interest to dress more ladylike. Keep in mind, I'm not a tomboy by any stretch of the imagination, but I do prefer pants when the windchill factor is ten below zero. She also demonstrated for me how to flirt shamelessly with each and every man who walked into her office. She smoked long, skinny cigarettes and took the bread off her tuna sandwiches so she could avoid the carbs. Every time I got a salad for lunch, she would affirm my suspicion that my value, even at work, was predicated on my appearance: "Look at you! You are so good!" And it was not only what she did say that disappointed me but also what she *didn't* say. She knew little about my life or my aspirations beyond the four walls of our tiny office. She seemed to speak only in exclamation points and periods, never in question marks.

A friend who was trying to break in to the film business contacted a female director she greatly respected and asked if they could speak. After a few rescheduled meetings, Paula* finally got to meet her potential mentor. But as soon as she arrived in the office, she realized that there was a glaring contrast between the woman she had built up in her mind and the one sitting before her. The director complained about many of her peers, telling Paula all about their character flaws and poor choices while describing herself as a "martyr for truth." She said, "I would give you some names so you could network, but they're all bitches." She detailed her physical ailments. She lamented having to pay so much for a decent script. She didn't ask Paula a thing. She ended by talking about how grueling and political the industry is, advising Paula: "If you like anything else a fraction of how much you like film, do that instead." Paula was crushed. She shook her fallen idol's hand, but in the elevator on the way down, she cried. I'm sure the director would have called it "tough love," but Paula called it devastating.

Despite a gallant effort to make connections with female academics in her field, my friend Mara* has been repeatedly dismissed and ignored. She doesn't know if it is simply a matter of time, although she acknowledges that the women professors are usually the primary caregivers for children in addition to being full-time faculty members. "It also feels like they're threatened by me or something," she admits. "I hate to say that, because it confirms everything bad about women, but I honestly feel that way."

Male professors are more interested in Mara, perhaps too interested. One male academic with whom she felt a very close platonic bond cut off their friendship when he confessed he had romantic feelings for her—an admittedly respectable choice. The life of the mind is titillating, but if Mara could keep her romantic feelings under wraps, you would think a man fifteen years her senior and supervising her could as well. Mara has ended up feeling like her femaleness is a strike against her no matter which coach she plays for.

Even those in the traditional corporate workforce, where you would think that mentoring would be institutionalized, complain of a lack of female guidance from above. Pamela,* a new lawyer at a major New York City law firm, explains: "There are very few women partners to begin with, so I struggled to even find a mentor who shared some of my concerns about balancing family and being taken seriously. When I did find a woman mentor, she was so bitter about all the sacrifices she has made that she couldn't imagine a different path for me. It was like, 'I suffered, so you're going to suffer. I had to be thin and perfect and have no free time, so that's what you're going to have to live with.'"

Women my age learn quickly that the only way to find and retain mentors, especially if you aren't from a "connected" family, is to take everything with a grain of salt. We are stripped of our delusions about finding the "perfect" mentor and must, instead, accept the idea that mentors are as flawed as human beings at large. I have had great success in creating relationships with older, wiser women by deciding to be realistic about what I am looking for in a mentor and never throwing the baby out with the bathwater. Dr. Robin Stern is a brilliant, sometimes irritating, always visionary and supportive mentor, and has been for six years. If I had run the other way the first time she was fifteen minutes late or checked her e-mail instead of listening to an answer I offered to one of her questions, I would have missed out on one of the most fortifying relationships of my life.

But the responsibility doesn't fall only on our young shoulders. It is also unfair that so many older women dismiss, ignore, or compete with those just starting to make their way in the world. You may have earned your cynicism; let us earn ours too. You may have had bad experiences with women in the past; let us be the first women who don't backstab or take you for granted. Protect us from your unresolved weight issues to whatever extent feels authentic. Celebrate us not for our slim waists but for our strategic planning. You certainly paid your dues, but don't punish us by making sure we pay them as dearly as you did. You labored for the working world to be more egalitarian and compassionate toward women. Now enjoy what you've birthed.

The Woodhull Institute preaches the "psychology of abundance"—the idea that women don't need to feel deprived or competitive or stingy anymore. They advocate the notion that there *is* enough in the world to go around, and that the more we share our resources, the more we gain. This includes not despising a skinnier woman because of her weight, giving a younger woman much-needed advice, sharing your wisdom and wealth with those who can benefit from it. Abundance, not accumulation, is the goal. Generosity, not perfection, is the way to get there.

Unfortunately, our shared psychology is still one of scarcity. Many older women lament the lack of dedication and feminist passion in the next generation, yet many young women are floundering, alone.

Looks as the Last Salvation

Once a perfect girl has wrestled with disappointment long enough, and lost, she succumbs to the new reality that she will not be the CEO of a Fortune 500 company by the time she is, say, twenty-five. There comes a point when she admits that she has a bit to learn about the business. But that same perfect girl, newly sober about career mobility, can still be intoxicated by the notion of being thin and hot. Even if she can't be the boss, she can be the secretary everyone is talking about. If she can't afford the Armani suit, at least she can get a knockoff and look better than her supervisor, who shelled out for the real thing.

The perfect girl focuses her energy on controlling her appearance. She spends her paycheck before the ink dries, buying trendy outfits that make her feel remade. (Never mind that they will bore her before the month is out.) She compulsively buys makeup, gets a membership at the tanning salon, purchases the same pair of shoes in a variety of different colors—all so she can feel worthy of attention when her job garners her none. The upkeep of her appearance, in essence, becomes her preferred full-time job. She feels good at it. She feels special again, if only on the surface.

This frivolous spending is no passing thrill. The economic damage is long-term. A 2002 study by the Women's Institute for a Secure Retirement found that over half of single young women are living paycheck to paycheck. Part of this may be because a woman still makes seventy-three cents for every dollar a man does, but if the gaggles of young women in trendy outfits buying out Urban Outfitters at the first of the month are any indication, I dare to argue that young women are also trying to buy self-esteem.

Ultimately the ritual is empty. No matter how much she "improves" her look or buys the latest gear, she is just a disillusioned postgraduate in an expensive outfit. None of it makes her feel any more hopeful on Sunday when the clock ticks down to another week of administrative blah. If anything, the reality of her dwindling bank account—or more likely, her amassing debt—hits home, and she fires up the burner for another ramen-noodle night (trying not to remember that the cosmopolitan she drank last night is equivalent to fourteen of these now traditional Sunday-night delights).

Sometimes, when the new shoes or the makeover or the Friday-night fix stops making her feel a sense of momentum, she resorts to more drastic measures . . .

Jane couldn't stand it anymore—not the after-hour calls from her boss, not the little judgments from her mom about her ballooning weight, not her Friday-night bar tabs (no guys asking to buy *her* a drink). She decided to take matters into her own hands and do something that she believed would push her life in the right direction. At twenty-two, she got liposuction.

Jane's mom had mentioned the option (and offered to pay for it), explaining: "You just have one of those body types where you can never really lose the stomach." Jane was hesitant until a coworker confessed that she had done the same and lost five dress sizes. When work was unbearable, Jane began to fantasize about what it would be like to leave on Friday and come back a week later with a toned and tightened body. She could almost hear the compliments that would be lavished on her. She could almost feel her hand, waving away the praise. Then her computer would let out a piercing ding, dragging her back into reality—another one of Calvin's inarticulate requests via e-mail.

Two hours and seven thousand dollars later, Jane had lost two inches around her waist. She had also lost some innocence—in the middle of the surgery, her anesthesia wore off and she woke up to the sound of the machine sucking away her insides.

When she healed, the compliments weren't exactly lavish. She explained: "I have a few friends who know about it, and they'll comment and say I look thinner or whatever, but I'm not really happy with it. No one else really notices."

As with any quick fix, nothing was actually fixed. A few months after our interview, six months after her surgery, I get an e-mail from Jane. She has moved away from New York City. She has started writing for a local newspaper. And she has begun to binge and purge habitually: "It has taken me weeks to formulate this email to you. I have fallen into a really bad bout of bulimia since leaving New York. It's odd that one of my reasons for leaving the city was because I felt it made me overly appearance conscious, and then I get to Bellevue and I end up having even bigger problems. I started therapy today again, which is perhaps why I am able to admit this to you now."

I read her e-mail sadly, as I do all of the e-mails I get these days from former interviewees who are updating me on their precarious conditions. If only there were some way to make Jane and all post-college wanderers believe that thinness is not a prerequisite for success, that self-esteem cannot be bought, that their wandering and waiting are justified. I am amused to see that Jane's e-mail signature line is "Forget the clock and take your compass because the direction you're headed is more important than the time it takes to get there." I can just imagine her typing it in—desperate to remind herself, to make herself believe. If only she did. If only any of us did.

Plastic surgery is becoming increasingly common among women of all ages and socioeconomic backgrounds. The most popular procedure, liposuction, was performed on 455,000 Americans last year, according to the American Society of Plastic Surgeons. Almost every kind of cosmetic surgery is on the rise, including a 25 percent increase since 2000 in breast augmentations (264,041 were performed in 2004). A staggering amount of money is being made off women's (and some men's) dissatisfaction with the bodies they were born with—almost $8 billion in 2004. Americans spent $890,610,213 buying bigger breasts alone.

An option that was once considered couth only among aging women, or those with "glaring" abnormalities, is now a fairly common high school or college graduation gift from Mom and Dad. The American Society of Plastic Surgeons reports that 335,000 teenagers, eighteen and younger, had plastic surgery in 2003. BBC News reports that 40 percent of teens in the UK want cosmetic surgery. Nose jobs, disguised as oh-so-necessary deviated septum surgery, are done all over the country for girls whose noses aren't even done growing yet.

What was once a wealthy woman's indulgence has now been marketed to middle- and low-income women, complete with financing programs claiming to help even those with bad credit. Many travel abroad for cheap cosmetic surgery procedures—dubbed "medical tourism" by the agencies popping up to make a buck off uninsured and low-income Americans—which are often unregulated and dangerous.

One young woman from a middle-class background in Texas told me this story about being a teenager and watching her mother suffer through multiple plastic surgeries: "She came home with vials filled with fat that had been taken out of her stomach, and she wasn't overweight to begin with, because her surgeon had suggested that would be a cost-effective way to have her cheekbones highlighted once a month. After she recovered from the liposuction, she returned to this surgeon to have one vial injected into each cheek once a month. Her face would bruise so badly from her injections that she had a purple tint under her makeup for most of the month. Then, by the time the purple had dissipated, she'd have the process repeated all over again."

What was once a "big deal"—something associated with serious medical risks that required ample recovery time—is now becoming a stop-and-shop pastime. *The New York Times* reports that women are upgrading their bodies the way they do their cars. In "the designer-body approach . . . an increasing number of doctors are using a technique known variously as precision, selective or micro liposuction"—in which a woman can have just an ounce of fat taken from her ankle, for example. Dr. Luiz S. Toledo, a plastic surgeon from São Paulo, Brazil, explains, "It's liposuction for skinny people." Dr. Howard D. Sobel of Manhattan describes his patients: "Some of them are perfect 10's who want to be 10.5's."

Precision plastic surgery is a dramatic example of how far perfect girls—and their older, though not wiser, counterparts—will go to make sure that their bodies are unnaturally flawless. The health risks and costs are not enough to deter them from a practice that gives them ultimate control—the ability to reconstruct their own forms, eradicate their imperfections, sculpt their bodies into visual symbols of how far they will go for the illusion of perfection.

The rub is that they can never go far enough. This kind of "lunchtime liposuction" encourages women to see their bodies as never-ending projects to be fine-tuned until death. Plastic surgery addiction is not a joke. Like diet or exercise obsession, it sucks the life, energy, time, and money out of otherwise brilliant women, resulting—ironically—in their being completely and totally out of control.

So What Next?

This island of success that we have imagined, this place where we would finally feel full, where that nagging emptiness inside would dissipate once and for all . . . it doesn't exist. We learn this the hard way—trapped in identical cubicles, deep in debt, out of control, stuffing our faces to numb the disappointment. The adolescent relationship with food that once plagued us has changed but not improved. We have new vices to tempt us into betraying our diets: lunch breaks at fast-food joints, snacking through the dull day. We have idle evening hours in our new apartments, endless bad reality television to make it through, Saturday nights at 2:00 A.M., alone at home, after a string of slobbering drunks asked for our phone number. Not exactly *Sex and the City.*

We don't really feel as if we have enough control to compose a life; life seems to be composed for us, and we tolerate it. We don't even choose what to eat in the end. It feels more as if it chooses us, and we deal with the guilt/shame/hopelessness that follows.

At stake here is not just our career goal or our vision of ourselves as thin, successful adult women, but our faith in the idea that we have a purpose. Before this time, we projected our personal purpose into the future, rehearsing for a day when we would be launched into the world. *Someday I will be rich and famous. Someday I will feel beautiful. Someday I will change the world.* But suddenly the future is now. Suddenly we realize that none of the answers we had for the ultimate question—*What will make me complete?*—have held up. It's not a paycheck from a fancy corporation. It's not a nice apartment, trendy clothes, a new car. It's not a nonprofit job that guarantees a spot in heaven. It's not even thinness.

None of these things makes us feel perfect or even good enough. None of these things fills up the emptiness inside, the one that Anna Quindlen warned us about: "If you have been perfect all your life and have managed to meet all the expectations of your family, your friends, your community, your society, chances are excellent that there will be a black hole where that core ought to be." When you turn twenty-five and you look up from the toilet bowl or the keyboard or the steering wheel and you realize that there is nothing where there should be something at the center of your life, at the center of your body, at the center of your soul, what do you do? When you realize that the hunger you feel is for something much larger, much more substantial than a paycheck or a flat stomach or a cute boyfriend, where do you look for spiritual sustenance?

12

Spiritual Hunger

Lacking spiritual sustenance, there is genuine hunger and thirst.
                                                —Marion Woodman

At the center of my generation's struggle with food and fitness is identity, and at the center of identity is spirit. Perfect girls were raised on the striving rationality of the eighties and the dot-com optimism of the nineties. For some of us, the closest thing we experienced to religion was a few Easter Sundays at church and some serious praying before the SATs. We were not conditioned to think of our religious affiliations as crucial on our path to success. Religion, instead, was the stuff of grandparents and world history classes. There was no real place for grand religion in a world growing smaller and smaller. The miracles we witnessed were technological. Efficiency, not piety, became the highest virtue.

Yes, some of us spent Sundays being wowed by big-screen theatrics in megachurches. Yes, some of us grew up reveling in the long summers away at Jewish camps. But even those of us who did grow up with a strong religious diet were often fed it in a fairly benign way. *You don't really have to wait until marriage, just be sure you are in love. I know Daddy isn't supposed to drive on Saturday morning, but we need milk. Fasting doesn't mean we can't have a few snacks.*

All of this ambiguity has led to a generation of relatively lost souls. We have studied divinity but never experienced it. We have read about religious wars in faraway lands but are unable to identify with people who would blow themselves up for a god for which there is no hard-and-fast evidence. We have affiliated when it was convenient—having a religious club to attend in the first weeks of college is a great way to get dates.

Some of us, for lack of a "capital G" God, have searched out little gods. We worship technology, celebrities, basketball players, rock stars, supermodels, video games. We try to emulate those who are quick, rich, beautiful—not steady, giving, or honest. We move fast all the time—fast food, fast cars, fast loans, fast promotions, fast diets. Instant gratification, not eternal salvation, is our primary concern.

We are a generation devoid of authentic rituals. The closest thing to a lasting coming-of-age ritual—the bat mitzvah—has turned into a consumption circus. Bling, not brakhot (blessings), is the central theme of the once holy event. Thirteen-year-old girls beg their parents for celebrity performances, outlandish party favors, designer dresses. The MTV reality show hit *My Super Sweet 16* demonstrates what happens across America three years later: sickening decadence that only serves to feed the insatiable appetites of already spoiled brats. As one young woman I interviewed explained, "My friend got to choose, either a car or a boob job for her sweet sixteen. She chose the boob job but got the car anyway."

Perfect girls turn themselves into their own little god projects. We strive to become the perfect human being, not in terms of service or soul but in terms of size. We go to the gym religiously, deny the foods of messy mortals, sculpt our bodies into the only divine we know. As Marion Woodman writes of these lost women, "They create their own rituals, but because they don't realize what they are doing they may invoke the wrong god, and be subject to that power whether they like it or not."

These empty substitute rituals, this misguided worship, intellectualization, addiction to moving fast has led my generation to a dark and lonely place. In the inevitable stillness that frightens the hell out of a perfect girl, she must ask herself not *What is the size of my stomach?* but *What is the quality of my soul? What do I believe in? What is my purpose? Is there a black hole where my core should be? Is there any-*

thing inside of me that can sustain rejection, disappointment, loneliness? Is there something solid, like resilience, instead of something hollow, like perfection?

Marion Woodman writes of our generation: "They have no sense of everlasting arms to uphold them through the crisis of life." We are not truly resilient, in part because we have little faith. We are not satisfied, because we are always waiting for evidence of our worth. We are not strong of soul, because we spend so much time obsessing about our bodies. In Nicole Blackman's beautiful poem "Daughter," she promises to teach her unborn daughter that within her is an "army" . . . "that can save her life."

Do you have such a belief?

Substitute Gods

Heather's* religion was running. Something about flying over the trails was transcendent. She pounded her barely cushioned joints into the dirt until a fog took over her brain. During these long, methodical runs, she felt most right with the world. The usual ache at her center was rocked to sleep by the rhythmic pounding of her feet against the earth.

While running, she was not just an ordinary human being, subject to the monotony of daily diet choices and messy relationships. She was not Heather from a middle-class family in Maryland. She was not typical or ordinary. She hovered above all that, better somehow, more holy. She was special—a star runner on her college cross-country team, an Olympic hopeful, a fast and fierce competitor. When she ran, she shed the flesh of an imperfect world and became something untouchable.

If running was Heather's religion, then food was her gravest sin. She began starving herself in high school, very deliberately whittling away her daily intake of food until family dinners were the only times she would indulge in meals. The small snacks she did allow herself— nonfat yogurt in the morning and a glass of orange juice, a piece of fruit or some veggies for lunch, a juice box and a few pretzels after track—became ritualistic. She examined every grain of salt sticking to the pretzel she was about to put in her mouth and scraped every speck of yogurt out of the container.

Some of her friends told her track coach how little she was eating, and he pulled her aside after practice one day. His wife, also a runner, had suffered from anorexia and eventually been hospitalized. As a scare tactic, he told Heather about his wife's struggles. Heather remembers, "I could tell how he was trying to show how bad it was, but in my mind it was like, *Wow, I want to be like that.* The extremity of her devotion was something to aspire to in my mind." The coach's wife had ripped out her feeding tube while in the hospital. Heather thought of her, secretly, as a role model.

The coach also spoke to Heather's parents, but her mother insisted that Heather ate dinner every night and seemed just to be truly dedicated to her sport. Heather's mother walked through life with a perma-grin. "Put on a happy face. Everything is fine all the time. Be the kind of person that gets along with everyone and doesn't ever cause a scene" were the lessons that Heather's mother most adamantly communicated to her growing up.

Her father, though overshadowed by Heather's domineering mother, did manage to bring up her disease once. Heather remembers that one random Sunday night, as they put away the dinner dishes, he simply blurted out, "Do you think you have an eating disorder?"

"Yup," she replied, without looking over at him.

"I am a dry alcoholic,"† he responded.

They never spoke about it again.

---

†Alcoholics who abstain from drinking are known in Alcoholics Anonymous slang by two different terms—either they are sober or they are dry. A "dry drunk" is an alcoholic who doesn't technically drink alcohol any longer but still thinks like an alcoholic, still feels ravaged by addiction, still obsesses and plans rigidly, judges others harshly, and has an inflated sense of self. Sound familiar? It should, because these are some of the most common characteristics of an anorectic. She is capable of staying away from food in general but obsessed with it. She sees herself as above others, as a more evolved human being. She puts every ounce of her energy into avoiding calories and, as a result, often also avoids pleasure, camaraderie, spontaneity. Anorectics, like dry drunks, see their body as the enemy—a messy combination of needs and emotions too childish to be indulged. Both kinds of addicts strive to transcend the monotony of everyday life. See www.alcoholicsanonymous.org.

Many perfect girls, like Heather, pursue weight loss with a religious fervor. They become ritualistic about their eating habits, describe food as forbidden or sinful, grow extremely dogmatic in their views on nutrition or fitness, and in the process develop a view of themselves as almost saintlike figures—pounds away from messy human existence. Starving or running becomes their religion. They become their own demigods. The bona fide higher power is anorexia itself.

This is nowhere more evident than in the phenomenon of "pro-ana" websites popping up all over the Internet. As Mark Morford, a *San Francisco Gate* columnist, put it: "Girls have anthropomorphized anorexia." Women, mostly teenagers, have created sites that glamorize and worship anorexia, exchanging tips on how to cut back on food without anyone noticing, creating communities of disappearing women who support one another in the pursuit of skin and bones. There are also "pro-mia" websites, similarly devoted to praising bulimia. A tip found on one reads, "Don't eat/drink anything that is a red color. When vomiting, in some cases bleeding may occur and you won't know if it's serious, or just what you ate/drank." These teens have found their "thinspiration," as many of them call it, in cyberspace. They pray to Ana and Mia, their designated goddesses of thin.

The women who frequent these sites claim that they have not a disease but a chosen lifestyle. After all, some claim, they are only reflecting what is already in the culture. They feature photographs of celebrities and fashion models curving over lecterns at award shows or posing for pictures in skimpy bikinis that show off their ribs. One website, designed to question the mainstream media's shock at the pro-ana and pro-bulimia movement, reads: "Our culture is pro anorexia in every sense, long before these websites emerged. At least they are being honest about what they promote."

Beyond the official "pro-ana" and "pro-mia" sites, many young women fill message boards or individual blogs (on LiveJournal or other free hosting sites) with tips for how to eat as few calories as possible or how to get out of hospitalization. Some of these girls post pictures of themselves wasting away, followed by captions describing how much more weight they want to lose. On the community boards, I found the following posting by a user named hipbones on January 13, 2006:

> I am starting a five-day fast tomorrow. I just got my hoodia pills[†] back. So I'll take two a day and some whenever I get hungry. I am going to be fucking skinny.

And on the same day, a user named ana_blush writes:

> I have only signed up for this account this week, but before that i was writing things on paper, what does that do? I'm just glad to be sharing things with people who i know wont frown upon it. no matter what it is you're doing you have support here.
>   why the hell cant the real world be more like this?

These girls, many of them as young as eleven and twelve, are searching out more than girlfriends to dish with. They are searching out a place that is less unpredictable, more supportive, more pure than the world around them. All of the elements of religion are present: the god, the worship, the dedication, the ritual, the community, the sin, and the salvation. Just as Heather was looking for an identity that felt special— the star runner, the paragon of willpower and dedication—these girls are hungry for some kind of recognition, some community in a world that seems so big and uncontrollable it simply swallows them up.

The desire to be thin is, at base, a desire to be recognized, a desire to be loved, a desire to be accepted. These are all things that the average religion promises. When women don't have that fundamental

---

†According to Mike Adams, an independent journalist on health and wellness, "There have been no widespread clinical trials examining the safety of Hoodia gordonii, the natural appetite suppressant herb now gaining widespread popularity as a potential weight-loss pill." "*Hoodia Gordonii* Is No Miracle Weight Loss Pill, Health Investigation Reveals," NewsTarget.com, December 5, 2004.

sense of belonging, of being seen and appreciated, they often decide that the culprits are their waistlines. Instead of seeking to understand and fulfill their needs through a spiritual practice or philosophy, they look to the most immediate quick fix. As they struggle over pounds, they become distracted from the deeper reality. The food, not the pain or the neglect or the discrimination, becomes the ultimate enemy. And in turn, their bodies are the battleground.

We find substitute gods—Ana, Mia, ourselves, supermodels, celebrities—because the authentic kind are hard to conceptualize. Our bodies are immediate, the reality of our wide hips or our round stomachs with us every minute. We face the prospect of eating three times a day—that is three times a day when we put ourselves up to the challenge of being "virtuous" or "sinful," three times a day when our worship of thinness is reinforced. How can that possibly compete with the biannual drop-ins at church, or even the once-a-week visits to temple?

Few in my generation were raised with the notion that seeking an individual spirituality is integral to success—at least not explicitly so. Many of us were raised by ex-Catholics, Buddhist converts, and reform Jews traumatized by their own dogmatic upbringings and determined not to push their children in any religious direction. But without a push of any kind, some of us missed the touch. We gravitated toward ideas, not faith. And as anyone who has been knocked down by sadness or sickness or exhaustion knows, ideas don't make a great cushion.

Taking the Leap

One of the biggest challenges young women face is the jump across the abyss that separates our intellectual understanding from our daily reality. We know in theory that balance and wellness are the goal, but in our day-to-day lives, balance seems boring and wellness geriatric. Jumping across this abyss requires some maturity. It also requires faith that you can get to the other side and that, once you are there, you will still resemble yourself.

Faith is not something smart girls come by easily. We are taught to be analytical. Young women, especially those on rigorous academic tracks, spend a lot of time training to stay in their heads instead of their hearts, an essential skill for moving forward in the world and expressing themselves. But perhaps we spend so much time stuffing our brains with information that our other psychological muscles— like the muscle to hope, the muscle just to be, the muscle to experience sensuality—grow weak. You can't *understand* that your body is okay the way it is. You have to just know it, to pay attention to what it tells you through the ache in your belly or the tiredness in your feet.

As a high-achieving senior at a private eastern college, Becky took a class titled "Reading the Anorexic Body." She had chosen it because of her own battle with bulimia. Becky also studied Buddhism that semester—learning about the Buddha's long journey to nirvana, his eightfold way, the depressing and integral concept that "life is suffering." She wrote different types of meditations on three-by-five index cards and memorized them for the test, but she didn't actually try them out.

When she graduated, she moved to San Francisco to teach preschool. One cloudy Saturday she stumbled into a yoga class and geared up for an hour of torture, but the instructor opened by asking them all to get in a restful position. She started chanting and lighting incense and encouraged them to feel the light and energy of a greater force, to fill the room with their own offering of loving-kindness. It was a culture shock after the rigidity and rationality characteristic of Becky's upbringing. She says, "I had grown up on the East Coast. I had a lot of East Coast intensity to me." She was unaccustomed, she realized, to listening without judgment. She was more used to analyzing, critiquing, and arguing.

Becky no longer binged and purged with regularity, but she still critiqued the size of her stomach daily. She still sought out the latest diets to fix her unacceptable physique. She was recovering from the disappointment of the weight she had gained back after scrapping the South Beach Diet.

But sitting in that light-filled yoga studio, smelling the pungent aroma of patchouli, listening to the sounds of strangers offering their voices—however untrained—to one united hum, she couldn't help noticing that her consciousness sank from her brain down into her body for the first time in years. The instructor said, "Meet your body where it is." Becky got goose bumps. She actually felt the strain of her shoulder blades pulling back in downward dog. She noticed how heavy her head was when she leaned over for forward bend. She experienced the movement of each one of her precious vertebrae as she straightened back to standing.

That one statement affected her enormously: "I thought of it constantly—'meet your body where it is.' It was in such opposition to the mentality of squeezing every ounce of fat out of your body, use it and abuse it. 'Meet your body where it is' became my mantra in terms of really being aware and mindful and listening. It changed things for me, it really did."

Throughout the next few years, Becky resurrected her ability to live inside her body without constantly judging and evaluating it. She said her mantra to herself on the walk to work, while shopping in the organic grocery store, when she woke up, and when she went to sleep. "Not only did yoga physically change my body," Becky explains, glowing, "but I started to think about eating in a different way. I started thinking about how I was fueling my body." She gave up dairy, because she realized that her body was rejecting it—her skin cleared up and her chronic congestion finally ended. She fed her body when it was hungry. She didn't feed it when it was sleepy or emotionally overwrought. She started taking yoga constantly, thriving off her renewed relationship with her body, in that moment, right there and then.

Her Buddhist class was finally making sense. All the concepts she had put on flash cards became part of her daily practice. Buddhist mindfulness, the practice of staying truly aware in the moment rather than thinking of past or present, was changing her entire experience of the world—*Now I am brushing my teeth. How does the brush feel against my gums? What does the toothpaste taste like? How many muscles are coordinated in spitting it out?* She was finally understanding harmful attachment—the concept that clinging to a desire can be poisonous to your well-being. When she faced a plate of cookies and heard the starving-daughter voice inside her mind shout, "I just can't help it! I have to have it," she took a step back and drew a deep breath, as she taught her preschool students to do. Usually there was a powerful message underneath if she listened hard enough. Usually it was not cookies she desired but rest or laughter or recognition.

Her mind was changing, and so was her body. One day she noticed that her belly button was a different shape. "That was the moment that I could see that there was actual physical change in my body," she remembers. She lost weight that she had once been desperate to get rid of, without being so attached to its significance. It seemed to fall away. In "meeting her body where it is," she had come to understand that she was okay, that her body was okay, that everything was okay. Years of therapy, hundreds of antidepressants, sleeping pills and tranquilizers, and a $150,000 education had not given her that knowledge.

———————

Knowledge is power, but cognitive knowledge is not the only kind that makes us strong and happy. In fact, it appears that cognitive knowledge rarely makes anyone strong and happy on its own. It also doesn't make people any more interesting or kind.

Becky found in that yoga studio and in the years afterward something she had been searching for throughout college. She had been in such pain, huddled over the toilet, vomiting her guts out, sometimes twice a day. In those moments, it was not her religion textbook or her feminist reader that she most longed for. It was self-acceptance. It was comfort. It was faith in the beauty of her body regardless of its size. These things don't come from the intellect alone. They come from the soul. You can rationalize until you are blue in the face, but you are never going to believe that you are beautiful unless you believe it in the regions below your brain. I have tried numerous times to "think my way" into a healthy relationship with my body, and it always backfires. A well-intentioned commitment to eating a balanced diet often leads to guilt and criticism. An innocent fitness schedule can become boring, militaristic workouts. These attempts fail if the heart, the senses, and the soul are missing. Spontaneity is crucial to health. Listening to when your body is hungry, and for what, is a mindful act anathema to most young women. In fact, the majority of those I interviewed for this book don't even know how to identify when they are hungry or when they are full. They have so intellectualized the rights and wrongs of feeding themselves that they can't feel a damn thing.

Becky learned to listen again, but even more important, she learned to believe. Studying religion is far different from experiencing spirituality, for which the brain must be shut off, the heart turned up. Spirituality requires that perfect girls stop thinking, planning, judging, and start sensing. It requires that we start listening to the quiet but insistent starving daughter within us—the part that cries and wants and hungers so voraciously when ignored or when fed paltry substitutes for what it craves.

It also requires us to embrace the possibility that the most basic of our needs and desires, the most average of everyday life, will have to feed us. Perhaps true spirituality is found not in our grandparents' tall-steeple religions but in the joy of a walk in the snow on a Sunday afternoon or the warmth of a bowl of split pea soup. Perhaps the very thing we are trying to run from—our ordinariness, the ordinariness of everyday life—is where divinity dwells.

Transcendence

Heather watched other women in the dining hall and secretly felt superior—as if she had evolved above the need to make petty little decisions about what to eat and when. "They are in a different category of people," she remembers thinking. "Their perceptions are different. They aren't on level one, where I am." The negotiation that once went on in her head had been minimized to one easy and clean word: *No.* No, she would not eat that. No, she would not go out drinking. No, she would not have a relationship with any of her shaggy-haired suitors. No, she would not stop running when everyone else did. *No* became her hourly, sometimes minute-to-minute, prayer.

Her commitment to the safe and powerful *no* became even stronger as she watched another woman on her track team and "on her level." She remembers: "You could see all of her ligaments and muscles, a lot of her bones. Everyone would say, 'Oh my gosh, she is so disgusting,' but I just thought that was so attractive. I wanted to be like that." Heather never approached this woman about their shared romance with the word *no,* but she watched and took notes. She strove to become even more "evolved," even more in control. One rainy night on a bus trip home from a big race, her partner in starving leaned over and whispered, "You know, if you ever need to talk, I'm here." Heather smiled and whispered, "Thanks."

Heather explains, "We both knew that would never happen. It is a very private thing and a very individual thing. I secretly took pride in being anorexic, and she threatened that. She was the competition, not someone to unite with." They were each aiming to rise higher above the mess of human existence than the other, become more holy, more pure, more powerful. Unlike bulimics, who sometimes binge and purge together, or share war stories about their worst episodes, many anorectics see their disease as an individual journey toward lightness—as a religious pilgrimage of sorts that no one can possibly understand or experience with them. They strive toward a state of being that they believe is too difficult for the average person to endure.

And they are right. In the process of all that striving, two things shattered for Heather. One was her body. Slowly but undeniably, Heather's body started to break down. She suffered from stress fractures, from fatigue, from a pulled hamstring. Her injuries made her feel suddenly human—an intolerable state for her at the time. Running was her entire identity, so when her coach recommended she take a couple of days off, it felt like a death sentence. Who was she if she wasn't maniacally circling the track or pounding through the woods around campus? Who was she if she wasn't transcending the need to stop or slow down? Her body became her enemy in an even more pronounced way—it was the weakness standing between her delusions of invincibility and her reality.

The other thing that broke loose despite her painful effort to hold it all together was her will. She started slipping, started giving in to her hunger, started acting like the girls she had once secretly loathed in the dining hall. With her body disobeying her pledge for perfection, her mind followed.

At first it began under the guise of prerace carbo loads—a common practice among runners. "I started going to the dining hall alone the night before a meet," she remembers, "and eating a ton of food. But then I would end up feeling really ashamed. I would think, *I'm disgusting. I am this huge pig.* That's when I started purging too." No longer able to fit the world into tiny, manageable boxes, Heather was forced to reckon with her own humanness again.

"Reading back in my journal," she tells me, "I see this very obvious division in myself, even in the handwriting. When I was in perfectionist mode, I wrote long lists of goals in this tiny little print. Then the next day, when I'd failed to meet those goals, the entry would be this big scrawling handwriting: 'I hate myself. I'm disgusting.' It was like this whole different person." Heather's journal reads like a chronicle of the perfect girl–starving daughter dichotomy. Its neat and clean plans for eating less, running more, studying, excelling at ways to fix her unacceptably messy life (perfect girl) were etched next to long, loopy lists of foods she had succumbed to (starving daughter). She was, quite simply, torn in two.

———————

Eating disorders are enticing to perfect girls because they are a kind of release from the monotony and frustration of daily life. Eating disorders, and eating-disordered behaviors, are like shortcuts—an anorectic doesn't have to struggle with the daily choices of what to eat and when, she merely doesn't. The bulimic gets to mute her loneliness or sadness or anxiety in a pile of the sweets and carbs she thinks she desires, then purge her system of it before it gets absorbed (this is actually an illusion of transcendence . . . many bulimics remain at a normal body weight or actually gain weight, because their bodies get hip to the routine and start sucking up whatever calories they can find before the food gets purged). Overexercisers fly high above the mundane world on endorphins, truly transcendent for a short time.

Perfect girls aren't attracted to the "stuff" of everyday life. We watched our moms juggle the stuff—the plumber, the laundry, the dinner, the hole in the stockings—and collapse at the end of the day. We weren't raised to be domestic, to respect balance, or to think of ourselves as cogs in a giant societal machine. We have a collective delusion that we will create lives less messy than our parents'.

Eating disorders fit into this delusion and provide a way to rise above diets and mundane concepts about weight gain. We will be thin and brilliant and funny, all with no fuss. We will be "effortlessly perfect."

But effortless perfection is an exhausting, futile pursuit that requires a tremendous amount of self-denial and emotional control. There is a mentality, among young women who strive to be perfect but among runners in particular, that there is something weak about listening to the body. You must dig down and muster the strength to overcome your pain or fatigue. You must not listen to the signs or signals from your feeble body. You must, in essence, overcome your humanness.

Central to the oppressive effort to be perfect is the notion that the body is tainted, that its urges are primitive and embarrassing. Anorectics want to transcend this "dirty" system by becoming pure, weightless, unfettered by earthly desires. This idea of transcending the dirtiness of the body has ancient roots. In *Holy Anorexia,* Rudolph Bell explores how those in religious orders during medieval times starved themselves as evidence of their devotion to Jesus Christ. Those who triumphed over their earthly needs—food, comfort, sensuality—were lauded as holy martyrs. Their ultimate reward was death.

Modern anorectics may not be starving for the sake of Christ, but they certainly buy into the ancient idea of hunger as weakness. Though they take this notion to the extreme, in truth they are not far off from the attitude the rest of society often takes toward the body and its pesky needs. Work and success, not balance or sensitivity, are our ultimate virtues. Growing up in the superwoman eighties and the dot-com nineties, younger women believed that success was achievable if we were dedicated and self-sacrificing enough. The message today has not changed much. Reality TV gives us fine examples of women transcending weakness to beat everyone else—*Survivor*, *The Apprentice*, *America's Next Top Model*.

Successful women are not supposed to be weighted down with the average tasks of everyday life; they are supposed to be able to pay someone else to do them and get on with being fabulous. Complaining about sticking to workout plans or struggling with restrictive diets is the stuff of the dowdy, the unsuccessful, and the powerless. The women whom my generation looks up to seem to fly above the messiness of life, their bodies like well-crafted statements of who they are. But any woman who appears to be effortlessly perfect is spending hours a day sweating and grunting in a gym, or undergoing messy cosmetic surgery.

When "real" women try to get to perfection by transcending the messiness of life, they get in trouble. They get sick. They get sad. They get, as Heather did, split in two. They spend so much energy denying their sensible hungers and cravings that their inner starving daughters start asserting themselves in big, aggressive ways. Instead of escaping the mundanities of earthly existence, they become ravaged by them. What was once an easy process—*Do I want that sandwich? No. Do I want that burger? No. Do I want that salad? Half*—becomes a much more complex and painful conversation.

No Less Than a Holy War

Like many young born-again Christian women in America, my twenty-one-year-old cousin Anna was raised on God and country. The church she grew up in was nestled in the beautiful mountains of Colorado, just outside her town, population ninety-two. She lived in a trailer until she was thirteen years old and my uncle Allan got the money to build a house. He's a fireman. My aunt keeps the books at the local inn.

Anna is gorgeous. She has almost frighteningly large eyes with thick, deep black lashes. Her hair is straight and shiny brown, her lips full and pink. She went to the prom with the prom king when she was just a first-year in high school. If anyone had escaped a poor self-image, I always assumed, it would have been Anna.

And then I asked. Anna was visiting me one March, and we were walking around the Metropolitan Museum of Art, when our conversation started to shift to eating disorders and nutrition. Anna had taken a nutrition class the previous semester, and we talked about all of the obsessive girls who filled the class, tilting their heads to one side and feigning innocence while asking questions like "What would happen if someone ate half of the daily calorie recommendation?"

We both laughed at these desperate girls. We talked about our love of sports and our hearty mothers (sisters), who had raised us to run and jump and flirt to our hearts' content. Finally we got around to talking honestly about our own negative feelings about our bodies. I told her about my experience in college—how I always felt on the edge of an eating disorder. She looked at me with those wide eyes, wet with relief, and admitted that she felt that way most of the time.

Not my Anna! I was screaming inside my head. *She isn't rich like all those girls I went to school with, the ones with the disappearing mothers and the absent fathers! She grew up sledding and hiking and praying. She grew up sheltered from fashion trends and personal trainers.*

But it was true. A working-class background, a small town, a religious upbringing . . . none of it could protect her from the slow creep of food and fitness preoccupation. In fact, when I asked Anna to describe what it was like on days she felt particularly in danger of falling over that edge, she answered, "It is a constant battle in my head. My academic training tells me what's good for me and what I should be eating, but then the insecure devil in my head takes over and is like, 'You're fat, you shouldn't be eating that.' The thing that keeps me from giving in is the other voice, the God voice. I pray, 'God, let me see me through your eyes and not the world's.'"

She paused then, looked up as if communicating with her savior, and said, "I think that's the constant walk with God that you have to do. You're never going to be the perfect Christian, but you have to learn to trust Him. You have to learn not to lean on your own understanding of the world, but His."

Women's struggle with their bodies is a holy war going on inside their own minds. The devil, whether the one found in the Bible or the one in the diet industry, is there, and he is telling you that you are bad, that you deserve nothing, that you have already screwed it all up. Your intellect is there, trying to be rational about calories, carbs, and cardio, chastising you for being so emotional, so needy. The little-girl you, or the middle-school you, or the first-day-at-college you might be there too—hungry, scared, alone. Your mother is also there—maybe judging, maybe criticizing, maybe trying to protect you. And if you are lucky, and have a God to call upon, or a guardian angel, or a kind, dead grandmother, maybe he or she is there too—trying to be heard above the shouting match among the rest of the voices. No wonder we are in so much pain.

I first understood the extent of this battle in the brain because of Anna, but I heard it echoed in hundreds of girls' stories in the course of researching this book. Another woman, who preferred to stay anonymous, explains: "My issues with eating and when to work out and all that is basically spiritual warfare. I have all these lies in my head, and it takes my faith in God to rebuke them." Another woman, who does not identify with a specific religion, explains: "I know, in my heart of hearts, that I was created by some energy that thinks I am okay the way I am, but I have so many other voices in my head—evil, destructive ones—that make me think otherwise."

We are not just negotiating the mass markets' claims about food, diet, fitness, beauty, sex, and success, we are negotiating the mixed messages inside our own minds, refereeing our own complex psychologies. Like puppets on invisible strings, we are played by our own thoughts. Perfect girls may make passing comments about feeling gross because we drank or ate too much the night before, but we rarely, if ever, expose this battle in our brains. This cacophony of voices is kept hidden, buried beneath layers of political correctness and pride—a meticulously, if unconsciously, protected image of who we want the world to understand us to be. We are hardly conscious of these voices ourselves. We experience the emotional aftermath of their shouting—the guilt, shame, confusion, frustration, loneliness—but we rarely tune in to the content of the messages, rarely interrogate them for validity, rarely even trace them to their sources.

Does this sound familiar?

You walk past your bedroom mirror and catch a glimpse of your ass in sweatpants. *Gross! Am I really that fat? Have I been walking around all this time with that big, fat ass, not even realizing how huge it is? That is unforgivable. I am such a mess. I need to get my life under control. Today I'm not going to eat even breakfast—set the tone from the start. I should go make some coffee.*

Maybe your go-girl feminist tries to sneak in: *Oh, come on. It's not that bad. I'm just one of those girls who has a big ass. Some guys like big asses. I should just eat healthier. I'm probably not getting enough protein. I should have a shake for breakfast.*

And the little girl, the lonely searcher, the starving daughter: *I just want to be pretty. Why is that so frickin' hard to achieve? I don't have to be a supermodel. I just want to be attractive. I just want to look in the mirror and feel good about what I see. Is that impossible? It feels impossible. I am so tired of this. I feel like just staying home from school. I feel like sitting in front of the TV all day and eating bowls of cereal. I'm so sick of everything.*

No wonder my generation is distracted by this obsession with our weight; it is the running commentary in our heads—like a whole team of sportscasters commenting on every grab and pass that we make throughout the day. The external voices are obvious and straightforward. You can disregard them or scoff at them. But turning off the voices in your head is not so easy. We go through life making choices without realizing that we are responding to these inner voices.

Some girls, unable to resist the starving daughter who wants food now, more, never enough, binge. This gluttonous act leads to temporary relief but is followed by unbearable guilt. As penance, they purge—rid themselves of their sin, pray to porcelain gods. The bulimic's experience of bingeing and purging is often a religious fervor—equivalent to the collapse and shake of Southern Baptists in the aisle—followed by the deep, dark shame of having gone astray. The starving daughter is awakened from her stupor of feeding (some women truly do eat in their sleep) by the outraged inner perfect girl who then tries to resurrect herself by ridding her body of its egregious imperfections.

For others, the answer to quieting the dull roar in the brain is a matter of willpower. These perfect girls rarely act compulsively, don't like to drink or feel too crazy about a guy. They believe the devil inside their own heads—there is evil out there, and they want to avoid it. They also believe the god—the messiness of life must be put into tiny compartments and managed. They want to make their lives, their bodies, into symbols of purity. They want to transcend the weakness of the common woman—the girl who lives down the hall who says, "Oh, I really shouldn't," and then takes another cookie. That kind of wavering disgusts the true-blue anorectic. She believes, profoundly, in control.

For either kind of perfect girl, there is a breaking point. Somewhere along the hilly road of the bulimic or the straight-and-narrow of the anorectic is a moment when she collapses, unable to perform the illusion of "effortless perfection" any longer, unable to say no one more time, unable to weather the bloat and disgust of a binge. At this moment, the light creeps in.

"Handing It All Up"

Heather,* the runner, had grown up with a very loose grasp of Christianity. She tells me, "I thought it was just about going to church a few times a year, singing some songs. I believed in God, but Jesus was just some guy to me." As her health got worse and worse—her injuries wouldn't heal; the therapists she tried to go to were unhelpful; her bingeing and purging had become a roller coaster—she agreed to go on a weekend retreat with some friends who happened to be pretty serious Christians.

It seems, in retrospect, like an incongruous choice. A woman hell-bent on privacy, rationality, planning goes on a retreat with people she doesn't know well in a place where she will not be able to control her eating. "I know, it doesn't make any sense, but at the time I just felt compelled," she explains. "I think God must have wanted me to go."

Heather was struck, throughout the weekend, by how joyful and loving everyone seemed to be. They accepted her without really knowing her, laughed easily, woke early with bright eyes. "Their quality of life seemed so different than mine," she remembers. "I thought, *If this is because of this guy Jesus, then I want to be a part of it.*" It is easy to picture the vast contrast for Heather—her tedious lists of calories and diary entries filled with self-hate versus the elated, communal rapture of a cabin full of born-again Christians celebrating their faith.

She started attending church on campus more frequently and studying the Bible with other Christians. "This guy Jesus" turned out to be a pretty fascinating character. She was drawn to the unconditional love that she was taught he possessed for her, for everyone. She was comforted by the idea that someone was beside her, invisibly helping her through the huge struggle that lay ahead.

And it *was* huge. Heather did not discover Christianity and then immediately resurrect herself—healthy, fleshy, at peace. Instead, she wrestled with her religious education. At times she used it to make herself sicker. She recalls, "I got this twisted sense of what holy was. I decided that it was the opposite of greed and gluttony. Not eating made me feel like I was holy or pure." But her new tendency to binge and purge offered no religious justification. It was simply devastating.

The hamstring injury refused to get better, so Heather was forced to stop running entirely. Her identity was, once again, shot. When her team made it to nationals, one of her most desired goals, she was further crushed, left behind with her broken body and broken heart.

At a time of real confusion and overwhelming defeat, she went on another Christian retreat with friends. This time a guest speaker mentioned in passing that eating disorders were an example of a sin that God could not tolerate. Heather's ears perked, and she started thinking hard about the way she had been reinterpreting the faith to fit her disease, about how tired she was, how hopeless. She remembers reading in the weathered Bible in her lap: "It is for freedom that Christ has set us free. Stand firm, then, and do not let yourselves be burdened again by a yoke of slavery" (Galatians 5:1). It dawned on her, with a violence so sharp it made her double over, that she was a slave to her eating disorder. She felt compelled to leave the lecture, as if God had spoken to her and told her that it was time to deal with her eating disorder once and for all. *Right now?* she remembers thinking. *In the middle of this lecture?* But God had a plan.

She went out on the porch, the sun practically blinding her, and started sobbing. It just flooded out of her, and for once, she did not restrain it. She did not try to stop it. She just gave in. She surrendered through her lifetime of tears, and she heard God speak very clearly to her again: "It is time to give this up. It is time to want to get better." Heather describes this moment as absolute revelation: "I just sobbed and I spoke to God. I just laid it all out, everything. And as I laid it out, I felt the Holy Spirit taking it away. Anything I could hand up, He could handle. I was just handing it all up."

This concept, "handing it all up," is anathema to perfect girls. Instead, we go through life trying to "take it all on." The idea that there is room to, in a sense, give up is hard to understand. That there is a time to admit that you are in over your head, that you have run out of options, that you are exhausted and unable to keep going, whether religious or not, is a revelation.

Our more-better-faster society doesn't talk a lot about these kinds of breaking points, especially for women. Women are expert, instead, at grinning and bearing it. Perfect girls are into control, into privacy, into performance. Handing it all up makes them feel vulnerable when they are aiming for invincibility.

But just as Heather was unable to transcend the chaos and messiness of life, all perfect girls attempting to do it right all the time do it wrong and lose it at some point (think Reese Witherspoon in *Election*). We are, after all, fallible, and one of the most beautiful, neglected parts of our humanness is our inability to handle everything on our own.

Stating aloud that you aren't happy with your relationship with food and fitness, asking for help, admitting weakness can be the first step toward becoming stronger. I chalk up my own rare admission of imperfection one promising spring day in Central Park as the moment that kept me safe from a full-blown illness. I was walking with my mom, who had come to pick me up from my first year at college, and I suddenly blurted out, "Mom, I think if I'm not careful, I could get an eating disorder." There was no premeditation. It just came out, blurted from some deep, unconscious place. It was almost as if the army that Nicole Blackman talked about wanting for her daughter, the one that lives inside you waiting to save your life, had rescued me from my own stubborn pride.

My mom was as shocked as I was that I had admitted to being on the edge, but she managed to respond calmly and constructively. She assured me that I could talk to a therapist at home that summer if I thought it might be helpful, that together we could reestablish a healthy pattern of wholesome and sometimes indulgent eating and fun exercising.

Truth is, I suffered long after that summer. Everything was not magically fixed by our mother-daughter bond or the afternoons in the mountains. The pull of perfection was much stronger than even those, my most precious gifts. However, whenever I got dangerously close to the edge again, I would think of that afternoon with my mom, those words I had unconsciously blurted out, and I would stop myself from slipping off. I knew, with that admission, I had committed myself to honesty. I couldn't stomach the idea of looking my mom in the eye and telling her that, despite all of her efforts, all of her fierce love, I had fallen.

Lynn Ginsburg and Mary Taylor, writers on food and spirituality, offer this perspective: "Accompanying an underlying sense of suffering is a feeling of emptiness. We feel something missing. Inside of us is a void, a longing deep within for some elusive satisfaction." Though perfect girls were not raised to believe that our devotion to any one religion is an integral part of our success, we long for some kind of cosmic reassurance, an unwavering sureness about our own worth in a world that constantly puts it into question.

The search for a god, this drive to understand mystery and meaning, is universal. But as my own mom explains, "Those of us who grew up with too many rules often didn't find our way back to a structured dogma that we could pass to our kids, so we left you searching for something. We didn't even show you the continent, much less the country, never mind the map."

We, the perfect girls, have been on our own version of a pilgrimage—going many miles and denying the most basic of our needs in the futile hope that all this will lead us to some kind of salvation. When we are thin, we have reasoned, we will be godlike and no longer need the reassurance of a higher power. We will possess a power within ourselves potent enough to get us loved and promoted and recognized.

We have sought perfect gods, and we have come up empty-handed. We have learned that, no matter how much we deprive ourselves, our bodies refuse to become holy. They are fleshy, curved, bleeding messes, made in an ancient form—certainly divine but not devoid of discomfort. We have learned that, no matter how much we control our appetites, a hunger remains at our cores. It won't be satiated by food or the swollen pride that results from refusing it. It certainly won't be satiated by perfection. As Anna Quindlen predicted, those of us who have tried to be perfect all of our lives will face a moment when we discover not an impeccably ordered soul within, but a black hole.

Only wonder will fill you and satiate your spiritual hunger— wonder at your little life, wonder at the struggle, wonder at minute and overlooked beauty. There is no secret path in the sky, there is only the very human work of slugging on the ground. It is at once mundane and miraculous, at once daily and divine. You will fail to bypass the nitty-gritty choices of life. Inevitably. You will fail to live life completely in your head. Inevitably. You will fail to lose weight, keep it off, stick to a diet. Inevitably. You will fail to deny your hungers, cravings, and desires. Inevitably. You will fail to be a perfect girl. Inevitably.

Ultimately you cannot organize a soul or a life. You cannot *achieve* well-being. You can only move toward wellness and peace of mind and happiness with a humble, transparent intention. You can only admit your smallness in a large and overwhelming world, and then be surprised by the power of that smallness. You can only see your body for what it is—a miracle of coordination, curves, resiliency, a partner in your life's journey.

Our generation's spiritual hunger is not a separate issue from our obsession with food and fitness. In fact, acknowledging the depth of our hunger is the beginning of the end of it.

13

Stepping Through the Looking Glass: Our New Stories

The only interesting answers are those that destroy the questions.
—Susan Sontag

The problems that exist in the world today cannot be solved by the level of thinking that created them.
—Albert Einstein

Back in the packed Marriott ballroom, surrounded by women much older and more versed in the language of pain than I am, the air is getting lighter as we anticipate the close of Carol Gilligan's keynote. Like antsy junior high students five minutes before the bell, the audience members start shifting in their seats.

I am overwhelmed. My questions have become a dozen nagging children all pulling on my heartstrings, and I have no answers or peanut butter sandwiches with which to appease them. My program is covered with notes in the adolescent language of absolutes, followed by a parade of exclamation points and question marks: "But what is the answer?! If we have 'lost' our voices, how do we 'find' them? How do we stop being perfect girls if this is all we have ever known? How can we stop when everything around us reinforces being thin all the time? Where is the power? Really?!?"

I look up from my ink and angst right as Carol Gilligan looks up from her notes on the lectern. Staring straight into the faces of her audience with determined, steely eyes, she says, "The seemingly impossible task is to tell a new story."

These words still echo inside me today.

———————

What could our new story be? I have wondered this as I listened to unique, beautiful women construct their individual histories out of eerily identical parts—diet that led to disease, ambition in overdrive, unspoken suffering. I have wondered this as I tried to blend in among a dozen fourteen-year-olds spilling their insecure lives and reveling in the spilling as only teenage girls can. I have wondered this when sitting at a Brooklyn diner and watching a woman pour water over her breakfast to prevent herself from eating it all. I have wondered this as I heard the voices of all those women I spoke to over the phone who seemed as if they could not stop talking once they started.

The studies on eating disorders say there will be few happy endings, but I can't believe them. I won't believe them. Yet as much as I don't want to accept that eating disorders are an inevitable epidemic in our spiritually bankrupt culture of thin-worship, when I try to think of a new story, it sounds an awful lot like a fantastical fairy tale.

———————

Once upon a time there was a generation of little girls born with furious cries and tiny hearts swollen with potential. They were raised in a world that told them daily how special and capable they were but also how unfinished and burdened with hope. A seed of anxiety was planted in the center of their beings. It sprouted and spread quickly. By the time they were twelve, they no longer remembered what it felt like to climb trees or become bored at meals. Their bodies, growing bigger and more uncontrollable all the time, became their enemies.

They wandered the world hungry, trying desperately to appease their anxiety with accomplishments—gilded little plastic trophies engraved with their names, report cards covered in A's and stuck to refrigerator doors with magnets, letters from colleges confirming their superiority. They wanted things other than these little tokens, but they couldn't quite remember what those things were. Their forgotten desires turned to bellyaches, numbed only by food or the refusal of it. They couldn't hear the whispers originating from deep within over the roar of their exercise bikes churning in place. They slept in fits and starts, waking with sweaty foreheads and pounding hearts; their dreams were full of monsters with their own faces.

They looked in mirrors, scrutinizing their reflections so long they forgot that a whole world existed outside the looking glass, a whole world that needed their ideas and their commitment and their passion. They were a generation of narcissistic Alices who forgot to step through.

But one day, one girl looked at herself in the mirror and was shocked at how beautiful her crooked nose was, how strange and lovely. Another girl noticed the striking curve of her big hips. Another suddenly relished her chest, flat as a board and ready for anything. Another discovered her rounded belly, and another her long, sturdy feet, and another her strong thighs.

And then these same girls started to wonder. If they were so surprisingly beautiful, what surprises did the world beyond the looking glass hold? One day, one brave girl stepped right through. And another followed her. And another and another and another . . .

And slowly, like the quiet creep of spring after a dry, brutal winter, this generation of girls remembered the power of their furious cries and the potential of their swollen hearts. They grew angry at the world that had told them daily how unfinished they were and started refusing to hear it. Instead, they started listening to the whispers from deep within, and as they listened, the whispers grew louder and they began to feel more and more complete.

They had much more time to do things they had always pledged to do, such as save the world and watch the sunrise with good friends on rooftops and hold the hands of their grandmothers. They had the resilience to pick themselves up and dust themselves off, because they realized that falling made them not more perfect but better somehow, more right with the world. They began to laugh at themselves, to like themselves, even, because they knew that imperfection and struggle were actually what prevented the day from being dreadfully boring.

The seed of anxiety that had once made them feel perpetually hungry withered and died, and in its place, a quiet power grew. It made them feel solid and satisfied, prepared to storm the boardrooms and bedrooms and battlefields of the world and save people. After all, they had already done the most difficult deed in saving themselves.

It just took the difficult but not at all impossible effort of stepping through the looking glass—leaving behind the world of someone else's making in order to enter one of their own.

And, of course, they lived . . .

I realize, however, that real girls with real lives, eating disorders, and real problems may not have the perfect ending. There is no glass slipper and certainly no Prince Charming. Our hair, no matter how much we deep-condition it, isn't strong enough or long enough to throw out the window for some hopeful dude to climb up. We don't live in houses made out of candy and gingerbread (thank God). Now I am sounding like Alice herself:

"I can't believe that!" said Alice.

"Can't you?" the Queen said in a pitying tone. "Try again: draw a long breath, and shut your eyes."

Alice laughed. "There's no use trying," she said: "one can't believe impossible things."

"I daresay you haven't had much practice," said the Queen. "When I was your age, I always did it for half-an-hour a day. Why, sometimes I've believed as many as six impossible things before breakfast."

How do we "step through the looking glass"? How do we recognize the world we live in for what it is—just one version of reality, of which there are many? How do we distinguish between our own truth and the dominant culture's dangerous views of beauty and ambition? We are beautiful in spite of our imperfections, even more beautiful as a result of them. And we are a generation of women on the brink of amazing things, regardless of our weight, held back, in fact, only by our preoccupation with it.

I close my eyes. Gilligan did say "the *seemingly* impossible." This time my fantasy is less fairy tale and more manifesto:

We were a generation of women raised to believe that power was outside ourselves. Sure, the expression "girl power" was thrown around as we came of age, but we recognized it for what it was: a marketing campaign to get us to buy T-shirts and plastic diaries with flimsy aluminum keys. We were too smart for that. Instead, we observed what was deemed powerful in the real world, and we took copious notes: beautiful, thin women with flawless business suits and easy laughs, and always men with lots of money. Our mothers' intuition, their curvaceous, often neglected bodies, their intensity and easy tears were nowhere in the landscape of real-world power.

So we did what any smart, observant newbies in a cutthroat climate do—we prepared to play the game. We cultivated our lists of accomplishments and attempted to sculpt our bodies to fit the template we saw everywhere. We hid the pain, the blood, sweat, and tears, the exhaustion, behind expensively straightened smiles. We posed as the great, thin hope—the next wave of women who were too competent to need feminism and too cool to admit to the time and energy wasted on appearing so.

But the running and the deprivation, the controlling and the self-hating finally caught up with us. We couldn't pretend any longer that ambition was enough to fill the void where our faith should be.

So we started admitting to our own vulnerability. We started yawning when we were tired and crying when we were sad. We started talking to our mothers and fathers and friends and lovers about our fears—describing the ugliness underneath all of our prettiness. We acknowledged the existence of the black holes at our centers. We admitted that we were scared and unsure of what to do to make things better.

And soon after we started to admit to our own weakness, we started to feel strangely free and strong. We started talking to one another and recognizing our stories told a thousand times over by strangers' voices. We stopped seeing one another as fierce competition and started recognizing fierce collaborators.

Most important, we discovered that power was not outside ourselves but inside, that it dwelled, hidden by the shadows of those black holes growing lighter all the time, at our centers. Eventually we exploded with light.

Now, that feels a little better, but I distrust the cohesion and ease of the story. My generation has grown up in a time devoid of grand, sweeping social change. Our activism is mostly relegated to point-and-click campaigns. Most of us have never fought for anything that didn't promise a community service award at the end. We have individual values, to be sure, but outside of hip-hop and indie rock shows, we hardly ever connect the dots between our frustration with the culture and others'. Maybe it is part of our delusion of specialness. Maybe it is the result of living in the shadow of massive corporations and an all-powerful television culture. Organizing a boycott of a sexist magazine or having a Love Your Body Day event feels like looking for a needle in a haystack.

Social change has crept up on us primarily as trends and new technology. E-mail and cell phones have changed the way we communicate. Online dating has altered our expectations for relationships. Protest is usually dressed up in our favorite tone: sarcasm.

Biographies change before culture. Our new story will not be *a* new story. It will be thousands of new stories, maybe even millions, that would together constitute a cultural shift in the way we think about our bodies. These stories may share common themes, protagonists, and villains, but they will all read differently depending on each author. What do *you* find when you step through the looking glass? Where does *your* power lie? What will *your* new story be?

Mine began with anger. As I started taking account of all the friends whose passion and intellect were being wasted on their weight, as I forced myself to be honest about my own wasted time and energy, I got pissed. I felt duped. Here we were, the brightest, best-educated, freest generation of women to walk the earth—protected by all kinds of institutional laws and social mores—and we were afraid of our own power. We were distracted from great opportunities by nagging insecurities.

My initial anger was made even bigger and harder to ignore when my concerns were dismissed and I was told that weight preoccupation is an unavoidable part of being a woman. Then my anger became a conviction that there had to be girls out there as frustrated and disillusioned as I was.

Then my words led to listening. I got to hear from these girls. I got to have my conviction confirmed over and over again. In listening, I became more reflective, which led me to think about culture, to ask myself: How did we get here? I began considering the past, assembling a narrative about who we were and who we had become. I went back to find the sources of our fears, the cataracts and dams that were misdirecting our energy.

Here is what I have learned.

Ask the Experts

There is no catchall treatment for an eating disorder; there is only very personal healing. If you are sick, you need professional help. No cultural loophole or superwoman strength is getting you out of this one. Professionals use a variety of time-tested models for healing. These heroes and sheroes know far more about the delicate work of reenvisioning a self-image than I do. It is with my utmost respect and humility that I refer the sickest and most pained among us to them.[†] They have listened, observed, studied, developed, innovated, collaborated, evaluated, reevaluated, and continue to do so day in and day out.

In the biopsychosocial model, therapists take account of the wide variety of factors contributing to an eating disorder and try to treat them simultaneously. In the medical model, the focus is on restoring a biochemical balance, usually with antidepressants or antianxiety medication. Cognitive behavior therapy (known as CBT) is a time-limited process in which patients, primarily bulimics, are asked to identify their irrational thoughts and destructive behaviors, and, through awareness, heal them. Some girls with eating disorders go through family therapy. Some are taught to see their disease through a feminist lens. Most also see nutritionists who help them develop reasonable meal plans. Professionals usually incorporate a variety of these models to treat one patient.

One of the most promising new approaches is called Maudsley, named after the hospital in London where it was developed. In this approach, the family is seen as the home of healing for anorectics. Rather than being blamed for their daughters' diseases, parents are encouraged to become active in helping their sick daughters "get better." There are three phases of this medical approach, culminating in the daughter earning the power to make independent food choices again once she has gained back 95 percent of her ideal weight. This cutting-edge approach is gaining popularity in America.

There are treatment programs and residential centers, private and public, short term and long term, all over the country and all over the world. The problem, in most cases, is not finding help but affording it. Most of these programs are outrageously expensive, as much as a college education in some cases. Families are strapped, dipping into their retirement savings or taking out second mortgages just to get their daughters the care they need. Many parents spend the time they aren't mourning the loss of their daughters' well-being, or wrestling with their own guilt for not recognizing that loss sooner, fighting with insurance companies or applying for loans. It is one more undeniable piece of evidence that our health care system is unjust and horribly broken.

Given the intractable nature of anorexia and bulimia, it is critical that you own up to your eating-disordered inclinations early and try to get help before they grow into full-blown disease. I have heard so many stories of girls and their parents who approached doctors early on and were turned away—told to come back if things got worse, if they dropped more weight. They lost a critical window of prevention and intervention. Many medical doctors process weight in pounds and ounces, rather than in the more relevant units of measure in our culture: anxiety and obsession.

The sad thing is that most of these parents and their daughters left the doctor's office with a surface feeling of relief undergirded by a deep feeling of unease. They knew—in their hearts of hearts—that sickness was imminent. We respect doctors as the final authorities in our culture, so we take their word as fact. You have to listen to your own body, mind, and spirit. If you are dissatisfied with how much you are thinking about food and fitness, if you have an intuition that there is something wrong with your body, if you feel like you need help— you do. End of story.

The Power of Being Young and Mad

Perfection and thinness are not your most potent sources of authentic power; your potential is. We dwell in the most powerful of places, a place reserved expressly for those who are young and naïve: a land of nothing to lose.

Our obsession with weight is not simply pathology; it is a message about our anxiety and ambition. We are poised to change the world forever—we are that powerful. The preoccupation with food and fitness itself is disempowering but not a waste. Settling for that preoccupation most certainly would be. Accepting self-hatred as an inevitable part of being a woman would be tragic.

It takes tremendous will and determination to fight your natural cravings each and every day. It takes finely tuned control to resist the excess all around you. It also takes profound depth of emotion to buckle under this pressure, to eat until you are bloated with the evidence of your own fragility. And revolting as it is, it takes real, physical strength and strategy to find a toilet where you can rid yourself of this fragility. If you harnessed just a fraction of this will, determination, control, emotional depth, strength, and strategy to get better, to take care of yourself, to resist the culture's monotonous messaging, imagine how powerful you could be.

Our teacher will be our struggle. The wisdom we will gain from having been sick, to one degree or another, and gotten better will be more powerful than never having suffered. The therapist James Hillman writes, "Psychology regards all symptoms to be expressing the right thing in the wrong way." We hunger because we are hungry for the world. We starve because we are overwhelmed by this hunger. We binge because we want love and recognition and peace. We purge because we are ashamed that we don't know how to get it in the right way. We run because we are eager. We chase perfection because we are idealistic. We obsess because we are determined. We will heal because we are too young and too strong not to.

I recently went to a reading where an old white poet chain-smoked cigarettes, pushing the words out of his tired mouth along with the smoke in between sips of whiskey. I liked his poetry—it was filled with profound declarations told in very small, ordinary ways. But sitting there and watching this old man read poetry about his dog and the moonlight, I realized that I am filled with rage. I felt incredibly young and beautiful and angry—as if there weren't enough poems about dogs or moonlight in the whole world to express how much I cared about people or despised the conditions that made them hurt. I realized that my words are filled with a bursting, slightly embarrassing, mad passion. And this is my power. If you are angry, like me, this is your power too.

Truth and Humility

There is no single prescription for eating disorders. Where do *you* fall on the spectrum of this disease? What have *you* lost by dwelling there? What truths do *you* need to tell and to whom? What practices do *you* need to adopt in order to feel less weighed down by the burden of your own self-loathing? Who do *you* trust to hold your hand when your pants or your expectations or your punishments don't fit? When and where and with whom do *you* feel most beautiful, and how can you be there with them for more of the time?

There is no one-size-fits-all mantra; there is only awareness of the voices inside our own minds and the fierce interrogation of their validity. Our power begins in our ability to be aware of the holy war going on in our heads and our dedication to disputing it on a daily, hourly, even minute-to-minute basis. We must reckon with our inner perfect girls, harness their ambition and optimism, and throw out the self-criticism. Teach them how to be quiet and listen, to be comfortable with slowness, to savor a victory. Teach them about the strength and knowledge born of failure, pleasure for pleasure's sake, the inevitability and beauty of imperfection.

Likewise, we must answer the cries of our starving daughters. We have resented them all of these years, thought them weak and embarrassing, when in fact they are the only things anchoring us to our authentic appetites. We must make them stronger by acknowledging their fears, cravings, intuitions. We must translate their aches into the language of emotion, identify loneliness and anger and boredom and disappointment before they become insatiable hungers. Our starving daughters' voices will sound less like whines and more like wisdom if we stop pretending they aren't there.

Listen to the whispers of the self-protecting voices and encourage them to speak louder. Sympathize with the insecure thirteen-year-old in you and the neglected five-year-old, but ask both to quiet down and let the wiser, stronger you lead. We must be able to laugh at our ridiculous parroting of the culture around us: *Did I really just watch that commer-*

cial for thigh cream and pull up my shorts to analyze my cellulite? Am I an automaton or a living, breathing girl? We must banish the critical bitches and the abusive ex-boyfriends and the tight-ass health freaks until we are left with only our "original minds," in the language of Buddhism, or our "God-created selves," in the spirit of Jesus. What does the kindest, wisest, strongest version of you know about your body?

What does the kindest, wisest, strongest version of you know about *other* women's bodies? Don't let the voices in your mind fall into the bottomless pit of jealousy and judgment. The more critically and less compassionately you view other women's bodies, the less you will have the capacity to accept yourself. You will fear that others are covertly criticizing you as much as you are them. The more you practice judgment and jealousy, whether consciously or not, the better you get at it. Instead, as Wendy Shanker wisely suggests, send a "little mini-vibe of compassion" to that beautiful old woman sitting across from you in the doctor's office or the round-bellied waitress who takes your order with a warm smile. Or better yet, give compliments honestly and often, especially to the kinds of women who don't get complimented by our culture.

We must raise our consciousnesses through raw conversation. We must talk about how bad it really is in order to get better. We must admit we are not invincible. We must ask brave questions so we can learn about our family histories and our genetic risks. We must face these and ourselves with brutal truth and fierce optimism. The self-help guru Geneen Roth writes: "The nature of obsession is that it protects you from the truth." The nature of truth, then, is that it delivers you from obsession.

Sometimes stopping the holy war in your head is possible only if you say your thoughts—even ugly—aloud, make them real. If I turn to my brother and admit that I have just looked at my profile in the mirror and thought, *I'll never be a successful writer until I get rid of this fat neck*, then I am forced to see that impulse for what it is: irrationality. Caroline Knapp wrote of her own path of recovery from anorexia: "Pain festers in isolation, it thrives in secrecy. Words are its nemesis, naming anguish is the first step in defusing it, talking about the muck a woman slogs through—the squirms of self-hatred and guilt, the echoes of emptiness and need—a prerequisite for moving beyond it." When you externalize the voices in your head, they lose power. They become silly and strange. You can hear them for what they are—destructive voices with an ulterior motive (money, usually), pretending to be looking out for your best interest. We are lousy ventriloquists.

Coming Home

Diets fail. Excess is a health risk. Starving can lower your blood pressure until your heart stops. Bingeing and purging can cause electrolyte imbalance so severe your heart stops. It is time to quit these unhealthy behaviors and addictions. It is time we blazed a new path home to our bodies.

One of the most effective ways to stop obsessing about your body is to start listening to it more. There is no magic diet or miracle fitness regimen; there is only tapping into your authentic appetites. You may need to relearn the hollow, surprising ache of hunger or the small satiation of fullness. You may need to remember how to like food without coveting it or how to taste it instead of calculating it. Your body does not know the diet language of "good" and "bad"; it knows only what it needs or wants at the moment. You may need to ride waves of cravings until they break. The less that wanting is mediated by your intellect, the less threatening it will seem. A cookie becomes a cookie again—sugar, butter, flour, and milk—not a statement about your worth as a woman. You may need to take it all less seriously.

Your body has ideas about what it wants to eat *and* how it wants to move. You may need to remember what you loved doing at five or ten or fifteen and start doing it again. When I am sweating and jumping and stomping my way through African dance class, I feel young and completely alive, freed from the boredom of listening to the same damn thoughts running through my head—*Is this done? Is that done?* I am just leaping. Skipping, jumping, playing soccer, dancing, diving, and making love are not fitness plans but ways to move in the world.

There is no there; there is only here. It makes sense that ambitious women are forward-thinking—it is our mojo. We plan, set goals, move on. We drive ourselves a little crazy. Try, every once in while, just being still. Try noticing the color of your bathroom tiles. Try feeling the shower while you are in it. Try appreciating the softness of your socks or the wide berth of your butt. It is good for sitting on. Try eating slowly and noticing the strange texture of a chip. Try eating Jelly Bellies with your eyes closed, one at a time, and guessing the flavors. Try reaching for your toothbrush very, very, very slowly. Try observing one interesting thing about every person in the waiting room.

The past is full of angst-inducing memories. Once you've eaten something, you've eaten it. Stop remembering that you've eaten it. Stop evaluating whether it was good or bad that you ate it. Don't reward yourself. Don't chastise yourself. Forget about it. It happened. It's over. No big deal.

There is no measure of a life well lived. You have to create joy and not push away sadness. Don't weigh yourself. The number is irrelevant. How do you *feel*? Stop being a perfect girl and start enjoying your life's little wonderful things. Rediscover or, in many of our cases, discover for the first time, the importance of small pleasures.

I'm talking about eating a slice of warm pizza when it's freezing outside, sharing a beer at the end of the day with your best friend, taking a nap without setting your alarm. I'm talking about laughing during sex. I'm talking about playing poker with the guys. I'm talking about dancing with the girls. I'm talking about Saturday-night board games and Sunday-afternoon softball. I'm talking about spontaneity—Popsicles in the snow, hot dogs on the street, calling in sick on the spur of the moment. Celebrate everything and anything—your first publication in a magazine, the anniversary of the day you paid off your college debt, a Thursday. You are young. Act like it.

There is no eternal reward for achieving; there is only believing. Believe in something, anything, that makes the day feel shorter and the night less lonely. If you are atheist, more power to you, but believe in your own strong moral center. If you are agnostic, dwell in that place of unknowing with a certain amount of wonder. If you have a set religious viewpoint, use it to liberate, not restrict, you. Don't let it become a new holy war in your head. Make it the bedrock of your kindness. Don't let any spiritual leader or religious dogma convince you that your body is anything but fine. It is not dirty. It is not dangerous. It is actually something of a miracle.

Whole Beauty

There is no perfection; there is only the beauty of imperfection. Gap teeth are so often endearing. Scars are intriguing. A big nose is memorable. Stray moles lead us places. I hated my toes for years—they bend in odd places, as if bowing to some formidable foot god. Then one day I was sitting waiting for the subway with my mom, both of us in open-toed shoes, and a stranger walked up and said, "You must be mother and daughter. You have the same toes." I looked down, and lo and behold, we were cut from the same cloth. I've had a secret affection for my crooked toes ever since. Quirks can push people head over heels into love. A set of formidable hips can make a man swoon. It is our strangeness, not our sameness, that attracts people to us.

Thinness is unremarkable. Everyone and her mother are thin. As a matter of fact, everyone and her mother have those same expensive highlights, those trendy new boots that cost a fortune, and those flat stomachs that fit very little inside. Sure, it seems pleasing to the eye at first—you recognize it instantly, it doesn't challenge you to think at all, it matches what you have seen on television and in fashion magazines. But there is also nothing to explore, nothing to learn, nothing to be surprised by. How dreadfully boring.

You know what is really, powerfully sexy? A sense of humor. A taste for adventure. A healthy glow. Hips to grab on to. Openness. Confidence. Humility. Appetite. Intuition. A girl who makes the world seem bigger and more interesting. A girl who can rap. A loud laugh that comes from her belly. Smart-ass comebacks. Presence. A quick wit. Dirty jokes told by an innocent-looking lady. Hooded sweatshirts. Breakfast in bed. A girl with boundaries. Grace. Clumsiness. A runny-nosed crier. A partner who knows what turns her on. Sassy waitresses. Pretty scientists. Any and all librarians (okay, maybe this is my issue). Truth. Vulnerability. Strength. Naïveté. Big breasts. Small breasts. Doesn't matter the size, they all fascinate. A girl who can play the blues harp. A girl who calls you on your bullshit but isn't afraid to love you in spite of it. A storyteller. A genius. A doctor. A new mother. A woman who realizes how beautiful she is.

Strength in Numbers

There is no recipe for a collective uprising; there are only friendships strengthened by truth and suffering. There are you and your best friend, making a pact to stop supporting each other's delusional diet schemes. There is a compassionate coed lying on her standard-issue dorm bed, feet sticking off the end, composing what she will say to her roommate when she gets back from the bathroom. There is air so thick you feel like you could choke on it during that confrontation, and then the air afterward, so clear and weightless it feels like you are walking on the moon. There is a phone call in the middle of the day. Nik answers, and I admit, through tears I am embarrassed to shed but will anyway, that I am feeling terribly sad and alone.

There is no social change in isolation; there is only the power and the poison of the company you keep. Don't date guys who have unrealistic expectations about your body or say mean things to you. Don't surround yourself with friends who compete, undermine, or belittle you. Indulge your girl crushes. When you meet an amazing woman you admire and feel is way out of your friend league, take a chance and ask her to hang out. It has worked for me with many of the women you have read about in this book, and I feel smarter and better just being around them.

And as important and more often overlooked, enjoy creating close relationships with guy friends who start out all hard and witty on the outside and end up being even mushier and more insecure than your girlfriends on the inside. They are good for your soul and your perspective.

Don't worship women who make it all look easy. Seek out mentors who are wise and generous and evolved most of the time and amusingly flawed the rest, women who are honest about the hard work and the small and profound rewards—such as getting to know a young woman like you.

There are no total and instantaneous solutions to a problem so intractable, so cultural, so institutional; there are only individual choices made each day that add up to change. Take responsibility instead of resigning yourself to a life of passive consumption and benign neglect. Your money is your mouth, however small and insignificant the voice coming out may seem. Support companies and causes that make the effort, even if based on the bottom line, to support your healthy body image. Dove's Real Beauty campaign may have had its flaws, but it sent a message to the rest of the corporate world: Women will pay for respect. Nike is running in Dove's footsteps. More will follow. Laugh at advertisements that try to make you believe you need a certain brand of suit or a certain color of hair or a certain miracle pill to feel okay in the world. The joke is on them. You already feel okay, and you are sitting on the couch in your ratty pajamas with your unwashed hair and not so much as a Dexatrim in the kitchen cabinet.

Don't read magazines that make you feel like shit. You probably don't need expert studies to confirm what you already feel—that flipping through the latest *W* has a direct correlation with your body anxiety—but just for kicks: researchers at the University of Kentucky found that girls exposed to average-weight model images were less likely to endorse thinness or restricting behaviors than were those exposed to Kate Moss and her crew. Pick up *BUST* for a change and experience how nice it is to look at hot ladies wearing clothes you could fit in *and* afford—a combo seemingly impossible between the pages of the average newsstand fare.

Don't see movies or buy albums by celebrities who think women's bodies are more interesting than their minds. Don't spend your hard-earned money on gimmicks that make people much richer than you. Don't buy thigh cream. It doesn't work. Don't diet, ever. Kathy Davis, a feminist scholar, writes of this need to say no in an era when we are constantly being pressured to say yes: "In our present 'culture of mystification'—a culture that constantly entices us with false promises of power and pleasure—we need to be concerned with domination rather than freedom and with constraint rather than choice." In this extreme-makeover, instant gratification, excess-for-less world, your power often comes from what you don't do rather than what you do. Don't, first and foremost, be a sucker for the commercial culture's version of beauty.

The Beginning

No one story describes our healing, but there will be moments when the light is let in. You can call them tipping points. You can call them intervening moments. You can call them, as the Zen master and mindfulness teacher Thich Nhat Hanh does, the first step in a journey of a thousand miles. We all have the responsibility to recognize these moments in our lives and do what is hard to do.

You may need to sleep in one day instead of making yourself go to the gym. You may enjoy an ice cream cone without once thinking about the calories involved. You may choose to order a burger instead of a salad simply because you feel like it. Or you may choose to order a salad instead of a burger because you realize that your pleasure in life comes from many sources, not just food. You may think about leaning over to your friend and whispering something mean about the girl sitting across from you but decide otherwise. You may force yourself to look in the mirror for five minutes straight, disputing every judgmental thought that comes your way. You may play a pickup game of basketball one Saturday. You may just learn to love yourself again.

There is no healing without help.
There is no power as potent as possibility.
There is no transformation without truth.
There is no change without vulnerability.
There is no wisdom greater than that found inside you.
There is no beauty without struggle or aberration.

There is no statement like your life.

There is no end.

There are only beginnings.

Here are some beginnings that I experienced along the way: When I set out to run the three-mile loop in Prospect Park, just blocks away from my house in Brooklyn, I begin determined and relieved. Finally a chance to get out of my bedroom, stacked with unread books and piles of red-marked drafts threatening to swallow me up. I breathe deeply, feeling grateful for the fresh air. My apartment, I realize upon leaving it, smells like garlic and old beer. I need to take out the recycling.

I put my iPod buds in my ears and fall in line beside a spandexed woman jogging and pushing a stroller. I briefly admire her dedication and her flat stomach. She must have really worked off that pregnancy fat fast. The little one asleep in a mountain of blankets doesn't look much older than a few months.

I try to imagine myself at that stage of life. Will I have the willpower to put my baby in a stroller and push it all the way around the loop in the park? I can barely motivate myself to run, without the added complication of a potentially cranky baby. In fact, it seems I'm still my own baby most of the time.

I start shuffling through my to-do list in my head and instantly feel overwhelmed. *Why did I ever agree to write that book review? I have so many papers to grade. What am I going to get my mom for her birthday?* As if there is a straight line connecting my left brain to my right knee, I feel an ache. *I need better running shoes. Tough it out, Courtney. It's just three miles. You used to be able to do this with no problem.*

And the more I tell myself how easy it used to be, the harder it becomes. *My knee is really hurting. Or is it? Come on, Courtney, buck up. Run out the pain—it is just momentary. Don't make a big deal out of it. You planned to run the loop today. It is on your to-do list. You won't have time to run tomorrow, so this is your only chance.*

The woman with the stroller leaves me in the dust without a bead of sweat on her brow. She looks light as a feather. I feel heavy as a boulder. I feel competitive. I feel cranky. I cling to control. *Keep running. Run through the initial pain and your body will loosen up and you'll get in that zone. Maybe I should pause and stretch. No, that will take extra time you don't have. Shut up. Keep running.*

But I am tired and I am stiff and I am writing a book about women's rigid obsession with fitness and I don't want to be a hypocrite. I want to listen to my own body. I want to be kind to myself. I want to be smarter than the voice inside my head that tells me I am nothing if I can't run a three-mile loop without stopping.

And so I stop. Before I have even consciously decided to do it, I feel my body slowing down, and I am walking, one foot in front of the other; my arms swing, and the pain in my knee subsides, and I hear the music again—as if planned, "Oh, Happy Day," my favorite gospel song. My breath comes easily. The relief floods in. I see the trees, just beginning to grow green and lush again, all around me. I am awed by the shimmering light on the surface of the lake. I see a little boy throwing handfuls of smashed stale bread at a grateful party of ducks, and I smile to myself.

I am not superwoman. I did not stick to my plan. I won't burn as many calories. I am not even in great shape. But I am not a hypocrite. I am not in pain. I am not in a mental arm-wrestle with myself. I am breathing deeply. I am moving. I am seeing the world around me. I am healthy. I am not perfect, but I am happy.

And here is another beginning:

I am sitting at a picnic table with a chattering gaggle of eight-year-old girls high on their morning Pop-Tarts. They are sprinkling sparkles over pools of glue and telling me stories about their moms and sisters, who "get worried and then eat, like, only grapefruit and stuff for days but then screw up and eat chips or something and then feel bad and then eat more grapefruit and stuff." I ask them what they think "pretty" is.

The ringleader, a stocky blonde with a gap between her two tiny,

Chiclet-like front teeth, jumps up from the table and practically screams: "You want to see my impression of a prom queen?"

"Yes, definitely," I reply, trying to move my voice recorder so it will pick up her performance.

She puts one hand on her head, palm facing up, apparently symbolizing a crown, and the other on her hip, and then starts sashaying around the picnic table in circles, shouting, "Hey, boys, look at me! Look at me, boys! Look at my royal heinie, boys! Isn't it so cute?" The rest of the gaggle erupts in exaggerated little-girl laughter, throwing themselves on the picnic table and dragging their knotty hair through the pools of sparkles.

One little girl, with a voice as small as any I have ever heard and hair black as the crows perched in the piñon trees surrounding us, leans over to my notebook and writes with a stubby, orange-colored pencil, "You are pretty. I think you have nice hair," and encircles her secret messages in a big lopsided heart.

"Thank you," I whisper in her ear, tears threatening to sneak out of the corners of my eyes. This little girl thinks I am asking these questions because I really don't know the answers. Suddenly it occurs to me that she is probably right. I am looking for wisdom from eight-year-olds with puff-painted shirts and stacks of brightly colored rubber bracelets.

I am not looking in the wrong place. I ask, "What about in the future? Do you think you will worry about stuff like your moms and big sisters in the future?"

A spindly little animal of a girl made entirely of bone and muscle jumps off the picnic table with her arms splayed out from her sides in the shape of wings and shouts, "In the future there will be flying cars! In the future, we will all be beautiful!"

And here is another beginning:
    You.

Resource Guide

Treatment Centers
Caringonline: www.caringonline.com
Eating Disorder Referral and Information Center: www.edreferral.com
Hyde Park Counseling Center: www.hydeparkcenter.com
Mirasol: www.mirasol.net
Rader Programs: www.raderprograms.com
The Renfrew Center: www.renfrewcenter.com
Remuda Ranch: www.remuda-ranch.com

Advocacy Organizations
Academy for Eating Disorders: www.aedweb.org
Alliance for Eating Disorders Awareness: www.eatingdisorderinfo.org
American Obesity Association: www.obesity.org
Council on Size and Weight Discrimination: www.cswd.org
Dads & Daughters: www.dadsanddaughters.org
Eating Disorders Coalition: eatingdisorderscoalition.org
Eating Disorders Anonymous: www.eatingdisordersanonymous.org
HEED Foundation: www.helpingendeatingdisorders.org
National Association of Anorexia Nervosa and Associated Disorders:
    www.anad.org
National Center for Overcoming Overeating: www.overcomingovereat
    ing.com
National Eating Disorders Association: www.nationaleatingdisorders.org
National Eating Disorders Screening Program: www.mentalhealthscreen
    ing.org
Overeaters Anonymous: www.oa.org

Feminist Nonprofit Organizations and Centers
Barnard Center for Research on Women: www.barnard.edu/bcrw
Girls Inc.: www.girlsinc.com
Ms. Foundation for Women: ms.foundation.org
NARAL Pro-Choice America: www.naral.org
National Council for Research on Women: www.ncrw.org
National Organization for Women: www.now.org
Planned Parenthood Federation of America: www.plannedparenthood.org
Soapbox Inc. speaker's bureau: www.soapboxinc.com
Third Wave Foundation: www.thirdwavefoundation.org
V-Day movement: www.vday.org
Wellesley Centers for Women: www.wcwonline.org
Woodhull Institute for Ethical Leadership: www.woodhull.org
Younger Women's Task Force: www.ywtf.org

Feminist Publications, Blogs, and Companies
Alternet: www.alternet.org
Babeland: www.babeland.com
BUST magazine: www.bust.com
Bitch magazine: www.bitchmagazine.com
Bluestockings Bookstore: www.bluestockings.com
The Scholar & Feminist online: www.barnard.edu/sfonline
Feministing: www.feministing.com
Lilith magazine: www.lilith.org
Ms. magazine: www.msmagazine.com
New Moon magazine: www.newmoon.org
off our backs: www.offourbacks.org
The Real Hot 100: www.therealhot100.org
Seal Press: www.sealpress.com
Women's eNews: www.womensenews.org
World Pulse magazine: www.worldpulsemagazine.com

Size Acceptance Activism
Adios Barbie: www.adiosbarbie.com
Big Fat Blog: www.bigfatblog.com
Body Positive: www.bodypositive.com
Fat! So?: www.fatso.com
National Association to Advance Fat Acceptance: www.naafa.org
Wendy McClure: www.poundy.com
Wendy Shanker: www.wendyshanker.com
Jessica Weiner: www.jessicaweiner.com

Books

Albers, Susan. *Eating Mindfully: How to End Mindless Eating and Enjoy a Balanced Relationship with Food.* New Harbinger Publications, 2002.

Bateson, Mary Catherine. *Composing a Life.* Grove Press, 1989.

Bordo, Susan. *Unbearable Weight: Feminism, Western Culture, and the Body.* University of California Press, 1995.

Brashich, Audrey. *All Made Up: A Girl's Guide to Seeing Through Celebrity Hype and Celebrating Real Beauty.* Walker Books for Young Readers, 2006.

Bruch, Hilda. *Eating Disorders: Obesity, Anorexia Nervosa, and the Person Within.* Basic Books, 1973.

Brumberg, Joan Jacobs. *The Body Project: An Intimate History of American Girls.* Random House, 1997.

———. *Fasting Girls.* Harvard University Press, 1988.

Chernin, Kim. *The Hungry Self: Women, Eating, and Identity.* Harper-Perennial, 1985.

———. *The Obsession: Reflections on the Tyranny of Slenderness.* Harper & Row, 1981.

Dalton, Sharron. *Our Overweight Children: What Parents, Schools, and Communities Can Do to Control the Fatness Epidemic.* University of California Press, 2004.

Davis, Kathy. *Embodied Practices: Feminist Perspectives on the Body.* Sage Publications, 1997.

Duncan, Karen A. *Healing from the Trauma of Childhood Sexual Abuse: The Journey for Women.* Praeger, 2004.

Ellin, Abby. *Teenage Waistland: A Former Fat Kid Weighs In on Living Large, Losing Weight, and How Parents Can (and Can't) Help.* Public Affairs, 2005.

Ensler, Eve. *The Good Body.* Villard, 2004.

Fraser, Laura. *Losing It: America's Obsession with Weight and the Industry That Feeds It.* Dutton Press, 1997.

Friday, Nancy. *My Mother/My Self: The Daughter's Search for Identity.* Delta Books, 1977.

Gilligan, Carol. *In a Different Voice: Psychological Theory and Women's Development.* Harvard University Press, 1982.

Ginsburg, Lynn, and Mary Taylor. *What Are You Hungry For?: Women, Food, and Spirituality.* St. Martin's, 2002.

Greenfield, Lauren. *Girl Culture.* Chronicle Books, 2005.

Hornbacher, Marya. *Wasted: A Memoir of Anorexia and Bulimia.* Harper-Perennial, 1999.

Kabatznick, Ronna. *The Zen of Eating: Ancient Answers to Modern Weight Problems.* Perigee, 1998.

Knapp, Caroline. *Appetites.* Counterpoint, 2003.

Levy, Ariel. *Female Chauvinist Pigs: Women and the Rise of Raunch Culture.* Free Press, 2005.

Maine, Margo. *Father Hunger: Fathers, Daughters, and the Pursuit of Thinness.* Gurze Books, 2004.

Maine, Margo, and Joe Kelly. *The Body Myth: Adult Women and the Pressure to Be Perfect.* John Wiley & Sons, 2005.

Miedema, Baukje, Janet Stoppard, and Vivienne Anderson. *Women's Bodies/ Women's Lives: Health, Well-being, and Body Image.* Sumach Press, 2000.

Nolen-Hoeksema, Susan. *Eating, Drinking, Overthinking: The Toxic Triangle of Food, Alcohol, and Depression—and How Women Can Break Free.* Henry Holt, 2006.

Orbach, Susie. *Fat Is a Feminist Issue.* Berkley, 1978.

Paul, Alice. *Pornified.* Henry Holt, 2005.

Pipher, Mary. *Hunger Pains: The Modern Woman's Tragic Quest for Thinness.* Ballantine, 1997.

———. *Reviving Ophelia: Saving the Lives of Adolescent Girls.* Ballantine, 1994.

Quindlen, Anna. *Being Perfect.* Random House, 2005.

Roth, Geneen. *Breaking Free from Compulsive Eating.* Penguin, 1984.

———. *Feeding the Hungry Heart.* Bobbs-Merrill, 1982.

———. *When Food Is Love: Exploring the Relationship Between Eating and Intimacy.* Penguin, 1992.

Sachs, Brad. *The Good Enough Child: How to Have an Imperfect Child and Be Perfectly Satisfied.* HarperCollins, 2002.

———. *The Good Enough Teen: How to Raise Adolescents with Love and Acceptance (Despite How Impossible They Can Be).* HarperCollins, 2005.

Sacker, Ira M., and Mark A. Zimmer. *Dying to Be Thin: Understanding and Defeating Anorexia Nervosa and Bulimia—A Practical, Lifesaving Guide.* Warner, 1987.

Schwartz, Mark, and Leigh Cohn, eds. *Sexual Abuse and Eating Disorders.* Taylor & Francis, 1996.

Shandler, Sara. *Ophelia Speaks.* HarperPerennial, 1999.

Shanker, Wendy. *The Fat Girl's Guide to Life.* Bloomsbury, 2004.

Simmons, Rachel. *Odd Girl Out: The Hidden Culture of Aggression in Girls.* Harcourt, 2002.

Steiner-Adair, Catherine, Nina Piran, and Michael P. Levine, eds. *Preventing Eating Disorders: A Handbook for Intervention and Special Challenges*. Edwards Brothers, 1990.

Steiner-Adair, Catherine, and Lisa Sjostrom. *Full of Ourselves: A Wellness Program to Advance Girl Power, Health, and Leadership*. Teachers College Press, 2005.

Wann, Marilyn. *FAT! SO?: Because You Don't Have to Apologize for Your Size*. Ten Speed Press, 1999.

Weiner, Jessica. *Do I Look Fat in This?: Life Doesn't Begin Five Pounds from Now*. Simon Spotlight Entertainment, 2006.

White, Emily. *Fast Girls: Teenage Tribes and the Myth of the Slut*. Berkley, 2003.

Wolf, Naomi. *The Beauty Myth: How Images of Beauty Are Used Against Women*. William Morrow, 1991.

———. *Promiscuities*. Random House, 1999.

Woodman, Marion. *Addiction to Perfection: The Still Unravished Bride*. Inner City Books, 1982.

———. *Conscious Femininity: Interview with Marion Woodman*. Inner City Books, 1993.

———. *The Owl Was a Baker's Daughter: Obesity, Anorexia Nervosa, and the Repressed Feminine*. Inner City Books, 1980.

———. *The Pregnant Virgin: A Process of Psychological Transformation*. Inner City Books, 1985.

Artists
Marina Abramovic
Judy Chicago: www.judychicago.com
Lauren Greenfield: www.laurengreenfield.com
Wynne Greenwood, Traci + the Plastics
Jenny Holzer
Miranda July: www.mirandajuly.com
Barbara Kruger: www.barbarakruger.com
Nikki S. Lee
Kiki Smith
Two Girls Working: www.twogirlsworking.com

Films
The ABC's of Eating Disorders: www.zakto.com/abc
Dying to Be Thin

The Education of Shelby Knox
Killing Us Softly: www.jeankilbourne.com
Perfect Illusions
Speak Out: I Had an Abortion: www.speakoutfilms.com
THIN

Notes

Introduction

1   *"When we try to pick out"*: Quoted in Hilde Bruch, *Eating Disorders: Obesity, Anorexia Nervosa, and the Person Within* (Basic Books, 1973), 8.

1   *Eating disorders affect more than 7 million:* National Association of Anorexia Nervosa and Associated Disorders (ANAD), "Eating Disorder Info and Resources," http://www.anad.org/site/anadweb/content.php?type=1&id=6982.

1   *Ninety-one percent of women recently surveyed:* National Eating Disorders Association, http://womensissues.about.com/od/eatingdisorders/f/EatDisorder.htm.

1   *In 1995, 34 percent of high school–age girls:* Emma Bothorel, Lizzie Dunlap, and Melissa Walker, "Love Your Body: Body Image Survey," *ELLEgirl*, February 2006.

1   *Over half the females between the ages of eighteen and twenty-five:* Ibid.

1   *The single group of teenagers:* Abby Ellin, "Dad, Do You Think I Look Too Fat?," *New York Times*, September 17, 2000.

1   *A survey of American parents:* Laura Fraser, *Losing It: America's Obsession with Weight and the Industry That Feeds on It* (Dutton Press, 1997).

5   *"obsessive perfectionists":* Steve Inskeep and Patricia Neighmond, "New Evidence Shows Childhood Anxiety Increases a Young Girl's Risk of Having an Eating Disorder Later in Life," National Public Radio, December 3, 2004.

5   *"Someday, sometime, you will be sitting":* Anna Quindlen, *Being Perfect* (Random House, 2005), 47.

6   *"effortless perfection":* The Women's Initiative, Duke University,
        http://www.duke.edu/womens_initiative/.

10   *"To move toward perfection":* Marion Woodman, *Addiction to
        Perfection: The Still Unravished Bride* (Inner City Books, 1982), 52.

12   *Recent research confirms that more than forty countries:* Margo
        Maine, *Father Hunger: Fathers, Daughters, and the Pursuit of Thin-
        ness* (Gurze Books, 2004), 40.

12   *Japan's "culture of cute":* Amy Borovy and Kathleen M. Pike, "The
        Rise of Eating Disorders in Japan: Issues of Culture and Limitations
        of the Model of 'Westernization,'" *Culture, Medicine, and Psychi-
        atry,* December 2004.

12   *A 2003 study of high school girls in Hong Kong:* Maria Fung and
        Mantak Yuen, "Body Image and Eating Attitudes Among Adoles-
        cent Chinese Girls in Hong Kong," *Perceptual & Motor Skills,*
        February 2003.

12   *Another in an all-female kibbutz:* Yael Latzer and Sarit Shatz, "Dis-
        turbed Attitudes to Weight Control in Female Kibbutz Adolescents:
        A Preliminary Study with a View to Prevention," *Eating Disorders,*
        Fall 2001.

12   *Almost a quarter of girls from the United Arab Emirates:* Valsamma
        Eapen, Abdel Azim Mabrouk, and Salem bin-Othman, "Disordered
        Eating Attitudes and Symptomatology Among Adolescent Girls in
        the United Arab Emirates," *Eating Behaviors,* January 2006.

13   *more than 1 million people in Britain:* Jeremy Laurence, "Anorexia
        Linked to Brain Defect Rather Than Social Pressures," *The Inde-
        pendent,* April 7, 2005.

13   *An unprecedented law passed in Buenos Aires:* Erika Kumar, "The
        Law of Sizes," *Adbusters,* July–August 2006.

1. Perfect Girls, Starving Daughters

18   *Social psychologists call this:* Author interview with Robin Stern,
        January 25, 2006.

19   *"In an effort to be mature and independent":* Marion Woodman,
        Addiction to Perfection: The Still Unravished Bride (Inner City
        Books, 1982), 62.

25   *Anorectics starve themselves:* National Association of Anorexia Ner-
        vosa and Associated Disorders, http://www.anad.org/site/anadweb/
        content.php?type=1&id=6982.

25   *"body dysmorphic disorder":* Kate Ravilious, "How the Brain Builds
        Its Image of the Body," *The Guardian,* November 29, 2005.

25   *Many are suspected of having a genetic predisposition:* Jeremy

Laurence, "Anorexia Linked to Brain Defect Rather Than Social Pressures," *The Independent,* April 7, 2005.

26 *5 percent of those who have anorexia:* Ibid.

26 *With both bulimia nervosa and binge-eating disorder:* Ibid.

26 *bulimiarexia:* Ibid.

26 *A grab-bag . . . does appear:* Robin Marantz Henig, "Sorry. Your Eating Disorder Doesn't Meet Our Criteria," *New York Times,* November 30, 2004.

26 *Binge-eating disorder was distinguished:* Ibid.

26 *Experts expect that the DSM-V:* Ibid.

26 *large numbers of young women binge and purge:* Ibid.

27 *"partial-syndrome eating disorder":* Ida Dancyger and P. E. Garfinkel, "The Relationship of Partial Syndrome Eating Disorders to Anorexia Nervosa and Bulimia Nervosa," *Psychological Medicine,* September 1995.

28 *"treating eating disorders as aberration":* Ronald Bishop, "The Pursuit of Perfection: A Narrative Analysis of How Women's Magazines Cover Eating Disorders," *Howard Journal of Communications,* October 2001.

30 *During the 1870s:* Author's reporting at a keynote speech, "Fast Girls: Then and Now," given by Joan Jacobs Brumberg at the Renfrew Center National Conference, November 12, 2005.

31 *the Victorian era marks the birth:* Ibid.

31 *Around the same time in America:* Ibid.

31 *Brumberg herself remembers:* Ibid.

32 *One of the first public memories:* Adena Young, "Battling Anorexia: The Story of Karen Carpenter," http://atdpweb.soe.berkeley.edu/quest/Mind&Body/Carpenter.html.

32 *"In the nineteenth century a woman":* Author's reporting at a keynote speech, "Fast Girls: Then and Now," given by Joan Jacobs Brumberg at the Renfrew Center National Conference, November 12, 2005.

32 *"vision of autonomy and independence":* Catherine Steiner-Adair, Niva Piran, and Michael P. Levine, eds., *Preventing Eating Disorders: A Handbook for Intervention and Special Challenges* (Edwards Brothers, 1990), 173.

33 *"We are forced to question":* Janell Lynn Mensinger, "Eating Disorders and the Superwoman Ideal in the Twenty-first Century" (unpublished paper), 22.

33 *Dr. Ruth Striegel-Moore:* Ruth Striegel-Moore et al., "Eating Disorders in Black and White Young Women," *American Journal of Psychiatry,* July 2003.

34   *The 7 million American women and girls:* National Association of
        Anorexia Nervosa and Associated Disorders, http://www.anad
        .org/site/anadweb/content.php?type=1&id=6982.

35   *"brain drain":* Joan Jacobs Brumberg in introduction to Lauren
        Greenfield, *Girl Culture* (Chronicle Books, 2005), 6.

2. From Good to Perfect

37   *"I had no doubt that":* Lorene Cary, *Black Ice* (Alfred A. Knopf,
        1991), 131.

45   *wives' marital satisfaction decreased:* Lawrence A. Kurdek, "Par-
        enting Satisfaction and Marital Satisfaction in Mothers and Fathers
        with Young Children," *Journal of Family Psychology,* 1996.

46   *Women with jobs outside the home:* U.S. Department of Labor,
        Bureau of Labor Statistics, www.bls.gov.

47   *According to the Women's Sports Foundation:* The Women's Sports
        Foundation, http://www.womenssportsfoundation.org.

49   *According to the Bureau of Labor Statistics:* "Women in the Labor
        Force: A Data Book," Bureau of Labor Statistics, May 13, 2005.

51   *A survey of almost six hundred tenth-graders:* Tracy L. Dunkley,
        Eleanor H. Wertheim, and Susan J. Paxton, "Examination of a Model
        of Multiple Sociocultural Influences on Adolescent Girls' Body Dissatis-
        faction and Dietary Restraint," *Adolescence,* Summer 2001.

51   *"young people were 50 percent more likely":* Jean M. Twenge, *Gen-
        eration Me: Why Today's Young Americans Are More Confident,
        Assertive, Entitled—and More Miserable Than Ever Before* (Free
        Press, 2006), 117.

51   *girls are internalizing their mothers' lessons:* Catherine E. Freeman,
        "Trends in Educational Equity of Girls and Women," *Education
        Statistics Quarterly* (National Center for Education Statistics),
        2004.

52   *Women outnumber men on college campuses:* Ibid.

52   *In a recent* New York Times *op-ed:* Jennifer Delahunty Britz, "To
        All the Girls I've Rejected," *New York Times,* March 23, 2006.

52   *" 'gender norming' is the dirtiest little secret in higher education":*
        "Colleges Slam the Door on Girls" (letter to the editor), *New York
        Times,* March 23, 2006, http://query.nytimes.com/gst/fullpage
        .html?res=9C06E6D71730F936A15750C0A9609C8B63.

53   *"How much better I might have been":* Jane Fonda, *My Life So Far*
        (Random House, 2005), 88.

53   *"The girl is left with the perception":* Nancy Friday, *My Mother/
        My Self: The Daughter's Search for Identity* (Delta Books, 1977), 7.

55   *"Up until then I had been a feminist"*: Jane Fonda, *My Life So Far* (Random House, 2005), 558.

55   *"more and more midlife women"*: Melba Newsome, "Empty Inside: For Older Women, the Quest for Perfection Leads Increasingly to Eating Disorders," *AARP: The Magazine*, November–December 2005.

55   *400 percent increase*: Ibid.

56   *Fifty years of attachment theory*: Lauren Lindsey Porter, "The Science of Attachment: The Biological Roots of Love," *Mothering*, July–August 2003.

58   *women are more prone to depression*: Society for Women's Health Research, http://www.womenshealthresearch.org/site/PageServer?page name=hs_sbb_suffer.

59   *studies show that women's bodies*: Author interview with Karen Kisslinger, January 22, 2006.

60   *"Because our mothers could not love themselves"*: Marion Woodman, *Conscious Femininity: Interviews with Marion Woodman* (Inner City Books, 1993), 15.

3. The Male Mirror

70   *"A lot of fathers feel such guilt"*: Author interview with Brad Sachs, January 30, 2006.

70   *"Many of the men"*: Author interview with Robin Stern, January 23, 2006.

71   *two-thirds don't believe*: Dads and Daughters, http://www.dadsand daughters.org/Poll_Results.html.

73   *Dads and Daughters was started*: Abby Ellin, "Dad, Do You Think I Look Too Fat?," *New York Times*, September 17, 2000.

74   *"We came to the idea"*: Ibid.

74   *sixteen hundred members*: Ibid.

75   *"Anorexia was the only way"*: Naomi Wolf, *The Beauty Myth: How Images of Beauty Are Used Against Women* (William Morrow, 1991), 204.

75   *one in seven Caucasian girls now start*: Michael D. Lemonick, "Teens Before Their Time," *Time*, October 20, 2000.

75   *"The invasion of hormones turns the child"*: Emily White, *Fast Girls: Teenage Tribes and the Myth of the Slut* (Berkley, 2003), 16.

84   *According to the U.S. Census Bureau*: U.S. Census Bureau, http://childstats.ed.gov/americaschildren/pop6.asp.

84   *"a deep, persistent desire for emotional connection"*: Margo Maine, *Father Hunger: Fathers, Daughters, and the Pursuit of Thinness* (Gurze Books, 2004), 21.

89   *"The things we saw women doing"*: Naomi Wolf, *The Beauty Myth: How Images of Beauty Are Used Against Women* (William Morrow, 1991), 204.

90   *"If we look at modern Athenas"*: Marion Woodman, *The Pregnant Virgin: A Process of Psychological Transformation* (Inner City Books, 1985), 85.

90   *"All my life I had been a father's daughter"*: Jane Fonda, *My Life So Far* (Random House, 2005), 565.

91   *"Often she is caught"*: Marion Woodman, *The Owl Was a Baker's Daughter: Obesity, Anorexia Nervosa, and the Repressed Feminine* (Inner City Books, 1980), 9.

4. (Perfect) Girl Talk
92   *In 1982 Carol Gilligan argued*: Carol Gilligan, *In a Different Voice* (Harvard University Press, 1982).

93   *teenage girls becoming 'female impersonators'*: Mary Pipher, *Reviving Ophelia: Saving the Lives of Adolescent Girls* (Ballantine, 1994), 22.

100   *"stress-induced vomiting"*: Rebecca Traister, "Return of the Brainless Hussies," Salon.com, May 19, 2006.

103   *44.8 percent of girls look to their friends*: Tracy L. Dunkley, Eleanor H. Wertheim, and Susan J. Paxton, "Examination of a Model of Multiple Sociocultural Influences on Adolescent Girls' Body Dissatisfaction and Dietary Restraint," *Adolescence,* Summer 2001.

103   *girls were more likely to worry*: Eric Stice and Katheryn Whitenton, "Risk Factors for Body Dissatisfaction in Adolescent Girls: A Longitudinal Investigation," *Developmental Psychology,* September 1, 2002.

106   *Girls Inc., though a 140-year-old organization*: Girls Inc., http://www.girlsinc.org.

5. Sex as a Cookie
114   *"Something happens to some girls"*: Mary Gordon, *Pearl* (Pantheon, 2005), 129.

114   *"All of these are about emptiness"*: Caroline Knapp, *Appetites* (Counterpoint, 2003), 10.

122   *the average girl lost her virginity*: Jean M. Twenge, *Generation Me: Why Today's Young Americans Are More Confident, Assertive, Entitled—and More Miserable Than Ever Before* (Free Press, 2006), 162.

122   *A teenage girl today is twice as likely*: Ibid.

122   *Eighty-four percent of college-educated single women:* Ibid., 163.

122   *60 percent of high school juniors:* Ibid., 168.

123   *"What teens have to work with":* Ariel Levy, *Female Chauvinist Pigs: Women and the Rise of Raunch Culture* (Free Press, 2005), 157.

124   *the more dissatisfied a teenage girl is:* Gina M. Wingood et al., "Body Image and African American Females' Sexual Health," *Journal of Women's Health & Gender-Based Medicine,* June 2002.

128   *"Whereas men tend to externalize stress":* Susan Nolen-Hoeksema, *Eating, Drinking, Overthinking: The Toxic Triangle of Food, Alcohol, and Depression—and How Women Can Break Free* (Henry Holt, 2006), 6.

131   *In a study of six thousand students:* Robin Warshaw, *I Never Called It Rape: The Ms. Report on Recognizing, Fighting, and Surviving Date and Acquaintance Rape* (HarperCollins, 1988).

131   *13 percent of college women indicated:* I. M. Johnson, E. F. Morgan, and R. T. Sigler, "Forced Sexual Intercourse: Contemporary Views," in *It's a Crime: Women and Justice,* 2nd ed. (Prentice Hall, 2003).

131   *In a study of 477 male students:* Scot B. Boeringer, "Associations of Rape-Supportive Attitudes with Fraternal and Athletic Participation," *Violence Against Women,* vol. 5, no. 1 (1999).

132   *In a recent study, 80 percent:* Leigh Cohn and Mark Schwartz, eds., *Sexual Abuse and Eating Disorders* (Taylor & Francis, 1990).

132   *"blame their bodies":* Author interview with Karen A. Duncan, June 9, 2006.

132   *"She was self-injuring":* Ibid.

135   Resources: http://www.addresources.org/article_medicines_mandelkorn.php.

6. The Revolution *Still* Will Not Be Televised

141   *"The body has become":* Lauren Greenfield, *Girl Culture* (Chronicle Books, 2005), 150.

142   *The seventeenth season of* The Real World: Kay Arthur, "On MTV's 'Real World' Paula Meronek Deals with a Grim Reality," *New York Times,* May 2, 2006.

144   *she admitted to* Vanity Fair: Evgenia Peretz, "Confessions of a Teenage Movie Queen," *Vanity Fair,* February 2006.

144   *"Fashion insiders have whispered":* Leslie Bennetts, "Nicole Richie Talks About Her Weight, Being a Role Model, and What Happened with Paris," *Los Angeles Times,* June 2006.

144 *"I think she's motivated to be scary-little"*: Ibid.

144 *"putting a sledgehammer to your vocal cords"*: Ericka Sóuter and Monica Rizzo, "Katharine McPhee's Bulimia Battle," *People,* June 22, 2006.

145 *"everyone look like"*: Jeff Leeds, "As Pop Music Seeks New Sales, the Pussycat Dolls Head to Toyland," *New York Times,* April 17, 2006.

147 *there are females in top positions: Hollywood Reporter,* http://www.hollywoodreporter.com/thr/film/feature_display.jsp?vnu_content_id=2043236.

150 *Hispanic, Asian-American, and Native American girls tended to report:* Dianne Neumark-Sztainer et al., "Ethnic/Racial Differences in Weight-Related Concerns and Behaviors Among Adolescent Girls and Boys," *Journal of Psychosomatic Research,* November 2002.

150 *In her 2000 study, Dr. Ruth Striegel-Moore:* Denise Brodey, "Blacks Join the Eating-Disorder Mainstream," *New York Times,* September 20, 2005.

150 *Other studies she has conducted:* Farai Chideya, "African-American Women and How They Confront Body Image, Eating Disorders, Obesity, and Cultural Stereotypes," National Public Radio, June 9, 2005.

150 *"What we think drives"*: Ibid.

150 *"unrecognized by the health-care system"*: Ibid.

151 *In a recent Florida State University study:* Quoted in Denise Brodey, "Blacks Join the Eating-Disorder Mainstream," *New York Times,* September 20, 2005.

163 *"It's acting. Halle Berry can go on film"*: Quoted in http://www.femalefirst.co.uk/entertainment/7252004.htm.

163 *"This is a grown woman that told me"*: http://www.msnbc.msn.com/id/6011814.

163 *White Chocolate has made a cottage industry:* Author reporting at the New York City National Organization for Women panel on Love Your Body Day, October 20, 2005.

163 *"I'm not representing anybody"*: Sonia Murray, "No One Is Exploiting Me: Some Women in the Business Deny Claims They Are Mistreated," *Atlanta Journal-Constitution,* September 27, 2004.

164 *"These girls are smart entrepreneurs"*: Ibid.

164 *"Hip-hop culture is the 800-pound gorilla"*: Anya Kamenetz, "Russel Simmons, Tax Man," *Village Voice,* April 13, 2005.

165   *"Adolescents are not inventing this culture"*: Ariel Levy, *Female Chauvinist Pigs: Women and the Rise of Raunch Culture* (Free Press, 2005).

165   *"Proving that you are hot"*: Ibid., 33.

166   *"Raunch culture, then, isn't an entertainment option"*: Ibid., 40.

7. What Men Want

171   Men's Health *is filled*: *Men's Health,* http://www.menshealth.com.

171   *three of the four afflicted main characters*: Review of *Starved, People,* August 8, 2005.

171   *1 million men have eating disorders*: "Officials See More Eating Disorders in Men," Associated Press, September 21, 2004.

171   *The age at which men develop*: Margo Maine, *Father Hunger: Fathers, Daughters, and the Pursuit of Thinness* (Gurze Books, 2004), 57.

171   *"New terms such as muscle 'dysmorphia'"*: Ibid., 91.

175   *Girls Gone Wild empire*: Ariel Levy, *Female Chauvinist Pigs: Women and the Rise of Raunch Culture* (Free Press, 2005), 12.

175   Maxim *has a section specifically*: *Maxim,* http://www.maxim magazine.com/articles/index.aspx?a_id=6956.

176   *"23 ways to get bare-faced confidence"*: *Cosmopolitan,* UK edition, January 2005.

179   *Harrison, one of the men Paul interviews*: Pamela Paul, *Pornified: How Pornography Is Transforming Our Lives, Our Relationships, and Our Families* (Henry Holt, 2005), 97–103.

180   *the most downloaded woman*: Lauren Greenfield, *Girl Culture* (Chronicle Books, 2005), 32.

187   *girls and boys as young as five years old*: Simon Gowers et al., "Children's Perceptions of Body Shape: A Thinness Bias in Pre-Adolescent Girls and Associations with Femininity," *Clinical Child Psychology and Psychiatry,* October 2001.

187   *"Who wouldn't want to have sex"*: Seth MacFarlane, *Family Guy,* "When You Wish Upon a Weinstein," December 10, 2004.

8. All-or-Nothing Nation

194   *"The slender girl in our culture"*: Kim Chernin, *The Obsession: Reflections on the Tyranny of Slenderness* (Harper & Row, 1981), 71–72.

194   *"This is a culture where"*: Marya Hornbacher, *Wasted: A Memoir of Anorexia and Bulimia* (HarperPerennial, 1999), 154.

198   *"According to the 'set point' theory"*: Susan Albers, *Eating*

Mindfully: How to End Mindless Eating and Enjoy a Balanced Relationship with Food (New Harbinger Publications, 2002), 123.

199 *"Our understanding of how and why"*: Clinical Guidelines on the Identification, Evaluation, and Treatment of Overweight and Obesity in Adults, http://www.nhlbi.nih.gov/guidelines/obesity/sum _intr.htm.

199 *"Fat is a social disease"*: Susie Orbach, *Fat Is a Feminist Issue* (Berkley, 1978), 6.

201 *64.5 percent of U.S. adults*: American Obesity Association, http://www.obesity.org/subs/fastfacts/obesity_US.shtml.

201 *"Fat is the leprosy of the 1990s"*: Mary Pipher, *Hunger Pains: The Modern Woman's Tragic Quest for Thinness* (Ballantine, 1997), 91.

202 *According to the World Health Organization*: World Health Organization, http://www.who.int/en.

202 *According to the National Institutes of Health*: Sharron Dalton, *Our Overweight Children: What Parents, Schools, and Communities Can Do to Control the Fatness Epidemic* (University of California Press, 2004), 25.

202 *inexplicably, the NIH spends*: American Obesity Association, http://www.obesity.org/subs/fastfacts/Obesity_Research.shtml.

202 *30 percent said they would rather be thin*: Emma Bothorel, Lizzie Dunlap, and Melissa Walker, "Love Your Body: Body Image Survey," *ELLEgirl*, February 2006.

202 *Dieting is ineffective 95 percent of the time*: National Eating Disorders Association, http://womensissues.about.com/cs/bodyimage/a/bodyimagestats.htm.

202 *That means, in America alone*: Ibid.

202 *Thirty-five percent of those who diet*: Ibid.

202 *25 percent of those who diet develop*: Ibid.

203 *"The dieting mindset is akin"*: Albers, *Eating Mindfully: How to End Mindless Eating and Enjoy a Balanced Relationship with Food* (New Harbinger Publications, 2002), 2.

203 *In a two-year study by nutrition researchers*: Quoted in *Medical News Today*, http://www.medicalnewstoday.com/medicalnews.php ?newsid=25384.

203 *Being fat, he maintains, is not equivalent*: Steven Shapin, "Eat and Run: Why We're So Fat," *New Yorker*, January 16, 2005.

203 *being underweight actually kills*: Ibid.

203 *"like saying 'whiter teeth'"*: Quoted in ibid.

203 *Even a group of researchers at the Centers for Disease Control*: Ibid.

204 *"The perception is that fat folks"*: Author interview with Wendy Shanker, January 17, 2006.

204 *"Above all, the fat woman"*: Susie Orbach, *Fat Is a Feminist Issue* (Berkley, 1978), 33.

206 *"There is such an emphasis on the body"*: Author interview with Dr. Janell Lynn Mensinger, June 23, 2006.

206 *"She segued right into talking"*: Ibid.
"Despite the nondenominational nature": Natalie Angier, "Who Is Fat? It Depends on Culture," *New York Times,* November 7, 2000.

206 *Dr. Michael Myers, a physician who has been treating obese women:* Weight.com, http://www.weight.com/psychosocial.asp?page=3.

209 *The 250 ads the average American: Consumer Reports,* http://www.consumerreports.org.

210 *"Many people believe that having"*: Author interview with Sharron Dalton, February 1, 2006.

210 *"The best lesson that I learned touring"*: Author interview with Wendy Shanker, January 17, 2006.

214 *"Here's where the all-or-nothing thinking"*: Susan Nolen-Hoeksema, *Eating, Drinking, Overthinking: The Toxic Triangle of Food, Alcohol, and Depression—and How Women Can Break Free* (Henry Holt, 2006), 115.

219 *"inevitable. The cultural pressure is internalized"*: Author interview with Susie Orbach, June 1, 2005.

9. Past the Dedication Is Disease

223 *One in 27 high school girls:* "The New Girls," *O: The Oprah Magazine,* May 2004.

223 *"Across socioeconomic lines"*: Ibid.

223 *13 percent of female athletes:* "Girl Athletes and Eating Disorders," *Dads & Daughters Newsletter,* March 1, 2002.

224 *out of 695 male and female athlete respondents:* National Association of Anorexia Nervosa and Associated Disorders, http://www.anad.org/site/anadweb/content.php?type=1&id=6982.

226 *"They're everywhere"*: Joanna Cagan, "Objects of the Game: Olympic Female Athletes Are Disrobing for the Cameras at a Record Pace," *Village Voice,* August 30–September 5, 2000.

226 *To date, Olympic and professional athletes:* Ibid.

226 *"crouching"*: Mark O'Keefe, "Sexploitation or Pride? Female Olympians' Revealing Poses Stir Debate," Newhouse News Service, 2000.

226   *a group of fourteen- to eighteen-year-olds felt:* Steven Thomsen, Danny Bower, and Michael Barnes, "Photographic Images in Women's Health, Fitness, and Sports Magazines and the Physical Self-Concept of a Group of Adolescent Female Volleyball Players," *Journal of Sport & Social Issues,* August 2004.

230   *investigators found that perfectionism:* Vikki Krane et al., "Relationships Among Body Satisfaction, Social Physique Anxiety, and Eating Behaviors in Female Athletes and Exercisers," *Journal of Sport Behavior,* September 2001.

230   *The Centers for Disease Control recommend:* Centers for Disease Control, http://www.cdc.gov/nccdphp/dnpa/physical/recommendations/index.htm.

233   *About 80 percent of the girls and women:* Renfrew Center http://www.renfrew.org.

233   *inpatient services can cost:* National Association of Anorexia Nervosa and Associated Disorders, http://www.anad.org/site/anadweb/content.php?type=1&id=6982.

233   *At Mirasol:* Mirasol, http://www.mirasolteen.com/enrollment.php.

233   *Ninety-six percent of eating-disorder professionals:* David France, "Anorexics Sentenced to Death," *Glamour,* November 1999.

235   *Dr. Craig Johnson, who studies women and sports, explains:* Girl Athletes and Eating Disorders," *Dads & Daughters Newsletter,* March 1, 2002.

236   *"by exercising excessively, with their dads":* Margo Maine, *Father Hunger: Fathers, Daughters, and the Pursuit of Thinness* (Gurze Books, 1991), 126.

242   *the female athlete triad:* Elizabeth Joy et al., "Team Management of the Female Athlete Triad," *Physician and Sports Medicine,* March 1997.

242   *There is a type of anorexia:* "Eating Disorder Athletes: Female Athletes Who Are Obsessed by Food and Body Weight Can Develop Anorexia Athletica," Peak Performance Online, http://www.pponline.co.uk/encyc/0301.htm.

242   *93 percent of trainers felt:* J. L. Vaughan, K. A. King, and R. R. Cottrell, "Collegiate Athletic Trainers' Confidence in Helping Female Athletes with Eating Disorders," *Journal of Athletic Training,* January–March 2004.

10. The College Years

247   *this kind of neurosis usually starts:* National Institute of Mental Health, *Eating Disorders: Facts About Eating Disorders and the*

Search for Solutions (2001), http://www.nimh.nih.gov/Publicat/
eatingdisorders.cfm.

247   *Ninety-one percent of women surveyed:* National Eating Disorders
Association, http://www.nationaleatingdisorders.org/p.asp?WebPage_
ID=286&Profile_ID=41138.

247   *56 percent of college first-years:* Melody A. Graham and Amy L.
Jones, "Study Refutes Commonly Held Belief That Freshmen Gain
Significant Amount of Weight During Their First Year," *Journal of
American College Health,* January 2002.

248   *"this annual weeklong bacchanalia":* Alex Williams, "Before
Spring Break, the Anorexic Challenge," *New York Times,* April 2,
2006.

248   *"contagious":* Ibid.

248   *Stonehill College . . . was sued:* "Stonehill College Denies Enroll-
ment to Former Student Because of Anorexia," *Chronicle of Higher
Education,* January 19, 2001.

249   *women have outnumbered men:* U.S. Department of Education,
http://nces.ed.gov/pubs2000/2000030.pdf.

249   *60 percent of women were trying:* Megan Madden, "Eating Disorder Rates Quadruple at Penn," *Daily Pennsylvanian,* February 24,
2005.

249   *At Georgetown, as many as 25 percent:* Laura Martin, "Eating Disorders Ignored by Brown," *Brown Daily Herald,* September 24,
2004.

249   *Take twenty-three-year-old Jennifer Boevers:* Lori Head, "Mills
College Students Respond to Death of Alumna from Anorexia,"
Mills College Weekly, December 23, 2004.

252   *42 percent of undergraduate women:* Kristin Rowe-Finkbeiner, *The
F Word: Feminism in Jeopardy* (Seal Press, 2004), 67.

252   *"social scene in which women feel pressed":* The Women's Initiative, Duke University, http://www.duke.edu/womens_initiative/.

253   *"If I had to pinpoint a defining moment":* Caroline Knapp,
Appetites (Counterpoint, 2003), 9.

255   *women both in and outside of sororities:* Kelly C. Allison and Crys-
tal L. Park, "A Prospective Study of Disordered Eating Among
Sorority and Nonsorority Women," *International Journal of Eating
Disorders,* April 2004, 354–58.

256   *"The fact that nobody talks about it":* Megan Madden, "Eating
Disorder Rates Quadruple at Penn," *Daily Pennsylvanian,* February
24, 2005.

257   *"walking question marks"*: Naomi Wolf, *The Beauty Myth: How Images of Beauty Are Used Against Women*, 206.

258   *"awareness of ideals versus our internalization"*: Helga Dittmar and Sarah Howard, "Thin-Ideal Internalization and Social Comparison Tendency as Moderators of Media Models' Impact on Women's Body-Focused Anxiety," *Journal of Social and Clinical Psychology*, December 2004.

259   *"education appears to be more important"*: Lindsay McLaren and Diana Kuh, "Women's Body Dissatisfaction, Social Class, and Social Mobility," *Social Science & Medicine*, May 2004.

264   *"be a good role model"* . . . *"compliment your friend's wonderful personality"*: National Eating Disorders Association, http://www.nationaleatingdisorders.org/p.asp?WebPage_ID=286&Profile_ID=41175.

11. The Real World Ain't No MTV

268   *"All of us failed to match our dreams of perfection"*: Interview with William Faulkner, http://www.littlebluelight.com/lblphp/quotes.php?ikey=8.

269   *"Ambition, we imply, should be focused"*: Mary Catherine Bateson, *Composing a Life* (Grove Press, 1989), 6.

274   *"I guess at the crux of it was this transition"*: Author interview with Sara Shandler, July 12, 2005.

277   *"Sometimes, there is so much disparity"*: Author interview with Robin Stern, February 2, 2006.

279   *"the medical community doesn't even consider"*: "Eating Disorders in Pregnant Women Are Often Undetected," PR Newswire, March 22, 2005.

279   *nearly one in five patients at an infertility clinic*: Ibid.

279   *pregnant women with eating disorders have a higher incidence*: Ibid.

285   *"psychology of abundance"*: Woodhull Institute for Ethical Leadership, http://www.woodhull.org.

286   *A 2002 study by the Women's Institute for a Secure Retirement*: Women's Institute for a Secure Retirement, http://www.wiserwomen.org/pdf_files/asr_femalefact_v3.pdf.

286   *a woman still makes seventy-three cents for every dollar*: National Committee on Pay Equity, http://www.pay-equity.org.

288   *liposuction, was performed on 455,000 Americans*: Natasha Singer, "Do My Knees Look Fat to You?," *New York Times*, June 15, 2006.

288 *25 percent increase since 2000 in breast augmentations:* American Society of Plastic Surgeons, http://www.plasticsurgery.org/public_education/2005Statistics.cfm.

288 *almost $8 billion in 2004:* Ibid.

288 *The American Society of Plastic Surgeons reports that 335,000 teenagers:* American Society of Plastic Surgeons, http://www.plastic surgery.org/public_education/2005Statistics.cfm.

288 *BBC News reports that 40 percent of teens in the UK want cosmetic surgery:* BBC News, http:///news.bbc.co.uk/1/hi/health/ 4147961.stm, January 5, 2005.

288 *Many travel abroad for cheap cosmetic surgery:* www.medretreat .com.

289 *"the designer-body approach":* Natasha Singer, "Do My Knees Look Fat to You?," *New York Times,* June 15, 2006.

289 *"It's liposuction for skinny people":* Ibid.

289 *"Some of them are perfect 10's":* Ibid.

289 *"lunch-time liposuction":* Ibid.

12. Spiritual Hunger

292 *"Lacking spiritual sustenance":* Marion Woodman, *Addiction to Perfection: The Still Unravished Bride* (Inner City Books, 1982), 28.

293 *"They create their own rituals":* Ibid., 30.

294 *"They have no sense of everlasting arms":* Ibid., 21–22.

294 *"within her is an army":* Nicole Blackman, *Aloud: Voices from the Nuyorican Poets Café* (Henry Holt, 1994), 395.

296 *"pro-ana" websites:* Mark Morford, "Hideously Skinny White Girls/It's Called the Cult of Ana: Just Another Savage, Moronic Icon to Ensnare Teenage Girls," *San Francisco Gate,* June 8, 2005.

296 *"Girls have anthropomorphized anorexia":* Ibid.

296 *"Don't eat/drink anything that is a red color":* http://winkin.php webhosting.com/~joeic/privet/thin/index2.html.

296 *"Our culture is pro anorexia":* http://www.anorexicweb.com/InsidetheFridge/proanorexia.html.

297 *"I have only signed up":* Ibid.

304 *many bulimics remain at a normal body weight:* National Eating Disorders Association, http://www.nationaleatingdisorders.org/p.asp?WebPage_ID=286&Profile _ID=41141.

305 *those in religious orders in medieval times:* Rudolph M. Bell, *Holy Anorexia* (University of Chicago Press, 1987).

310 *some women truly do eat in their sleep:* National Eating Disorders

Association, http://www.nationaleatingdisorders.org/p.asp?WebPage_ID=286&Profile_ID=41141.

313   *"Accompanying an underlying sense"*: Lynn Ginsburg and Mary Taylor, *What Are You Hungry For?: Women, Food, and Spirituality* (St. Martin's, 2002), 5.

13. Stepping Through the Looking Glass

271   *"The only interesting answers"*: Quoted on About.com, http://womenshistory.about.com/od/quotes/a/susan_sontag.htm.

271   *"The problems that exist"*: Quoted in Jon Kabat-Zinn, *Coming to Our Senses* (Hyperion, 2005), 62.

319   *"I can't believe that!"*: Quoted on Wikipedia.com, http://en.wiki pedia.org/wiki/Through_the_looking_glass.

323   *In the biopsychosocial model*: National Association of Anorexia Nervosa and Associated Disorders, http://www.anad.org/site/anad web/content.php?type=1&id=6901.

323   *In the medical model*: Ibid.

323   *Cognitive behavior therapy*: Ibid.

323   *family therapy*: Ibid.

323   *feminist lens*: Ibid.

323   *Most also see nutritionists*: Ibid.

323   *Professionals usually incorporate a variety*: Ibid.

323   *Maudsley*: ANAD, http://www.altrue.net/site/anadweb/content.php ?type =1&id=6981.

325   *"Psychology regards all symptoms"*: Quoted in Rob Brezsny, "Secrets of Pronoia: How the World Is Conspiring to Shower You with Blessing," *The Sun*, November 2005.

327   *"little mini-vibe of compassion"*: Author interview with Wendy Shanker, January 17, 2006.

327   *"The nature of obsession"*: Geneen Roth, *When Food Is Love: Exploring the Relationship Between Eating and Intimacy* (Penguin, 1992), 197.

327   *"Pain festers in isolation"*: Caroline Knapp, *Appetites* (Counterpoint, 2003), 158.

332   *Dove's Real Beauty campaign*: Lisa D'Innocenzo, "Who Are You? Is Your Brand Just a Product or a Solution?" *Strategy*, September 2005, http://www.strategymag.com/articles/magazine/20050901/who .html?print=yes.

332   *girls exposed to average-weight model images*: Suzannah Fister and Gregory Smith, "Media Effects on Expectancies: Exposure to Real-

istic Female Images as a Protective Factor," *Psychology of Addictive Behaviors,* December 2004.

333   *"In our present 'culture of mystification'"*: Kathy Davis, *Embodied Practices: Feminist Perspectives on the Body* (Sage Publications, 1997), 11.

Acknowledgments

I am never as happy as when I am grateful, so consider me ecstatically joyful at this moment.

Thanks to Beth Evans, at the Brooklyn College library, and my research assistant, Yeva Jermakyan. Thanks to Rebecca Watson and Girls Inc., Santa Fe, Rachel Ammon and the Renfrew Center, the Brooklyn and Hunter Colleges' women's studies departments, my endlessly entertaining and often brilliant students, and all of those who responded to my e-mail survey with such honesty and clarity.

If it takes a village to raise a child, it takes a football stadium of supporters to make a child a writer. Thanks to all of my inspiring writing teachers over the years—you have the most important job in the world, whether society or salary indicates otherwise: Mary Johnson, Stacy Pies, Robert Boynton, Ellen Willis, Ted Conover, Vincent Puzick, Mary Gordon, and the first author I ever knew, Donna Guthrie.

Thank you to Tara Bracco, Susan Devenyi, Wende Jager-Hyman, Karla Jackson-Brewer, Deborah Seigel, Erica Jong, Joan Finsilver, and all of the other incredible women of the Woodhull Institute for Ethical Leadership, who taught me how to ask, and thank you also to all of those who first said "Yes!"—*New Moon, Clamor,* and Women's eNews. A special thanks to Naomi Wolf, who demystified the industry.

Thank you to Tracy Brown for making me feel like a big deal without ever making a big deal, Leslie Meredith for seeing with new eyes, and Andrew Paulson for making it all more fun.

Thanks to my mom's crew of women who support me back home—especially Kelli, Diana, and the late and great Rosemary—and my second mom, Pam Hinton.

Thank you to all the ladies proving that feminism isn't dead: Jennifer Baumgardner, Amy Richards, the Real Hot 100 and feministing crews, and the rest of you card-carrying third-wavers.

Thank you to my infamously named writers' group for their wine, work, and words—especially Kate Torgovnick for her bulletin pride and southern charm, Ethan Todras-Whitehill for harmonica lessons and, yes, cognac, Felice Belle for making me laugh so hard the whole restaurant stares, and Jennifer Gandin for being the minister's daughter who taught me about faith that had nothing to do with a ministry.

Thank you to my mentors—a girl was never so blessed with so much wisdom. Karen, your serendipitous arrival in my life seems divined; thank you for sharing yourself so honestly and expertly. Selena, your work in the world is trumped only by your presence in it—thank you for walking your talk and talking so profoundly. Janet, your generosity and vision are nothing short of heroic—you are already a mother of so many, including me. Robin, thank you for dragging me along, making me laugh, and believing in me so unwaveringly. Your spirit is infectious. D.D., you are the change.

Thanks to all those I interviewed—expert and survivor, healed and struggling, young and old alike. Your time and truth were what shaped this book. I am deeply indebted to Melissa Mannis, my favorite teenage cultural critic, and Allison Baker, my source in so many ways.

Special shout-outs to the friends who hashed over the book with me when it needed it and then dragged me away to go dancing when that was sorely in order: Dr. Z, Kate the Great, Tiffany, Yana, Jen, M.C. Coy, Becky, Ramin, and the poker boys. Mugs, thank you for fifteen years and counting. Anna, my sister-cousin, you are my spiritual adviser. Your beauty helps me understand my own. Gareth, thank you for teaching me the beauty of anger and kapusta. You are fiercely lovely.

Thank you to my families: Sam and Ben, the Kuhns, the Guthries, and the Johnsons, especially Momma J, for her macaroni and cheese and enlightening hugs.

Bub, it's silly how much we make sense. Your kindness is your genius. With you, it's always peanut-butter-and-jelly time. I like you.

Momma and Papa, thank you for the Santa Fe sanctuary, totally impartial editing, and interrupting each other on the phone. Papa, you are my spirit. Momma, you are my soul. Thank you both for being my best friends in the world.

Christopher, please shut up. I have something to say. You are the most courageous, big-bottom-lipped, genius big brother in the galaxy and beyond. If I were a horse, you would be a unicorn.

Index

Page numbers followed by *n* indicate notes.

as superwomen, 46–47, 58, 88–89
See also parenting; parents
MTV, 14, 141, 170, 293
Muir, John, 1
music, 153–61, 170
See also hip-hop; rap
Myers, Michael, 206

Nelly, 162–63, 163*n*
new stories, 316–36
and beauty, 330–31
beginnings of, 333–36
and conversations about eating
disorders, 327–28
and culture, 321–22, 326–27
and fantasies, 317–20
and power, 317, 319, 320–21, 322,
324–25, 328, 333
and spirituality, 327
and treatments for eating disorders,
322–24
and truth and humility, 326–28
uprising for, 331–33
Nolen-Hoeksema, Susan, 128, 214
nutrition/nutritionists, 98, 111, 323

obesity
causes of, 199
in children, 206
definition of, 199*n*
emotional and psychological aspects of,
201–2, 202–3, 206
as epidemic, 29, 95, 197, 202, 204
and fat bitch, 215–20
and health/disease, 201–2, 202–3
ignorance about, 200–204
images of, 203–4
and personality, 203–4
and race/class issues, 206
and sports, 242
See also diets; eating disorders; fat;
weight
obsession
and legacy of feminism, 51–52, 59–60
as only dangerous when lethal, 28
prevalence of, 30–31
and quality of life, 35–36
See also specific topic
Oliver, J. Eric, 203

Olsen twins, 144
one-size-fits-all beauty standard, 193, 326
Orbach, Susie, 29, 199, 204, 219
"otherize," 28

parenting, 44–47, 64, 70–71, 79–84, 91
parents
and competition among teenagers, 103
and new stories, 323, 324
pressure from, 236
and sex, 118–19
See also fathers; mothers
"partial-syndrome eating disorder," 27,
72, 73, 203
Paul, Pamela, 179
perfect girls
characteristics of, 5, 6, 20–23
contradictions of, 20–21, 257–61
as daughters of feminists, 21
double consciousness of, 257–61
and failure, 250, 314
Gilligan's views about, 39, 40
as god projects, 293
and "good girls," 39, 40
impatience of, 273
pilgrimages of, 314
as privileged, 278
starving daughters compared with,
24–25
stop being, 330–36
See also specific topic
perfection
and admission of imperfection, 313
and beauty of imperfection, 330–31
books/writings about, 9–10, 11–12
characteristics of, 52, 53
in college years, 248–49, 250, 252,
254–55, 257–61
correlation of eating disorders and, 6,
32–33
"effortless," 6–7, 252, 259, 305, 306,
310
Fonda's views about, 90–91
from good to, 41–52
and history of eating disorders, 32
as impossible to attain, 110, 313, 326
and legacy of feminism, 49, 50–51, 52,
53, 63–64
never enough, 6

and obsession with perfect girl,
246–47
perfect girl compared with, 24–25
and perfection, 5–6
and spirituality, 302–3, 304, 305–6
and sports, 236
Steinem, Gloria, 42
Steiner-Adair, Catherine, 32
Stern, Robin, 70, 277, 285
Stonehill College, 248
stress, 58–59, 88, 128, 150
Striegel-Moore, Ruth, 33, 150–51
success, 260, 288, 298, 305–6
superwomen, 9, 40, 46–47, 58, 63, 64
Susan, 2, 211–14

tattoos, 219–20
Taylor, Mary, 313
teenagers
and boys, 106–8
coded communication among, 93–94
competition among, 100–105, 108
credit cards of, 107
dysfunctional, 62
fathers' views about bodies of, 73–77
as "female impersonators," 93
hyper-awareness of, 94
as just being a girl, 112–13
Manhattan, 94–95, 96–97, 100–102,
103–4, 106, 107–8, 109–11, 112–13
meanness of, 96–100, 101, 104
perfect-girl talk among, 92–113
perfection projection of, 108–12
power struggles among, 96–100
pregnancy of, 115, 118, 123n, 124
Santa Fe, 96–100, 102, 106–7, 108–9
sarcastic joking among, 104–5
therapy, group, 233–34
THIN (HBO), 234
thinness
and attractiveness, 186–87, 193
and being seen, 175
in college years, 254–55, 258
as desirable, 107–8
fantasies about, 209–10
and "father hunger," 84
and hip-hop, 162
media emphasis on, 107–8

and media-literacy fatigue, 147–48,
148–49
negative perceptions of, 216–17
and new stories, 330
obsession about, 6–10
and perfect-girl talk among teenagers,
107–8
and pop icons, 144
in post-college years, 270–71, 286
as prerequisite for perfection, 18
as prerequisite for success, 288
qualities associated with, 198
and self-talk about fat, 208–9
and spirituality, 297–98
and sports, 223–24, 230–31, 232–33
statistics about, 202
too much, 147–48, 211–13
See also diets; eating disorders; weight
Third Wave Foundation, 63
thyroid problems, 96
Title IX, 222–24, 226
Toledo, Luiz S., 289
"toxic triangle," 128
transcendence, 302–6, 310, 313
Trice, Obie, 162
truth, 189–90, 191–92, 326–28
"truth talks," 99, 100
tummy tucks, 153
Twenge, Jean, 51

vegetarianism, 212–13, 256
virgins, 123n, 141, 142
vomiting. *See* bulimia nervosa

weight
emotional and psychological aspects of,
205–6, 206
obsession about, 1–4, 18–19, 258–59,
306–10
and perfect-girl talk among teenagers,
94–102, 106–7, 111–12, 113
as in personal control, 19
See also diets; eating disorders; fat;
"freshman fifteen"; obesity; *specific
person or topic;* thinness
Weight Watchers, 204
Wendy, 222–23, 224, 229, 235, 237–38,
240–41, 243–44

Readers Guide

by Courtney and her mom, Jere E. Martin, MSW, LCSWII

1. Do you think food and fitness obsession is a normal part of being a woman?

2. Does the description of the perfect girl resonate with you?

3. How does the starving daughter part of you—your unspoken needs, fears, desires for comfort—get expressed? Are you comfortable with this part of you? Why or why not?

4. What do you see as the biggest losses of the epidemic of eating disorders and the larger culture of food and fitness obsession?

5. How do you differentiate between healthy ambition and unhealthy perfectionism? How did your mother and/or father influence your perspective? How do you think you might influence your daughter's perspective?

6. How did your mother's relationship with her body influence your relationship with yours? What was the talk about health and beauty in your family? Was there one person whose comments were particularly influential? If so, why do you think that was?

7. Courtney writes that feminists taught their daughters that they could be anything, and that their daughters, instead, decided that they had to be everything. What do you think about that interpretation? Do you consider yourself a feminist? Why or why not? Do you think feminism means different things for different generations?

8. Courtney describes her relationship with her own father as a "walk in the park" compared to that with her mother, which resembles a "jungle hike." Is this true for you? What are the benefits and losses of having less intimate but steadier relationships with our fathers? What kind of father-daughter relationship best supports a daughter's healthy self-image?

9. What was your self-image like at age thirteen? Are the insecurities you felt then still with you in some way today? In what ways do they show up? Do you keep them hidden? If so, how?

10. Who was *the* perfect girl in your middle school or high school? What do you think she might be doing now?

11. Do you think of eating and fitness issues as a rich, white girl's disease? Were you surprised that so many working-class girls and girls of color were affected by these issues?

12. Instead of developing an authentic sense of their own sexuality, Courtney and her friend Jen struggle within a society that still reduces young women to virgin/slut stereotypes. Did or do you experience this same dichotomy? How has it changed since the 1950s and in what ways is it still the same today? What do those women labeled as prudes lose in terms of options for expressing the full range of who they are? What about those labeled as easy?

13. In what ways do you think women's appetites for sex mirrors their appetites for food? What would have to change about our culture in order for women to be more in touch with their authentic appetites?

14. Who do you see as healthy role models in pop culture for young women today? Why is there such a lack of contemporary heroines? Were there more in the past, and if so, why?

15. In what ways does hip-hop culture strengthen young women's sense of self? In what ways does it stifle it?

16. As mass media provides us with a more diverse range of female images, in terms of body type and race, how does this affect your perspective of the ideal body?

17. How does a woman's relationship with her own body affect her relationships with those she dates?

18. Were you surprised that the majority of the men Courtney interviewed emphasized how important humor was as opposed to a particular body type? Is this your experience? Do you think that porn socializes young men to have unrealistic expectations for women's bodies? Why or why not?

19. Courtney writes about the difference between being noticed—cat-called, picked up in bars, etc.—and being truly seen. Does one form of getting attention make you feel more beautiful than the other? Why?

20. In what ways do you see the epidemics of obesity and eating disorders as related? Do you agree that we live in a "bulimic culture," as Marya Hornbacher attests?

21. Courtney's friend Gareth helps her become aware of her own inner judgment about other women's bodies, particularly fat women. After reading that chapter, have you become aware of any subtle judgments in your own mind?

22. In what ways do you think involvement in sports has strengthened women's sense of self and in what ways has it exacerbated body insecurities?

23. Whose responsibility is it to create a sports culture where young

women are encouraged to maintain a healthy relationship with food, fitness, and their bodies? Whose responsibility is it to identify when athletes cross the line between dedication and disease?

24. Why is food and fitness obsession so rampant on college campuses?

25. In what ways do single-sex environments (all-women's schools, sororities, etc.) help and/or hinder the development of positive relationships with food and fitness?

26. Do you have friends with disordered eating or fitness addiction? What have you done to help them? Looking back, do you have any regrets about your decisions to either confront or not confront friends in trouble?

27. What do your spiritual beliefs teach you about the body? Do these coincide with or contradict the views of Western medicine? What about Western beauty standards?

28. In what ways can religious dogma exacerbate women's unhealthy relationships with their own appetites? In what ways can spirituality foster self-acceptance?

29. In what ways does the lack of ritual in our culture contribute to women's antagonistic relationship with their bodies, especially when in transition (puberty, menopause, etc.)? In what ways could you reintroduce body-affirming rituals into your life or the life of your daughter?

30. When have you felt most and least healthy about your relationship with your body? What influenced you at these times?

31. What woman's story in this book did you find most interesting, and how has that changed your understanding of these issues?

32. What is the ideal relationship for women to have with their bodies? Does it vary from woman to woman?

33. What is one small step you can commit to taking right now that will help end the culture of self-hatred for you and for other women?

About the Author

Courtney E. Martin, originally from Colorado Springs, Colorado, is a writer, speaker, and teacher.

Her work has appeared in *The Washington Post*, *The Christian Science Monitor*, *Glamour* magazine, and *Utne Reader*, among other national publications. In addition, she is a columnist for the American Prospect Online and a contributing blogger at feministing, a Woodhull Fellow, and a Women's Media Center expert. She was awarded the Elie Wiesel Prize in Ethics in 2002 and founded the Secret Society for Creative Philanthropy in 2006.

Courtney has a BA in political science and sociology from Barnard College and an MA in writing and social change from New York University's Gallatin School. She currently lives in Brooklyn where you can often find her conspiring to create unself-conscious dance parties.

You can read more about her work at www.courtneymartin.com.